The Comintern: Historical Highlights
Essays, Recollections, Documents

Hoover Institution Publications

The Comintern:
Historical Highlights
Essays, Recollections, Documents

Edited by

Milorad M. Drachkovitch and Branko Lazitch

Published for
The Hoover Institution on War, Revolution, and Peace
Stanford University, Stanford, California
by
Frederick A. Praeger, Publishers
New York • Washington
Pall Mall Press, London

Frederick A. Praeger, Publishers
111 Fourth Avenue, New York, New York 10003, U.S.A.
77–79 Charlotte Street, London, W.1, England

Published in the United States of America in 1966
by Frederick A. Praeger, Inc., Publishers

•

Preface

In the course of several years' research on a history of the Third International, the editors of this volume have gathered a rich assortment of materials, too extensive to be incorporated into a necessarily condensed historical account and too significant to be buried in the archives. Therefore it was decided these materials should be organized, combined with original essays by several authorities on the history of communism, and published as a separate volume to stand on its own. Hence this volume has two purposes: to illuminate some controversial or insufficiently explored aspects and problems of the Third (Communist) International, the "Comintern," and to offer to specialists and interested readers certain recollections of former Comintern leaders and unpublished documents from Comintern archives.

The eight original essays contained herein explore essential and in some instances neglected aspects of the Comintern. Stefan T. Possony discusses its claim to Marxist legitimacy and shows, on the basis of documentary evidence, that Marx's concept of an international revolutionary workers' movement differed from Lenin's. Bertram D. Wolfe examines the same problem of Lenin's Marxist orthodoxy from a different angle; he concludes that in the most sensitive field, that of organization, Lenin basically "revised" the established practice of the Second International, and that his party decisively influenced the destiny of the Third International. Branko Lazitch, in his first essay, makes a pioneering attempt to show how the Comintern from its earliest days controlled its sections by sending its emissaries abroad and calling representatives of foreign parties to Moscow. (Although this essay covers only the experience of the French Communist Party, it is legitimate to assume that the French case is characteristic for the Comintern's modus operandi in other countries.) Richard C. Thornton uses official Comintern and Chinese Communist sources to demonstrate that in its 1928 directives to Chinese Communists the Comintern already foreshadowed the strategy of protracted guerrilla warfare applied later by Mao Tse-tung and his followers. Babette

Gross examines the intrinsic inability of German Communists to establish a common front with other leftist forces against Hitler after their earlier Moscow-prescribed tactics had helped the Nazis to seize power. Branko Lazitch, in his second essay, and Boris Souvarine analyze and comment on the tragedy of foreign Communist leaders massacred in the 1930's by Stalin's police and, until recently, largely condemned to oblivion. Milorad M. Drachkovitch closes the essays with a discussion of another neglected episode of Comintern history: how the Communist Party of Yugoslavia, considered in the middle 1930's one of the most unreliable Comintern sections, was able during the war to put into practice the theoretical postulates of the Comintern's last congress.

The three recollections which form the second part of the volume are significant because of their topics and the personalities of the authors. Henri Barbé and Albert Vassart were at different times members of the top hierarchy of the French Communist Party and were able to observe personally from a privileged position the unfolding of Comintern history. The excerpts published in this volume are part of unpublished memoirs which are now in the possession of the Hoover Institution. Barbé relates an incident that occurred at a meeting of the Comintern's Executive Committee in December 1928, when probably for the last time foreign Communist leaders dared to disagree with Stalin publicly and in his presence. Célie and Albert Vassart offer an account of the background of the birth of the French Popular Front in the 1930's which varies from the official Communist version of the event. Similarly, Eugenio Reale challenges the official record in his recollection of how the Cominform, in which he played a part as a delegate of the Italian Communist Party, was founded in 1947. His recollections, written for this volume, supplement in part the Italian and French versions of his book, not translated into English, on the founding of the Cominform.

The documents assembled in the third part of the volume pertain to the internal problems of the German and French parties in the earliest years of their existence and should provide valuable material for the study of the relationship between Comintern headquarters in Moscow and individual sections of the Comintern. The apprehensions of the German Communist leader Paul Levi about the negative course of events among the European Communist parties as a consequence of Moscow's dictates, and the ignorance on the part of the earliest leaders of the French Communist Party of Bolshevik methods and mentality, both tend to explain how and why the Comintern evolved as it did. To put the documents in perspective, the editors have provided introductory notes and biographical sketches of the persons mentioned in them.

All the essays, recollections, and documents deal with the Comintern as it was forged by its two supreme rulers: Lenin, who founded it according to his precepts, and Stalin, who molded it in his own way. The downgrading of Stalin in the Soviet Union has fostered a tendency to glorify Lenin as an infallible leader of the international proletariat. But here we have evidence of a multidimensional Lenin— not a mythical and flawless hero, but a political leader of exceptional abilities whose ideas and achievements, nevertheless, put the international Communist movement on a track which led irretrievably to Soviet predominance when he had to leave the stage. As for Stalin, the various contributions to this volume reveal yet another "cult of personality" aspect—the aspect of his behavior in connection with the international Communist movement. Thus, an essay on the Cominform also is included to provide an expanded understanding of Stalin's handling of international Communist affairs.

In tying together the volume, several persons have been helpful to the editors. Mr. Claude Harmel and Professor Wiktor Sukiennicki have provided biographical data in some instances. Messrs. Savel Kliachko and James Sattler, as well as Mrs. Grete Heinz and Miss Lisa Hoffman, have translated and rechecked some of the individual pieces. Mr. Max Knight has read the manuscript several times, offered pertinent criticism, and given it its definitive linguistic form. To all these persons, who obviously are not responsible for the content of the volume, go the editors' deep-felt thanks. Thanks are also due the Library for Political Studies in New York and its director, Mr. Joseph Buttinger, for permission to reproduce two documents from Paul Levi's Archives.

THE EDITORS

CONTENTS

Contributors

STEFAN T. POSSONY was born in Vienna in 1913 and educated in Austria, Germany, Italy, France, and the United States. He was a Carnegie research fellow at the Institute for Advanced Study at Princeton University in 1941–42; special adviser to the U.S. Air Force in Washington, D.C., 1946–61; and professor of international politics at Georgetown University, Washington, D.C., 1946–61. Since 1961 he has been Director of International Political Studies at the Hoover Institution. In 1953 Dr. Possony published *A Century of Conflict: Communist Techniques of World Revolution 1948–1950* (Chicago: Regnery). His most recent book is *Lenin, The Compulsive Revolutionary* (Chicago: Regnery, 1964).

BERTRAM D. WOLFE was born in 1896 and as one of the founders of the left wing of the American Socialist Party which became the American Communist Party, he was a founder of the Comintern. Mr. Wolfe attended the Fifth Comintern Congress as a delegate of the Mexican Communist Party and the Sixth Congress as a delegate of the American party. In 1929 he represented the American party at the Executive Committee of the Communist International (ECCI) and engaged in a long controversy with Stalin which resulted in his break with the Comintern in July 1929.

Mr. Wolfe has M.A. degrees from the Universities of Mexico (1925) and Columbia (1932) and an LL.D. from the University of California (1962). He has alternated teaching with freelance writing in Russian history, sociology, and political science. His last academic appointment was as Distinguished Visiting Professor of Russian History at the University of California (Davis). He is at present a Senior Research Fellow at the Hoover Institution. During the Korean War he set up and directed the Ideological Advisory Staff for the Department of State and the Voice of America.

Among his published works are *Three Who Made a Revolution*

(1948, revised 1964, New York: Dell Publishing Co.), *Communist Totalitarianism* (Boston: Beacon Press, 1956), *Khrushchev and Stalin's Ghost* (New York: Praeger, 1957), *Marxism: One Hundred Years in the Life of a Doctrine* (New York: The Dial Press, 1965), and *Strange Communists I Have Known* (New York: Stein and Day, 1965).

BRANKO LAZITCH was born in Užice, Yugoslavia, in 1923. He obtained his B.A. and Ph.D. in Political Science from the University of Geneva, Switzerland. Mr. Lazitch also holds a diploma in European studies from the College of Europe, Bruges, where he teaches frequently as a visiting professor. Since 1951 he has been living in Paris, working as an editor of the review *Est & Ouest* and lecturing occasionally at various European universities. His *Lénine et la Troisième Internationale* was published in 1951 (Neuchâtel: Edition de la Baconnière), with a preface by Raymond Aron. His other works include *Les Partis Communistes d'Europe, 1919–1955* (Paris: Editions Les Iles d'Or, 1956), and *Tito et la Révolution Yougoslave, 1937–1956* (Paris: Fasquelle, 1957). Mr. Lazitch now is collaborating with Milorad M. Drachkovitch on a "History of the Third International."

BABETTE L. GROSS was born in Potsdam in 1898, joined the German Communist Party in 1921 and from 1923 to 1933 was in charge of a Communist publishing house. A close working associate and common-law wife of Willy Münzenberg, she emigrated from Germany in 1933 and settled in Paris. She accompanied Münzenberg on his trips to Moscow and arranged for the publication of Communist literature in Paris. In 1938, when Münzenberg was expelled from the German Communist Party, she herself broke with the German party and also with the Comintern. In 1941, after the defeat of France and Münzenberg's death, she went to Mexico, but she returned to Germany in 1947 and since has been writing in collaboration with her sister, Margarete Buber-Neumann.

RICHARD C. THORNTON, born in 1936, is a doctoral candidate in Far Eastern and Russian history at the University of Washington, Seattle. Mr. Thornton spent part of 1964 doing research in Taiwan and is now completing his dissertation, "The Comintern and the Chinese Communists, 1928–1931."

BORIS SOUVARINE was born in 1895 and joined the French Socialist movement while still a youth. At the end of the First World War, he was one of the three secretaries of the Committee for the Third International. Although his arrest in 1920 prevented him from attending the Congress of Tours at which the French Communist Party was founded, he was able, in his prison cell, to draft the final resolution of the congress and was named in absentia a member of the comité directeur (later called central committee).

Mr. Souvarine was one of the French party's delegates at the Third Congress of the Comintern and subsequently became the French representative on its Executive Committee. He also was promoted to membership in the Presidium and the Secretariat of the ECCI. Confirmed in these duties by the Fourth Comintern Congress in 1922, he continued to discharge them for a brief period after Lenin's death in January 1924.

Because of Souvarine's opposition to the campaign against Trotsky, whose book, *Cours nouveau,* he had just published in France, he was investigated by a special commission at the Comintern's Fifth Congress in 1924 and relieved of all official functions. Upon his return to France in 1925, he became the leader of an anti-Stalinist Communist group. At first he edited the *Bulletin communiste,* then the review *La Critique sociale,* and finally broke completely with communism in all its forms.

In 1935, Mr. Souvarine published *Staline: Aperçu historique du bolchévisme,* and for years his comments on events in Russia appeared in the daily *Le Figaro.* He took refuge in the United States during the war, returned to France in 1947, and has since contributed a number of analytical articles on Communism to the review *B.E.I.P.I.* (today *Est & Ouest*). One of these "Un Caligula à Moscou. Le cas pathologique de Stalin," published in 1953, bore an astonishing resemblance to Khrushchev's revelations in his secret speech of February 1956. Boris Souvarine is now living in Paris, where he edits the review *Le Contrat social.*

MILORAD M. DRACHKOVITCH was born in Belgrade in 1921. His academic degrees include a doctorate in Political Science from the University of Geneva, Switzerland. During the 1950's he was warden and later director of studies at the College of Europe, Bruges. Since 1958, Dr. Drachkovitch has taught at Brooklyn College and the University of California at Berkeley and spent a year at the Russian Research Center, Harvard University. In 1961 he became a senior staff member at the Hoover Institution on War, Revolution, and Peace, and Lecturer in the Department of Political Science at Stanford University. Among his publications are *Les socialismes français et allemand et le problème de la guerre, 1870–1914* (Geneva: Droz, 1953), *De Karl Marx à Léon Blum* (Droz, 1954), *United States Aid to Yugoslavia and Poland* (Washington, D.C., 1963), and, as editor, three volumes of essays from the Hoover Institution's October 1964 conference on "One Hundred Years of Revolutionary Internationals." Currently he is conducting research for a "History of the Third International," in collaboration with Branko Lazitch and under the advisership of Boris Souvarine.

EUGENIO REALE was born in Naples in 1905, a member of a family of intellectuals. He studied medicine and practiced as a surgeon in his native city and in the early period of Fascist rule joined the Communist Party. In 1931 Dr. Reale was arrested, sentenced to solitary confinement, and in 1937 exiled to France. There he became editor of *La Voce degli Italiani,* a daily newspaper published in Paris. Interned in 1940 by the French and extradited to Italy in 1943, he was once more incarcerated, but was finally released in September 1943.

Dr. Reale occupied important state and party posts during the last phase of the Second World War and during the immediate postwar years: he has been a member of the Italian Communist Party secretariat (March 1944), under-secretary for foreign affairs in various governments prior to 1947, Italian ambassador to Poland from August 1945 to January 1947, a member of the Italian delegation at the peace conference in Paris, a member of the central committee of the Italian Communist Party from its fifth congress in 1946, Italian delegate to the founding meeting of the Cominform in 1947, a member of the Italian Consultative Assembly, a deputy to the Constituent Assembly, and a senator of the Italian Republic.

In 1948 Reale left the party secretariat, in 1952 he resigned from the central committee, and in 1953 he refused to accept candidacy for election to the Senate. After the Twentieth Congress of the Communist Party of the Soviet Union and then the Hungarian insurrection, Reale declared his hostility to the policies of the leaders of the Italian Communist Party and his opposition to the "dictatorship of the proletariat" and the Soviet system of government.

With the eighth congress of the Italian Communist Party (December 1956), his dispute broke into the open, and Reale was expelled from the Party on December 31, 1956. In June 1957, with the collaboration of friends, he started a new weekly, *Corrispondenza Socialista,* the tenor of which has been Social Democratic and anti-Communist.

Essays

The Comintern's Claim to
Marxist Legitimacy

by

STEFAN T. POSSONY

"The sole heir of the First International is the Communist International. It is not only the guardian of the traditions of the First International in the domain of theory, but also its executor in the realm of the practical. . . . The Communist International is the realization, on a much vaster scale, of the global party that the First International was supposed to be, in accordance with the ideas of Marx and Engels."—From the theses elaborated by the Comintern on the occasion of the sixtieth anniversary of the First International.

Ever since Lenin launched the Bolshevik movement in 1903, legitimacy has been of the greatest importance to communism. Lenin made every effort to trace his intellectual genealogy back to Marx and Engels and took great pains to conceal the Russian origins of many of his theories and practices. After Lenin had seized power in Russia and Bolshevism was broadened into a world revolutionary movement, the need for legitimacy became greater than ever before: the Third International would never have become a powerful force if Lenin had not succeeded in presenting himself as the continuator of Marx and if the Comintern had not been accepted as the direct descendant of the First International. Thus, the statutes of the Communist International, adopted at the Second Comintern Congress in August 1920, at the very outset quoted several paragraphs from the provisional rules of the First International, written by Marx himself, and proclaimed that the Third International's objective was "to continue and to carry through to completion the great work begun by the First International Workingmen's Association."

3

The alleged Marxist inheritance and orthodoxy were the crucial elements which enabled the Kremlin to outpace the Socialist Second International and to develop the Comintern as a genuinely multinational organization rather than as an instrument of strictly Russian political warfare. To be sure, the Comintern was to degenerate into precisely such a tool within about ten years after its founding, but the presumption of the Marxist succession was so firmly entrenched that the substitution was at first barely noticed.

But was the Comintern really the heir of the International Workingmen's Association? Certainly, Lenin and Bolshevism were an offshoot of the Russian Social Democratic Labor party, which was Marxist in orientation and which at its inception, largely through Vera Zasulich and Georgii Plekhanov, had maintained sporadic contacts with Marx and Engels. (Actually, the founders of Marxism had maintained far closer personal contacts with Russian revolutionaries like Danielson and Lavrov, who were connected with the populist movement, and they evinced great skepticism about Russian Marxists.) But apart from these personal links, the First and Third Internationals had very little in common. Their ideological orientation, organizational concepts, objectives, and "methods of struggle" were in fact quite different.

The First International was not Marxist. The few Marxists who participated in the organization occupied a balancing center position. Marx himself exercised a strong intellectual influence within the General Council, but he was careful to phrase the papers he wrote for the Association in such a manner that they were, as Engels wrote, "acceptable to the English trade unions, to the followers of Proudhon in France, Belgium, Italy, and Spain, and to the Lassalleans in Germany."[1] The program was drafted by Marx "to the satisfaction of all parties," not just of those Engels mentioned, but also of liberals, free traders, suffragettes, and Positivists on the right, and of Blanquists, Bakuninists, and anarchists on the left. The Association's membership varied, and splits occurred, resulting, for example, in the expulsion of American suffragettes and of left radical Bakuninist elements. But there was no attempt to keep the Association "monolithically" restricted to one single ideology. The Association was a very loosely organized "united front" and not a "world combat party."

The objectives of the Association were far more "reformist" than revolutionary. In his programmatic statement of 1864, Marx did not speak of the abolition of classes but only of the "destruction of class rule." The "abolition of classes" did become an objective in 1872, but the pertinent amendment to the program was not proposed by Marx or Engels. In any event, the Association worked for two far more concrete objectives: first, to influence the foreign policy of the big European powers to bring about the weakening of tsarist Russia and to support progressive causes (such as the Polish independence movement, German and Italian unification, and, in the American Civil War, the Union against the secessionists); and second, to coordinate the various national labor movements to achieve the "economic emancipation of the working class."

The Association did not consider itself to be either the "general staff" or "the leader and organizer" of a world revolutionary movement fighting "for the establishment of the world dictatorship of the proletariat."[2] It was constituted as a liaison committee and was, above all, anxious to provide material and legal support to industrial strikers. The power of the General Council, Marx stated in 1872, was not one of arms, of soldiers, nor of the law, but rather a moral power.[3] This attitude was based on the belief that violence and conspiracy were inappropriate methods of realizing the aims of the First International.

It is true, of course, that Bakunin and his followers disagreed sharply with the antiviolent and anticonspiratorial tactics propounded by Marx. It is also true that Marx himself, as a result of his experiences as a practical politician connected with the Association, gradually veered to the right. In this reformist course, Marx, naturally, was supported by all reformist and semirevolutionary elements. The fact is that notions of gradualism dominated the thinking of the majority.

Therefore, the ancestral lineage of the Comintern went back to the Bakuninist minority rather than to the First International. Marx contrived the expulsion of this minority precisely because Bakunin adopted those very strategies which the Comintern emulated fifty years later.[4] Perhaps the Comintern's true ancestry may be detected in the rump Association which vegetated for a few years after 1874, when the Marxists and the moderate elements abandoned the organization. In brief, the Comintern took over from the Association what was not Marxist, and did not take over what was Marxist.

Let us now look more closely at some characteristic features of the Comintern's paternity claim.

THE ROLE OF CONSPIRACY

The conditions for admission into the Third International, formulated by Lenin, stipulated the need for illegal organizations and work.[5] Marx and Engels admitted the need for secret organizations in countries where the proletarian party could not function openly, but they strictly distinguished between "secret organizations" and "secret societies." In his speech of September 22, 1871, when Marx propounded this difference, he added that the "result" of secret societies is "always negative." "This type of organization is not compatible with the development of the proletarian movement. Instead of educating the workers, it subjects them to authoritarian and mystical laws which restrict their independence and turn their consciousness in the wrong direction."[6]

Marx joined the International precisely because he deemed it a nonconspiratorial and *therefore* a promising effort; and he objected to early drafts of the inaugural address because he felt they would have launched the International as a conspiratorial society. Marx and Engels objected to secret societies because, according to their experience, conspiratorial organizations were particularly vulnerable to police infiltration. They also believed that conspirators became easily corrupted morally and politically, that conspiracy often played into the hands of "reaction," and that conspiracy could be derailed by provocation.[7]

In a letter of November 23, 1871, Marx wrote to Friedrich Bolte, a German Socialist living in New York:

> The *International* was founded in order to replace the socialist or semi-socialist sects by a real organization of the working class for struggle. . . . The development of socialist sectarianism and that of the real working class movement always stands in inverse ratio to each other. Sects are justified (historically) so long as the working class is not yet ripe for an independent historical movement. . . . The history of the International was a *continual struggle of the General Council* against the sects and amateur experiments. . . . Where the working class is not yet far enough advanced in its organization . . . it must . . . be trained.[8]

Marx explained, in the same letter, that whereas pressure to force a shorter work-day in a particular factory is a purely economic move, an attempt to "force through an eight-hour, etc., *law* is a political movement . . . a movement of the class with the object of enforcing its interests in a general form . . . possessing general, socially coercive force." Clearly, such an objective was believed unattainable by conspiracy. The rejection of conspiracy as a method therefore involved more than just a dispute about means; it also *implied* divergent ends.

The conflict between Marx and Bakunin often has been described as a power struggle between two ambitious men: Marx was accused of not being able to tolerate a second towering figure beside him. This interpretation, however, is one-sided, for the dispute had broad political significance.

There was Bakunin's financial and personal behavior, which, if it had become known more widely, would have entailed unfavorable publicity for the International. More significant, however, was the series of foolish and invariably unsuccessful uprisings which Bakunin organized, notably in France and Italy. As early as 1867, the "leaders of the International" refused to support a hopeless rising in Paris, and they were promptly accused by the anarchist elements of being secret agents of Napoleon III.[9] Bakunin's actions were in part motivated by his desire to die on the barricades. But suicidal mania was hardly what the labor movement needed, and when Bakunin and his followers did not desist, there was no choice but to draw a sharp line against insurrectionism. Hence, shortly after the discovery of a bomb plot against Napoleon III, which led to the arrest of many French members of the International, the General Council, on January 25, 1870, issued a statement to the effect that an association identified with the working class must act openly and exclude secret societies in any form. "If the working classes are conspiring . . . they are conspiring openly, as the sun conspires against the darkness.[10]

Furthermore, as a result of the Paris Commune, the European governments were becoming apprehensive about the International. To prevent strong police repression all over Europe—and various agencies were using quotations from Bakuninist writings to discredit the International—it was necessary to keep the labor movement operating in the form of open political parties. This did not mean that the conquest of political power was to be abandoned, but this conquest was to be accomplished by political methods. Nor did it mean that secrecy was ruled out, but conspiracy was rejected. Therefore, at the London conference of the International in September 1871, a resolution was adopted stating that in countries where the regular organization of the International could not function because of gov-

ernment intervention, "the Association or its local groups may recon-
stitute itself under other designations. All so-called secret societies
are and remain, however, formally excluded."[11]

The notorious Nechayev affair brought the conflict with Bakunin to a boiling point. The Russian government had decided to make
a *cause célèbre* of Nechayev, not only because fraud and murder
were involved, but also because the entire revolutionary cause could
be discredited through the blood-curdling text of the *Revolutionary
Catechism*. Marx complained that Bakunin's friends had shifted to
the International the responsibility for Nechayev's "silly and in-
famous maxims."[12]

In 1874 and 1875, Engels sharply criticized P. N. Tkachev, one
of Lenin's intellectual forerunners, for his conspiratorial talk. Engels
specified that he was not opposed to conspiracy under all circumstances, but rather wished that the Bakuninists, for once, would carry
out an *effective* conspiracy against the Russian government. Instead,
they were just indulging in *Schwindelverschwörungen* (phoney con-
spiracies).[13] Engels contended, not too fairly, that Bakunin's plan
really was to set up a secret society designed to subjugate "the European workers' movement to a hidden dictatorship of a few adven-
turers."[14]

Engels took the opportunity of criticizing Blanqui's notion that
revolution was to be conceived as a *coup de main*. This concept of
revolution by a small revolutionary minority implies "the necessity of
dictatorship after success: the dictatorship . . . not of the whole revolutionary class, of the proletariat, but of the small number of those
who carried out the *coup de main* and who from the very beginning
were organized under the dictatorship of one or a few men."[15] This
statement was prophetic, but it hardly can be classed among the intellectual roots of "Leninism."

THE ROLE OF VIOLENCE

After the Hague congress in September 1872, Marx made a public
speech at Amsterdam. He disclosed that the congress had just decided to fight the collapsing bourgeois society on political as well as
social grounds. There had been a lengthy dispute with the Bakuninist
anarchist element about the need for "political struggle." The terminology is slightly bewildering,[16] but the question was whether the proletariat should participate in day-by-day political struggles and
strengthen its political power through organization and the winning

of elections,[17] or rather devote its energies to the preparation of uprisings. The worker, Marx explained in his speech, must one day seize political power and "overthrow the old policy which is upholding the old institutions," but the road to this objective need not be the same everywhere.

It is necessary, Marx argued at Amsterdam, to take into consideration the institutions, mores, and traditions of the various countries. "We do not deny that there are countries like America and England," and perhaps Holland, "where the workers can reach their objectives by peaceful means. But if this is true we also must recognize that in most countries of the continent, violence must be the lever of revolution;[18] one day it will be necessary to appeal to violence in order to establish the dominion of labor."[19] Marx's point had been presaged in the inaugural address, in which he stressed the importance of "numbers." England and the United States had a system of democratic elections and parliamentarism. Institutions of this type were indeed suitable for the conquest of political power by the proletariat, once it constituted an "immense majority."

The exact text of Marx's Amsterdam speech has not been established. The version printed in the German party press de-emphasized his statement on violence, whereas the French text published in Belgium stressed it.[20] The version of the *Algemeen Handelsblad,* a Dutch bourgeois paper, did not coincide entirely with the two other versions, but on September 10, 1872, this paper reported as follows:

> The speaker defends the use of violence where other means do not help. In America, the barricades are unnecessary, because there, if only they want to, the proletariat can win victory through the polls. The same applies to England and some other countries where the working classes have the right to speak out. But in the great majority of states, revolution has to be substituted for legality, because otherwise—by wrong generosity, by a falsely directed sense of justice— one would not attain one's ends. Strong, vigorous propaganda will have to prepare and support the revolution.

The surprising thing, of course, is not that Marx mentioned the need for violence in "most countries of the continent," but that he explicitly admitted the possibility of a nonviolent seizure of power in the two industrially most advanced countries, as well as in "some other countries." Apart from a few tongue-in-cheek suggestions about proletarian tactics in the United Kingdom and a remark in the preface to *Das Kapital,* this statement was the first which envisaged a strategy totally different from revolutionary violence. What makes the statement particularly important is that it resulted from a formal decision by the International. Its trenchant implication was that violent revolution is a method applicable to backward but not to modern and democratic countries.

F. A. Sorge, the Association's general secretary and a close collaborator of Marx, followed the master to the rostrum and delivered an even more revealing speech. The old philosophers, he argued at Amsterdam, preached peace but there had always been war. Christianity preached love, but hatred had always prevailed. The revolution of 1789 preached liberty, equality, and fraternity, but the bourgeoisie wanted liberty for itself, equality for the preservation of its privileges, and fraternity only among the members of its own class. Those three great forces, therefore, had proved unable to give the world a system of love, peace, liberty, equality, and fraternity. "The International wants to employ a fourth approach: labor. Labor will restore peace between the classes and reform society." Not only was revolution abandoned here in favor of reform, but Sorge, a true-red Marxist, even introduced the notion of class peace!

In a letter to Bebel of March 18–28, 1875, Engels clarified much of this when he talked about "the organization of the working class as a class by means of the trade unions. . . . This is the real class organization of the proletariat in which it carries on its daily struggles with the capital."[21]

In 1891, Engels explained explicitly that it might be possible to "grow peacefully" into the new society in those countries where the parliament (*Volksvertretung*) wields decisive power and where the constitution allows the majority to do what it wants. Engels named the countries where this peaceful transfer was possible: like Marx, he mentioned England and the United States, but he added France to the list. He denied this possibility for Germany but argued that the German Social Democrats should include in their goals the "concentration of all political power in the hands of the *Volksvertretung.*" He also stated, "One thing is certain: our party and the working class can come to power only under the form of a democratic republic;" and to this statement he appended the somewhat ambiguous comment, "This [democratic republic] is even the specific form for the dictatorship of the proletariat."[22] To explain what such a "dictatorship of the proletariat" would actually mean, Engels, in his introduction of March 1891 to Marx's *The Civil War in France,* invoked the Paris Commune as a classic example, stressing that one of the surest expedients used by the commune was to fill all posts by election on the basis of universal suffrage, with the voters retaining the right to recall their delegates at any time.

In 1895, in his last publication, Engels argued that the ballot could replace the bullet and that a peaceful transition to the proletarian state had become possible in Germany also.[23] The German Social Democratic party was growing in numbers and influence and was strengthening its discipline. It had been demonstrating to its comrades abroad a new weapon: the ballot. The *Communist Manifesto,* Engels explained, had called for general suffrage as one of the first objectives of the proletariat, and indeed the ballot proved to be one of the sharpest weapons. Bismarck was compelled to introduce general suffrage in order to gain mass support for his plans. The workers used this right to the fullest and thus changed the ballot from *moyen de duperie* into *instrument d'émancipation.*

The two million voters of the German Social Democratic party, Engels claimed, had become the most important and decisive force of the international proletarian army. The further growth of this force must be secured. If there were to be a collision with the military, the decisive battle might be delayed and rendered more costly. It was important to keep the Socialist force intact for the day of decision. "The irony of world history has stood everything on its head. We, the 'revolutionaries,' the 'insurgents,' we strive much better with legal means than with illegal means. The so-called parties of order perish as a result of the legality which they created themselves." Engels concluded by pointing out that the Christians, after long periods of persecution, ultimately won state power in the Roman Empire not through violent revolution but because, as a result of their propaganda, Christianity was proclaimed to be the state religion. The Socialists, he implied, should imitate this example.[24]

The passages in which Engels referred to the continuing possibility of violent action were deleted by Wilhelm Liebknecht, who as Engels wrote to Lafargue on April 3, 1895, had for some time been addicted to "the tactics of peace at any price and of opposition to force and violence."[25] He also complained that an overly edited version had been published in *Vorwärts,* which made him appear a "peaceful adulator of legality."[26] In his private correspondence with Lafargue, he left no doubt that peaceful tactics and opposition to force and violence were preached by him "only for *the Germany of today*," adding that such tactics may become inapplicable tomorrow. With respect to France, Belgium, Italy, and Austria, he commented, "these tactics could not be followed in their entirety."[27]

Despite Engels' disclaimer, it appears that Liebknecht eliminated only a few sentences, which, in every single instance, read as though Engels attempted to argue against his better judgment. He obviously felt obligated to pay homage to the traditional revolutionary tactic, perhaps in the conviction that he could not do otherwise. The letter to Lafargue, after all, was written to a man whose wife was the daughter of Marx. In his text he had proved quite convincingly that violent revolutionary tactics could not succeed against a well-prepared army.

What occasioned Marx's and Engels' change in strategic orientation? The failure of the Commune in 1871 undoubtedly was a key factor. A second factor was the dispute with Bakunin and the Blanquist elements, and the obsession of the radical wing with insurrection. The insurrectional follies of these preachers of violence undoubtedly sharpened Marx's and Engels' understanding of the limitations of violent strategy and, by contrast, showed what could be done by nonviolent means. Hence it was his *practical* experience as a member of the General Council of the International which modified Marx's thinking about the role of violence. The political conclusion he drew was that it would be useful to put the International into a milieu (that is, the United States) where it could learn the arts of the nonviolent political struggle more effectively than in any European country.

In his Amsterdam speech, Marx discussed the bewilderment which many of his friends had expressed about the Association's transfer to the United States. "Don't forget that America is becoming the workers' continent *par excellence,* that every year half a million men, workers, emigrate to this continent, and that the International must sink strong roots in the soil where the workers dominate." The *Algemeen Handelsblad* reported that Marx referred to America as "the country of the workers." He clearly considered America a "new and fertile field indeed for the efforts of the International." Hence he obviously expected good results from the transplantation of the Association. That this experiment failed, largely because the industrial worker of America did not consider himself to be a proletarian, is another matter.

Lenin later interpreted Marx's speech (and Stalin repeated Lenin's interpretation) to the effect that Marx envisaged a possibility of nonviolent revolution because at that time "militarism and bureaucracy were absent" in England and America, but that between 1914 and 1917, "the last representatives . . . of Anglo-Saxon 'liberty' . . . have slid down entirely into the all-European, filthy, bloody morass of military-bureaucratic institutions to which everything is subordinated and which trample everything underfoot." Stalin commented that "monopoly capitalism and imperialism" also had been added, and that therefore "the special conditions for peaceful development in England and the United States had disappeared."[28] Stalin's comment that there was no "imperialism" in 1872 is too silly for words. As to "monopoly capitalism"—where did Marx get his theory on the "concentration" of capital?

Actually, Marx did not believe that England had no militarism or standing army. To the contrary, he had argued that if the independence of Ireland could be achieved, the need for the British standing army would disappear. Yet Ireland had not become independent by 1872, and the standing army, though small, was still there; and so was English "militarism," which often had been criticized by Engels. With fresh memories of the American Civil War, it is unlikely that Marx discounted the military capabilities of the American government. The differences between Anglo-Saxon and European bureaucracy were plain, but Marx hardly assumed that the English and American administrations were anything but instruments of class rule, and he knew enough about English bureaucracy not to discount it.

Lenin's interpretation therefore was invalid. Lenin also failed to mention Marx's reference to Holland, where militarism surely had not grown, and he skipped the fact that Engels had added France and later Germany to the list of possible peaceful transfers of power. Since France and Germany were militaristic, bureaucratic, imperialistic, and so on, it was clear that in Engels' mind these factors had no bearing on the possibility of peaceful power seizures, and that the existence or non-existence of effective democratic parliamentarism was the decisive point. But Lenin ignored the question of democracy. He and Stalin thought that since 1872 the number of countries where peaceful transition was possible had declined to zero. By contrast, Engels believed their number was increasing.

It can be argued persuasively that the acknowledgment of peaceful means signified a basic change in Marx's thinking. He did not rule out the need for violence (including war), but considered the applicability of violence to be diminishing. In this breaking with the tradition of violence, Marx applied the new approach to the most advanced capitalist countries, where, according to his theory, society had to be most ready to adopt socialism. After Marx's death, Engels, albeit with qualifications, became an outspoken supporter of democratic "methods of struggle," and went far beyond Marx. Several decades later, a genuine Marxist—one who believed in the notion that the new society was being created in the womb of capitalism—should have believed that the possibility of peaceful transition existed in many additional countries. Lenin's and Stalin's *global* denial of this possibility showed not only their deviation from the tactical principles laid down by Marx and Engels but, more importantly, their abandonment of the key theorem in the Marxist doctrine.

WAR AND REVOLUTION

The historical link of the Third International with the conferences of Zimmerwald (1915) and Keinthal (1916), as well as with Lenin's insistence that the "imperialist war" must be turned into a civil war everywhere, needs no elaboration. Lenin's First World War policy was codified and broadened in 1928 by the Comintern's resolution on war, which was drafted by Bukharin and issued by the Sixth World Congress. This is not the proper place to investigate whether Lenin or his successors actually pursued the policy which he preached. We proceed on the assumption that Lenin did call for revolution in all belligerent countries (which is at least half of the truth) and that he showed no interest in the war aims of the Powers. Besides, the Comintern war resolutions contain definitions of just and unjust war, to the effect that the class character of a belligerent decides whether he is fighting for a just or an unjust cause, and that the aggressor is not necessarily in the wrong: a proletarian aggressor, for example, would always be fighting a just war. Are these "lines" in the Marxist tradition?[29]

In July 1870, the General Council asked Marx to write an address[30] on the International's attitude toward the Franco-Prussian War. Marx explained that Germany was fighting a defensive war (France was the ostensible aggressor) and intimated that Napoleon III probably would be overthrown. (At the time the true origins of the war were not known.) However, "if the German working class allows the present war to lose its strictly defensive character and degenerate into a war against the French people, victory or defeat will be equally harmful." While official France and official Germany were fighting a fratricidal war, Marx suggested that the workers "send each other messages of peace and friendship." He made no proposal for actions of greater significance.

This initial policy of supporting Germany's war was the result of three different considerations: Marx and Engels hoped that Napoleon III would be eliminated; they were convinced that the unification of Germany would create more favorable conditions for the development of the German workers' movement; and they believed that as a result of a German victory the center of gravity of the workers' movement would shift from France to Germany, and therefore from Proudhonism and Blanquism to Marxism. In other words, the differences between the various bourgeois states were significant; the issue of aggression versus defense was important; and it did make a great difference whether the war was won by one or the other capitalist government.

Marx, at that time, was able to manipulate the International. Yet he chose to pursue a policy of almost complete passivity. Though the statutes of the Association specifically envisioned the convocation of emergency meetings, he maneuvered to postpone the congress scheduled for 1870. Bakunin, with his Leninist tactics *avant le mot,* wanted to convene the congress in neutral Amsterdam "immediately" after the outbreak of the war.

In late August 1870, Marx and Engels warned the German Social Democratic party that the war might turn into a *Raubkrieg* by Germany against France. On September 4, Napoleon III abdicated. After the Germans had thus presented France with a republic—*"et laquelle!"*—the new rulers of France thought the Germans should leave immediately the holy soil of France; otherwise there would be a *guerre à outrance.* But this, Engels commented sharply, was unrealistic.

The General Council, upon a suggestion by Charles Longuet, Marx's future son-in-law, agitated for the recognition of the new republican government by England. On September 6, Marx in a letter to Engels expressed the fear that French members of the International were going from London to Paris "to overthrow the provisional government and establish a Commune de Paris." Marx was opposed to this policy. Actually, he went so far as to approve provisionally of Jules Favre, the main figure of the new government: Favre had always favored the unity of Italy and Germany.[31]

Nevertheless, the end of the Bonapartist regime called for a new policy. Marx wrote a second address[32] for the General Council in which he pointed out that Germany had won its defensive war; but even before this victory, the Prussian government had decided to transform the defensive war into a war of conquest. The German working class had supported the war it had been unable to prevent. The German proletariat had deemed it to be a war for Germany's independence and for the liberation of Germany and Europe from the oppression of the Second Empire. Now the workers wanted guarantees that their sacrifices had not been in vain, Marx continued. They demanded an honorable peace for France and recognition of the French republic.

Marx expressed the fear that the republic might be just a transitional step toward the restoration of the Orléans dynasty. Nevertheless, "every attempt to overthrow the new government . . . would be desperate folly. The French workers must do their duty as citizens." Their job now was not to rise but to use the new republican freedom to establish an effective organization of the proletarian class.[33] Remarkably enough, Marx's address ended with *"Vive la république!"* If Lenin, in 1917, had followed the spirit of this second address, he would have resolutely supported the provisional government of Prince Lvov and Alexander Kerensky.

Rudolf Meyer, a progressive historian who knew Marx and Engels personally, asserted that "undoubtedly" Marx planned, after Napoleon's downfall, to instigate Socialist uprisings in "about all European countries."[34] But this plan failed, because the moderates kept the upper hand in France, and the German military arrested the revolutionaries. Thereupon, Meyer alleged, Marx advised consolidation of the "blue republic."

There is no evidence that such an insurrectional plan ever existed, though relevant documentation still may come to light.[35] The second address contained merely this lame passage: "May the sections of the International Workingmen's Association in all countries call the working class to activity [*tätige Bewegung*]. If the workers should forget their duty and remain passive, the present dreadful war will be only the forerunner of still more dreadful international struggles." Such language hardly was a precursor of Lenin's pan-revolutionism.

On September 5, 1870, James Guillaume, a close collaborator of Bakunin, sent a manifesto to the sections of the International in which he stated that Prussia was threatening the independence of the French people. Republican France represented the freedom of Europe, while monarchist Germany stood for despotism and reaction. All republicans must rise and march to defend the French republic. In all other countries, members of the International must arm themselves and march to fight at the side of their French brothers. The cause of the French republic was the cause of the European revolution. "The moment has come to give our blood for the liberation of the workers and of all of humanity." Guillaume told the German internationalists that whereas their previous attitude had rightly been one of passive protest, now their duty was to help their French brothers destroy the common enemy, the military power of Prussia. They should rise in the name of a German republic, so that in Berlin as in Paris only the International would be on the march.[36]

Bakunin dispatched twenty-four letters to get the revolution started. The theme of these messages was that since the army no longer could save France, salvation must be achieved through a popular uprising, to be coordinated with uprisings in Spain and Italy. Paris could not assume the initiative; it therefore must be taken by the provinces. "The people everywhere must arm and organize themselves, to launch against the German invader a war of destruction." "Paris and France cannot be saved except by an immense popular uprising."[37] The friends of Prussia *in France* had to be destroyed before the Prussians, who were coming from the outside, could be stopped.

To start the revolution, Bakunin picked Lyon, the second largest city in France. The uprising which he instigated late in September 1870 lasted less than a day. Its easy suppression probably was due to the work of police infiltrators. Bakunin tried his hand again in Marseille, but thereafter desisted from further attempts.

In the meantime, Engels was watching operations with an expert eye. Immediately following Napoleon's overthrow, he discussed in the English press the possibilities of guerrilla war against the Germans. He was thinking of partisan war to be waged by trained soldiers under centralized professional direction—that is, guerrilla war by the army remnants augmented by newly mobilized volunteers and conscripts. He vigorously supported Gambetta's partisan operations in his press articles. There is even a strong possibility that through Paul Lafargue, Marx's son-in-law, he submitted operational suggestions to the resistance leaders around Gambetta. In January 1871, Marx, who had received secret information from Germany, presumably about the difficulties experienced by the German army in France, transmitted intelligence via Engels and Lafargue to the chief of French counterintelligence. On January 16, 1871, Marx wrote a letter to the *Daily News* asserting that the French cause was not yet desperate. France was continuing to fight, not just for her independence but for the freedom of Germany and Europe.[38] In brief, Marx and Engels were supporting the war effort of the French republic against Germany.

On March 18, 1871, as a result of events which had nothing to do with any actions of the International, let alone of Marx himself, the Commune of Paris came into being.[39] This was the first "seizure of power" by the "proletariat," and Marx provided advice on various questions of policy and finance. But he did not maintain serious contacts with the leaders of the Commune. The members of the International who did participate in the Commune failed to identify themselves fully with its governing body, constituting themselves instead as a separate party.

It is understandable that Marx should have acted with great restraint in his relations with the Commune, which was divided into a majority of Blanquists and a minority of Proudhonists. But there was at least one task for which Marx's and the International's enthusiastic support was needed: to keep the Paris Commune going, additional communes had to be established all over France. Now was the time to adopt Bakunin's strategy and implement it through realistic tactics. But, on that score, Marx did nothing.[40]

He did seek to mobilize political (though not financial) support from abroad and, to judge from the scanty information available, suggested demonstrations of "solidarity"—a tactic dear to the Positivists. Although he asserted that he wrote several hundred letters to all parts of the world where the International had connections, so far virtually no traces of this extensive correspondence have been discovered. In several letters to editors of English newspapers calling for sympathy with Paris, Marx protested strenuously against accusations that he or the International had been responsible for establishing the

Commune. Since September, many sections had been acting on the invitation to agitate for recognition of the republican government. This agitation continued, most incongruously, throughout the life of the Commune.

Toward the end of the struggle, Marx communicated to Paris secret information which he had obtained from Germany to the effect that Bismarck had been offering German credits to the French government. The French refused lest prominent members of the government lose their personal commissions, which French bankers were willing to pay for the internal indemnity loan of two billion francs. Marx also reported that the French government had asked Bismarck's permission to postpone the payment of the first indemnity installment until after the fall of the Commune and that Bismarck had agreed to this request. Since Prussia was in urgent need of money, it therefore could be expected that Bismarck would "give the Versailles government every possible facility for hastening the occupation of Paris."[41] The Commune was in no position to take proper precautions, and Marx subsequently expressed satisfaction that the Communards perished fighting, instead of capitulating in complete demoralization.

On August 10, 1871, Marx disclosed in a private letter that before the armistice the French government had approached the International in order to arrange public demonstrations in London in favor of the "government of defense." It had asked that the demonstrators speak not of the "republic" but only of "France." The General Council refused to provide assistance under this condition. But, added Marx, "this goes to show that the French government itself considered the *International* an ally of the French republic against the Prussian conqueror—and in fact it was the only ally France had during the war."[42] *Qualis pater, talis filius?* The Comintern really should have purged Marx.

A Party of a New Type

THE FOUNDATION STONE OF THE COMMUNIST INTERNATIONAL

by

BERTRAM D. WOLFE

Lenin began his career as a Social Democrat, a disciple of Plekhanov, who was himself an orthodox disciple of Marx. He revered, too, Plekhanov's contemporaries, Paul Axelrod and Vera Zasulich. His own closest comrades-in-arms were two men of his own generation, Martov and Potresov. With these he formed a "triple alliance" or *troika*. He was to form many *troikas* in the course of his subsequent political life to give the cover of "collective leadership" to his own strongly original ideas on power, on organization, and on *de facto* one-man leadership. But this first *troika* was different from all the others. It was in his eyes an "alliance," not a team of three with himself as undisputed lead-horse. Despite his headstrong self-assurance, there was a sense of equal partnership which was lacking in all his later teams. And toward Plekhanov, Axelrod and Zasulich he evinced a genuine reverence which he was never again to accord to any living man.

At the beginning of the present century, these six persons formed an editorial board to impose their views on the various Socialist or Social Democratic movements, the embryonic unions, and the working class of Russia. Together the six edited the journal *Iskra*, together faced all other trends in the nascent socialist and labor movement, together fought the battle for what they regarded as the only true orthodox Marxism. Yet within three years Lenin had broken with the other five and was posting guards to keep four of them out of a meeting of the *Iskra* caucus at a party congress. Another fourteen years and these one-time close comrades were to find themselves on "opposite sides of the barricades."

The story of this union to impose orthodox Marxism on the Russian movement and then the break as to the meaning of orthodoxy, is the story of Lenin's development of his own distinctive views on the nature of Party organization and of the conquest of power. What Lenin founded in the course of his struggles with the other five he himself was to call "a party of a new type." It is with this party that Lenin seized power, and so completely did his success in seizing power seem to him to justify all that he had done that when he stepped on the arena of world politics to found his Communist International and push for a world revolution, into the basic documents of the Comintern he wrote his prescriptions for a "party of a new type." Thus when we study the history of *Iskra,* its rise and fall, we get a key to the organizational forms and spirit of the Communist International, for its foundation stones were so many replicas, as far as Lenin could make them so, of his own Russian "Party of a New Type."

Between 1900 and 1903, this foundation stone was chiseled. While in exile in 1900 in remote Siberia, Lenin corresponded with Martov, also in Siberian exile, and with Potresov, working out in meticulous detail his plans for the new Marxist journal, *Iskra,* to be ²dited and published abroad and smuggled into Russia. The triple alliance, as he saw it then, would add its youth and vigor to the prestige and wisdom of the *troika* of the older generation, headed by Plekhanov.

The older *troika* had been in exile abroad since the beginning of the eighties. Living out their homesick lives through long decades of isolation from their native land and the movement, they were delighted when they were visited by this energetic young man with a practical bent for organization. To be sure, there was a nasty moment when Plekhanov, taking it for granted that he would be the editor of the new journal (was he not one of the most distinguished Marxists in the whole Socialist International?), found that Lenin took it for granted that he himself would be the editor. Plekhanov was haughty, Lenin in a rage—a kind of tempest which welled up from the depths of his being at intervals throughout his life.[1]

In a letter to Martov intended to serve as a report to his faction, "How the Spark Was Nearly Extinguished,"[2] a document which takes up twenty-five pages in his *Works* and is written in a language more suited to a Russian novel than a political report, Lenin told how he had been "enamored" of Plekhanov, had "courted him out of the great love I bore him." "Never, never in my life," he lamented, "have I regarded any other man with such sincere respect and reverence . . . never stood before anyone with such humility, never been so brutally spurned. At times I thought I should burst into tears." But not veneration nor love nor grief nor humility suggested to him that perhaps Plekhanov, and not he, should be editor. "My infatuation disappeared as by magic. . . . An enamored youth receives from the object of his love a bitter lesson: to regard all persons without sentiment; to keep a stone in one's sling."

At that moment, the "youth" grew up. Never would he speak of himself as a youth again. On the granite of his character the lesson thus engraved would last a lifetime. Three years later, when he was outvoted at the Second Party Congress on an organization question, he would show that he could "regard without sentiment" not only the "elders" but the other two members of his "triple alliance" as well. In 1900, however, the "lovers' quarrel" was patched up with a cold agreement to live together "without infatuation"—and, of course, with Lenin having his way. *Iskra* would be printed in Germany, where Lenin lived, not in Switzerland, where Plekhanov made his home. Lenin's wife was to be its secretary, keep the confidential addresses, code and decode letters, develop the invisible ink in which they were written, handle correspondence with the underground, consult with her husband and, on his order, dispatch items of correspondence to the others. Lenin assumed the burden of rewriting correspondence from Russia into articles, the task of answering letters, assigning themes to the other editors subject to their agreement, nagging contributors, dummying, proofreading (with Martov's help), cutting, arguing with authors to get consent to revisions. He it was who wrote the exhortations and instructions to the agents in Russia, developed the apparatus for smuggling, dispatched escapees and exiles as agents, selected people to come abroad, be briefed by him, then return to Russia. His fellow editors were glad that he took upon his shoulders these unrewarding tasks. Thus, from the outset, Lenin was the machine man, the master of the *apparat* which he himself had conceived.

He was better than any of the others at his self-chosen chores. Plekhanov had a wider-ranging mind, more learning in Marxist theory, history, philosophy, and literature; Vera Zasulich was more concerned with the sufferings of the masses; Axelrod had more respect for the autonomy and dignity of the workingmen and their organizations; Martov was a better journalist and popular agitator; Potresov was a better provider of funds—mostly from his own private fortune. But Lenin was the systematic, doctrinaire thinker on organization questions and the fulfiller of his own doctrines.

LENIN, THE ORGANIZATION MAN

Indeed the most obvious trait setting Lenin apart from his associates was this absorption with the mechanics and dynamics of organization. In a world where most intellectuals were in love with ideas, and accustomed—whether by temperament or the pressure of circumstance—to a yawning gap between the dream and the deed, Lenin was an *organization man*—indeed, *the* organization man—of whatever movements he planned or took part in.

He was an enemy alike to the slippered sloth and dusk-to-dawn discussion of the Russian intellectuals, and to the "spontaneous" and "unreliable" flareups, subsidings, and very conceptions of their own interests on the part of the Russian masses. All his life he was at work on a machine to harness the force of the waves and tides, to convert their fluctuating, unreckonable rise-and-fall into a single stream of energy. It was his aim, as he wrote, "to collect and concentrate all the drops and streamlets of popular excitement that are called forth by Russian conditions . . . into one single, gigantic flood." Tidily, yet passionately, he assumed the task of "choosing the people who are necessary and verifying the practical execution of decisions." In a world of intellectuals who lived by ideas, organization was his idea. "In its struggle for power, the proletariat has no other weapon but organization." "*Now* we have become an organized party, and that means the creation of power, the transformation of the authority of ideas into the authority of power, the subordination of the lower party organs to the higher ones." Amidst men dedicated to dreams, organization was his dream. "Give me an organization of revolutionaries," he cried, echoing Archimedes, "and I will turn Russia upside down."[3]

When, at the Second Congress, delegate Popov spoke of the future Central Committee in liturgical language as a "Spirit, omnipresent and one," Lenin cried out from his seat, "Not Spirit, but *Fist!*"[4] Before there was a Party congress or a central committee, Lenin was already dreaming of this, his fist, which would hold all reins in its grasp, control all levers and springs of action. In 1902, a year before the congress, he wrote:

> The committee should lead *all* aspects of the local movement and direct *all* local institutions, forces and resources of the Party. . . . Discussion of all Party questions, of course, will take place also in the district circles, but the *deciding* of all general questions of the local movement should be done only by the committee. The independence of the district groups, it follows, would be permitted only in questions of the technique of transmitting and distributing. The composition of the district groups should be determined by the committee; i.e., the committee designates one or two of its members (or even of those not members of the committee) as delegates to such and such a district, and entrusts these delegates with *setting up the district group,* all the members of which should be in their turn confirmed . . . in their positions by the committee. The district group is a local branch of the committee, receiving its powers only from the latter.[5]

Thus the central committee was to be the brain, the local organizations the limbs; the committee would decide, the locals execute; the committee would designate and confirm the local leaders in their posts, then the local leaders would in due course become delegates to a congress which would approve the central committee which had designated them. Such a central committee would be spirit and fist in one.

To his associates (as distinct from his admiring followers) there was something disconcerting in this zealotry of centralization. Yet their minds were on other aspects of the movement, its doctrine, its theory, its journalistic exposition. Organization was an unattractive concern. Not unwillingly, they handed over its burdens to this dedicated expert on organization. For their part, they dreamed of the day when Russia would know sufficient liberty that the masses of workingmen might form their own organizations and democratically control and designate their central organs, which would then serve rather than use and command the working class. But meanwhile, Russia was police-ridden and proper Socialist organization practically impossible. "Whether this revolutionary practice," Potresov was to write later, "which had not been so much experienced as thought up in the head of its future organizer, was really the practice which corresponded with the aims and methods of international social democracy, it was still difficult to judge." Later, "we had to pay dearly for this misunderstanding."

The others might dream of the day when Russia would be free enough for the workingmen to organize freely and freely select their officials and determine their own program. Then the Party, they thought, would become a simple instrument of the class, its creature and servant, willing, expert, and dedicated to the task of helping the working class to achieve its own aims and its own freely decided goals. But Lenin did not see it that way. This was to him not Marxism, but a species of treason to Marxism. This was "bourgeois politics," he wrote in one of his most uncompromising, and to his colleagues incomprehensible, early utterances: "The task of the bourgeois politician is to 'assist the economic struggle of the proletariat.' The task of the Socialist is to make the economic struggle assist the Socialist movement and the victory of the revolutionary labor party."[6]

Could authoritarianism go further? To the question whether the workers exist for the Party or the Party exists for the workers, Lenin had found his uncompromising answer.[7]

Moreover, Lenin had conceived an especially large, and indeed unique, role for the journal, *Iskra*. Plekhanov, Martov or Potresov could have edited it, too, but it would have had another character. On the masthead was the old message of hope from the Decembrists to Pushkin: "Out of the spark [*iskra*] shall come the flame." To Lenin the "spark" was more than a figure of speech. *Iskra* was to be "an enormous pair of bellows that would blow every spark of popular indignation into a flame." It was to be "not only the collective agitator but the collective organizer." It was to become the guardian of the purity of doctrine, the destroyer of rival revolutionary theories (heresies in Lenin's mind) and competing tendencies (enemies to him).[8] It was to be "the scaffolding" of an all-Russian revolutionary party, the convoker of a unifying and homogenizing all-national congress, for the party that should issue from it must not only be unified but uniform, not only integrated but systematized, rigorously intolerant of variety, pluralism, and multiformity, whether in ideology or structure.

Iskra's "network of agents" must become the vanguard and elite of the revolutionary movement. They must "devote to the revolution not only their spare evenings, but the whole of their lives." They must make revolution their profession and be professional in their revolutionary skills. No mere vendors or distributors of a clandestine journal, they must "introduce strict division of labor in the various forms of work," become "accustomed to fulfilling the detailed functions of the national 'all-Russian' work . . . test their strength in organization of various kinds of revolutionary activities . . . form the skeleton of an organization . . . sufficiently large to embrace the whole country," sufficiently self-assertive, ubiquitous, and omnipotent to "utilize" every flare-up of discontent in "every layer" of society, whether *zemstvo*, or student, or peasant, or worker. The aim of the journal was "to gather a clandestine circle of leaders and to set in motion the greatest possible mass." Clearly this was not a group of newspaper vendors or even a party; it was more exalted and exclusive than a party, for a party might embrace *all* who agreed with its general aims. The network of agents would seek rather to become the "officers' cadres" of future armies, which it would lead in a storm attack against the citadel of tsarism. Their work for the paper "would serve as an exact measure of the extent to which . . . our military activities had been firmly established. . . . This degree of military preparedness can be created only by the constant activity of a regular army."[9] Not an ordinary army either, but an officers' corps capable of expansion at any moment of unrest into the staff of a multitudinous host. "The paper will bring forward not only the most competent propagandists but the most skillful organizers, and the most talented political leaders, who will be able at the right moment to issue the call for the decisive battle, and to lead that battle."[10]

While the other editors thought of themselves as agitators, propagandists, ideological guides, and teachers, telling *Iskra* readers what to think and believe, only the rough-hewn, repetitive, audacious articles signed Lenin told them what to *do* and how high a value to set upon themselves and their routine-seeming work. In due course Lenin elaborated all these articles into an epoch-making brochure called, after the celebrated utopian novel of Chernishevsky, *Chto Delat'*? or *What Is to Be Done?*

Was ever a journal given so large a role in history? No wonder the *Iskra* agents in their narrow, suffocating underground were attracted to this wise old-young man. Here was a dream that seemed to give one's small tasks enormous meaning. Here was a commander one could follow, worship. Even his amoralism seemed engagingly attractive as he wrote instructions on how to circumvent rival tendencies and journals, how to be sure that "our people" are elected as delegates to the coming ("Second") congress, how to put "ours" into committees by taking advantage of police arrests of "theirs." With the representatives of other Socialist groups, some older and better organized than the Iskrists—like the adherents of *Rabochee Delo* (The Workers' Cause) and of the Bund (the Jewish Workers' Union)—he wrote, "be wise as serpents and gentle as doves."[11]

By building an *apparat* for *Iskra* within the general revolutionary movement, Lenin was building a machine of personal loyalty to himself alone among the six *Iskra* editors. Though they did not yet know it, among the Iskrists there were already Leninists.

THE BIRTH OF BOLSHEVISM

By 1903, the Iskrists had succeeded in establishing their ideological ascendancy, thanks chiefly to their organizational predominance and to the prestige of the learned and venerated Plekhanov—and thanks to the detailed plans and directives of Lenin. Having managed to sidetrack or blow up all rival plans for a nationwide Socialist congress, *Iskra* now invited all local and national groups to send delegates to a congress called by it. Out of respect for an abortive congress in 1898, all of whose members had been arrested by the police, the convention called by *Iskra* was designated the "Second" congress. But its announced aim was to found an all-Russian Socialist party on the basis (or so the *Iskra* editors intended) of *Iskra*'s program.

At the congress, the Iskrists had a safe majority. Lenin had seen to that. The Iskrist majority held together while they worsted rival tendencies and had their program adopted. Then they themselves fell to quarreling over what seemed a trivial difference in the definition of a party member.[12] When Lenin was outvoted on this organization question, his fury knew no bounds. In one of his famous rages, he split the *Iskra* caucus and convoked a faction meeting of the "true Iskrists," posting guards to keep out all his fellow *Iskra* editors except Plekhanov, who for the moment was siding with him. It was only two years since he had written to Martov that he would henceforth "regard all persons without sentiment and keep a stone in his sling." Now he kept Martov out of his own caucus. How well he had learned his lesson!

Could this be the unifying congress that was to give birth to a single, all-Russian party? Lenin was the first to realize that it had given birth to two parties instead of one, that the clash of temperaments concealed differences on organization, on relation of the Party to the working class and to society, on the nature of the revolution itself—differences so profound that they could be resolved only by one faction's destroying the standing of the other. It took his five associates of yesterday (as it did the Russian underground) more than a decade before they realized it, too. During that decade, Lenin often would be forced by Party public opinion, including that of his own faction, to work together with those whom he thought of as ineluctable enemies, but no pretense at unity for tactical reasons ever caused him to give up his faction organization or alter by one iota his unique views.

Though he had his slight majority during the congress for only a brief interval, his awareness of the power impact of words caused him to arrogate to his faction the title *Bolsheviki* (Majorityites), and to dub his opponents *Mensheviki* (Minorityites). Ineptly, the Mensheviki accepted his label, coming to wear its stigma as a badge of pride. Actually, at the congress itself, the vote on which the Iskrists split into two factions—the vote on the "definition of a member"—was twenty-three for Lenin against twenty-eight for Martov, a clear majority for the "Minority." Only at the end of the congress, when a number of delegates already had left or withdrawn in protest, did Lenin manage to muster nineteen votes against seventeen on the personal issue,[13] with three abstentions. Even then he did not have a majority of those present and recording their votes, and his nineteen was a mere third of the full congress. Between 1903 and 1917, his opponents usually would have the majority of the Party members behind them, but Lenin clung to the power-redolent name which gave his faction and his acts prestige among the inexperienced.

When the congress adjourned, there were three central organs: the editorial board of *Iskra*, consisting now of Lenin and Plekhanov[14] (for the next ten years Plekhanov was to waver between Bolsheviks and Mensheviks); a central committee, handpicked by Lenin, to function underground in Russia; and a Party council, made up from the first two. Within a year, Plekhanov too broke with him because of his merciless attitude toward the other old editors, and Lenin lost his post on the central organ. His handpicked central committee broke with him because of his "splitting tactics," his henchmen thereby becoming in his eyes "worse than Mensheviks." The Party council, of course, turned against him. Then the underground let him know that it wanted "unity."

Unshaken, he picked himself a new *troika* of men who had not even been at the congress, had not been elected to anything. He managed to gather twenty-two random signatures to an endorsement of what he had done and what he contemplated. The twenty-two included his wife, his sister, and himself! But he called this tiny fraction by the large name "Bureau of the Committees of the Majority." Like all future *troikas* and faction committees, these were emanations of his own person, handpicked from those who were willing to agree with a position which in his strong-minded self-confidence he alone had elaborated. To the secretary of this new Bureau of the Committees of the Majority, he wrote characteristically on January 29, 1905: "For God's sake don't trust the Mensheviks and the central committee [i.e., his own handpicked central committee of yesterday] and everywhere, unconditionally and in the most resolute fashion force splits, splits, and again splits."[15]

But whatever the future might hold in store, in 1903, when the "unifying" Second Congress adjourned, it was Lenin and his wife who held in their hands all threads leading to the underground agents and hence to the locals in Russia. As one of his opponents, Rafael Abramovich, was to tell me years later: "Though Lenin was virtually isolated abroad where everyone had been able to follow the congress fight closely, he had all the connections with Russia and we had none."

Thus did Lenin in his first big test prove himself a master of the twin arts of organization and power—power for the Iskrists within the many-colored Socialist and revolutionary movement, then power for himself and his faction in the underground. In 1917, when power was lying loose in the streets, he would demonstrate his skill in using his machine to seize power in the state and hold on to it. So was his belief to be confirmed that it did not matter how many he lost in the course of the building of the party machine, so long as the machine remained effective and those he won accepted his organization conceptions and his leadership.

Marx had been vague on how the working class would take power, deliberately silent on what it would do with power once it had it. In Lenin, however, he had an innovating disciple who was a theoretician, technician, and virtuoso of organization and power. Lenin's speciality was the *how*, rather than the why or what. Conspiracy, centralized organization, military discipline, the ability to stir, manipulate and coalesce the sources of discontent for one's power purposes—a technique and indeed a technology of the art and science of taking power, of devising the instruments for seizing, holding, wielding, and maximizing power—what are these if not the levers of modern revolution? Here indeed was a revolutionist of a new type, determined to form what he himself would call "a party of a new type," to make, as it turned out a revolution of a new type. In 1903, his five associates on the *Iskra* editorial board contemplated the fury of his dictatorial centralism with uncomprehending wonder. In 1917, it would be the world's turn to stare and wonder.

For the three years from 1900 to 1903 the six editors of *Iskra* had been using a common vocabulary: *Marxism, orthodoxy, socialism, working class, party, central committee, member.* Plekhanov had written, and they all had approved, a common program.[16] But at the congress their confident, self-chosen band of leaders had been rent in two over *the definition of a member!* It dawned on them then that every word they had been using in common was subject to directly opposite interpretations.

Factionalism has a logic of its own. It compelled five of them to ask for the first time how they could ever have permitted these strange organization doctrines to be uttered in their name by their specialist on questions of organization.[17] And it led Lenin to invent for the other five a heresy undreamed of by Marx: "opportunism in the organization question." For this "deviation," Lenin invented a completely new language of reprobation, derision, and condemnation: *khvostism* ("tailism," or dragging at the tail instead of leading); "cringing before spontaneity," "slavish kowtowing to the backwardness of the masses," "dragging the Party backward," "glorifying unpreparedness and backwardness," "bourgeois trade unionism in the organization question," and many related heresies. (These expressions are culled from the rich new vocabulary of disparagement and abuse which Lenin introduced in his ground-breaking *What Is to be Done?* Some of them are analyzed below.)

A PARTY OF THE CLASS OR A PARTY FOR THE CLASS

"Only" a question of organization (since they still kept the common Program)! Only a question of organization, but what a gulf it opened! Of course both Lenin and his opponents appealed to Marxism, for both sides looked on Marxism as truth and science. But here, as elsewhere, Marx is ambiguous. Among these champions of ortho-doxy and slayers of revisionism, one text from the sacred canon could be made as probative as another. As against Marx's certitude con-cerning his own theoretical ideas, there was his insistence that ideas play only a minor role in history, as a reflection of more fundamental self-acting material forces. Though Marx fought ruthlessly for the supremacy of his doctrine in the International, always he insisted that in the long run the working class itself would elaborate its own "con-sciousness" and organization, while "doctrinaire sects" would be out-grown or absorbed into mere servants of mass workingmen's parties. "The emancipation of the working class must be conquered by the working class itself," he wrote as the first point in the Statutes of the International Workingmen's Association. And, even as he criticized the unity of Lasalleans and Marxists in Germany, which had come about without his advice and on a program which seemed to him un-sound, nevertheless he declared: "Every step of a real movement is more important than a dozen programs."[18] The working class, be-cause of its conditions of life, he thought, would develop its own rev-olutionary consciousness. From its increasing numbers and urban concentration, its mounting polarization at one pole of society, its ever-widening struggles and deeper experiences, its growing humilia-tion, degradation, despair, and indignation, it would generate its own mass working-class party, correct its own errors, coming at last to the point where "the conditions themselves would cry out: *Hic Rhodus! hic salta"!* The "class *in* itself" would become a "class *for* itself," would elevate itself to the ruling class, then revolutionize society.

If one goes from isolated texts to the overall context of Marx's thought, or if one takes the mighty German movement which Marx and Engels (and until August 1914, Lenin, too) regarded as the model, there can be no doubt that Marxist theories assigned a deci-sive role to the spontaneous development, the self-organization, the *class* consciousness, the conditions of life and experiences of struggle of the working class. As Engels wrote, "For the ultimate triumph of the ideas expounded in the Communist Manifesto, Marx put his trust only and exclusively in the intellectual development of the working class as it must necessarily result from action and discussion in com-mon."[19] But in less than three years, from 1900 to 1903, Lenin put out quite a body of literature in the name of *Iskra* and of "orthodox" Marxism which made it clear that he did not share Marx's confidence in the working class.

LENIN'S CENTRALISM

The first striking peculiarity in Lenin's doctrine is its extreme central-ism, coupled with an extreme distrust of the rank and file of his party and the local organizations. When Lenin was in control of the central organ of the Party, he asked defiantly: "What is bad about the com-plete dictatorship of the central organ?"[20] Chided with suppressing party democracy, Lenin answered for himself and his band of profes-sional revolutionaries: "They have no time to think of the toy forms of democracy . . . but they have a lively sense of their *responsibility* and they know by experience that to get rid of an undesirable mem-ber, an organization of real revolutionaries will stop at nothing."[21]

This is surely one of the most unresponsive answers in political literature. Lenin argues that under the conditions of police spying in Russia, party democracy is a "useless and harmful toy." But the con-text reveals that even in a free country the chief function of party "democracy" to him is to provide "the general control, in the literal sense of the term, that the Party exercises over every member," a control which enables the Party to decide whether to assign to a mem-ber one function or another, or to get rid of him altogether as unfit. He believes that, in the context of illegality, democracy can be re-placed completely by the mutual trust of Socialists in each other, the absolute trust of all in the self-selected leading committee, and faith in the ability of the latter to get rid of those who cannot be trusted.

Even more uncompromising is Lenin's championing of "bureau-cratic centralism" as against the democratic autonomy of the primary or local organizations and their control over the center. This bureau-cratic centralism he considers as appropriate to a Socialist party in any country. The language of his celebration of "bureaucratism" is prickly and rough-hewn, but its meaning is startlingly clear:

> Bureaucratism *versus* autonomy, such is the principle of revolu-tionary social democracy as against that of the opportunists. . . . The organization of revolutionary social democracy strives to go from the top downward and defends the enlargement of the rights and plenary powers of the central body.[22]

Of course it was hard, indeed impossible, for this power-cen-tered man to imagine that he would not be in control of the center. To Lunacharsky he said:

> "If we have in the CC or in the central organ a majority, then we will demand the firmest discipline. We will insist on every sort of subordination of the Mensheviks to party unity . . ."

I asked Vladimir Ilyich: "Well, and what if it should turn out after all that we are in a minority?"

Lenin smiled enigmatically and said: "It depends on the circumstances. In any case we will not permit them to make of unity a rope around our necks. And under no circumstances will we let the Mensheviks drag us after them on such a rope."[23]

Not until Lenin had been chided by his opponents for more than half a decade for his rejection of party democracy did he finally seek to conceal somewhat his arch centralism and aversion to any local autonomy or to control from below. For the purposes of his concealment, he coined his celebrated term, *democratic centralism!* Even after he was in power and no longer could give as his justification the tsar's police, in the third year of his rule he defined that self-contradictory term as "meaning only that representatives from the localities gather and choose a responsible organ. . . . The responsible organ must do the administering."

When Lenin's concept of democratic centralism was transplanted to the Communist International, it was formulated this way:

> The main principle of democratic centralism is that of the higher cell being elected by the lower cell, the absolute binding force of all directives of a higher cell to a cell subordinate to it, and the existence of a commanding [*vlastnogo;* i.e., endowed with, or clothed with, power] Party center [the authority of which] is unchallengeable for all leaders in Party life, from one congress to the next.[24]

Lenin's division of spheres between what should be "centralized" and what "decentralized" would be comical were it not for its tragic implications for Russia and for communism. In his "Letter to a Comrade on Our Organizational Tasks," Lenin wrote:

> We have arrived at an extremely important principle of all Party organization and Party activity. In regard to ideological and practical *direction* the movement and the revolutionary struggle of the proletariat need the *greatest possible centralization,* but in regard to *keeping the center informed* concerning the movement and concerning the Party as a whole, in regard to *responsibility* before the Party, we need the *greatest possible decentralization.* The movement must be led by the smallest possible number of the most homogeneous groups of trained and experienced revolutionaries. But the largest possible number of the most varied and heterogeneous groups drawn from the most diverse layers of the proletariat (and of other classes) should take part in the movement. And in regard to each such group the center of the Party must have always before it not

only exact data on their activities but also the fullest possible knowledge of their composition.[25]

If we add to this rule (quoted on page 24) which prescribes that the "committee should lead *all* aspects of the local movement and direct *all* local institutions, forces . . . decide all general questions" and leave "independence of the district groups . . . only in the questions of the technique of transmitting and distributing," then Lenin's conception of hierarchical centralism becomes terrifyingly clear. All power, all command, all decision should be with the center ("the district group receives its powers only from the latter"), but the duty to carry out, obey and report should be "decentralized" and accorded as a "privilege" to every local organization and individual member, and even to party sympathizers.

Afraid that his readers might not get its full implications, Lenin repeated it all again, as was his wont, with only slight variations and different underscorings:

> We must centralize the direction of the movement. We must also (and we must *for this reason,* for without the informing of the center its leadership is impossible) decentralize as much as possible the *responsibility before the Party* of each circle which forms part of the Party or inclines to it. This decentralization is the necessary condition for revolutionary centralization and *its necessary corrective.* In order that the center may not only give advice, persuade, and argue (as has been done up to now), but may really direct the orchestra, it is essential to know exactly who is playing which fiddle and where; who, where, is learning to master which instrument or has mastered it; who, where and why, is playing out of tune (when the music begins to grate on the ear); and who, how, and where should be transferred to correct the dissonance, and so on.[26]

From the outset Lenin's "center" was self-appointed. He began with himself, then gathered around him those who agreed with him. Again and again he removed players from his orchestra when *their* playing grated on *his* ears, gathering others more in harmony with his directing. Thus his "Leninist" center was self-perpetuating.

The same ideas reappeared in the years of comparatively open activity between 1907 and 1914, when *Zvezda and Pravda* were legal journals and the Bolsheviks could campaign openly and elect deputies to the Duma. They continued during the six months of 1917 when Russia, in Lenin's words, was "the freest country in the world." And they continued when Lenin held power in party and country. At first he sought to justify his centralism before its critics by pointing to the harsh conditions of a conspiratorial underground movement, but in time it became clear that his centralism sprang from the deepest necessities of his temperament, his confidence in himself, and his pessimistic view of his fellow men. He has been compared to a schoolmaster commanding his pupils (by Edmund Wilson) and to a general commanding an embattled army (in his own figures of speech on military discipline). Here, in any case, is "a revolutionary of a rare type: a revolutionary with a bureaucratic mind,"[27] to whom the complete centralization and control of all activities is—of all things—the road to a stateless, partyless utopia!

Hence Lenin's Archimedean cry for an organization of revolutionaries "to turn Russia upside down" did not cease when Russia was turned upside down. As before, Lenin continued to repeat the cry for "organization, organization, organization." In power, as when fighting for power, he said: "Our fighting method is organization." But now he had something new to add. To the old dream of centralized organization of the Party, which he did not for a moment abandon, he added the new dream of total organization by the Party. Of what? Why, of Russia. Its industries and its agriculture, its feelings and its thoughts, its habits, even its dreams—total organization of slackness, of the waywardness of will, of all deeds and desires. "We must organize everything," he said in the summer of 1918, "take everything into our hands."[28]

THE BIRTH OF TOTALITARIANISM

Thus to the authoritarian trend inherent in an infallible doctrine, possessed and interpreted by an infallible interpreter who ruled an infallible party, from above, infallibly, Lenin added the further dream of an authoritarian doctrine and *apparat* with the determination to "organize everything, take everything into our hands"—and totalitarianism was born.

Indeed, this ambition totally to organize everything was actually inherent in his doctrine from the start. The outbursts against "spontaneity" and "elementalness" in the first "Leninist" pamphlet (*What Is to Be Done?*) show that the longing to give ordered and organized form to the spontaneously developing life of the masses was always at the core of Lenin's thought. After he had taken power he wrote in 1920: "Petit-bourgeois spontaneity is more terrible than all the Denikins, Kolchaks, and Yudeniches put together."

If it seems strange in a "democrat" to distrust the rank and file of the party and the local organizations, it seems stranger still in a Marxist to express distrust of the very class from which "proletarian consciousness" was to issue and whose destiny it was to achieve socialism. But Lenin thought this distrust necessary and obvious. "Cut off from the influence of the social democracy," he wrote in his first signed article for *Iskra,* "the workingmen's movement becomes petty and inevitably bourgeois."[29]

That dictum, only a single sentence in his first *Iskra* article, became the central thought of *What Is to Be Done?* There he spelled out his distrust, underscored it, repeated it tirelessly and monotonously.

An entire chapter, entitled "The Spontaneity of the Masses and Consciousness of the Social Democracy," stresses the distinction between "spontaneity" and "consciousness," which brings us to the core of Lenin's spirit. The Russian word *stikhiinost'* means both spontaneity and elementalness. *Soznatel'nost',* for Lenin, means ordered and order-producing consciousness.[30] He opposed the two words to each other as one might light and darkness. The elemental and spontaneous were incorporated in the working class and the masses generally. It was the way they thought, felt, fought, when they had no guidance from "consciousness." Consciousness was the Party. The Party without leadership over the masses was mind without body. The masses without the leadership of the Party was body without mind.

As his emphasis on centralism as against democracy had led him to invent the heresy of "opportunism in the organization question," so his emphasis on consciousness as against spontaneity led him to invent the heresy of "slavish kowtowing before spontaneity." The language is strange, the idea of the heresy stranger still. "Kowtowing" is the act of worship by which the devout in the Russian church prostrate themselves before a revered image. To call it "slavish" and "shameful" makes it clear that Lenin regarded it as evil. But why? Because the working class, left to itself, without the tutelage of the Party, would never in its life attain to so much as the conception of socialism! Socialism turns out not to be, as Marx believed, the quintessential thought of the proletariat, but a doctrine understood, possessed, and propagated by an intellectual elite, and at that an elite not of the working class. Hence to look to the working class to work out its own salvation, to seek only to serve the working-class movement rather than to take it in tow, is in Lenin's eyes to renounce revolution and socialism. Lenin describes this as dragging behind the working class instead of dragging it after you. This is the heresy of *khvostism* which we have already noted. Thus Lenin's distrust of "spontaneity" and his heresy of "tailism" are bound up with his distrust of the working class itself.[31]

In the introduction to *What Is to Be Done?* Lenin apologizes— for the first and last time—for the work's "numerous literary shortcomings." Actually, it has no "literary" form at all. It does not develop its ideas; it proclaims them, repeats them, insists on them, hammers them home. Repetition of his main points, not merely until they sink in, but until they "condition" the reader, hypnotize him, take possession of him, take on the air of indisputable truisms,—this was, in his speaking as in his writing, the essence of Lenin's styleless "style."

He took a backward glance at the yesterday of the Russian workers. Their struggles had not made them Socialists, nor could any amount of experience in struggle ever turn the working class into a Socialist class or a consciously revolutionary one. For this there was needed a vanguard of professionals—professionals of theory, organization, consciousness; professionals who made revolution their profession. There had not been, there was not,

> nor *could there be* Social Democratic consciousness in the workers. This can be brought to them only from the outside. The history of all lands testifies to the fact that alone by their own forces the working class is capable of working out only a trade union consciousness. . . . But the teachings of socialism have grown out of those philosophical, historical, economic theories which were worked out by the educated representatives of the possessing classes, the intelligentsia. By their social position, Marx and Engels, the founders of contemporary scientific socialism, belonged to the bourgeois intelligentsia, too. This is true for Russia also, where the theoretical doctrine of Social Democracy arose in complete independence from the spontaneous (elemental) growth of the workers' movement—arose as the natural and inevitable result of the development of thought among the revolutionary intelligentsia.[32]

The workers have to be "pushed from the outside." There has never been, nor can there be, enough of this "pushing from the outside." Conversely, to "flatter" the workers, to arouse in them "a sense of distrust toward those who bring them political knowledge and revolutionary experience from the outside" is to be a demagogue—a unique, Leninist definition of this term—"and a demagogue is the worst enemy of the working class."[33]

Since there can be no talk of an independent ideology being worked out the *only choice is:* either bourgeois or Socialist ideology. There is no middle term (for no "third" ideology has been worked out by mankind, and, furthermore, in a society torn by class contradictions in general there can never be an outside-of-class or above-class ideology). Hence *any* diminution of Socialist ideology, and *departure* from it, signifies by that very fact a strengthening of bourgeois ideology. But the *spontaneous* development of the workers' movement leads precisely to its subordination to bourgeois ideology . . . for the spontaneous workers' movement is trade unionism, etc., is *nur Gewerkschaftlerei* [the German term for trade unionism pure and simple], and trade unionism means precisely the ideological enslavement of the workers to the bourgeoisie.[34]

Class political consciousness can be brought to the worker *only from the outside,* that is, from outside the economic struggle, from outside the sphere of relations between workers and bosses. The sphere from which alone it is possible to derive this knowledge is the sphere of the relation of *all* the classes and strata and the state and the government—the sphere of interrelations among *all* classes. Therefore, the question, what is to be done to bring to the workers political knowledge, cannot be answered . . . by "go to the workers." To bring to the *workers* political knowledge, the Social Democrats must *go into all classes of the population,* should send *in all directions* the detachments of its army.[35]

We [what Lenin chooses to italicize is always of special interest] must take upon ourselves the task of organizing such an all-sided political struggle under the direction of our party. . . . *We* must develop from the practical activists of the Social Democracy such political leaders as will be able to direct all the manifestations of this all-sided struggle, be able at the necessary moment "to dictate a positive program of action" alike to rebellious students, and to dissatisfied *zemstvo* figures, and discontented religious sectaries, and indignant schoolteachers, and so on.[36]

A DICTATORSHIP FOR ALL CLASSES

Aided now by historical hindsight, we can see that Lenin was driving at a party not merely to direct the working class but to direct the entire populace, a party that, given the opportunity, would conceive it its duty to "dictate the positive program" of every class of society. "Dictate" was no empty figure of speech to Lenin, as became clear from the outset of his career. When he was still a member of the *Iskra* editorial board he explained in a memorandum to his colleagues that he proposed to show every kindness to the peasantry, "but not yield an inch" in our "maximum program." "If the peasants do not accept socialism when the dictatorship comes, we shall say to them: 'It's no use wasting words when you have got to use force.' " On the margin of this memorandum Vera Zasulich wrote, "Upon millions of people? Just you try!" When he and his party came to power, that is just what they did try.

It was to be neither a party "of" the entire populace nor "of" the working class. It was to be a carefully selected elite, offering itself as leader, director, guardian *for* the working class and for all the discontented from religious sectaries to *zemstvo* councilors.

> The economic struggle against the bosses and the government does not in the least require—and therefore such a struggle can never give rise to—an all-Russian centralized organization, uniting in one general attack each and every manifestation of political opposition, protest, and indignation, an organization consisting of revolutionaries by profession and led by the real political leaders of the entire people.[37]

Thus *stikhiinost'*, spontaneity, the natural liberty of men and classes to be themselves—this spontaneity was for Lenin the enemy and opposite of "consciousness." In Marx spontaneity and consciousness coincided, or would eventually coincide, for, though Marx had his own idea of consciousness, he thought that historical experience would be the connecting link to bring the proletariat to that consciousness in the course of its struggles. But for Lenin spontaneity and consciousness were irreconcilable opposites. The Party did not give expression to the consciousness of the class but the Party had that consciousness as its own infallible possession which it must inject into, impose upon, the class. The Party was the institutional organization of consciousness, which needed the elemental or spontaneous movement, its rebelliousness and its numbers, to give it force, even as a general staff needs an army. But it is the general staff which possesses military science, does the planning of battles and campaigns, gives orders, decides on offensives and retreats, and—where general staff and political party are one and the same—decides on objectives as well. The army is needed to provide numbers, muscle; the general staff is the brains. What general worthy of his stars would let his army determine its own tactics and actions? That way lay chaos. He must drill the army, give it experience under fire, keep it in a fighting mood, train it to obey automatically and completely, harden it in battle, supply officers for every detachment, discredit and eliminate the willful and insubordinate.

Obviously this is far removed from the original Marxist conception of a party of the working class, growing more and more inclusive as modern industry and experience develop, engendering more and more solidarity and consciousness in the course of its repeated struggles. To Lenin the crowd was but a rabble, its spontaneous thoughts and feelings mere false understanding—unless it could be turned into a disciplined, obedient force by officers who alone knew the aims and the art of war.

One question remained to be answered, and this Lenin did not altogether spell out. Yet, if we wander through the repetitive pages of his brochure, Lenin gives us answers again and again to this question. *Who were these revolutionaries by profession?* From what class or classes would they be recruited? To what class would they belong?

If "consciousness" comes not from the working class but only from outside, if its bearers and formulators are "by their social position educated representatives of the possessing classes, the intelligentsia," then it is clear that the members of his elite band would come chiefly from those layers of society which were able to master this doctrine—namely, the students and the intellectuals.[38] True, by becoming professional revolutionaries they were in a sense declassing themselves. But they would not thereby become members of the working class; rather would they withdraw from their professions and economic functions, withdraw from the existing "classes" of society and from society itself, live in its interstices as masters of a profession new in history, the profession of sapper or revolutionary. They were not to be part of the present at all, but its challengers—bearers of the future which they, and they alone, foreknew.

As a concession to the "working-class" element in Marxist theory, Lenin acknowledged that "the best of the workers" might also attain to this consciousness. Russia in due time would beget its own "Bebels," and, he hoped, many of them. But these too would have to leave the factory and the workbench, be extruded from their class—in short, declassed:

> The worker-revolutionary for full preparation for his job must also become a professional revolutionary. . . . A worker-agitator who shows any talent and is at all "promising" *should not* work in the

factory eleven hours a day. We must see to it that he lives on party support, that he should be able in time to go over to an underground status.[39]

Even when Lenin was in power and exercising the "proletarian" dictatorship, he repeated this judgment:

> It is understood that the broad masses of the toilers include very many people who . . . are not enlightened Socialists and cannot be, because they have to work at hard labor. [Lenin uses the term *katorzhno,* derived from the word *katorga,* meaning penal labor] in the factory and they do not have the time or the possibility of becoming Socialists.[40]

Among professional revolutionaries, whether declassed representatives of the propertied classes or declassed workers, *"all distinctions as between workers and intellectuals* must be obliterated."[41] This classless band of priest-guardians must "form a clandestine group of leaders, to set the largest possible masses in motion," become the leader, and "dictate the program" to all the discontented of all classes, and lead them all in an all-Russian struggle against the existing order.

A UNIQUE VANGUARD PARTY FOR A UNIQUE REVOLUTION

There was yet another sense in which Lenin held his organization of classless professional revolutionaries to be "the vanguard" of a particular class, the proletariat. When his opponents accused him of being nothing but a nineteenth century revolutionary conspirator like those of the old *Narodnaia Volia,* Lenin answered proudly:

> The very idea of a militant centralized organization, which declares determined war upon tsarism, you describe as Narodovolist. . . . No revolutionary tendency that seriously thinks of fighting can dispense with such an organization . . . a powerful, strictly secret organization which concentrates in its hands all the threads of secret activities, an organization which must of necessity be centralized.[42]

Yes, in all these things he was a *narodovolets,* and "flattered" to be so described. Like them, too, he sought "to recruit *all* the discontented and hurl this organization into decisive battle . . . that was their great historic merit." Only two mistakes did the *narodovol'tsy* make, and only in these did Lenin differ from them. Their first mistake was not to realize that Russia would and must develop modern industry and modern capitalism, and with this a modern proletariat.

Their second mistake, which followed from the first, was to believe that the main mass of discontented, the main battering ram to use against the gates of the fortress, was the peasantry. But the industrialization of Russia and the teachings of Marxism combined to show that the main mass force to be used as a battering ram, more concentrated, more organized by the barracks discipline of the factory, more accessible to the teachings and leadership of his elite—that main battering ram was the working class.

Herein lay the "proletarian" heart of his "Marxism." This it was that made it essential that his elite, regardless of class origin, should proclaim itself the "vanguard of the working class." This it was that made it so necessary for the "vanguard of society" to claim recognition as the vanguard of the class which must in turn be recognized as the vanguard class in society. For this his vanguard must penetrate the working class, enter into its "essentially bourgeois" trade unions, indoctrinate it with the vanguard doctrine which was at the same time, whether the proletariat accepted or rejected it, the "proletarian" doctrine. For this it must seek to guide and control the workers' struggles, divert them from their "spontaneous" purposes to its conscious purpose, manipulate and utilize their numbers and penetrate their organizations for the aims of the vanguard elite, "dictate to them a positive program of action," force their organizations to transcend their natural aims and limitations, inject into the working class "from outside" the "consciousness" of the revolutionary mission assigned to it by its vanguard, by Marx and by History.

Indeed, the workingmen and their organizations would be measured by this standard—a standard developed outside their movement and in opposition to its "spontaneous" aims, a standard impossible for the workingmen themselves to develop under any circumstances. For the workers, "consciousness" was neither more nor less than *acceptance of the leadership,* guardianship, guidance, program, and decisions of this elite band of professionals of revolution.

Thus Lenin's vanguard was the vanguard of the proletariat by definition. Its doctrine was the doctrine of the proletariat by definition. And its organization was the "highest form" of organization of the working class by definition.

He who regarded himself as the most orthodox of orthodox Marxists could rightly claim that the party he was to build was a party of a new type, which Marx and Engels would have been astonished to contemplate. It was not only new and unique; it was exclusive. For while there might be many parties with differing programs,—even many rival parties, all alike claiming to be Socialist—there was room in any society for only *one* party claiming to be *the* vanguard of the working class and then the vanguard of the "ruling class" and of society.

There have been attempts to find "predecessors" and "influences" for Lenin's conception, in Babeuf and Blanqui, in Pestel, Nechaev, Tkachov, Chernishevsky. But when all these, or the relevant fragments from their writings, are added together, they do not make Lenin's theory or practice. He is unique as its begetter, systematizer, developer, realizer in life, and—what gives it its great importance—the architect of its successful seizure of power.

NOT "RIPENESS IS ALL" BUT "READINESS IS ALL"

Such a classless elite well might seize power, not as Marx had foretold, where the economy was most advanced and the working class most numerous, organized, cultured and "conscious," but just as easily, nay more easily, where the economy was backward, the workers neither "mature" nor "conscious," and all political organization of all parties and classes rudimentary.

Once in power, it might continue to hold power *in the name* of the proletariat, since it was the vanguard of the proletariat by definition and self-proclamation. It might dictate to the rest of society in the proletariat's name, and dictate to the proletariat as well in the proletariat's name, for the vanguard knows best.

Moreover, this vanguard-elite theory would make it possible for restless intellectuals to seize power in the name of the proletariat even in the lands where the proletariat was in its infancy. In the name of this doctrine, Mao Tse-tung could seize power "for the proletariat" by means of peasant armies in an overwhelmingly agrarian land of rudimentary industry. Ho Chi-minh might do the same in a land where the only workers were plantation hands and handicraftsmen plying their ancient trades. All that was needed was opportunity and will, plus the acceptance of the idea of the Leninist *apparat*.

Once in power, they could do as did Lenin, and after him Stalin and Khrushchev: use the "proletarian power" to rule society as a whole, including the proletariat, for, as Lenin put it, "just because the revolution has begun, that does not mean that people have turned into saints." Far from it. One of the important duties of the proletarian power is "to resist the inevitable petit-bourgeois waverings of

these proletarian masses." Indeed, one of its first tasks is to combat
the demoralization which war and the Party's own war against the
Provisional Government had introduced into the masses. "Only by
an extraordinarily difficult, prolonged, stubborn road can we overcome this demoralization and conquer those elements who are aug-
menting it by regarding the revolution as a means of getting rid of
their old shackles by getting out of it as much as they can."[43] Surely,
a proletarian party of a new type! And out of such a party as model
could come only a "proletarian international" of a new type, which
would prove to be as "international" as it was "proletarian."

Two Instruments of Control by the Comintern: The Emissaries of the ECCI* and the Party Representatives in Moscow

by

BRANKO LAZITCH

The arsenal of Moscow's practices to tie together the sections of the Communist International included two semisecret activities: the sending of "emissaries" to inspect the work of the national Communist parties and the institution of "representatives" of the national parties assigned to the Comintern in Moscow.

The following essay is based on conversations with several former leaders of the French Communist Party who have never made public their experiences with Moscow, and on some unpublished documents obtained from them. Five of these leaders served as the French party's representatives in Moscow: Boris Souvarine, André Ferrat, Pierre Célor, Albert Vassart, and Henri Barbé (a former secretary of the Central Committee). Others were Louis Sellier and Albert Treint, both former secretaries-general of the French party.

MOSCOW'S EMISSARIES IN FRANCE

After the Bolsheviks had seized power in Russia, they no longer were obliged to conform to the rules of conspiracy, but they required that these rules be followed by all sections of the Comintern. One of these rules was that there should be a constant combining of both legal and illegal methods of action and that no trust should be placed in "bourgeois legality." This rule was made explicit for all Communist parties

* Executive Committee of the Communist International.

in the twenty-one conditions for admission adopted at the Second Congress of the Comintern in 1920. Consequently, the Comintern itself was obliged to adhere to this conduct from the start of its activity in the West, especially because the revolutionary attempts in Europe during 1919–20 often resulted in vigorous counteraction by the "bourgeois" authorities. On the other hand, Soviet Russia was engaged during this period in a difficult civil war and in a war with Poland, a situation which did not facilitate the establishment of contacts with the first Communist groupings of Western Europe, such as the French group.

The Leninist Period of the Comintern

From 1919 on, Moscow succeeded in breaking through the blockade and sent its first secret emissaries to Western Europe. First, three special envoys settled in Berlin where, usually under false identity, they established the Comintern's western secretariat: J. Reich (*pseud.* Thomas, Rubinstein), N. Krebs (*pseud.* N. Rakov, Felix Wolff, Inkov), and A. E. Abramovich (*pseud.* Albrecht, Zalewski). They were aided in their work by several couriers whose job it was to get into neighboring countries.

Beginning in 1919–20, two types of envoys from Moscow arrived in France: simple couriers (liaison agents) and emissaries on political or financial missions. The first category included a number of female Communist party workers, since the Bolsheviks knew from experience that the police paid less attention to women than to men. Two of these women were Helen Unszlicht (sister of Józef Unszlicht), who operated in France with false papers of identification bearing the conspiratorial name of Jeanne, and Helen Yakovliev (wife of a Bolshevik). Among those in the second category were three faithful followers of Lenin since the time of his residence in Switzerland before the revolution: Vladimir Diogotte, who had lived in France before the revolution and had maintained contact by correspondence with Lenin's wife, and who returned to France in 1920 together with Helen Yakovliev;[1] S. Mineff, a Bulgarian physician who had enlisted in Lenin's cause and had come to France under the false name of Lorenzo Vanini (he later became well known under three successive pseudonyms—Dr. Chavaroche, Lebedev, and Stepanov), and finally, Abramovich-Zalewski, who became the object of a political-financial scandal.

Abramovich, the Old Bolshevik (a rare title), returned to Russia on the same train as Lenin, Zinoviev, and other Russian revolutionaries who had found refuge in Switzerland until the February Revolution. After the Communist revolution, Abramovich was sent to Berlin where, using the pseudonym Albrecht, he was active in the work of the western secretariat of the Comintern and served as "Moscow's eye" in the ephemeral Soviet Republic of Bavaria. Beginning in 1920, Abramovich traveled in the name of the Comintern in France, Italy and Austria. For example, he arranged the trip to Russia of Alfred Rosmer, who in 1920 became president of the Second Congress of the Comintern. Abramovich himself made a second trip to Western Europe armed with a substantial checkbook, assigned the job of furnishing aid to Communists for their activities, particularly for their press. Tracked down by the French police early in 1921, he was arrested together with two members of the comité directeur of the French Communist Party, Antoine Ker and Amédée Dunois. After this occurrence, the French party leadership requested Abramovich's recall (just as previously Diogotte had had to leave France upon request of the Committee for the Third International)[2] and, upon his release from prison, he went first to Berlin and then to Russia. On December 8, 1921, the Secretariat of the Comintern, over the signatures of Jules Humbert-Droz and Otto Kuusinen, informed the comité directeur of the French Communist Party: "In response to the request by the French party for an inquiry into the case of [Abramovich-] Zalewski, the ECCI has named a special commission including two representatives of France to the ECCI, which will give Zalewski a hearing in order to settle this matter once and for all."[3] However, as a result, not only was the matter liquidated but so was Abramovich as the Comintern's emissary in Europe. He continued to be active for a time in the secret apparatus of the Comintern, but he was never to deal again with the affairs of the French Communist Party.

With the advent of relatively normal conditions in Europe and the end of the civil war in Russia, it became easier to make contacts. Newly arriving emissaries were strictly on political missions (financial matters were handled by a special Comintern service), such as, for instance, Henryk Walecki, who attended the Marseille congress of the French Communist Party in December 1921; he played a behind-the-scenes role but made no speeches and did not even appear before the delegates. The same was true of Dmitrii Manuilsky, who spoke French well. In 1919 he arrived in Boulogne-sur-Mer with Inessa Armand, ostensibly to fulfill a Red Cross mission for prisoner-of-war repatriation. Actually, he was to establish contact with the French Communists.

The French authorities, however, foiled Manuilsky in his attempt; he did not succeed even in making contact by correspondence. He returned in 1922 as the Comintern's delegate to the French Communist Party congress at Paris, and in the spring of 1924 made a secret visit to Paris as an emissary of the Comintern or, more accurately, as Zinoviev's emissary. He had a specific mission: to draw to Zinoviev's side a part of the former leftist faction of the French party, including Treint, in order to isolate Souvarine, who was opposing the campaign against Trotsky. Manuilsky did succeed in winning over Treint, who soon was raised to membership in the Presidium of the Comintern, but he failed with respect to the former revolutionary trade unionists grouped around Pierre Monatte. In his conversation with the latter, Manuilsky, trained in Bolshevik methods informed Monatte that Souvarine was going to get himself expelled from the Party, to which Monatte, ignorant of Bolshevik methods, retorted, "You're crazy!"

Jules Humbert-Droz was another man who enjoyed Moscow's confidence. As such he was sent to France in order to get acquainted with the situation inside the French Communist Party and to prepare confidential reports for Zinoviev and Trotsky. He reached Paris at the end of 1921, and stayed there for longer intervals in 1922 and 1923. The French party was split at that time, and one of the leaders of its left faction, Souvarine, was at the same time the representative of the entire French party in Moscow, while the secretary-general of the party, Louis-Oscar Frossard, belonged to the party's center. Nevertheless, Moscow wanted to have its own man on the spot who would correspond directly with Zinoviev over the heads of two official bodies: the secretariat of the party in Paris, and its representative in Moscow.[4]

Soon another "eye of Moscow" was sent to France: Suzanne Girault, who had been a teacher of French to children of wealthy Russian families and had joined the Bolshevik cause after its victory. She began her career with the Comintern as an interpreter and "home help" for the Rosmer family. Thanks to her connections with the GPU, where her son worked, she was "promoted" to the status of a political person and assigned in 1923 to the politburo of the French Communist Party.

Thus, already during the time of Lenin, the clandestine activity of all-powerful emissaries began, about whom Paul Levi, president of the German Communist Party wrote as early as 1921: "They never work with the leadership of individual Communist parties, but always behind their backs and often against them. They enjoy the confidence of Moscow, but the local leaders do not. . . . The Executive Committee [of the Comintern] acts as a Chrezvychaika [i.e., Cheka, the original Soviet Secret Police] projected outside the Russian borders."[5]

The Zinoviev Period

When Zinoviev and Stalin launched their open campaign against Trotsky, they apparently insisted upon the loyalty of the leaders of the foreign parties. Under the pretext of ideological purity, the formula of "Bolshevization" of the International was a useful aid in getting rid of those who were not considered completely devoted. This period marked a new phase in the system of Comintern emissaries.

These new delegates did not remain in France for restricted periods in order to accomplish a specific mission (get rid of a leader or attend a congress); rather, they settled in France, apparently unknown to either the bourgeois police or the Communist press. Later, after earlier emissaries evidently had found it difficult to impose Moscow's point of view (Manuilsky suffered a reverse at the Paris congress in 1922), the delegate became the personification of Moscow's will, and the law of the party was increasingly of his making.

Two Zinoviev emissaries succeeded each other in France: August Guralsky (*alias* Kleine and Lepetit) and Mikhailov (Boris Mihailovich, *alias* Williams).

Guralsky had first been a delegate in Germany; he was Bela Kun's lieutenant in the "March action" of 1921 in Germany, which ended in a bitter defeat;[6] he had been part of the Comintern group involved in the insurrection of October 1923, which also ended in failure.[7] In 1922 he settled in Berlin under the pseudonym Kleine and served on the politburo of the German Communist Party. He remained there until the beginning of 1924 when he left for Moscow, in the wake of the disputes that broke out after the abortive action of October 1923, the German party having no more use for him. To clarify matters, however, the politburo of the German Communist Party, on May 1, 1924, addressed a letter to the ECCI stating: "The central committee of the German Communist Party declares that there is nothing for Comrade Kleine to do in the German party, and his return to Germany is not desired."[8] Composed on the eve of the

Bolshevization, this letter was probably one of the last repudiations
of a Comintern emissary by a party.

At this moment Kleine was already in France, conducting his
activities under the name of Lepetit. He had been sent on an urgent
mission ahead of Manuilsky to exercise pressure on the comité directeur and to prevent Souvarine, who likewise had returned from Moscow, from winning over the comité to his point of view. It was Kleine-
Lepetit's task to make sure that the French party made no pronouncements in opposition to the anti-Trotsky campaign, as the Polish party
had already done. Lepetit's way of maneuvering was never to appear
at the meetings of the politburo, but to meet separately with each
leader of the French party or to bring together several leaders at a
time in secret meetings. He carried on, in fact, a "factional" activity,
which would have been considered a crime if directed against Zinoviev's leadership, but which, since it was favorable to Zinoviev and
unfavorable to Trotsky, had become a leading Bolshevik virtue. He
succeeded in his mission and, in the summer of 1924, his efforts produced a "monolithically Bolshevik" delegation to the Fifth Comintern Congress, a delegation which denounced Souvarine's activity
and viewpoints. A member of the French delegation at the same congress, who during two subsequent years in the Soviet Union had
numerous contacts with "Lepetit," has sketched the following por-
trait of him:

> Guralsky was a veritable virtuoso of "dialectic." Excessively
> shrewd, devoid of all scruples and sense of morality, he permitted
> himself to perform every imaginable political pirouette. He thrust the
> party leadership into the most hazardous ventures, then disavowed
> this leadership on the grounds that it had altered his instructions. We
> named him "the juggler". . . . Guralsky was recalled to Moscow at
> the beginning of 1925. He left behind a dispirited and partially dis-
> organized French Communist Party. The solidarity existing between
> Guralsky and Zinoviev continued unflaggingly until the end. As a
> matter of fact, Guralsky was imprisoned at the same time as his
> patron and met his end shortly before him.[9]

"Williams" was Guralsky's successor. Upon his arrival, he
moved into the apartment of Georges Marrane, a member of the central committee. He did not arrange any meetings with the party leadership, the politburo, or the central committee, but contented himself
with seeing Treint, Pierre Sémard, Barbé, Jacques Doriot and others
separately. He was familiar with the political situation in France and

in the world at large and fluent in French, German and English. In contrast to preceding Comintern emissaries, such as Manuilsky and Guralsky, who were products of the Comintern's central apparatus, Williams apparently had come from a special Soviet agency.

He did not remain in Paris for long. He was injured in 1925 in a traffic accident, which left permanent scars on his cheek and forehead that made him particularly conspicuous thereafter. After leaving France, he traveled to Germany, India, Chile, Argentina, the United States, and other countries on secret missions. In 1945, after the Second World War, he returned to Paris under the name of Boris Mihailovich as a correspondent for *Izvestia*.[10]

The Stalinist Period

In 1927–28 during the Bukharin period of Comintern leadership, the practice of assigning an emissary to the French Communist Party was abandoned. It was not necessary; the man in charge of the Comintern's "Latin secretariat" (France, Italy, Spain, Portugal), Humbert-Droz, had firmly in his hands the reins of direct control over the French Communist Party, with which he had numerous contacts. (In his capacity as Comintern representative he had attended the Lille congress of the French party in June 1926.) Nor was there any special delegate from Moscow in France later during 1928–30, when Barbé served at the same time as secretary of the French Communist Party and of the Communist International.

With the elimination of Bukharin from the leadership and the replacement of Humbert-Droz by Stepanov, the old system was restored, marked formally by the selection of Eugen Fried as emissary in 1931. He was a Slovak or a Sudeten German but born in Brno, an active member of the Czechoslovak Communist Party since its founding, and one of his party's delegates to the Fifth Comintern Congress in 1924, remaining in Moscow the following year as a member of the organizational section (Orgburo) of the Comintern's Secretariat.[11] He occupied his post in Paris until 1939, aided from time to time by other emissaries then known as "instructors." Their task consisted in overseeing not the whole of the French Communist Party's activity, but only certain sectors. From 1930 on, there were several successive instructors, in particular Anna Pauker, Ernö Gerö, a Russian party worker named Seraphine (*alias* Suzanne) and Leon Purman. Purman, who at the second congress of the Polish Communist Party in 1923 was elected a member of its central committee, was demoted to the rank of candidate-member by the fourth congress in 1927. He committed suicide in Moscow. Fried, however, far exceeded these instructors in importance.

His first mission, together with Anna Pauker, was to lay an effective groundwork for the elimination of the Barbé-Célor faction. (Manuilsky also made one more visit to France, to participate in this enterprise, just as he had been dispatched in 1925 to consolidate the leadership of Treint, Suzanne Girault and Pierre Sémard.) The enthronement of Thorez as leader of the French party according to the will of Moscow had to be implemented by the presence of a large though clandestine delegation of the Comintern, headed by Fried. Several members of his Moscow apparatus were among the delegates. Notable among them were Anna Pauker (under the pseudonym "Marina"), another woman called "Suzanne," the only Soviet Russian member of the delegation (her husband was a Soviet officer), a Pole under the name of "Witowski," and another Pole whose real name was Georges Kagan and who had studied at French and Belgian universities before joining the Comintern's apparatus.[12]

Albert Vassart, a member at the time of the French Communist Party's secretariat, was well acquainted with Fried. Here is what he had to say about his work:

> There were many different forms of liaison between Fried and the leadership of the French Communist Party. He would see each party secretary personally and frequently about those matters with which each was especially charged. He also met, although less often, many other members of the politburo and the central committee, sometimes even the leaders of the most important regions. Still, to enable Fried to participate in meetings of both the secretariat and the politburo, special meetings were arranged at least once weekly through the efforts of the French apparatus of the OMS [Comintern section for international liaison directed at Moscow by Osip Piatnitsky, who served simultaneously as the Comintern's treasurer]. It was often in the course of these get-togethers, numbering up to ten or twelve people, that Fried held his separate rendezvous.[13]

Fried's influence was especially strong over Maurice Thorez, notes Vassart:

> Fried played a decisive role in completing Thorez' political training. Although Thorez had little initiative or political courage, he was an excellent "spokesman" for developing whatever was proposed to him. But Fried did not simply use Thorez as a front with

himself as the actual leader of the French party; he applied himself to correcting Thorez' inadequacies and faults in order to make a real leader out of him.

After the Seventh Congress of the Comintern in 1935 and the French Communist Party's successes in the initial period of the Popular Front, Fried's mandate in France underwent important changes in form. On the one hand, since Thorez had become secretary-general of the party and a member of the Presidium of the ECCI—while Marty was simultaneously secretary of the Comintern and a member of the French party's politburo—it was Moscow's judgment that these promotions within the hierarchy should be taken into account in order to establish new contacts between the Comintern and the French Communist Party. Consequently, Fried ceased to be the Comintern's delegate in France and became instead a "political counselor," with the special assignment of working with Thorez. On the other hand, Fried's many-sided activities became less "conspiratorial." From 1936 on, he lived and acted, for all practical purposes, as a French citizen, or, in any case, as a foreigner legally residing in France.

As a cover, Fried used part of his time for research among historical documents to enrich the holdings of the museum of revolutionary history which the Communist municipality had established at Montreuil. In 1935 he was living with Thorez' first wife, Aurore, while Thorez himself was living with Jeanette Vermersch—without benefit of matrimony. This situation did not in the least disturb the political relations between Fried and Thorez. Still, they were both required to provide Moscow with some explanations.[14]

Concerning Fried's relations with Moscow, Vassart reports:

In the course of his long stay in France, Fried made rather frequent trips to Moscow. Every time a delegation of the French Communist Party leadership was summoned by the Comintern, Fried accompanied it; sometimes he would precede the delegation or would remain for a while in Moscow after its departure. Fried submitted complete reports on his mission to no one but the Russian delegation to the Comintern, that is to Manuilsky and Piatnitsky, principally. (Stepanov joined the others in this capacity just before Piatnitsky's liquidation.) As regards Fried's contact with Moscow during his stay in Paris, it was all the same whether he was operating entirely under cover, as in 1931, or in complete legality, as in 1938—he still maintained permanent liaison outside and over the head of the French Communist Party. Directives intended for Fried were put into code by the OMS in Moscow and sent to the headquarters of the French party in Paris on Rue Lafayette. No French organization knew this code. In order to decipher it, there was no recourse but to forward it to the OMS section in Paris. But the OMS section, upon translating the coded dispatch, communicated its contents to the Comintern delegate exclusively and transmitted nothing to the French party.[15]

THE REPRESENTATIVES OF THE FRENCH COMMUNIST PARTY WITH THE ECCI

The evolution of the Comintern from 1919 to 1939 was as discernible in this phase of its secret and semisecret activities—that of assigning Communist party representatives to the Comintern in Moscow—as in the above-described related phase—that of sending "emissaries" to check up on the work of national Communist parties. At the start, the representative of a relatively important foreign Communist party (such as that of Germany, France, Italy or Poland) influenced the course of affairs in his own party and participated in the important decisions of the Comintern; later he was unable to do either. At the beginning, it was possible for a Polish or French representative to express his point of view about the struggle within the Bolshevik Party and to refrain from joining either Stalin or Zinoviev. Later this became impossible: a representative would not think of dissociating himself from the master of the Kremlin; he would not have even the opportunity, since no one would ask for his opinion. All he had to do was to approve unconditionally what had already been decided. Also, at the beginning the name of a Communist party representative with the ECCI at Moscow was made public and known to everybody, whereas later it was kept secret from both the "bourgeois enemy" and rank-and-file Communists.

The Years 1921–24

The first representative of the French Communist Party at Moscow during the years 1921–24 was Boris Souvarine. Less than a month after his arrival in Moscow in June 1921, he had his first brush with the "eye of Moscow," a Soviet confidence man attached to the French delegation at the Third Congress of the Comintern, Taratouta (Victor, *alias* Kemerer). Even a "commission of inquiry" was set up, with Anatolii Lunacharsky and Mikhail Olminsky representing the Bolshevik party and Fernand Loriot and Paul Vaillant-Couturier representing the French party. The commission found Souvarine in the right and found justified the request for the withdrawal of Taratouta as the representative of the Russian Communist Party with the French delegation. (The point was that Souvarine had visited some Soviet prisons and had made certain protests. As the commission phrased it, "It was because of the brusque way in which Souvarine expressed himself that he was denounced by Taratouta.")

The first half of Souvarine's stay in Moscow was marked by a dispute with the leadership of the French Communist Party (in which he had the support of the Comintern). During the rest of his stay, however, he came into conflict with the Comintern leadership itself. In the former situation, he found himself in the minority because of the vote taken at the Marseille congress of December 1921, which refused to elect him to membership on the comité directeur. But because the left faction of the French Communist Party stood solidly behind him and because the Comintern was closer to this left than to the centrist majority, Souvarine remained a member of the ECCI. During the first part of 1922, Souvarine was not, however, the only representative of the French party in the top hierarchy of the Comintern. In February of 1922, when a delegation of the majority of the French Communist Party came to Moscow to defend a viewpoint hostile to the United Front, Louis Sellier, a member of that delegation, remained in Moscow as a second French representative with the Presidium of the ECCI which was elected at the First Enlarged Plenum held also in February. Sellier remained there until the Second Enlarged Plenum in June 1922. During that time he came closer to the official line of the Comintern and, by the same token, estranged himself from Frossard, head of the party and of the majority hostile to "Moscow's ukases." At the meeting of the Fourth Comintern Congress, on December 1, 1922, in his report on the French question, Trotsky praised Sellier in the following terms: "Louis Sellier has been representing the French party for some time here in Moscow. He returned to France and was the proposed alternate secretary-general of the party, an important post which indicates that this comrade is highly esteemed in the French party. We who have been acquainted with him in Moscow share that esteem for comrade Louis Sellier."[16]

While the conflict between Souvarine and the majority of the French party could have been more or less smoothed out in 1922, the dispute which arose between Souvarine and the directing body of the Comintern at the end of 1923 had much more drastic repercussions.

When the Zinoviev-Stalin-Kamenev *troika* declared war on Trotsky over the succession to Lenin, the Comintern suffered the attendant consequences. In the course of this behind-the-scenes struggle, Souvarine expressed his disapproval to Zinoviev, orally at first, then in a letter sent from Paris on January 6, 1924, on the eve of Lenin's death. Zinoviev replied to him rather dryly and accused him of waging a "factional struggle," and of lending his support to "an opposition which represents no more than one per cent." Souvarine sent him a long letter on March 22 declaring,

> I cannot accept your arbitrarily imputing to me a "factional" point of view. It is not enough merely to assert these things; one must prove them. What I disapprove of is the war being waged against Comrade Trotsky and all those who are suspected, rightly or wrongly, of "Trotskyism." I do not consider that there is anything to be gained by my assuming the role of defender of such a comrade as Trotsky, who knows very well how to defend his own point of view, nor have I become a "Trotskyist," because an active French party member has quite enough to do in his own party and in the activity of the International without, in addition, meddling in a factional dispute within the Russian party. But it is my opinion that the blows directed at Trotsky are injuring not Trotsky but the Party itself, the revolution, and the International.[17]

What followed was typical of Bolshevik methods. Two emissaries, Guralsky and Manuilsky, were sent to Paris; a French delegation completely loyal to Moscow was dispatched to the Fifth Congress of the Comintern where a resolution was passed "concerning the Souvarine case."[18] Souvarine was accused of lack of discipline and petty bourgeois spirit. The resolution concluded, "There must be satisfaction of the demand made by the French Communist Party delegation at the Fifth Congress of the Comintern calling for the expulsion of Souvarine."[19] After this, Souvarine was deprived of his accommodations at the Hotel Luxe and, upon leaving Russia in 1925, was shadowed on the train by an agent of the Cheka. He was searched at the border, and all his personal notes, documents and correspondence were confiscated.

The Years 1924–27

Albert Treint was the French Communist Party's man at Moscow during the Zinoviev period of Comintern leadership. Since he had reached the apex of his party and then achieved simultaneous membership on the ECCI, the Presidium, and the Comintern Secretariat, he was marked for elimination soon after Zinoviev. He attended the enlarged plenums of the ECCI in 1925 and 1926 and stayed a long time in Moscow. When it became clear that Zinoviev's partisans were going to be the victims of the campaign Stalin was preparing against Zinoviev, Treint only partly realized what was happening; he observed the fact of the matter but did not comprehend its genesis. In a letter sent from Moscow on September 15, 1926, he wrote:

> Upon returning to Moscow, I found myself confronted by a veritable pogrom organized against me on the basis of a Tass wire reporting that I was leaning toward the League of Nations, based also on the fables being peddled by Humbert-Droz. I must have put my foot in it following a stupid article by Bernard in *Bolshevik,* organ of the Russian Central Committee, dealing with the congress of Lille in the most fantastic manner. I protested in the Presidium, and Bukharin took it upon himself to have published in *Pravda* and *Bolshevik* the necessary corrections of the articles by Bernard and Humbert-Droz.[20]

Henry Jacob, a member of the French party's central committee, stayed in Moscow during Treint's absence. Jacob was simultaneously a delegate of the CGTU (French Communist trade unions) to the Profintern and of the French party to the Comintern. As secretary of the Textile Federation, he could attend sessions of the Profintern, and he belonged to the Comintern because of his membership on the French party's central committee. He was promoted to the ECCI's Secretariat at the close of the plenum in February–March 1926. But this promotion did not last long; at the next plenum in November–December 1926, Pierre Sémard, secretary-general of the French party, attacked not only his predecessor, Treint, but also Jacob, who "had come out in favor of the opposition in the Russian Communist Party." Thus Jacob was fated to follow Zinoviev and Treint in their fall.

During the Zinoviev period, a third French leader was frequently in Moscow: Jean Cremet, member of the politburo of the French party who in 1926 became a member of the Comintern's Secretariat and Presidium. He enjoyed the honor of a compliment by Stalin, who proposed that Cremet be included in the directing nucleus of the French party.[21] But Cremet became seriously implicated in a Soviet espionage case, and at the next plenum (May 1927) his name no longer appeared in the leading organs of the Comintern.[22]

Trotsky, in exile, wrote in a letter to the attorney-general of the
Republic of Mexico: "The general pattern of the GPU's foreign organization is as follows: included on the central committee of each
section of the Comintern is a responsible GPU chief from the country
in question. Generally speaking, the fact that he is a representative
of the GPU is known only to the party secretary and one or two members of the central committee."[23]

Applied to the French Communist Party, this pattern leads one
to conclude that, during 1924–27, first Suzanne Girault and then
Jean Cremet were the representatives of the GPU. After this period,
and until the outbreak of the Second World War, the role of confidence man for the GPU was probably played by Jacques Duclos.
Treint reasons that by logically eliminating as possibilities all other
French Communist leaders (Thorez, André Marty, Marcel Cachin,
Pierre Sémard, Benoît Frachon), Duclos remains the only plausible
candidate. André Ferrat recalls Duclos' arrival in Moscow in 1930
to prepare for a secret mission in Spain as an agent of the Comintern
and how, in the main, he was "worked on" for this purpose by the
GPU apparatus. Barbé asserts:

> In 1931, the Party assigned Duclos the task of controlling and
> supervising the special work being done by the "worker correspond-
> ents." This organization was exposed in 1932. It was revealed in the
> indictment that a special bureau, headed by a certain Philippe, con-
> solidated all information received by *L'Humanité*. Through the inter-
> mediary of a Soviet agent, Bir (nicknamed Fantomas), Philippe
> maintained contact with the Soviet military attaché in Paris. The
> moment this situation was uncovered, Duclos left abruptly for
> Berlin, where he spent several months. As for Bir and Philippe, they
> were placed on trial and, in December 1932, sentenced to imprison-
> ment—three years for Bir, thirteen months for Philippe.[24]

The Years 1928–29

During the period 1928–29, before and after the elimination of Bukharin from the leadership of the Comintern, Henri Barbé had three
functions: secretary of the French Communist Party's central committee; the party's representative at Moscow; and member of the
directing organs of the Comintern (Executive Committee, Secretariat and Presidium). The difference between the new situation and
the one preceding it began to assume shape: hitherto the representatives of the French party with the Comintern (such as Souvarine and

Treint) could come to the defense of one of the factions of the Bolshevik party, but with the advent of the new period there was only one faction—that of Stalin. From now on, consequently, the representatives could become victims for reasons other than those formerly valid.

As a member of the directing organs of the Comintern, Barbé was probably the last representative of the French Communist Party to hold such an important position—or title, rather—within the central apparatus. But he did not belong to the Comintern's real directing organ, one nowhere stipulated by the Comintern's statutes and one which had never been reported on in the Communist press: the Little Commission (*malaia komissiia*). The Political Secretariat consisted of nine to eleven members, before and after the Sixth Comintern Congress, but its restricted bureau, the Little Commission, actually held the reins. Before the congress it was composed of Bukharin, Manuilsky, Piatnitsky, Remmele, and Ercoli (Togliatti). After Bukharin's fall, Molotov, Manuilsky, Piatnitsky, Ulbricht and Kuusinen took over. Their decisions had the force of law; the meetings of the Secretariat or of the Presidium of the Comintern consisted merely of discussing the application of decisions already agreed upon. It was evident that the Little Commission, through the intermediary of one of its members (Bukharin at first, then Molotov), maintained direct contact with Stalin and his private Secretariat—from which quarter emanated the orders that were simply to be carried out.

Nevertheless, Barbé had occasion during his sojourn at the Comintern to be summoned, accompanied by Bukharin and Humbert-Droz, to attend a session with Stalin discussing the election campaign strategy of the French Communists in 1928. This privilege was not to be granted to the next representatives of the French Communist Party—Ferrat, Célor and Vassart.

The Years 1930–31

André Ferrat, former secretary of the Young Communists of France and former member of the French Communist Party's politburo, was a party delegate during the period 1930–31. He arrived in Moscow on January 1, 1930 and remained there until June 1931, leaving the city only during the summer of 1930 for an excursion into the Caucasus and a trip near Yalta, where he met Bukharin and Kamenev—to whom no one talked any more.

Ferrat's nomination as the French party's representative, proposed by Barbé, Thorez and other leaders, was decided upon by a restricted committee without participation by the politburo or the central committee. Since he had been operating underground in France, with the threat of a five-year prison sentence hanging over him for antimilitarist activity, Ferrat accepted this nomination.

He went from France to Brussels, where a secret reception center for French Communists was maintained. There he received false Swiss passports for himself and his wife to travel to Moscow.

Ferrat lived at the Hotel Luxe and worked from 8 a.m. to 5 p.m. at Comintern headquarters on Mokhovaia Street. He was paid a modest salary, but he was able to supplement it amply by the publication of his articles. A single article of his would be printed in several Soviet newspapers or periodicals, and every time one appeared Ferrat would receive a special "bonus."

His contact with the French Communist Party leadership in Paris was neither close nor frequent; he had no private courier of his own, and the ties between the ECCI and its emissary in Paris were far more systematic and better organized than those existing between the French party and its representative in Moscow. When the ECCI sent instructions or other communications to its Paris delegate (Fried had just arrived), the representative of the French party at Moscow was not apprised of their content. Conversely, the incoming correspondence of the French party did not reach its representative in Moscow first and the Comintern later. Instead it was channeled directly into the offices of the Comintern's Latin secretariat, bypassing the French official. In the secretariat the mail was scrutinized by Varia Lebedeva, formerly Stepanov's wife and later Manuilsky's mistress, who then had it distributed to Stepanov, Manuilsky or Piatnitsky—whereas Ferrat rarely received anything. While the Comintern practice of sending directives and information to its delegate in Paris without informing the representative of the French party in Moscow could at least outwardly be justified, the fact that the same representative was deprived of getting acquainted with the material dispatched by his own party represented a flagrant violation of the prerogatives of the party's representative.

The Comintern had at its disposal a sizable network to get information about the French Communist Party. Ferrat lists as this network's components the secretariat of the French party itself, the ECCI's delegate in France, the Soviet Embassy, the GPU in France, and the ties of friendship that Stepanov had established during his various sojourns in France. By collating the information from these sources, the leadership of the Comintern was able to form an idea about the situation within the French party.

The paramount organ of the Comintern was, as already mentioned, its restricted Political Secretariat (Little Commission), composed in 1930–31 of five members: Manuilsky, Piatnitsky, Kuusinen, Ercoli and Pieck.[25] Ferrat was assigned to the Latin secretariat, headed by Stepanov. The staff was small: Varia Lebedeva, who had overall responsibility for the leadership cadres of the Latin Communist parties—a kind of auxiliary, so to speak, of the Soviet political police; Ferrat for the French party; and R. Grieco (Garlandi) and Aquilla for the Italians (the latter often wrote for the press of the Comintern). A young Swiss Communist in this group died very soon. Serving as adviser to the Latin group was Anna Pauker, *alias* Marina.

On rare occasions when it was deemed necessary to evaluate the situation in France, Ferrat, together with Stepanov, was summoned before the restricted Political Secretariat (Little Commission) and asked to present a report. In March 1930, Ferrat criticized the "leftist" position of the French party's leadership in regard to the law on social insurance.

He had little contact with any Soviet organs outside the Comintern. Among the young Communists in the Comintern he was well acquainted with two secretaries, Khitarov and Gorkić. At the Profintern, the French Communist trade unions were represented by Léon Mauvais. Ferrat taught courses at the Comintern's Lenin School; among some fifteen students from the French group was Waldeck Rochet, at present secretary-general of the French Communist Party.

Ferrat had little contact with the Soviet secret apparatus. He gave two lectures at the special GPU school near Moscow, where his audience consisted of five Frenchmen, three Belgians, and two Swiss. (Once he had occasion to concern himself with the financial affairs of the French Communist Party when Piatnitsky wanted to reduce its budget—that is, the subsidy it was receiving from the Soviets. Ferrat argued against reduction.)

The Years 1931–32

From June 1931 to October 1932, the French Communist Party representative in Moscow was Pierre Célor, one of the secretaries for the central committee. Upon his arrival in Moscow, he immediately assumed posts in the Presidium and Secretariat of the ECCI, a double promotion accorded him at the close of the Eleventh Plenum of the ECCI in April 1931. However, he was not to remain in his new functions for very long; he and Barbé were the chief victims of a purge embarked upon in Moscow when the Comintern decided to settle accounts with the "youth group" in the leadership of the French party after having itself imposed this group upon the leadership two years earlier. The Comintern entrusted André Marty with the investigation in Paris of the Barbé-Célor faction, while a special session of the so-called Commission on Cadres was organized at Moscow on March 8, 1932—and lasted for twelve hours. Present were Manuilsky, Piatnitsky, Stepanov and Lebedeva, for the Comintern; Barbé and Auguste Havez, chief of the underground organization of the French Communist Party; and five Russians in leather jackets, the required uniform at the time for members of the Cheka. As Célor was ill, a physician was summoned and kept available throughout this "trial" in a nearby room. The technique to be used in the great purge trials of the future, which were to be staged with such theatrical flamboyance from 1936 on against the leaders of the Russian party, was being "broken in" in the course of Célor's trial. Using some discrepancies in details given in several autobiographical depositions by Célor, the prosecution charged that Célor had concealed the truth from the Comintern and that he was an *agent provocateur* of the police. Finally, after many vicissitudes, Célor and his wife obtained an exit visa. They were subjected to surveillance by one Cheka man in the train until their departure and then by another at the Gare du Nord in Paris.

The Years 1932–34

André Marty, who had brought the Barbé-Célor case under investigation in Paris, was rewarded by being appointed to Célor's post at Comintern headquarters. This was the beginning of Marty's career within the central apparatus of the Comintern, a career which led him later to the very summit of the hierarchy (member of the Presidium of the ECCI and chief organizer of the International Brigades during the Spanish civil war), only to fall later like all preceding representatives of the French party in the Comintern. As a final touch of irony, Marty was to be charged with being in contact with the police, an accusation similar to that he himself had leveled twenty years earlier against Célor.

The Years 1934–35

In 1934 and 1935 the French party's representative was Albert Vassart. His experience in the early days of the Popular Front is reviewed elsewhere in this book. Casting a retrospective glance at his role, Vassart wrote:

> The real content of the Communist International's policies was always settled upon by an exclusively restricted general staff. After having made its sovereign decisions as to the political line to be followed, however, this general staff did acknowledge the possibility of opening to discussion the actual methods of applying this line. Moreover, this was always the way—and the only way—in which "discussion" took place at the various echelons of the Communist International. The policy decided upon by the "summit" was never to be brought into question, but the carrying out of this policy was not necessarily mechanical in its operation. A certain degree of initiative was still permissible; there was no prohibition against adroitness in executing a directive.[26]

The Last Three Representatives of the French Party at Moscow

After Vassart, it was Marty's turn to go once more to Moscow, from the end of 1935 to the middle of 1936; after this he was assigned to service in Spain. His successor was Georges Cogniot, a member of the central committee, who was in Moscow from the end of 1936 to October 1937. Cogniot was succeeded by Jules Decaux, an alternate member of the central committee, who departed for Moscow in 1938.

But the great purge of 1936–38 had profound repercussions among the personnel of the Comintern; an overwhelming part of the old apparatus had disappeared (more precisely, had been liquidated), while Georgi Dimitrov's Secretariat was now functioning with a much reduced and predominantly Russian staff. Reduction of the Comintern to a state of suspended animation was actually the expression of Stalin's will.

It was in order to adjust to this new situation that Cogniot was replaced in 1938 by a second-echelon party worker, Decaux, whose articles had appeared in the press of the Comintern but who had never carried any weight in Moscow or, for that matter, in Paris. Moreover, he returned to France in the spring of 1939 without being replaced. Marty, on the other hand, released from his duties in Spain, was recalled to Moscow a few weeks before the signing of the Nazi-Soviet pact in August 1939. Another French leader, Raymond Guyot, was also there at the time. Guyot had been made secretary of the Communist Youth International in 1935 and won election as a Communist deputy a year later. He had to leave Moscow abruptly about September 20, 1939, to convey the new defeatist instructions to French Communist Party headquarters in Paris.[27] What made this action especially urgent was the fact that on September 2 the Communist parliamentary group had voted in favor of the war credits requested by the Daladier government.

The two institutions of the Comintern—the emissaries of the ECCI and the Communist party representatives at Moscow—had undergone a far-reaching evolution, culminating in the affirmation of Russian omnipotence in the Comintern. This situation was officially characterized by the euphemism "the leading role of the Bolshevik party."

This leading role rested upon a threefold foundation. The first was a historical fact: during the entire existence of the Comintern, Soviet Russia was the sole viable Communist state. Consequently, foreign Communists saw this Russian hegemony as "the inevitable result of circumstances," as the head of the German Communist Party, August Thalheimer, emphasized at the Fifth Congress of the Comintern: "The hegemony of the Russian party in the International is a historical necessity. The other parties must first install the dictatorship of the proletariat in their own countries."[28]

The second foundation was the multitude of organizational and institutional ties woven together by Moscow within the Communist International—ties which made this hegemony of the Soviet party possible. Among these ties were the two organs described.

The third foundation was personified by the figure of Stalin, who had acquired unlimited personal power in both the Bolshevik party and the Communist International.

Viewed as historically inevitable even by the Communists themselves, however, these three foundations were subject to evolution. (The Russians, accustomed to the old and long-maintained state of affairs, seem to have forgotten the role of changes in historical dialectics.) The first foundation ceased to exist the moment the Bolshevik Revolution was no longer unique, when other revolutions triumphed in Europe and Asia. The second foundation disappeared when the Comintern was dissolved and with it most of the old organizational and institutional ties linking the foreign Communist parties to Moscow—including the two categories described. As long as the third foundation, Stalin, was still there, it was possible to ignore these changes or limit their consequences. After Stalin's death, however, the "historically inexorable" path, as the Communist formula puts it, was fully cleared for the new phase in the history of the world Communist movement which we are witnessing today.

The Emergence of a New Comintern Strategy for China: 1928[*]

by

RICHARD C. THORNTON

Major historians of Chinese communism seem to agree that Comintern policy toward China underwent a "leftward shift" in 1928, replacing the United Front of the previous period. They argue that the Comintern directed the Chinese Communists to follow a policy of large-scale armed insurrection to bring about the rapid overthrow of the Nationalist regime of Chiang Kai-shek. Perhaps the earliest proponent of this thesis was Harold Isaacs, who, in his book *The Tragedy of the Chinese Revolution,* says,

> In line with the general leftward lurch taken by the Comintern in 1928, the sudden discovery of the "third period," the final period of capitalism and the "stormy revolutionary upsurge," theoretical confusion was multiplied by the tactical madness of ultra-leftism; opportunism fused with adventurism.[1]

This thesis was followed closely by other historians, including Professors Benjamin I. Schwartz, Robert C. North, and John K. Fairbank. Professor Schwartz presents the most cogent formulation of this position in his book *Chinese Communism and the Rise of Mao.* He contends that the Comintern leadership called for the overthrow of the existing regime in China, for the establishment of a new soviet regime under the exclusive control of the Chinese Communist Party. It called for armed uprisings—or preparation for armed uprisings—both in town and country.[2]

---

* The author is indebted to Professor Donald W. Treadgold and to the members of the China Colloquium of the University of Washington for their valuable comments.

Professor North, too, considers that the Comintern's policy for the Chinese Communists after 1928 was "a program of armed insurrection essentially similar to the plan which failed at Canton"[3] in 1927—that is, a policy of direct attacks on large cities. Lastly, Professor Fairbank finds that the Comintern's directives for the sixth congress of the Chinese Communist Party in 1928 "laid the basis for the disastrous 'Li Li-san line' of 1929–1930,"[4] which was an attempt to capture a large urban base for the CCP by means of large-scale armed uprisings.

However, this version of events which prevailed for so long has come into question. New documents indicate that events took quite a different turn. They suggest that while a "leftward shift" undoubtedly occurred, the highly important reorientation which took place in Comintern policy toward China in 1928 was not toward large-scale urban uprisings. In the Ninth Plenum report on the Chinese Question and later in the resolutions of the sixth congress of the Chinese Communist Party, the Executive Committee of the Comintern (ECCI) introduced a new strategy of revolution for the Chinese Communists to follow which embodied a sophisticated conception of protracted guerrilla warfare and political subversion.

To examine and substantiate the emergence of this new strategy, it is appropriate to observe it within two different but complementary frameworks. The one relates to the debate within the Comintern on the Chinese situation, with Stalin's political maneuvering representing the key to the problem. The second, easier to understand if Stalin's position is present in mind, concerns the Comintern's (i.e. Stalin's) new line for China. This essay therefore will explore, successively, the two aspects of the same problem.

POLICY DEBATE ON CHINA WITHIN THE COMINTERN

The break between the Chinese Communists and the Kuomintang in April 1927 brought about a major shift in Comintern strategy for China. Whereas previously the Comintern had directed the Chinese Communist Party to cooperate with the Kuomintang, after 1927 both competed for power as separate political units. The change in the political situation in China required a change in Comintern strategy. Discussion of various policy alternatives began at the fifteenth party congress of the Soviet Communist Party in December 1927 and continued through the Sixth World Comintern Congress of July–September 1928. The alternatives which were put forward during this period reflected certain limits on the type of policy acceptable to the Comintern. Most important, there was no question of withdrawing from China. Nor was there any official doubt of an ultimately successful "Socialist" revolution in China, by which was understood the establishment of a Chinese Communist regime. All policy proposals centered around the manner in which the revolution would proceed and develop after the defeat administered to the Chinese Communists at the hands of Chiang Kai-shek.

The key issue was, should the Chinese Communists make an immediate and direct attempt to overthrow the newly established Nationalist regime, or should action be deferred until such time as the Chinese Communists would be in a stronger position? Three alternatives were proposed by three different groups. What may be called the "extreme left" position in this revolutionary spectrum was taken by a faction led by Heinz Neumann, Besso Lominadze, and Ch'ü Ch'iu-pai. This faction favored a vigorous policy of immediate action to overthrow the Nationalists. The "right," represented by Bukharin and Chang Kuo-t'ao, proposed continued though limited cooperation between the Communists and petty-bourgeois elements in China. This group saw no chance for the immediate victory of the Chinese revolution. Stalin, his man Pavel Mif, and—for the time being—Li Li-san, occupied an intermediary position but one which was closer to the position of the extreme left than to that of the right despite his alliance with the right. As we shall see in the second part of this essay, Stalin, as perhaps suited his crafty temperament, advocated a policy of protracted guerrilla war in China.

The Challenge from the Extreme Left: Lominadze's Theory of Permanent Revolution

From the fifteenth congress of the Russian Communist Party in December 1927 through the Sixth Comintern Congress in the summer of 1928, the extreme left faction made a serious and sustained attempt to direct the Comintern's China policy onto a more revolutionary path of immediate action.[5] At the fifteenth party congress, the main spokesman for immediate and direct attacks to overthrow the Nationalist regime was Besso Lominadze. He had just returned from China where he and Heinz Neumann during the latter half of 1927 apparently had been directing the series of uprisings which the Chinese Communists attempted at this time. Lominadze returned to Moscow in time for the fifteenth party congress. Neumann remained in

China for the Canton uprising which occurred while the congress was in session.

Speaking just after the Canton uprising had taken place, Lominadze said that the events at Canton were the "beginning of a new upsurge of the Chinese revolution" and, he argued, the Comintern's policy should be "immediate armed uprisings" to overthrow the reactionary Nationalist regime.[6] He attempted to justify his proposal in terms of Marxist theory, but by a different schema than the one which held that all revolutions passed through the stages of feudalism, capitalism, and socialism. Lominadze asserted that China was characterized by the Asiatic mode of production, not feudalism, and that the two were separate and distinct.[7] Under the Asiatic mode of production society was atomized. This explained, he went on, the collapse of the Chinese bourgeoisie, which no longer represented "any united political force," and which existed only as "separate groups . . . commanded by separate militarists."[8] Attempting to show how favorable the situation in China was to a policy of immediate uprisings, which, according to Lominadze, would propel the Chinese revolution directly into its "Socialist phase," he went so far as to claim that the Kuomintang itself was so fragmented that it no longer existed as a "political party." At this point in Lominadze's speech, Stalin—perhaps to disassociate himself from this view—interrupted him to ask, "and what is left of the bourgeoisie?" Lominadze replied, "a few bourgeoisie were left. (Laughter.) A few groups of bourgeoisie were left."[9]

In brief, Lominadze's argument was as follows: since China was characterized by the Asiatic mode of production, the bourgeoisie could not constitute an effective political force. Therefore, the Chinese revolution was not a bourgeois-democratic revolution. It was a workers' and peasants' revolution which, because of its "continuous, permanent character," would largely bypass the bourgeois-democratic stage and move into the Socialist phase.[10] According to Lominadze, it followed that the policy which the Comintern must adopt to secure this end was one of immediate and continued armed uprisings.

Lominadze's theoretical analysis carried some interesting implications. If the revolution in China were passing from the Asiatic to the Socialist stage, bypassing capitalism, then how could it be classified as a "workers' and peasants' revolution?" Would it not be simply a peasants' revolt? And if that were the case, where did the

Communist Party, the vanguard of the proletariat, come in? Indeed, there seemed to be an elementary flaw in Lominadze's position. To deny the existence of the bourgeois-democratic stage of the revolution was to deny the possibility of the development of a proletariat and any role in the revolution for the Communist Party if the Communist Party were supposed to be the vanguard of the proletariat.

It was perhaps with these implications in mind that delegates to the congress challenged Lominadze's proposals. Pavel Mif, Stalin's China expert, and Nikolai Bukharin, head of the Comintern at this time, immediately attacked the theoretical underpinnings of Lominadze's position. First, Mif disputed the assertion that the Asiatic mode of production prevailed in China:

> Comrade Lominadze has endeavored to oppose feudalism to the Asiatic method of production, in the sense that the latter has substituted [sic] feudalism in China. (Lominadze: "Marx has done that.") Marx did not oppose feudalism to the Asiatic method of production in this sense. Marx understood under Asiatic methods of production a variety of feudalism, and expressly stated that here there was no essential difference from ordinary feudalism, but only secondary differences of an external, partially historical, and juridical character.[11]

Next, Mif opposed Lominadze's assertion that the bourgeoisie no longer existed as a separate political force. "In China," said Mif, "the struggle between the bourgeoisie and the proletariat for hegemony commenced right at the beginning of the Chinese revolution," and

> those comrades who simply sweep away the bourgeoisie from the scene . . . actually sweep away the question of the ruthless struggle for hegemony in the Chinese revolution. The bourgeois tendencies have not ceased to exist in China, and the fight against them must be continued with unremitting energy. These bourgeois tendencies, striving for the liquidation of the revolution and the triumph of reaction are not only unweakened but are assuming aggravated forms.[12]

Mif opposed the two main theoretical propositions that Lominadze had used to support his proposal for immediate armed uprisings in China. He maintained that Lominadze was simply wrong to say that the Asiatic mode of production prevailed in China and equally incorrect to say that Marx held this view. It was Mif's, and indeed Stalin's, position that there was feudalism in China, that

capitalist relations were developing there, and that the Chinese bourgeoisie, far from being a negligible political force, was stronger than
ever before.

The Stalinist group must have believed that the views expressed
by Lominadze represented a potentially serious threat to their own
position, for Mif did not terminate his criticism with his comments at
the fifteenth party congress. He continued his attack in both *Bolshevik* and *Communist International*, two leading party journals. In *Bolshevik*, Lominadze was permitted to present his own case with Mif's
criticism appearing in the following article of the same issue.[13] These
articles appeared just before the meeting of the Ninth Plenum of the
ECCI in February 1928, and both authors entreated the Executive
Committee to decide in their favor. Later in 1928, while the Sixth
Congress of the Comintern was in session, Mif went to even greater
lengths in an article in *Communist International* to show that Marx
viewed the Asiatic mode of production as merely a variant of feudalism and not as a separate stage of development, as Lominadze contended.[14]

At the fifteenth party congress, Bukharin criticized Lominadze
in a similar vein. To declare, he said, that the bourgeoisie was split up
into various groups which were in mutual conflict was not at all to say
that the bourgeoisie had been completely eliminated as a social class
force.[15] Paralleling Mif's comments, Bukharin also criticized Lominadze's formulation of Chinese feudalism as "extremely vague."
Classifying China as feudal or Asiatic, he said, had a close relationship to the estimate of the classes existing in China, "for the denial of
the existence of feudalism has implied . . . the denial of the existence
of the landowning class, and this denial has again led to other conclusions."[16] These "other conclusions" were left unstated, but—especially for Bukharin—the implications of Lominadze's argument were
even more far-reaching than those already discussed.[17]

The Ninth Plenum of the ECCI, meeting some two months after
the fifteenth party congress, upheld the criticisms of Lominadze,
labeling his viewpoint a mistake similar to that which Trotsky had
made in 1905. The part of the resolution dealing with his argument
reads as follows:

> The characterization of the present phase of the Chinese revo-
> lution as one which has already grown into a Socialist revolution is
> incorrect. Equally incorrect is its characterization as a permanent
> revolution (the position taken by the representative of the Executive

Committee of the Communist International [Lominadze]). The tendency to skip over the bourgeois-democratic phase of the revolution coupled with the simultaneous appraisal of the revolution as permanent, is a mistake similar to that made by Trotsky in 1905. This mistake is all the more harmful since such a formulation of the question ignores the profound national peculiarity of the Chinese revolution as a semi-colonial revolution.[18]

The Extreme Left at the Sixth Congress of the Chinese Communist Party (June–July, 1928)

Stalin himself had coauthored the Ninth Plenum resolution cited above, clearly implying his rejection of proposals for immediate action to overthrow the Nationalist regime.[19] Yet this did not deter an extreme left faction in the Chinese Communist Party from attempting to obtain a reversal of the position expressed in the Ninth Plenum resolution on the definition of the stage of the Chinese revolution at that time. Ch'ü Ch'iu-pai, who, with Lominadze and Neumann, apparently had planned and directed the uprisings in China during the latter part of 1927, but who had since been removed from his position as leader of the Chinese Communist Party, belonged to the extreme-left faction in the Chinese party opposing the Stalinist position.[20]

At the sixth congress of the Chinese Communist Party, held some four months after the Ninth Plenum, this extreme-left faction seems to have attempted to change the definition of the stage of the Chinese revolution from bourgeois-democratic to Socialist, just as Lominadze had done at the fifteenth party congress earlier. One argument made by this faction was merely a repetition of Lominadze's argument given above. The rejoinder given by Pavel Mif in the official Comintern organ was simply that the Ninth Plenum had already dealt with the question of permanent revolution. He warned against the view that the Chinese revolution had skipped over the whole historical stage "when the attention of the struggling masses must be focused upon the elimination of imperialist control and feudal institutions in China," that is, upon the main tasks of the bourgeois-democratic stage of the revolution and not the Socialist.[21]

Another argument raised by Chinese extreme leftists was that if the slogan of the redistribution of land were raised, then the revolution had to assume a Socialist character. Mif disagreed, disposing of this argument by referring to the resolution of the sixth congress of the Chinese Communists in which it was stated that the new policy did not call for the redistribution of all of the land, but only the confiscation of the landlords' land.[22]

The final argument put forward by the extreme-left faction to change the definition of the stage of the Chinese revolution from bourgeois-democratic to Socialist was more formidable. The argument was that to a certain extent the Chinese revolution was anti-imperialist. To the extent that it was anti-imperialist, it was an international revolution, and to that extent it was a proletarian revolution. Given these premises, the extreme-left faction argued, the present stage of the revolution "bore the outlines" of a Socialist revolution.[23] The reply to this argument was based on the orthodox theory of dual revolution. Expressing the official view, Mif said that the Chinese "comrades" had failed to note an important distinction. In the first phase—the bourgeois-democratic phase—the Chinese revolution was only an auxiliary force in the international revolution and therefore it, itself, could not be Socialist. Only in its second phase —the Socialist phase—would it become a "direct constituent part" of the international proletarian revolution and assume a Socialist character.[24] But as yet, he maintained, the Chinese revolution was still in the bourgeois-democratic stage.

A puzzling question arises here: Why did the Chinese extreme-left faction oppose the Comintern in these terms? What difference did it make whether the revolution were designated a bourgeois-democratic or a Socialist one? To put this another way, what did this faction hope to accomplish by defining the Chinese revolution as being in a "Socialist" phase? This was not, to be sure, a mere academic exercise. As one Comintern official put it at the time, "the question of the character of the growing revolution in China has for us far from an academic character. The selection of the tasks of the revolution, the basic slogans, and our basic tactical line, all depend upon the resolution of this question."[25]

While a theoretical definition of the stage of the revolution would prescribe the policy to be followed, it also implied the limits to policy, which must have been the major reason the extreme left argued so strenuously for a change in definition. Such policy limitations were spelled out in unmistakable terms at the sixth congress of the Chinese Communists. In a lengthy (116 pages) and highly revealing speech about basic policy, an unidentified "representative of the

Comintern" explained the refusal of the ECCI to sanction immediate action to attempt an overthrow of the Nationalists. During the bourgeois-democratic stage of the revolution,

> the task before the workers, peasants, and our Party, the leader of the working class, is not to call for a direct seizure of power by the working class, it is not to destroy capitalism and to organize a Socialist economy. That is to say the basis of the revolution at present is not Socialist, it is not proletarian. . . . The present tasks are the elimination of feudal forces, the completion of the agrarian revolution, and the expulsion of imperialism. But these tasks cannot exceed the limits of the capitalist system. . . . They cannot exceed these limits because the task [of the bourgeois-democratic revolution] is only to eliminate the feudal system, not to eliminate the whole of the capitalist class. Its task is still not to attempt a seizure of power by the working class. [t'a hai pu shih ch'i-t'u yi ko kung-jen chiéh-chi tou-ch'u cheng-ch'uan te jen-wu.][26]

But there was more to making policy than merely making theoretical definitions. Defining the stage of the revolution, while supremely important, was insufficient grounds in itself for deciding on a tactical line. The balance of forces must be reckoned. The speaker raised the issue of imperialism. "To take the strength of imperialism lightly, no matter what, is impossible." To do so would result in an incorrect tactical line and a "completely incorrect general political position."[27] True, the imperialists are fighting among themselves for control of China, but they are united in their opposition to the Communists. Furthermore, the present concentration of imperialist forces in China is greater than ever before.[28]

Among the Nationalists there are also many contending factions: the bourgeois landlords are struggling against the feudal warlords; the South is against the North; the Chiang faction is against the former Wuhan faction, the Kwangtung faction, and so forth. "But, comrades, do not forget that all of these factions alike are striving to slaughter us . . . to suppress the workers' and peasants' revolution," and their combined forces are greatly superior to those of the Communists.[29]

In deciding upon a tactical line, therefore, these are the circumstances which have to be taken into consideration. "This is the position from which we should begin, not from some imaginary position," like believing that the revolution will be victorious in a short time if only we define its present character as Socialist, or that "imperialism almost does not exist because the imperialists themselves are in conflict over profits," or, referring to Lominadze's argument, "that the bourgeoisie almost does not exist because the various factions of the bourgeosie are struggling among themselves. . . . In this way nothing exists."[30]

The Comintern representative evaluated the present balance of forces as being a bloc of three forces aligned against the Chinese Communists: the imperialists, the landlord-warlords, and the national bourgeoisie. "Because this kind of powerful new bloc has arisen, our strength organizationally and technically is weaker than theirs and, in certain respects, politically we are weaker as well."[31] We must not underestimate the strength of the enemy or overestimate our own; if we do we will certainly adopt an incorrect line.

> Revolutionary courage does not consist in incessantly, under all conditions, making war. Revolutionary courage consists in making war only under certain conditions, or when a certain relationship of class forces makes war necessary.[32]

The Comintern representative said that the kind of "foolish, fetishistic doctrinaire" who sees every situation as revolutionary and who always raises the slogan of insurrection "is useless[!]"[33] In his concluding remarks the speaker explained that a revolution does not succeed over night and suggested that in general the Chinese Communists were too impatient for victory.

> The Party believes that only by employing the method of insurrection to overthrow, fundamentally, the existing regime in China, by employing the method of violent armed struggle to oppose the strength of imperialism, by employing the method of an all-China great workers' and peasants' insurrection to expel imperialism and to destroy the power of the capitalist-feudal class, is there a possibility of moving out of present conditions. However, this is not to say that in the enormously large country of China, where there are many different provinces and many different conditions, in an extremely short period of time, in one or two days, hundreds of thousands of people will suddenly rise up; this cannot happen. *An insurrection begins in some provinces and later spreads to other provinces; in some places it fails, in some places it succeeds, its area grows broader and larger; but this kind of situation, at present, still has not developed. Perhaps [China] must pass through a very long period before it can develop.*[34]

Now we have existing in some districts several soviets, which although they are very weak, do exist; this is good. In the future they will become centers around which the development of the revolutionary movement will be greater than in any other areas. This is completely correct. *But we cannot muddle together the matter of the victory of the Chinese revolution with the matter of the existence of several district soviets.* Although there now exist soviets in several provinces, although the comrades there have done good work, the Chinese revolution has suffered defeat; this is a definite fact.[35]

With these arguments the ECCI frustrated all attempts by the extreme-left faction in the Chinese Communist Party to redefine the revolution as having a "Socialist" character. In the tenor of these arguments an answer is suggested to the question of what the extreme-left faction hoped to gain by their theoretical arguments. If the revolution were recognized as being in its "Socialist" phase, by definition the bourgeois-democratic stage would have been completed. Then the immediate task facing the Chinese Communists—the task which Lenin said faced the Bolsheviks in his April Theses in 1917—would be the assumption of state power.

The Extreme Left at the Sixth Congress of the Comintern (July–September, 1928)

The extreme-left faction had suffered three consecutive defeats: at the fifteenth party congress, at the Ninth Plenum and then at the sixth congress of the Chinese Communists. Still, leading members of that faction considered the issue open and continued to press their views at the Sixth Congress of the Comintern. Lominadze recanted during the congress, but Heinz Neumann and Ch'ü Ch'iu-pai, the other two main leaders of the extreme left, expressed firm opposition to the Comintern's new China policy. However, they were forced to modify the arguments which had already been deemed incorrect by the Stalin group on the previous three occasions.

Lominadze was criticized severely at the Comintern's congress. Perhaps as a result of this criticism, or pressure from the Stalin group, he repudiated his earlier proposals for immediate uprisings in China to overthrow the Nationalist regime. In making his statement, he contrasted his now "incorrect" viewpoint with the newly adopted policy of the Comintern toward China.

> In order not to arouse the impression that I want to cover up my own mistakes on the Chinese question . . . I must openly declare

that, prior to the Ninth Plenum I made a serious mistake. . . . I did not look upon the Canton uprising as a rearguard action, did not consider it to be the concluding engagement which wound up a whole period of the revolution, but I held it to be the beginning of a new upsurge of the Chinese revolution. Events have disproved this position . . .

My mistakes consisted in that, proceeding from a false estimate of the situation, I continued after the Canton uprising to hold that the course for an immediate armed uprising was just as necessary as before the Canton uprising.

Now it is perfectly clear that this line was not tenable after the Canton uprising. The Ninth Plenum, and subsequently the Theses proposed to the Sixth World Congress, put this question absolutely correctly: the slogan for armed uprising can now be formulated only as a propaganda slogan. *Only in those districts where there is a spontaneous peasant movement should the [Chinese] Communists put themselves at the head of these peasant uprisings, to consolidate and to strengthen themselves there.*[36]

Lominadze's opposition to the Comintern's new China policy ends at this point. After the congress he apparently was assigned a post as a "youth leader," but in December 1930 he was ousted from his position and charged with organizing an "anti-Party 'left' right bloc." He committed suicide in 1936.[37]

Neumann, who had since returned from China, did not capitulate as Lominadze had done. Instead he presented a highly sophisticated and convincing argument, bulwarked by voluminous quotes from Marx and Lenin, for immediate action in China. His speech was so well stated that it was not challenged at the congress; it was, for the most part, simply ignored. Modifying the form of the argument presented by Lominadze earlier, but retaining its essence, Neumann focused on the concept of the "noncapitalist path of development" for China and other colonial countries. He avoided direct mention of China as Asiatic and agreed that the present stage of the revolution was bourgeois-democratic, but like Lominadze he argued that the Chinese bourgeoisie was a weak social force unable to solve the tasks of the bourgeois-democratic revolution. Quoting from Lenin's statement on the possibility of a noncapitalist path of development for colonial countries at the Second Congress of the Comintern in 1920 and calling it one of the "keenest thoughts Lenin ever expressed," Neumann maintained that with the assistance of the proletariat of the advanced countries China would be able largely to bypass the capitalist (bourgeois-democratic) stage on its way to Communism.[38] He did not propose openly a policy of immediate armed uprisings in China. To do so would have revealed his opposition to Stalin to all of the delegates at the congress. Instead, Neumann cleverly framed his remarks in such a manner that the only possible conclusion to be drawn was indeed a policy of immediate action.

Professing agreement with the Ninth Plenum's resolution on China, Neumann affirmed that there now existed the "soviet phase" of the revolution in China. But he said that "the soviet phase is only a political form,"

> the content of this political form is the phase of the transition to the Socialist revolution, which smashes the limits, the restrictions of the bourgeois-democratic revolution, even though this bourgeois-democratic revolution is still before us.
>
> Whoever does not understand that, whoever only speaks of having a bourgeois-democratic revolution in China, whoever does not want to recognize that we are in the midst of the transition to the Socialist revolution, is making a mistake.[39]

Again, quoting Lenin on the relationship between the bourgeois-democratic revolution and the Socialist, Neumann pointed out that there was no sharp dividing line between the two; "the first grows over into the second. The second solves in passing the questions of the first."[40] According to Lenin, he said, it was the "fight" which determined how far the second succeeded in growing out over the first. How must this term "growing over" be understood, he asked. Of course, the revolution will grow over on the basis of the relation of class forces, and so forth. But, as Lenin said, on the basis of these class forces, "the fight decides, and only the fight, about the transition to a higher phase of the revolution."[41]

In this way Neumann set forth his argument for immediate action in China. There could be no stopping of the revolution, not even temporarily, "to solve the tasks" of the bourgeois-democratic revolution; the revolution must be continued, pushed on to the Socialist phase. The only conclusion to be drawn from this argument, of course, was that the ECCI should adopt a policy of pushing on to the Socialist phase of the revolution in China, which could only mean a policy of "immediate action."

While Neumann's argument had relatively little effect on the actual course of the discussions at the congress, it seems to have been the cause of some modification of the official line in the final "Theses on the International Situation and the Tasks of the Comintern." There, in a paraphrase of Stalin's Ninth Plenum resolution, the Chinese revolution was designated as being in the bourgeois-democratic stage. However, a partial concession was made to Neumann about the necessity of the bourgeois-democratic revolution "growing over" into a Socialist revolution. Where the Ninth Plenum resolution read that it was incorrect to characterize the present phase of the Chinese revolution "as one which has already grown into a Socialist revolution,"[42] the final Theses read: the Chinese revolution was now in the bourgeois-democratic stage "which unavoidably must *grow over* into the proletarian [stage]."[43] Still, what the Theses did not say was equally important. It did not say, as Neumann had proposed, that the Chinese revolution was in the state of the "transition to the Socialist revolution."[44]

Three days later, Ch'ü Ch'iu-pai delivered his concluding remarks at the thirty-ninth session of the congress. As a member of the extreme-left faction, he undoubtedly believed that the Comintern should adopt a policy of immediate action in China, but he did not reiterate openly the theoretical arguments of Lominadze and Neumann. Instead he expressed his differences with the Stalinist group principally on "pragmatic" grounds. To support his position Ch'ü drew on the "experience" of the Chinese revolution and avoided all mention of "theoretical stages" on which both Lominadze and Neumann had based their arguments heavily.

Ch'ü Ch'iu-pai held that "in the near future there could be victorious uprisings in certain large cities"[45] (*pu chiu te chiang lai chiu k'o yi tsai mo hsieh ta ch'eng-shih ch'ü te pao-tung te sheng-li*). In order to bring these uprisings about, he apparently wanted the Comintern to adopt a policy of instigating the peasantry into widespread revolts directed by the Chinese Communist Party. The corollary to his argument, as he developed it in his speech to the congress, was a de-emphasis of the anti-imperialist movement, firm opposition to the national bourgeoisie, and temporary alignment with the petty-bourgeoisie (but far different from the alignment proposed by Bukharin).

In what seems to have been an impassioned speech, Ch'ü asserted that the anti-imperialist movement in China had been ineffective. "What is the anti-imperialist movement?" he asked. It is simply a combination of boycotts, demonstrations, meetings, and strikes. The strike in Hong Kong, for instance, lasted for nearly two years, during which time the Chinese Communists had led demonstrations and all the rest. "But this did not put an end to imperialism, and we cannot say that we will overthrow imperialist rule in China if we continue to fight only by such methods. Imperialism can really be overthrown only if the proletariat can rouse the mass millions of peasantry under the slogan of the agrarian revolution."[46]

Ch'ü, like Lominadze and Neumann, also argued the thesis of a weak bourgeoisie. The national bourgeoisie, he said, had betrayed the revolution and no longer warranted the support of the proletariat. Its betrayal, however, should not be confused with its strength as a class force. "It is said now that probably the national bourgeoisie has already established its reign in China. But this is not so. It is so weak that even when it engages in counter-revolution, it does so with the help of the gentry and . . . under the leadership of the imperialists."[47] In actuality, Ch'ü claimed, the past few years have witnessed the "denationalization" of the national bourgeoisie. Many have given up their factories; some have even sold them to the imperialists. Others have returned again to speculation in land and finance.[48]

We must be unalterably opposed to the so-called national bourgeoisie. The petty-bourgeoisie, on the other hand, are somewhat different. We can lead them, Ch'ü maintained, in the struggle against imperialism—so long as it does not require anything more than demonstrations and meetings. "If we think that our task consists only in arranging demonstrations, meetings, and so forth, then of course we will always have a strong alliance with the petty-bourgeoisie."[49] But we must not confuse the rural and urban petty-bourgeoisie with the rural and urban poor. "We must not be so foolish as to rouse the masses of the rural and urban poor only for demonstrations. We must rouse them for a more serious performance, beginning with ordinary activities, but not stopping short with these."[50] At the point where we go beyond mere demonstrations, at the "moment when the peasantry is rising in agrarian revolution, in uprisings," we must be prepared to cast the petty-bourgeoisie out.[51]

Emphasizing his main point, Ch'ü urged the Comintern to give its full support to the agrarian revolution—that is, to peasant insurrections in the countryside. In discussing this question, he revealed that the Chinese party "membership exceeded 100,000 . . . of which the great majority were peasants."[52] This should not mean, he went on, that we must refuse further admission of peasants into the party. Emphasis, however, should be placed on further broadening the "peasants' mass organizations, of course, simultaneously broadening the workers organizations and drawing workers into the party. Only by this means can we guarantee the proletarian composition of our party."[53] Here, Ch'ü pointed to what he considered a serious "shortcoming" in the Comintern's new policy. He thought that the number of peasants being organized for the agrarian revolution was too low but the number being admitted into the party too high. Ch'ü, it seems, held to an elitist conception of a Communist party. He favored expending the peasants as cannon fodder in insurrections, but was reluctant to admit them as party members. He attempted to illustrate what he meant:

> If local uprisings in the countryside or in districts are victorious, then soviets are organized. All participants in the soviets en masse immediately join the party. . . . In the majority of cases, the form of our soviets is identical with the party and the party with the soviets.[54]

"If," Ch'ü claimed, "non-party peasant revolutionaries could be drawn into peasant associations and soviets [but not into the party], then our own party cadres and party organizations could be much more clearly organized."[55] Otherwise there was a distinct tendency, which had been manifested in other Communist parties as well as in the Chinese, for the party "to take the place of mass organizations."[56]

Toward the end of his speech Ch'ü attempted to give some theoretical backing to his proposal of peasant insurrections by bringing up the theory of the "hinterland," or, as it also was known, the theory of the "world rural districts." The theory of the hinterland postulated that the growth of imperialism had not helped to develop "capitalist relations" in colonial countries; on the contrary, it had tended to retard such growth. According to the theory, colonial countries were becoming mere agrarian appendages for the imperialist countries. Or, to put it another way, the imperialist countries were becoming world cities and the colonies were becoming world rural districts. The similarity between the hinterland theory and the "Asiatic" theory was evident. The hinterland theory seems to have served the same purpose for Ch'ü Ch'iu-pai that the "Asiatic" theory did for Lominadze. It permitted the assertion that "capitalist relations" were not developing in China, and therefore not only the bourgeoisie but the proletariat was weak, if it existed at all. From this followed a policy of reliance on the peasantry, which was strong in agrarian countries, rather than on the proletariat, which necessarily was weak.

Ch'ü did not make the explicit conclusions which could be drawn from this theory. He only stated the initial premises.

> I think after all that the problem of the national revolution becomes clear if one considers that the colonies are the world rural district. If one takes into consideration that, on the whole, all of these colonies are agrarian and peasant countries, then we must realize that the [Communist] International requires a definite tactic in regard to the colonial peasantry as a whole. Only from this point of view can we work out proper tactics for the revolutionary movement in the East.[57]

However subtle Ch'ü may have believed himself to be in stating his position, there was slight chance that the Comintern would accept its premises. Lozovsky, one of Stalin's men who headed the international trade union apparatus, had anticipated Ch'ü and dissected the implications behind the "hinterland" theory for Bolshevik policy a few days before.

> If we speak of . . . colonies as "world rural districts" . . . all talk about proletarian and peasant dictatorship must cease automatically. In the "world rural districts," in the "continent of rural districts," there can be no industrial proletariat, and therefore no room for proletarian and peasant dictatorship. With such terminology the proletariat disappears as leader. [The proletariat] . . . could come into being only on the basis of the development—be it only a slow, meandering and very painful development—of capitalist relations in the colonies.[58]

And, of course, without a proletariat, a Communist party could scarcely exist—theoretically. Lozovsky's deduction was irrefutable and there was little that Ch'ü could have said to offset his remarks. The wonder is that he even attempted to do so. Later, in the final *Theses on the Revolutionary Movement in the Colonies and Semi-Colonies*, the "world rural district" or "hinterland" argument that capitalist relations were not developing in the colonies was explicitly rejected. The *Theses* reaffirmed that "the export of capital to the colonies accelerates the development of capitalist relations in them."[59]

Thus ended the attempts by the extreme-left faction to direct the Comintern's China policy onto a path of immediate revolutionary action to overthrow the Nationalist government. Led by Lominadze, Neumann, and Ch'ü Ch'iu-pai, this faction had engaged in an extended conflict with the Stalinist group which lasted for approximately ten months, from December 1927 to September 1928. After long months of debate and argument the Stalinist group, in alliance with Bukharin and the "right," had defeated the "challenge from the left."

Stalin and the Right

Stalin's relationship with the "right," that is, with Bukharin, was complicated by his temporary alliance with it against the extreme left. During the period of the "challenge from the left," Stalin's dependence on this alliance led him to make certain concessions to maintain it. Some of these concessions are discernible in his China policy, especially regarding the issue of cooperation with the petty-bourgeoisie as proposed by Bukharin. At the fifteenth party congress, Bukharin accepted the designation of the current stage of the Chinese revolution as "bourgeois-democratic," but advocated a new alignment of "class forces"—the social groups with which the Chinese Communist Party could ally itself. He proposed a policy of continued but conditional support of the Chinese petty-bourgeoisie.

Bukharin introduced his proposal by a seemingly irrelevant digression, discussing the conflict of views between Radek and Lenin over the Bolshevik attitude toward Ireland during the First World War. Radek held the position that since the revolutionary movement was led by the Irish bourgeoisie and not the working class, it was of little interest to the Bolsheviks. Lenin attacked this view, according to Bukharin, and voiced full support for the Irish revolutionary movement on the basis of his "dual action" strategy, which involved:

> firstly, an action on the part of the nationally oppressed proletariat and the peasantry, together with the nationally oppressed bourgeoisie against the oppressor nation, and secondly, an action on the part of the proletariat of the oppressor nation, or at least of the class-conscious portion thereof, against the bourgeoisie and any support the latter may find in the oppressor nation.[60]

Then Bukharin applied this "highly significant" formula of Lenin's to the Chinese revolution. In China, as previously in Ireland, similar situations prevailed in which the national bourgeoisie was engaged in a fight against British imperialism. According to Lenin's formula, "dual action" tactics were employed. In Great Britain, the proletariat was to oppose the bourgeoisie; in China, the proletariat, peasantry and nationally oppressed bourgeoisie were to oppose British imperialism.[61] But Bukharin believed the situation in China had changed; the national bourgeoisie had gone over to the counter-revolutionary camp and this demanded a struggle by the proletariat, the peasantry, and "part of the petty-bourgeoisie in the cities" against the combined forces of foreign imperialists, the feudal class, and the national bourgeoisie.[62]

The response of the Stalin group to Bukharin's proposal can be understood best after a brief comment about the general political situation. The fifteenth party congress had been the scene of the complete defeat of the Trotskyite opposition. Stalin had been able to accomplish this victory over Trotsky principally by means of an alliance with Bukharin. Therefore, while Stalin was still "allied" with Bukharin, especially at this crucial point in the political struggle with Trotsky, any disagreement with him could not be voiced openly.

Disagreement with Bukharin's views was expressed indirectly. Stalin's man Pavel Mif, in the speech cited earlier in which he vehemently criticized Lominadze, raised objections to Bukharin's proposals as well, but without mentioning the latter by name. Concluding his comments on Lominadze, Mif said that his remarks were intended only to draw attention to the difficulties of the Chinese revolution. "This revolution cannot hope for the aid of the bourgeoisie. Not only will the bourgeoisie refuse to support it, but will rise in arms against it." The Communists must be prepared for a relatively "long lasting reaction of the bourgeoisie and large landowners in China."[63]

Mif agreed with Bukharin that it was the future relation of class forces which would decide the course of the Chinese revolution. Thus far, the bourgeoisie and the landlords had been victorious, but "the struggle continues and is directed at the present time mainly against the Chinese bourgeoisie [and] against the class of large landowners." There were sections of the Chinese peasantry as well, Mif believed, which would also join this reactionary grouping.

> During the bourgeois-democratic epoch in Russia it was possible to calculate [sic] on the whole of the peasantry joining to overthrow the large landowners, but in China this is not the case. Not only must certain strata of the peasantry, the kulak elements, be excluded from the main mass of the peasantry on whom we can depend [the poor peasantry], but the Chinese proletariat and this main mass of peasantry must fight from the beginning against the Chinese bourgeoisie.[64]

Concluding his comments, Mif said that it must be the duty of the Chinese Communists to isolate the bourgeoisie and landlords and to win over the broad masses. Furthermore, the agrarian revolution "can only reckon on the help of the village poor and must take up the struggle against the kulaks, the landowners, and the bourgeoisie."[65]

Bukharin replied to Mif directly. First, he said that he "did not believe in the possibility," much less the probability, of a prolonged reaction in the form of an alliance of the bourgeoisie and landowners. A "Stolypin era" of land reform such as occurred in pre-revolutionary Russia could not occur in China because the bourgeoisie had no land reserves with which to explore solutions to current agrarian problems. Second, "I scarcely believe that Comrade Mif approaches the question of the struggle against the Chinese kulak from the right aspect."[66] Bukharin insisted that the main issue was not the struggle against the kulak, or rich peasant, but against the landowners.

> Of course it is obvious that the rich kulak, in such places where he sides with the landowner against the main mass of the peasantry . . . must be combatted. But this is not how Comrade Mif states the question.[67]

Clearly, the exchange indicated some fundamental disagreement over the question of the alignment of class forces and the Chinese Communist Party's relationship to it. As expressed by Pavel Mif, Stalin's position apparently was that the Chinese Communist Party should follow a strict policy of united front from below, with no cooperation with any part of the bourgeoisie. In practice (see chart below) this meant that in the countryside the Chinese Communists would ally only with the hired hands, the poor, and the middle peasants against the kulaks and the landowners. In the cities it meant that the Chinese Communists and the urban proletariat would oppose the bourgeoisie (without differentiating them into national and petty-bourgeoisie), feudal warlords, and foreign imperialists.

countryside	*cities*
landowners	foreign imperialists
kulaks (rich peasants)	national bourgeoisie
middle peasants	feudal warlords
poor peasants	petty bourgeoisie
hired hands (rural proletariat)	proletariat

Chinese Communists

Bukharin's interpretation of what the new alignment of class forces should be was quite different. In the countryside, he postulated, the Chinese Communists should ally with the hired hands, poor peasants, middle peasants, and that section of the kulaks (rich peasants) which had not yet gone over to the landowners, against the landowners and whatever section of the kulaks "sides with the land-owners against the main mass of the peasantry." In cities he urged cooperation between the Communists, the urban proletariat, and the "petty-bourgeoisie . . . against the combined forces of foreign im-perialists, the feudal class, and the national bourgeoisie."[68]

Comparing the two positions with the documents of the Ninth Plenum of ECCI, the sixth congress of the Chinese Communist Party, and the Sixth Comintern Congress, it appears that Stalin compro-mised with Bukharin on this issue. He agreed—for the time being—with Bukharin's proposals for limited cooperation between the Chi-nese Communists and petty-bourgeois elements in China in return for Bukharin's support against the extreme left, which, as we saw above, was challenging his China policy.

In the Ninth Plenum resolution in which Stalin's general China policy is adumbrated, there is no differentiation of the bourgeoisie into national and petty-bourgeoisie. Apparently, Stalin had not yet decided to compromise over this issue, for the resolution states simply that the "bourgeoisie has not only made a definite bloc with the counter-revolutionary feudalists and militarists, but has actually reached an agreement with foreign imperialism."[69] If anything, these words suggest that there would be no compromise.

However, by the time the sixth congress of the Chinese Com-munist Party had ended, a shift had become evident in Stalin's posi-tion regarding the issue of cooperation with parts of the bourgeoisie in China. In the political resolution and in the resolution on the peas-ant question, Bukharin's policy proposal was accepted. In the section concerning the anti-imperialist and anti-militarist struggle, the politi-cal resolution reads that in its urban policy the Chinese Communists should actively "draw the broad mass of the working class and petty-bourgeoisie" into the anti-imperialist movement, and further in-structed the party to "split off a significant portion of the petty-bourgeoisie . . . from the Kuomintang and the national bourgeoisie on the basis of the slogans of the anti-imperialist struggle."[70] In the peasant resolution the shift was no less evident for the party's rural policy. The relevant passage reads,

In places where the rich peasants have already become reac-tionary forces, the struggle against rich peasants should be carried on simultaneously with the struggle against warlords, landlords, and gentry. As long as the rich peasants have not yet lost their revolutionary potentialities, as long as they struggle against the oppression of warlords and bureaucrats, the CCP should endeavour to absorb rich peasants into the struggle against warlords, landlords, and gentry. Where the rich peasants waver between revolution and counter-revolution, the party, so far as the struggle of poor peasants and hired hands is not handicapped, should not intensify the struggle against the rich peasants.[71]

This compromise on Stalin's part was duly carried out by the Chinese Communist leaders upon their return to China. "Central" circular number two, which is a condensation of the main resolutions adopted at the congress in Moscow, stated the new line. It read that the party "need not intentionally step up the struggle against the rich peasants, but should not abdicate the class struggle against the landlord characteristics of the rich peasants."[72] It also stated that the sixth congress of the Chinese Communists had pointed out that the party should "unite with the petty-bourgeoisie and rich peasants to oppose all reactionary forces."[73]

Broadening the scope of analysis, it seems that Stalin was not the only one who compromised over the issue of cooperation or noncooperation. While Stalin agreed to a policy of limited cooperation with the bourgeoisie in China, Bukharin also compromised by agreeing to a policy of no cooperation with the Social Democrats in Europe. In a speech in which he discussed the results of the Sixth Comintern Congress, Bukharin said that the leaders of the Social Democrats in Europe were the "watchdogs of imperialism." It was this attitude of social democracy, he said, that "conditioned the tactical change already decided upon by the Executive Committee of the Communist International previous to the Congress . . . [which was a] turn toward a more energetic fight against social democracy."[74]

> At the sixth congress it became clear that this tactical change must be intensified and extended, because the tendencies of the social democratic parties to split the working class have become a general phenomenon. Our struggle against social democracy must be intensified.[75]

In the same speech, Bukharin confirmed that cooperation even in the colonial countries could be only temporary. In some colonial countries "certain temporary agreements with the bourgeoisie are possible in some cases," but of course there could be no thought of "any 'lasting agreement' with the bourgeoisie."[76]

Interestingly enough, although Bukharin compromised publicly, privately his views about the desirability of continued cooperation with the Social Democrats remained unchanged. In a letter to the Comintern secretary, Humbert-Droz, who was then being attacked by the Stalin group as a rightist-deviator, Bukharin expressed sympathy for the idea that the best interests of Communists in Europe would be served by alliances with the Social Democrats against the Fascists.[77] In the letter Bukharin apologized to Humbert-Droz for being unable to espouse this view in public because of the delicate position he occupied within the Soviet Communist Party.

Both men had altered their views for the sake of compromise. But as Stalin's political position became stronger over the next few months, he was able to dispense with Bukharin and in the process dispense with his compromise over the issue of cooperation with the petty-bourgeoisie as well. In June 1929, roughly two months before Bukharin was formally expelled from the Party, the Comintern sent a directive to the Chinese Communists ordering them to struggle resolutely against the kulaks for the leadership of the peasant masses.[78] The line of limited cooperation with the petty-bourgeoisie in China had been changed to complete opposition, the very position which Stalin had advocated through Mif at the fifteenth party congress in December 1927.

STALIN'S STRATEGY FOR CHINA

At the same time that Stalin opposed the extreme left and compromised with the right he was developing his own position. The gradual emergence of his strategy for China can be seen best in the ECCI Ninth Plenum resolution on the Chinese Question and in the resolutions of the sixth congress of the Chinese Communist Party. These documents with their subsequent qualifications and amplifications appear to have established the basic strategic policy which the Chinese Communists followed until coming to power in 1949.

It would be erroneous to assume that because Stalin opposed the extreme left his strategy was necessarily less revolutionary than theirs. The principal differences between the two lay in the time projected by each for the completion of the revolution and in the initial tactics to be pursued. The extreme left expected the victorious establishment of a Chinese Communist regime as a direct consequence of immediate and widespread uprisings against the Nationalists who, they believed, had not yet consolidated their regime. Stalin, on the other hand, emphasized protracted guerrilla warfare—which implied a long term process. Guerrilla warfare would require years, perhaps decades, until the necessary forces could be accumulated to challenge the Kuomintang.

Immediate action to overthrow the Kuomintang would require direct attacks on the centers of state power—the large cities held by the Nationalists. Guerrilla warfare, however, would have to be waged in areas where the Kuomintang's military forces were weakest —in the countryside far removed from the centers of state power. Under such a strategy, attacks on the centers of state power would ensue only when the military balance had been altered decisively in favor of the Communists. From the first Stalin appears to have favored the gradual accumulation of a military force. The idea is suggested in the ECCI's Ninth Plenum resolution on China, coauthored by Stalin, which says that one of the main objectives of the Chinese Communists is the organization of "Red army detachments in the expectation that these detachments will then gradually be unified into one general all-China Red Army."[79]

From 1923 to 1927 the ECCI had instructed the Chinese Communists to engage in a United Front, which involved cooperating with the Kuomintang in its drive to win state power in China while striving to gain control over that organization from within. The development of an independent military force had not been a part of this strategy. Unfortunately for the Comintern and the Chinese Communists, in April 1927, when the Kuomintang substantially had attained its objectives but when the Communists had not yet achieved the internal takeover of the Kuomintang, Chiang Kai-shek had broken with his ostensible allies and had begun a campaign to exterminate them.

The Chinese Communists had been disorganized by the break with the Kuomintang and were tactically unprepared for it. Their actions in the months that followed had displayed little evidence of a grand design directed by the Comintern.[80] Fleeing from the Kuomintang's "white terror"—the physical annihilation of Communists— remnants of the Communist leadership had assembled hastily whatever forces they could muster and had made several *ad hoc* attempts to upset the newly established Nationalist regime (in the Nanchang uprising in August, the Autumn Harvest uprising in September, and the Canton uprising in December). All had failed. Many Communists, including Mao Tse-Tung, had retreated to the comparative safety of mountainous South China—a bandit refuge for centuries— to reorganize their forces. Their fortunes were at low ebb. Within a few months a powerful political force had been reduced almost to insignificance. The altered situation clearly called for a new policy, and it was at this time that Stalin decided to bring forth his new strategy for China.

Directives of the Comintern's Ninth Plenum

When the Executive Committee of the Comintern convened its Ninth Plenum on February 9, 1928, the essentials of a new policy had already been worked out. Its basic components were adumbrated in the Ninth Plenum's resolution on the Chinese Question of February 25, 1928,[81] which contained, first, an analysis of the current situation (points one through four), then an outline of the new strategy (points five through eleven). The resolution stated the Party's objectives in cities and countryside and suggested the military, political, organizational, and propaganda methods necessary to achieve the desired ends.

In analyzing the current situation, the ECCI maintained the theoretical formulation which it had originally postulated—namely, that the revolution in China was in its bourgeois-democratic stage. Theoretically, this meant that the immediate objectives of the Comintern still were the establishment of a dictatorship of workers and peasants, the completion of the agrarian revolution, the elimination of all feudal relations, and the unification of China. The resolution emphasized that the Chinese revolution was neither a "Socialist" revolution, which would imply that the bourgeois-democratic stage had been skipped over, nor a "permanent" revolution, which would imply a policy of continuous and unabated armed insurrection in China.[82]

"The first wave of the broad revolutionary movement of the workers and peasants," the resolution stated, "is over," and has ended in "heavy defeats" for the revolution—especially for the Communists, leaders of the revolution. This situation, the resolution continued, marks "the transition of the entire mass revolutionary movement of China into its new, soviet phase."[83]

The ECCI, in its resolution, went on to state that "at the present time there is no mighty upsurge of the revolutionary mass movement on a national scale," but that "certain symptoms" indicated that the workers' and peasants' revolution was moving in the direction of a nationwide upsurge.[84] This prognosis was supported by the heroic insurrection of the Canton workers, the increasing number of mutinies among warlord armies, the complete political disorganization and continuous internecine warfare among the various militarist cliques, and "primarily by the development of the peasant movement in several districts (the sovietization of several districts . . .)."[85]

Finally, the ECCI observed that the revolutionary movement in China was developing extremely unevenly. "It proceeds unevenly in the various Chinese provinces with different historical conditions of struggle. It has, up to now, also developed unevenly in the towns and in the rural districts."[86] The current soviet phase of the revolution was further characterized by the fact that while the peasant movement was developing, the workers' movement "is experiencing a certain degree of depression."[87] This newly applied concept of "uneven development" to the Chinese revolution appeared to imply that, for the time being at least, there was no chance of a given condition existing on an all-China scale, and therefore no possibility that a nationwide revolutionary situation could develop as long as the Chinese revolution proceeded unevenly.

On the basis of this analysis the ECCI sketched the strategic policy which the Chinese Communists were to follow:

> The party must prepare itself for the broad upsurge of a new revolutionary wave. This upsurge will inevitably confront the party with the direct practical task of organizing and leading the mass armed insurrection, because only through insurrection and the overthrow of the existing power can the tasks of the revolution be solved. But precisely for this purpose, and because of it, *the center of gravity of party activity at present lies in winning over the mass millions of workers and peasants,* their political enlightenment, their organization around the party and its slogans (the confiscation of landed estates, the eight-hour working day, the national unification of China and emancipation from the imperialist yoke, the overthrow of the existing power, the dictatorship of the proletariat and peasantry, and the organization of soviets). The greatest danger in the entire present situation lies in the fact that the vanguard of the workers' and peasants' movement [i.e., the CCP], as a result of an incorrect appraisal of the present situation and an underestimation of the enemy forces, may break away from the masses, run too far ahead, pulverize its forces and allow itself to be smashed unit by unit. The

Communist party will surely be beaten and disorganized if it does not understand the entire necessity of *winning over the masses and organizing them,* if it does not oppose every effort to divert its attention from preparing the mass millions for a new, broad, revolutionary upsurge, a preparation which constitutes the principal task of today.[88]

The new strategy, then, apparently was not the immediate carrying out of armed insurrections everywhere to topple the national government, but, in order to prepare for the day when that became possible, the "winning over [of] the masses and organizing them."[89] The question immediately arises: did this slogan imply the proscription of all military activity? The Comintern's leaders did oppose certain kinds of military activity, condemning "putschist practices" and "scattered and uncoordinated guerrilla actions,"[90] both of which were considered to be "playing with insurrection."[91] It seems that the ECCI's position was that neither putsches (attempts by small groups to seize state power) nor spontaneous but random peasant uprisings, even though led by the Communist party, could become the "point of departure for a nationwide uprising"—the ultimate objective of Comintern strategy.[92]

The ECCI did not proscribe all military activity. The leaders of the Comintern urged the Chinese to engage in carefully planned guerrilla warfare in the villages and towns of the outlying countryside. "In organizing peasant actions," the resolution stipulated, "to which the party must devote serious attention in the future, it is always and undeviatingly necessary to take into account the various conditions of struggle in different provinces and parts of the territory of China," especially, the resolution continued, "in those districts in which soviet power has already been established under Communist leadership."[93] The ECCI further postulated that the two main objectives for the Chinese Communists in the rural soviets were the carrying out of the "agrarian revolution"[94] and the organization of "Red Army detachments in the expectation that these detachments will then be gradually unified into one general All-Chinese Red Army."[95] Here is suggested a military policy which can perhaps best be described as guerrilla war, with rural soviets employed as bases from which to advance the struggle. (Certainly the Ninth Plenum's resolution contains not much more than a suggestion of this strategy.) But this suggestion was to be developed into definite policy by the time the sixth congress of the Chinese Communists took place some four months later.

The slogan "winning over the masses" had concrete significance for the Chinese Communist Party's political work among the workers and peasants. Essentially, it meant creating new Communist organizations and infiltrating existing non-Communist ones. In the cities, the party was directed toward the organizing of trade unions by means of the so-called "workers' fraternities,"[96] Communist front organizations which provided assistance to workers in return for the opportunity to expose them to Communist propaganda. In addition, the ECCI ordered the party to penetrate the legal and even the "yellow" (Kuomintang) trade unions as another means to reestablish the party's influence among the workers. Terrorism and commandism (forcing of strikes) were to be abjured. In this period when the party's objectives were to win over "the unquestioned support and complete confidence of the masses,"[97] terror and compulsion could only alienate them.

In the countryside, as well, the ECCI outlined specific tasks for the Chinese Communists. Most important, the resolution stated, was the necessity of "creating and extending a network of peasant organizations (peasant leagues, committees, etc.)."[98] "Special attention," the ECCI noted, must be devoted to work among the poor peasantry, and a "special organization" must be created for the "proletarian elements of the village" (hired hands). Finally, the ECCI demanded that now, "more than ever before," the party must conduct systematic propaganda work among the masses in city and countryside to raise their level of class consciousness and to organize them under the party.[99]

The leaders of the Comintern deemed the reorganization of the Chinese Communist Party all-important. They stated emphatically, in the resolution, that "the most important condition for the further development of the revolution is the overall strengthening of the Communist Party of China itself, its cadres, its periphery, its center."[100] Specifically, the ECCI urged that the party recruit new members, strengthen contacts between the party's "central" and local organizations, and build a strong party apparatus. These, the resolution commanded, must be the immediate tasks of the day.

In the propaganda sphere, it went without saying, the Chinese party was to oppose unequivocally the Kuomintang regime. Further, the ECCI cautioned the Chinese leaders that they must also oppose the attempts of former Communists, like T'an P'ing-shan, to organize their own Communist parties. This "right-opportunist danger," the resolution stated, will be more easily neutralized the more effectively the party struggles "against the left 'putschist' deviations in its own ranks."[101] Just as important, the ECCI emphasized, the party must oppose the Trotskyist view that the Chinese revolution had been "liquidated."[102] There must be no pessimism about the future of the Chinese revolution, nor any question that the Chinese Communist Party was the leader of the revolution. Finally, formulating its international line for China, the ECCI made it "the duty of all sections" to support the Chinese revolution by fighting "for the recall of troops and ships from China, against all attempts at annexation and the division of Chinese territory, [and] against the policy of throttling the Chinese revolutionary movement."[103]

There appears to be nothing in the Ninth Plenum's resolution to suggest a stress on the policy of purely "urban insurrection," as opposed to insurrection in the countryside, especially if what is meant by this term are Communist-led uprisings in the larger cities like Peking, Shanghai, T'ientsin, Canton, the Wuhan complex, Changsha, Nanking, and so forth. The wording of the resolution does suggest Communist-led guerrilla activity carried out over a large area, which, to be sure, encompasses towns and villages. But direct attacks on the centers of state power—the key industrial and administrative cities where the strength of the Kuomintang was concentrated and where the position of the Kuomintang was far superior to that of the Chinese Communists—was not the immediate objective of the new strategy outlined by the Comintern resolution. Rather, as Chang Kuo-t'ao stated in correspondence with the author, Stalin's strategy for the Chinese Communists appears to have been for them to "occupy some outlying areas [pien ch'u]"[104] far removed from easy striking range of Nationalist forces, which were quartered mostly in the larger cities. In the hinterland the Chinese Communists could, presumably, gradually build up the military-political power necessary to carry out a successful revolution with a minimum of risk of annihilation by Kuomintang forces. (Of course, as we know, the Kuomintang was able to frustrate most of these early attempts by the Communists to make the new strategy work.)

The strategy of a guerrilla war of attrition, which I have suggested was the Comintern's new strategy for the Chinese Communists, seems to go a long way toward explaining the distinction—and apparent contradiction—in Comintern directives, between the proposition that the revolution must continue and the proposition that putschism must be avoided. The Ninth Plenum's resolution implies that the revolution would be carried on by means of guerrilla warfare, political subversion, and so forth. A putsch, on the other hand, is an attempt by a small group to seize state power. In China, as in most countries, state power was located in the administrative and industrial centers, the larger cities. Therefore, the Comintern's warnings against putschism appear to be warnings against attempts to seize the larger cities, where state power was held by the Kuomintang. The larger, key cities would be the last bastions to be stormed when the balance of forces in the guerrilla war of attrition shifted in favor of the Chinese Communists. As long as the Kuomintang was stronger than the Communists in the larger cities, it was only expedient not to attack them in those places with inferior forces.

Further Elaboration of a New Political Strategy

The sixth congress of the Chinese Communist Party, which was held in Moscow from June 18 until July 11, 1928,[105] gave shape to the Ninth Plenum's draft of the Comintern's new strategy. The Comintern's leaders, evidently suspicious that not all of the Chinese Communists would agree to follow the new "line," permitted only a trusted few party members to travel to Moscow to attend the Congress:[106] an official Chinese Communist source lists eighty-seven and a Western source lists only fifty.[107] Whatever the correct figure, it is evident that many Chinese Communist leaders were excluded from the Sixth Congress.

The Comintern's new strategy appears to have been communicated formally to the Chinese Communists in several resolutions which were "adopted" by the sixth congress. These resolutions were nothing more than directives composed by the leaders of the Comintern. The most important of these, which outline the new Comintern strategy, were the political resolution, the resolution on the peasant movement, the resolution on the problem of organizing soviets, and the resolution on the agrarian question.[108]

I propose to discuss the resolutions in detail, for it seems it is the dominant opinion among the historians noted above that the Comintern's directives in general were ambiguous, at times to the point of being unintelligible—and purposely so. In fact, one writer asserts that "decision makers in Moscow contrived directives which could be interpreted to their advantage no matter what course events might take."[109] It is my belief that with the proper concepts these directives are eminently meaningful and in no way "contrived" to be ambiguous, as I hope to demonstrate.

The political resolution is probably the most important of the four. It adds detail to the basic thesis postulated in the Ninth Plenum's resolution and is a more comprehensive statement of the Comintern's new strategy, touching on all aspects of the plan to be put into action. The resolutions on the peasant movement, the organization of soviets, and the agrarian question, on the other hand, are much more detailed than the political resolution, but are limited in scope to their respective subjects.

Part five of the political resolution—the immediate tasks of the communist party—provides a clear statement of the new strategy. In it are discussed the problems of the party's internal re-alignment, new tasks in the trade union and peasant movements, policy in the soviet and non-soviet areas, propaganda tactics in the anti-imperialist movement, and so forth. The major tasks for the internal reform of the party were seen to be the following:[110]

> First, the reconstruction of the party cells and local committees destroyed by the reaction. Special attention must be paid to the creation of party organizations (cells) in heavy production units, factories and mills where the principal masses of the working class are concentrated.
> Second, the development of an active campaign among the workers to recruit party members; the continuation of the policy of drawing the leaders of the workers movement into the leadership of party work . . .
> Third, to carry out the principle of democratic centralism, guaranteeing, to the extent permissible under illegal conditions of work, inner party democracy, and to carry out the policy of establishing a collective form of discussion and decision-making; at the same time to struggle against ultra-democratic tendencies in several organizations, tendencies which can lead to the disruption of party discipline, to the growth of irresponsibility, and to the detriment of the authority of the leading party centers.
> Fourth, to overcome all deviant attitudes in the [party] organizations toward cliquism and provincialism, which are harmful to the unity of the organization and lower its fighting ability; to liquidate

the system of "punishment" of comrades for errors in their work; if they have no systematic line and do not maintain their errors, they should be corrected. Allow those comrades to come back to work, but [on the condition that] they must now adhere to the correct party line.

Fifth, to intensify the work of the theoretical education of the masses of party members in order to raise their political level . . .

Sixth, to intensify propaganda for the correct tactical view of armed uprising,[111] and, similarly, for the problem of establishing soviets of workers', peasants', and soldiers' deputies.[112]

The instructions of the political resolution were equally precise on the party's tasks in the trade union movement.

First, the basic task of the party is to struggle for the majority of the working class, for the active support of their vanguard—the party—for their confidence and conscious acceptance of its leadership. Special attention must be paid to the trade union movement of industrial workers, and to the strengthening of the leading role of the proletariat in the peasant movement.

Second, to accomplish this task it is necessary to correct immediately some incorrect notions concerning relations between the working class and the party, which hold that the party, in its relations to the proletariat, stands apart from and is independent of the working class, commanding it. . . . It is still not fully recognized that the party is only the most forward, conscious element of the working class.

Third, to struggle decisively against the methods of compulsion and command in relations with our own class, against forcing involvement in the strike struggle or in armed uprisings . . .

Fourth, exert maximum efforts, simultaneously, to work for the reconstruction and leadership of the revolutionary trade unions and to penetrate into all reactionary and other organizations. . . . This penetration is necessary to [achieve] the objective of winning over the masses.

Fifth, to work systematically for the liberation of the working masses from the influence of Kuomintang ideology . . .

Sixth, all of this work is the necessary precondition for the winning over of the masses. It must be carried out in the process of the struggle. It is necessary to strengthen as much as possible the [party's] leadership of the daily economic struggles of the working masses.[113]

Next were the political resolution's instructions for the party's work in the peasant movement. The term "peasant movement," in the

Comintern's lexicon of revolution, evidently referred mainly to events taking place in those areas of the vast countryside which were not subject to direct control by either the Chinese Communists or the Kuomintang. The instruction below formed, it seems to me, the basic policy by which the Chinese Communists could gradually bring this area under their control. The policy included the exacerbation of class differences, the establishment of peasant organizations under Communist control, and the support of many of the peasants' demands for better conditions. When these activities bore fruit in the form of "spontaneous peasant outbursts or uprisings," the Communists were to direct this peasant guerrilla struggle along the same lines as the Communists' own guerrilla movement. Finally, in such areas of unrest, they were to attempt to establish soviets and to create detachments of a Red army. The instructions were as follows:

> First, the confiscation of all landlord land and its transfer over to the soviet of peasant deputies is the central slogan of the movement.
>
> Second, the strategic line: the principal enemy is the landlord-gentry; the basis of support of the proletariat in the countryside is the poor peasant; the middle peasant is a strong ally. To sharpen the struggle against the kulak at the present stage is incorrect as it would efface the basic contradiction between the peasant and landlord classes. But this does not mean that we must abandon the class struggle with the kulak-semi-landowner.
>
> Third, support, deepen, and unite the [non-Communist] peasant guerrilla movement. Lead it in the channel of [our] organized struggle for soviet power and the agrarian revolution. Coordinate the peasant movement with the struggle of the working class in the cities.
>
> Fourth, the creation of a worker-peasant Red Army, which is possible at the present time as a result of the existing political situation, must be the center of attention of the party's work in that [part of] the countryside enveloped by the guerrilla movement. Success in this affair can be one of the decisive factors in the growth of a new revolutionary upsurge.
>
> Fifth, increased attention must be given to peasant organizations (peasant unions, peasant committees, secret societies, and so forth). Strengthen the leading role of the proletariat in them.
>
> Sixth, support the partial slogans of the peasant movement, such as the struggle against taxes, debts, conflicts over non-payment of land, rents, or demands for their reduction.[114]

The Comintern instructed that those areas under the direct control of the Chinese Communists—the soviet areas—be consolidated to form the basis for further expansion of soviet power into nearby towns and adjacent countryside. These areas were to have been softened beforehand by Communist activities (as described immediately above) in order that they be susceptible to Communist penetration. The party's tasks in the soviet areas were as follows:

> First, the expansion of soviet centers, that is, the seizure and consolidation of areas, which can become bases for the further development of the mighty [soviet] movement.
> Second, the maximum development of a regular workers-peasants red army.[115]
> Third, the radical implementation of the agrarian program.[116]
> Fourth, the creation of soviet apparatuses of power and the drawing of the masses into the administration of these soviet areas.[117]
> Fifth, the decisive suppression of all counterrevolutionary attempts and the complete liquidation of the political and economic domination of the ruling classes.
> Sixth, the establishment of maximum ties with nearby urban centers and the workers' movement.[118]

In its propaganda activities, the Comintern directed the Chinese Communists to engage in a campaign designed to discredit the Nationalist government, to alienate the people from the government, and to play upon the existing conflicts in the social order. The party's chief tasks in this sphere were:

> First, to struggle for the leadership of the anti-imperialist movement. To draw into the struggle the broad masses of the working class and petty bourgeoisie; to expose the national bourgeoisie as a force supporting imperialism. Combine the struggle against imperialism with the struggle against the Kuomintang and the Nationalist government.
> Second, to achieve, under the conditions of the growth of the anti-imperialist movement, the legal or quasi-legal existence of revolutionary organizations of the working class . . .
> Third, to split off a significant portion of the petty-bourgeoisie —handicraftsmen, artisans, small-traders, those who do not exploit others' labor, part of the petty-bourgeois intelligentsia, the lumpenproletariat, and so forth—from the Kuomintang and the national bourgeoisie on the basis of the slogans of the anti-imperialist struggle, the abolition of militaristic oppression, the maximum reduction of the tax burden . . .
> Fourth, to support the economic demands of office employees,

apprentices and students in the arts and handicraft establishments, support the economic demands of the coolies . . .[119]

The relationship of the political resolution to the ECCI's Ninth Plenum resolution is explicit. By adding detail to the Ninth Plenum's outline, the political resolution brings out more clearly the main points of the Comintern's new revolutionary strategy. In brief, the party was called upon to establish or to re-establish its organizations (party cells, Red trade-unions, peasant associations, and so forth) wherever possible. At the same time the Comintern instructed the Chinese Communists to engage in a propaganda campaign to raise the theoretical level of its own party members, to win the masses away from the ideology of the Kuomintang, and to discredit the Nationalist government itself by identifying it as a tool of imperialism.

The Comintern instructed the Chinese Communists to play upon existing social conflicts, and, from the groups most likely to support them (workers, poor peasants, hired hands, and so forth), to recruit men for armed detachments, which would be consolidated into a Chinese "Red Army" as time and circumstances allowed. Finally, the Chinese were instructed to establish soviet bases in the countryside, to consolidate them by carrying out the agrarian revolution (redistribution of land, elimination of ruling classes, and so forth) within the soviet areas, and to use these soviets as bases for further expansion of Communist power in the countryside. Guerrilla warfare was the primary method by which the Communists were to extend the area of the countryside under their control; soviets were the political instruments with which these areas could then be consolidated.

It seems that, on the basis of the Ninth Plenum's resolution and the political resolution of the sixth congress of the Chinese party, there is little ground for the argument that the Comintern commanded the Chinese Communist Party to strive for the recapture of its urban bases as its first task—so that the Chinese Communist Party could achieve "true proletarian hegemony" within its ranks.[120] If anything, I believe, the Comintern saw that its main opportunity lay in the countryside. True, the leaders of the Comintern called for the party to continue its activities in the cities; no conceivable opportunity was to be disregarded. However, the function of urban activities, apparently, was to prevent the Nationalist authorities from concentrating their full forces on the Communist build-up (the soviet bases) in the countryside—a common tactic in guerrilla warfare.[121] In view of the Kuomintang's superior position in the larger cities, it does not appear likely that Communist activities in them were designed to capture complete political control. The more plausible explanation seems to be that Communist urban activity—at least in the larger cities—was a kind of diversionary activity.

A Revolutionary Policy for the Countryside

The scope, then, of the political resolution was broad, covering all major aspects of the party's work for the coming period. The resolutions that follow, on the other hand, are all limited to specific topics. The resolution on the peasant movement takes as its point of departure the corresponding section in the preceding political resolution and discusses in meticulous detail the various tasks raised by that resolution. It constitutes the tactical line to be followed in the countryside outside the soviet areas. On the problem of class differentiation in the villages, the poor peasant was to be the basis of Communist strength. The leaders of the Comintern considered that the alliance of the poor peasantry and rural proletariat with the middle peasantry was the key to the success of the agrarian resolution. The tactic adopted toward the rich peasant, however, varied according to circumstances.

> In places where the rich peasants have already become reactionary forces, the struggle against rich peasants should be carried on simultaneously with the struggle against warlords, landlords. . . .
> As long as the rich peasants have not yet lost their revolutionary potentialities . . . the CCP should endeavor to absorb rich peasants into the struggle against warlords, landlords, and gentry. Where the rich peasants waver between revolution and counterrevolution, the party, so far as the struggle of poor peasants and hired farm hands is not handicapped, should not intensify the struggle against the rich peasants, thus driving them all the more quickly into the counterrevolutionary camp and making them the aggressive enemies of the revolution. The task of our party at the present stage is to neutralize this type of rich peasant in order to reduce the strength of the enemy; but the struggle of the poor peasants and hired farm hands should be carried on simultaneously, and no concession should be made to the rich peasants for the sake of the united front.[122]

The resolution stated that the Chinese Communists should "support the slogan of equal distribution of land, but should also criticize it."[123] If the majority of the peasantry of a given area support this slogan, the resolution continued, the party also should support it, but the party must point out that real equality will be possible only after the completion of the proletarian revolution. Similarly, where the middle peasants are the majority, equal distribution of land should not be carried out by force, because this would only oppose their interests.[124]

The party must create independent organizations for the rural proletariat (hired hands) in the villages and enlarge and consolidate its leadership over the various peasant organizations—the peasant associations, peasant committees, secret societies, and so forth.[125] It is these organizations, especially the peasant committees, which the party must prepare to become the nuclei of future soviet power.[126]

"Guerrilla warfare," the resolution continued, "will be the chief instrument of struggle,"[127] by means of which effective control over an area of the countryside can be established, soviets created, a Red Army built up, and the agrarian revolution carried out. However, the Comintern cautioned, there are weaknesses to guerrilla warfare as a form of struggle which must be corrected:

> First, the conduct of guerrilla warfare separated from the masses has the effect of making them misunderstand the meaning of guerrilla warfare, or even respond to the propaganda of the landlords that guerrilla warfare is banditry. Hence, from now on, guerrilla warfare must begin with the spontaneous demand of the masses, and must be carried on simultaneously with propaganda and agitation work. Second, the tendency to destroy cities and kill, burn, and rob purposely. This tendency is only a reflection of a lumpen-proletariat and peasant mentality which may hamper the development of the party among the peasant masses or even among the proletariat. Therefore, every effort should be made to erase this erroneous concept within the party. Of course, our party should actively lead the peasant masses in their struggle to liquidate the landlords and gentry and to weaken the antirevolutionary forces. What is opposed by the party, however, is purposeless killing and burning which are irrelevant to our revolutionary mission. . . . Third, looseness and lack of organization. From now on, [we] must direct the peasant associations in a planned, organized, and centralized manner.[128]

Discussing the tactics to be employed in organizing local uprisings, the Chinese Communists were advised that under "the increasingly intensified class struggle at present, the setting up of a soviet regime in one hsien [district] or several hsien is possible."[129] It should be noted here that nowhere in the resolutions of the sixth congress of the Chinese Communists is there advocated as immediate, practical policy the organizing of a *nationwide uprising* to overthrow the Nationalist regime. The slogan "setting up a soviet regime in one hsien or several hsien" obviously did not have this meaning, but rather meant the organizing of local revolts in small "districts." Even the organizing of local revolts was to be done with extreme caution, and then only when the existing power in a given area was "tottering." "It is not necessary," the resolution went on,

> that guerilla warfare should turn into local revolts. Only when, during the process of struggle, the vast peasant masses are mobilized, when there arises a genuine demand on the part of the masses for a political regime of their own, and when the reactionary forces in the area are actually tottering, can guerrilla warfare develop into local revolts. Therefore, when the guerrilla forces have brought a large area under their control, have secured the participation of a large number of people, and the conditions are ripe for producing *a hsien or municipal local revolt,* the party must consider carefully its objective conditions and subjective strength, and proceed with the revolt well-prepared, well-organized, well-planned, employing suitable tactics under the leadership [of the CCP] and with the cooperation of the workers of the hsien or municipality. After the success of the revolt, the slogan of the mass struggle should be put into effect, and all of the reactionary forces should be liquidated in order that still greater numbers of peasants and workers may be mobilized and the policies of the soviet regime be realized.[130]

The significance of the resolution on the peasant movement should not be underestimated. It provides the basic tactical plan by which the Chinese Communist Party was to extend its influence in the countryside. It states that effective control over an area first must be established by means of guerrilla warfare. Once the Kuomintang forces could no longer provide protection for the area involved, the Communists could commence the next step. In conjunction with propaganda indicating that they were genuine revolutionaries and not bandits as they were called by the Kuomintang, the Communists were to organize the "déclassé" elements against the ruling group and support their demands against them—to the extent, if feasible, of backing a local revolt. Of course the party could engage in such activities only after the police power of the Kuomintang had been removed— but that was the aim of the guerrilla activity.

Does the peasant resolution imply the prior endorsement of the whole so-called "Maoist" development of Chinese Communism? It does not. To argue in the affirmative would be to claim clairvoyance for the Comintern. Posing the question in this way only circumvents the real issue,[131] for it certainly can be argued that the Comintern ordered the Chinese Communists to carry on a policy of guerrilla warfare in the countryside, thereby establishing the fundamental theoretical concepts which Mao Tse-tung was able to develop with success over the next two decades. In fact, Mao himself tacitly admits that the Comintern supplied the correct strategic framework for the Chinese revolution in an article written in 1936. "Without answering this question," he said, "of whether China's revolutionary base areas and the Chinese Red army could survive and develop, we could not have advanced a single step. The sixth national congress of the Chinese Communist Party in 1928 . . . gave the answer to the question. *Since then the Chinese revolutionary movement has had a correct theoretical basis.*"[132]

The Organization of New Chinese Soviets

If the resolution on the peasant movement was concerned mainly with the problem of how to extend Communist control over a given district or area of the countryside, the resolution on the organization of soviets was concerned mainly with the tactics which should be pursued after effective control over an area had been established. When the party decides, reads the resolution, that conditions exist in a given area for a successful revolt, it must undertake the task of establishing cells in that area, "so that these cells after the seizure of power, are prepared for all necessary work."[133] In all probability, the resolution added, these cells will form the basis for the establishment of soviet power. "In all areas where uprisings are planned," the party must disseminate, in advance, propaganda explaining the content of soviet rule.

> Outside of propaganda work, the party must carry out organizational work. Here can be used the old example of Shanghai, where delegates from the masses were elected secretly at meetings before the seizure of power. However, under present conditions of the underground in China, it is difficult to affirm that it is possible to elect delegates by such means. In all probability these conditions do not exist. Therefore . . . the party must carry out advance prepara-

tions through cells, individual party members, and through reliable workers.[134]

Until the formal establishment of a soviet in a given area, "the primary form of political power is the provisional power, that is, the Revolutionary Committee."[135] The Revolutionary Committee must be composed of the representatives of the various organizations taking part in a planned uprising. All responsibility for the uprising must be delegated to the Revolutionary Committee and to its headquarters. The headquarters must come under the control of the Revolutionary Committee and be quickly convertible to a headquarters of the Red Army. The headquarters must lead all military activities in its region, prepare the mobilization of workers, organize supply for the Red Army, and so forth.[136] Under no circumstances should the Revolutionary Committee come into conflict with the peasant associations, because these associations are the basis for the organization of soviets and their support is vital.[137]

As soon as a revolt is successful, the Revolutionary Committee must quickly begin work for the transformation of power to the official soviet. It must be understood, the resolution stated, that the Revolutionary Committee is only a temporary government. It organizes the soviet, whose members, at their first meeting, declare themselves to be the official government. Of course, the resolution went on,

> the composition of the Revolutionary Committees must absolutely guarantee the fulfillment of party directives. Elements having influence among the soldiers or among the local population must take part in the work of the Revolutionary Committees, but if, from the first, they cannot firmly guarantee the strengthening of our party's influence, then we must take measures to isolate them and to prepare various means of excluding them from the Revolutionary Committees at the appropriate moment.[138]

In the very first days after the establishment of a soviet in an area, the Revolutionary Committee with the help of the party "must reorganize the troops taking part in the uprising into a regular Red Army."[139] At first, the resolution continued, "revolutionary elements of peasant committees and trade unions" as well as "hopeful" elements may be recruited. Later, after the Red Army has become established in the area, enlistment for a "definite number of years" may be allowed.[140] Independent guerrilla units which take part in the uprising from that particular area also must be formed into regular army units and their command and political composition reorganized.[141]

After an uprising, stern revolutionary measures must be taken immediately. All bandits must be disarmed and suppressed—even if they have assisted in the uprising—to prevent any resurgence of opposition to the soviet regime.[142] Attempts to win the masses away from religious and semi-religious organizations must be made. Their leaders must be isolated and at the appropriate moment these groups reorganized under Soviet control.[143] Of course, all known counter-revolutionary leaders must be taken as hostages as soon as possible.[144]

Judging from this resolution, the concept of "proletarian hegemony"—the control of the Communist movement by party members from the working class—was an ideal condition for which to strive, but not an immediate practical possibility. The resolution goes on to state that from the peasants, workers and guerrillas taking part in a given uprising, the party must create a cadre of military leaders and political workers. Officers from the old army may be used in the cadre, the resolution continued, because of their understanding of military affairs. However, use only lower ranking officers, for the military understanding of the higher ranking officers is already obsolete.[145] "Political workers and members of political committees play an important role. This work can be done only by members of the Communist Party. Best of all, place party members from the working class or peasant leaseholders (tenants) in this work."[146] It appears that a party member was acceptable for work in the important political committees even if he were a peasant.

The soviets themselves must be organized on the basis of a direct vote by the toiling masses of the area and must insure the leading role of the workers. Soviets should be established like the one in Hai-lu-feng and, in part, like the one established in Shanghai, but not as in Canton, "where, in fact, there was only a revolutionary committee and no soviet."[147] Soviets should not be elected from representatives of only the highest organizations, but at meetings of all of the toiling masses—workers, poor peasants, members of trade unions, handi-craftsmen, and so forth.

The soviet is not merely a "mass meeting," nor is it an "organization of several leaders"; it is a governing body composed of representatives from the toiling masses. The number of members of the executive committee of a soviet should be from eleven to twenty-seven. From this group should be elected a "presidium," which holds actual power in a given area. The number of members in a presidium should be from five to seven.[148] Once a soviet is elected, it should establish various sections to carry out its governmental functions, such as sections for military affairs, for financial, economic and social affairs, and so forth.[149] Again, it must be emphasized that there must be a party fraction in every organ, and that "the party fractions of these organs absolutely must fulfill the directives of the party."[150] "In all soviets the party must have a party fraction. It is by means of these party fractions, through statements by party members, that the opinion of the party is expressed on the various questions of soviet work."[151] Communists working in the soviets should work openly to raise the influence of the party in them, by leading the work of the soviet.[152]

Finally, the basic objective of the soviets and the guerrilla movement as a whole was seen to be the gradual expansion of the territory controlled by the Communists and the gradual denial of control over territory to the enemy Kuomintang. "The important task of the revolutionary committees, party committees, and soviets in their respective localities is the expansion of their territory. This is the basic guarantee of their existence. The expansion of territory can be carried on in two directions: first, soviets should employ military force to carry out attacks on neighboring areas; [second] they should render assistance to mass uprisings in neighboring areas. . . . This activity should be connected with the activity of the Red Army."[153]

Agrarian Reform and Communist Power

Having described the methods by which the Chinese Communists were to gain control over a given area and to organize a soviet in that area, the Comintern, in the resolution on the agrarian question, proceeded to instruct the Chinese Communists in the basic economic and social policies of the agrarian program to be followed inside each soviet thus established.[154] In effect, the aim of the agrarian program appeared to be the complete and utter destruction of the existing social and economic order under the control of each soviet and the establishment of a new order based on a fundamental redistribution of land in favor of the poor and landless elements. Since the poor and landless generally constituted a majority, they would become a source of support for the Communists. The policies, which constituted the Communist agrarian program, were as follows:

> First, the overthrow of the power of the landowning gentry and bureaucrats . . . the arming of the peasantry, and the establishment of soviets of peasants deputies . . .

> Second, the immediate abolition of landlord ownership of land without compensation; the seizure of land must be carried out under the direction of the local soviets of peasants deputies, which will redistribute the land for use by the landless peasants and peasants with little land.

> Third, the transfer of ancestral temples, monasteries and other kinds of public lands, as well as empty and sandy land of a given [soviet] area to the soviet of peasant deputies for redistribution among local peasants for their use.

> Fourth, the creation of a special land fund from local governmental and other lands and a colonization fund for allotment to soldiers of the workers-peasants army . . .

> Fifth, the declaration of all usurious loans as invalid.

> Sixth, the abolition of all *land* and other one-sided agreements [entered into by] either oral or written transactions.

> Seventh, the abolition of all taxes and requisitions collected by militarists and local powers. The elimination of the farm tax system and the establishment of a unified progressive tax.

> Eighth, state assistance to agriculture: (a) organization of agriculture, (b) improvement and expansion of the irrigation system, (c) assistance in the struggle with natural calamities, (d) governmental organization of migration, (e) organization of cheap credit through agricultural banks and credit cooperatives, (f) organization of market and supply cooperatives, (g) establishment of a unified monetary system and a unified system of weights and measures.[155]

The effect of these policies, if carried out, would be to improve immediately the lot of the individual peasant, even if only for the short run and if only a little. However rudimentary the reforms may have appeared, it is possible that many peasants did come to believe the revolutionaries were worth supporting because of them. This belief then would be heightened to a conviction if the legal regime, upon its recapture of the area in question, attempted to undo these "reforms" and to restore the status quo ante. Unless the legal government were able to convince the local populace that its actions were the only proper course, or to make its own policies more attractive to them, then the areas once occupied by the Communists, even though recaptured by the government, would be a permanent source of support—either active or passive—for the Communists.

Comintern and the Chinese Communists in 1928:
A Recapitulation

It appears that Comintern strategy was suited to the conditions in which it was to be applied. In highly industrialized Western Europe, for instance, the Comintern directed its parties to concentrate their activities among the masses of industrial workers in the cities. In China, however, where urban industrial workers were few, the Comintern placed emphasis on the countryside.

The Comintern had directed the Chinese Communists to establish Soviet bases in the countryside out of easy reach of Kuomintang forces, to consolidate them by carrying out the "agrarian program" within the Soviet base areas, and to create, arm, and train small fighting detachments, which, in the course of the guerrilla war, would be merged to form a Chinese "Red Army." Once Soviet bases were consolidated in one locality, the Chinese Communists were to repeat the process in an adjacent area, gradually expanding the territory under their control.

In the Comintern's new strategy, the activities of the Chinese Communists in the larger cities were designed to prevent the Kuomintang from concentrating its efforts on the main force of the Chinese Communists in the countryside. Strikes, propaganda, terror and subversion were to be employed to keep the cities in turmoil. In terms of the strategy as a whole, the Communist Party's urban activities played a key diversionary role.

The immediate objective of the Comintern was not, it appears, the rapid overthrow of the Nationalist regime by means of armed uprisings carried out in the larger cities all over China. The Comintern seems to have envisaged a protracted struggle during which the Communists would gradually weaken the Kuomintang and build up their own strength. The strategy analyzed above is the essence of the one which Mao Tse-tung developed and perhaps refined in his conquest of China. The foregoing analysis, however, does show that, from the sixth congress of the Chinese Communist Party in 1928 onward, the Comintern instructed the Chinese Communists to carry out a broadly conceived strategy of guerrilla warfare and political subversion.   -

Thus, a detailed examination of the Comintern's strategy, as set forth in the Ninth Plenum's report on the Chinese Question and in the resolutions adopted by the sixth congress of the Chinese Communists in 1928, gives new significance to that congress as a turning point in Chinese Communist history and provides a framework for the re-evaluation of subsequent Comintern strategy in China. This re-evaluation may, in turn, lead to a reinterpretation of many events in Chinese Communist history.

The German Communists' United-Front and Popular-Front Ventures

by

BABETTE L. GROSS

More than a quarter of a century has elapsed since the Communist International gave orders to its parties to apply popular-front tactics. Carrying out these tactics represented a break with Leninist doctrine on the role of the Communist parties. Although Lenin in his writings occasionally had advocated an alliance of all democratic, liberal, and Socialist forces in opposition, in practice he seized every means for circumventing coalitions between Russian Socialists and leftist bourgeois parties even before the October Revolution.

After the October Revolution, the Third International accepted the claim of the Bolshevik party as the sole revolutionary vanguard of the working class. The struggle against capitalism and its representatives, the bourgeois parties, was to be unrelenting. No collaboration with the class enemy could be tolerated. Tactically motivated coalitions were ruled out. Assumption of power through reformist methods implying cooperation with the bourgeoisie was rejected. The Communist International opposed the leaders of the reformist parties and of the trade unions as obstacles to the advancing proletarian revolution.

When it turned out that in the other European countries the revolutionary road to power was barred, the Communist International began to concentrate its attention on winning over the "majority of the working class"—those belonging to reformist parties and organizations. The discussion about united-front tactics was opened.[1] It stressed that Communists should attempt to work together with the other members of their class and convert them as far

111

as possible to the Communist point of view, with the goal of defeating jointly the class enemy.

The united-front tactics were confined, in the view of the Comintern leaders, strictly to the working class as a whole and irreconcilably opposed to the whole of the bourgeoisie. When at the Linz congress of the Austrian Social Democrats (1926) Otto Bauer assailed the concept of civil war—while the program of the party adopted at the congress favored the strengthening of the republican state and of the democratic institutions—Bukharin bitterly attacked, in the official Comintern organ, the Austrians' "juridical cretinism." He declared that for a "really revolutionary party the radical democratic demands cannot be anything else but a means of destruction of the apparatus of the bourgeois state."[2]

The Communists clung to the conception of the bourgeoisie as the class enemy pure and simple even while the National Socialists were liquidating the Weimar Republic, including its democratic institutions and the achievements attained by the German working class. Only when Hitler had established firmly his totalitarian regime and was threatening the Soviet Union did the Communist International make an abrupt turnabout which found its expression in the popular-front tactic. It was Albert Vassart, the French representative at the Comintern, who in 1934 coined the expression *front populaire* as the slogan for the new policy of the French Communists. With the popular front he wanted to take the wind out of the sails of the French Fascists and their mass propaganda. At first, the Russians expressed misgivings about the term, which, in Russian translation, was reminiscent of the *Narodnaia Volia,* or more precisely the populist Socialist Revolutionaries, the large party of workers and peasants which had been liquidated by the Bolsheviks after 1917. A Russian philologist employed as a consultant declared that there was a fundamental difference between *Front Populaire* and *Narodnaia Volia;* the former did not mean "going to the people" but rather "a front, in which the people participate," and thereby the term *Front Populaire,* popular front, became acceptable.

The first prerequisite for applying popular-front tactics is the establishment of a collaboration between "class comrades"; i.e., between the Communists and the leaders of other, mainly Socialist, labor parties and their organizations. As soon as such a united front agreement has been concluded, the time is ripe for turning to the bourgeois parties and for proposing to them electoral alliances, coalitions, and other forms of collaboration—to create a so-called popular front.

This tactic is called for whenever the Communists are too weak and too isolated to "win a working class victory by violent means," and when they therefore have chosen collaboration with other labor parties and certain bourgeois groups to attain their objectives.

THE UNITED-FRONT TACTICS OF THE GERMAN COMMUNIST PARTY

The young revolutionary parties which split off from the Socialist parties in the various European countries in 1918–19 and adhered to the Third International as Communist parties were thoroughly disinclined to attempt to form a united front with the reformist parties. The German Communist Party hoped to persuade the German workers to rise up in arms and to create a soviet republic. When these efforts failed and it became apparent that the overwhelming majority of the German working class opted for the reformist path, the Communists began to consider the united front. The right and the left wings of the party harbored opposite notions as to how to put into practice Lenin's principle of winning over the majority of the working class.

The left wing was fundamentally opposed to the united-front maneuvers because it blamed the Social Democratic leadership for the collapse of the German revolution, and collaboration with this leadership seemed senseless. The right wing relied on the bulk of the Social Democratic party members and counted on winning over their leaders to revolutionary activities.

THE UNITED FRONT "FROM ABOVE"

The discussions about united-front tactics in the Communist International were motivated by the fluctuating needs and interpretations of Russian foreign policy and by the struggles for power within the Russian leadership which hinged on that policy.

In 1923, when the Soviet Union was making every effort to break out of its isolation and was counting at the same time on a revolutionary development in Germany, the pendulum swung far to the right. A "labor government" in Saxony served as a model for the "united front from above" with the Saxon reformist leaders, since Communists and Social Democrats collaborated in the government through joint top committees.

When the experiment failed and the hopes for a revolutionary development in Germany collapsed, the right and left wings of the German Communist Party found themselves in sharp disagreement. The Fifth Comintern Congress condemned particularly "the danger of rightist deviations," and blamed the right for its "opportunist interpretations" and its "attempt to make something more out of the united front than a revolutionary method of agitation and mobilization of the masses."[3]

Once again, in 1926, there was a united-front action—this time successful—between the Communist party on the one hand and the reformist parties and trade-union committees on the other. At the instigation of the Communists, a wide popular movement was set in motion in Germany to reject the claims by the German princes deposed in 1918 for financial compensations from the Weimar Republic. Two leftist bourgeois organizations, the *Liga für Menschenrechte* and the *Deutsche Friedenskartell*, had taken the initiative in founding a committee to oppose these compensations. This Kuczynski Committee (named after its chairman) was joined by a Communist leader, Willi Münzenberg. They organized a remarkably successful referendum, which was supported during the campaign by the Communist party, the Socialist party, and the trade unions; 12.5 million voters signed up. Although all bourgeois parties suggested abstention, the referendum resulted in 14.4 million votes against paying compensation to the princes, considerably more than the number of votes obtained by the Socialist and the Communist parties at the previous Reichstag elections in 1924 (10.5 million). Zinoviev, at that time still head of the Communist International, referred to the compensation campaign and the Anglo-Russian Unity Committee as successful joint actions and asked the left wing to apply these tactics for winning over the majority of the working class in the principal industrial countries.[4]

SOCIAL DEMOCRACY BECOMES THE MAIN ADVERSARY

The consolidation of the Stalinist apparatus and the "Bolshevization" of the Communist parties on orders from Moscow entailed a radical change in their relations with the other labor parties. In a 1924 article, "On the International Situation," Stalin had already designated social democracy "objectively speaking, as the moderate wing of fascism."[5] At the Tenth Plenum of the ECCI, in July 1929, Manuilsky justified this switch:

> We never believed that the united-front tactic constituted a universally valid prescription. There were times when we bargained with the Second and Second-and-a-Half Internationals, with the General Council and Purcell. We are now strong enough to apply more aggressive methods for winning over the majority of the working class.[6]

At the plenary meeting of the central committee of the German Communist Party in January 1931, Ernst Thälmann assailed German social democracy in the following terms:

> On the other hand, social democracy, above all the "left-wing" SPD, is still *the main obstacle* in the German proletariat's revolutionary struggle for liberation. The Party and the working class cannot possibly be successful in the fight against fascism and against the capitalist system in general, without beating this main obstacle and destroying this *most dangerous enemy in the camp of the working class*."[7]

Any possibility of collaborating with the Social Democrats was thus eliminated and social democracy became the prime Communist target.

COMMUNISTS OPPOSE BOTH SOCIAL DEMOCRATS AND NATIONAL SOCIALISTS

When the National Socialists rapidly increased their influence and carried off an unexpected electoral victory on September 14, 1930, the Communists tried to wage a simultaneous fight against the Social Democrats and Nazis. Rather than support all democratic forces opposed to the threats of national socialism, the Communists adhered to the suicidal general line assailing social democracy as "the most dangerous enemy in the camp of the working class." This line, laid down by Moscow, met with incomprehension and resistance among the members of the Communist party. For them the Nazi bully squads were the main adversary; they had to be counterattacked, their blows warded off. However, among the party officials demoralization had reached such a point that they tried to keep up with the zigzag course of the "head office" without even trying to find the reasons for it or denouncing this treason to the ideals of the Socialist movement.

The growing totalitarian threat constituted for even the German Communist leadership the principal source of concern. The growing National Socialist terrorism had to be resisted. Hardly a day went by in the last years of the Weimar Republic without the slaying of a worker. In the face of this, Stalin's spokesman at the Comintern, Manuilsky, still insisted in the spring of 1931, before the Eleventh Plenary Session of the ECCI: "The Social Democrats knowingly are duping the masses when they assert that the principal adversary of the working class is fascism. In truth, Hitler's version of fascism does not constitute the principal antagonist."[8]

STALIN BACKS TOLERATION OF NATIONAL SOCIALISTS

During these critical years Stalin personally intervened on several occasions in the policy of the German Communist Party. Forced collectivization was severely straining the Soviet Union. Under these circumstances Stalin was anxious to avoid bloody clashes between Communists and rightists in Germany. He favored a stable Germany, even at the price of dictatorship of the right. The German right could seize power, however, only after Social Democratic influence had been smashed by all available means.

On his visit to Moscow in April 1931, Heinz Neumann, who at the time shared the leadership of the German Communist Party with Thälmann and Hermann Remmele, was reproached by Stalin for conducting a "leftist sectarian mass policy." The dictator criticized the German party for pursuing a misguided policy in Thuringia because it had brought about there, with the help of the Social Democrats, a vote of no confidence against Wilhelm Frick, the National Socialist minister of the interior.[9] Neumann should have grasped Stalin's objective better. Neumann had drafted in 1930, with Moscow's support, a "program for the national and social liberation of the German people." By this program the German Communist Party was trying to emulate the nationalist clichés of the National Socialists, who were just organizing a plebiscite against the Young Plan.[10] The workers were urged to "turn their backs on the traitorous Social Democrats, the government coalition party, the party of the Versailles peace treaty, the Young Plan, the enslavement of the German working masses."[11]

The right-wing forces—the National Socialists, the German National Party, and the Stahlhelm (the veterans' organization)—decided to demand a plebiscite, in the summer of 1931, for the dissolution of the Prussian diet, in order to precipitate the overthrow of the Social Democratic government of Prussia. At first the Communists opposed this demand, holding meetings to protest against this "fascist plebiscite." Thereupon the politburo of the German Communist Party received instructions from Moscow to participate in the imminent plebiscite. A heated exchange ensued in the politburo. Thälmann bluntly refused to carry out this order. He, Remmele, and Neumann were called to Moscow to learn at first hand that this instruction had been issued to the Communist International by Stalin personally. The "Red plebiscite" thus took its course under the slogan: "All votes in favor of the Red plebiscite on August 9!" The Communist party suffered a severe loss of confidence. Large masses of Communists refused to heed the unrealistic command of their leadership and become collaborators of the National Socialists.

RUSSIAN ESTIMATES OF NATIONAL SOCIALISM

Leading officials of the German Communist Party displayed little foresight regarding the political significance of national socialism and its chances of success. Thälmann voiced the opinion in 1932 that Hitler had already lost much ground and was losing influence steadily, and that the German Communists' only adversary was social democracy. Wilhelm Pieck was equally mistaken in gauging the looming danger when he told a friend in early 1933: "If the Nazis come to power, they will be at the end of their rope in two months, and then it will be our turn!"[12] And Fritz Heckert, the German representative at the Comintern, wrote: "The Nazis will perform no miracles and will be at the end of their rope in no time."[13]

The German Communists were doing nothing more than expressing the opinion prevailing in Russian party circles. Stalin, who, in the relaxed mood of an evening party, had called Hitler a "great guy" in Heinz Neumann's presence, wished the Germans to shed their democratic illusions under a National Socialist dictatorship, illusions which German Social Democrats had fostered over the years. After Hitler's bankruptcy, it then would be easier for the Communists to seize power.

The following significant conversation took place at the end of 1931 between Neumann and Stalin: "Don't you agree, Neumann," the dictator wanted to know, "that if the Nationalists seize power in Germany they will be so thoroughly occupied with the West that we can build up socialism here in peace?"[14]

STRATEGIC RETREAT INTO UNDERGROUND ACTIVITY
AND UNITED FRONT FROM BELOW

After Hitler seized power, the bureaucracy of the Communist International did not swerve from the rut of its previous tactics. While Thälmann and hundreds of other Communists were arrested and an incredible wave of terror swept over Germany, Moscow did not believe that Hitler could stay in the saddle. In a resolution adopted in March 1933 by the Presidium of the ECCI then in session, it was decided that the united-front tactic from below, with Social Democratic workers, be continued in order to smash the fascist dictatorship by an armed uprising. The German Communists were told,

> The establishment of an outright dictatorship, which destroys all democratic illusions among the masses and frees them from the sway of social democracy speeds Germany on its road to a proletarian revolution. It shall be the task of the Communists to make clear to the masses that the Hitler regime is leading the country to disaster. With greater determination than ever we must make the masses understand that there is only one way to avert even greater misery and catastrophe, namely a proletarian revolution and the dictatorship of the proletariat.[15]

The German Social Democratic party meanwhile also had been outlawed, members of both parties were being persecuted jointly, and still the Socialists as a party remained the Communists' main enemy, even though the term "Social Fascist" fell by the wayside. A strident debate arose among the German Communist refugees abroad about the causes of the German catastrophe and about the political course of the German Communist Party and its miscalculations. The official Party declarations took no note of all this. According to the proper interpretation, the German Communist Party had suffered no defeat; it had not been swept away by the National Socialists but had retreated strategically to underground activity.

The Thirteenth Plenary Session of the ECCI which assembled in Moscow in December 1933 specifically declared that it "approved unequivocally the political course adopted by the central committee of the German Communist Party under the leadership of Comrade Thälmann at the time of the fascist upheaval." Under the heading, "Against Social Democracy, for a United Front from Below," it was stated that the Social Democrats were rejecting the proposals of the Communist party for unified class action and persevered in widening the division of the proletariat in the face of fascism and war.[16]

ATTEMPTED POPULAR FRONTS IN THE GERMAN
EMIGRATION AND THE THIRD REICH

A number of leading figures on the left had been arrested in the first days of the Hitler dictatorship. Those who felt directly threatened fled abroad. Soon exile headquarters for the Social Democratic and the Communist parties were set up in Czechoslovakia to keep in contact with underground groups in Germany across the Czech border.

Strong emigrant groups assembled in the Saar (which still remained under League of Nations supervision) and in France, Belgium, and other Western countries. Inevitably, contacts were established among the émigrés, irrespective of their party affiliation in Germany. There sprang up committees to aid the refugees and organizations to support the imprisoned and their families. German-language newspapers and periodicals were published; books were written about events in Hitler Germany, and material was gathered for Hitler's enemies inside the Reich.

Under the impact of political events in France, the German Communists altered their tactics toward social democracy in 1934.

UNITED FRONT IN THE SAAR

The plebiscite to be held on January 13, 1935, was to determine whether the Saar population wished to return to the German Reich, as was open to it under the Treaty of Versailles, or whether it preferred to remain under League of Nations administration; and whether the Saar mines were to stay under French administration.

The Hitler government used the appealing election slogan "Home to the Reich"; the Social Democrats argued against annexation by a Nazi Germany. The Communists, as spokesmen for "a Red Saar in a Soviet Germany," propagandized at first also for an annexation to Germany. The Comintern and the exile leadership of the German Communist Party changed their original line under the influence of the united-front negotiations of the French Socialist and Communist parties and decided to drop the "Red Saar" campaign and to support the status quo.

Wilhelm Pieck and Walter Ulbricht, who had made several visits to Moscow in 1934, were informed about developments in the French Communist Party. An additional factor was that Georgi Dimitrov had been released from his German imprisonment at the end of February 1934 (in an exchange of prisoners), had gone to Moscow, and had gained prestige in the Comintern as the "victor of Leipzig." He was considered a man on the make, and he had his own views on the united-front tactics. Nobody dared any longer to call him an opportunist, as had been done for years. He had been laid on ice by his Bulgarian party years before because of his "opportunistic conduct" and had been sent abroad. There he had worked in a subordinate capacity on the staff of the Comintern. He doubtless favored a united front with the Socialist leaders.

Several hundred German Communist émigrés had found their first refuge in the Saar territory. They helped the weak Communist party, already demoralized by the propaganda in favor of annexation, to reach a united-front agreement with the local Socialist leaders. Both parties joined in organizing meetings and proclamations, suitable appeals appeared in the Communist papers, the "united front from above" was carried out everywhere.

The combined efforts of the Social Democrats and the Communists failed to bring about a favorable outcome of the plebiscite. A mere 48,000 voted in favor of staying under League of Nations administration, while 477,000 votes favored annexation to Hitler Germany. Even granting that reintegration of Germans into Germany seemed the natural solution, the eyewitness had to admit that the bulk of the Saar population was applauding the National Socialists, expecting the dawn of a golden age under Hitler.

After the plebiscite, several thousand people from the Saar and all German émigrés left the Saar territory and gravitated toward France. The Saar Socialist leaders (Max Braun, Emil Kirschmann, and others) went to Paris and stayed in close touch with the Communist émigré organizations active there.

DIMITROV PROCLAIMS THE GREAT ABOUT-FACE

The exile leadership of the German Communist Party faced the crucial problem of entering into negotiations with the Social Democratic executive committee in Prague. For this purpose tactics pursued for years had to be abandoned. The step was taken at the Seventh Congress of the Comintern (held in Moscow between the end of July and the middle of August 1935) and at the so-called "Brussels conference" of the German Communist Party, which gathered in Moscow during October 1935.[17] At the Seventh Congress, the newly appointed secretary-general of the Comintern, Georgi Dimitrov, proclaimed a radical about-face calling for the establishment of an antifascist popular front and unified action with the Socialist parties. This constituted the official repudiation of the policy which the Comintern had supported for seven years, ever since the Sixth Congress. The bourgeoisie was no longer viewed monolithically; conflicts among one's opponents must be exploited; the Socialist parties must be approached, and the struggle against fascism must become the crucial objective; the Communist parties must join forces with all enemies of fascism and establish a broad united front. As the underground periodical *Das Banner*, published by the Sozialistische Arbeiter Partei (SAP)[18] was to write, if before 1934 any leading Communist had spoken up publicly in favor of such a stand, he would have been "branded an opportunist, a renegade, an enemy of communism, a bourgeois mercenary, a counterrevolutionary and expelled from the International."

The sensational reorientation did not come in response to a belated recognition of political realities but as a result of the altered requirements of Soviet foreign policy. Hitler had secured a firm grasp on Germany, contrary to all Soviet predictions. He had made use of the same totalitarian methods which the Bolsheviks had applied to assure their undivided power. Only one party was permitted, an effective political police had been established, and the opposition was physically wiped out. Germany had been poured into a single mold.

As soon as internal consolidation had been completed, the Third Reich undertook a strong diplomatic offensive. Ribbentrop courted England; Hitler attempted a rapprochement with Poland. To the capitalist West he presented himself as the friend of peace, whose sole target was communism. Soviet foreign policy assumed a new orientation. It tried to foster better relations with the Western democracies. Litvinov visited these countries to reactivate nonaggression pacts. In May 1934, in Geneva, he explored with the French foreign minister, Louis Barthou, the possibility of negotiating an East-European pact; in September of the same year the Soviet Union joined the League of Nations, which it had abused for more than a decade. Finally, on May 2, 1935, the Franco-Russian Pact of Mutual Assistance was signed in Paris (it was ratified by the French National Assembly in February 1936).

The Comintern adapted itself to the new line. It was to make every effort to strengthen the Communist parties in the democracies and to draw into its fold the antifascist elements of the population.

THE "BRUSSELS CONFERENCE" OF THE GERMAN
COMMUNIST PARTY

About fifty German Communists had gathered for the so-called Brussels conference. The exile leadership of the German Communist Party, the district secretaries doing underground work in Germany, and a few leading officials living as émigrés in Moscow submitted to the desired "auto-critique" and explained the defeat of the party in 1933. Not one of these men would have dreamed of subjecting the Comintern tactics of that time to criticism. There were scapegoats at hand; the "Neumann wing" was made to bear the blame for the mistaken policy toward the National Socialists. Another member of the politburo who identified himself with the Neumann faction was Hermann Remmele.

In truth, Neumann had been removed from German party leadership in February 1932, and the politburo under Ernst Thälmann would have had ample time to change its tactics during the critical year of 1932, instead of adhering slavishly to Stalin's policy toward Germany. In spite of their "satisfactory account" of their political mistakes, Neumann and Remmele were not admitted to the party conference and were excluded from activity with the party.[19]

With the exception of a few younger party workers sent to Germany from the Lenin School, the functionaries assembled in Moscow represented the old Thälmann leadership. Thälmann himself was in a German prison, and his most trusted lieutenant, John Scheer, had been arrested by the National Socialists and "shot while trying to escape." Thälmann's succession was now at stake.

Weeks of internal struggle had preceded the conference, and Ulbricht and Pieck had been the victors. They received the support of Dahlem, Ackermann, Merker, Funk, Mewis, Dengel, and others, while Thälmann's close friends, Florin, Schubert, Schulte, Kippenberger, and Creutzburg, were pushed aside. Of the latter, all but Florin, became victims of the same great purge as Neumann and Remmele and were liquidated in Soviet prisons and camps.

Pieck in his report denounced the German party policy in the years preceding Hitler's rise to power. "We directed our main attack at the Social Democracy," he declared, "at the time when the main attack should have been directed against the fascist movement."[20] That was something that most German Communists had already grasped by 1930, but would never have been permitted to say.

Pieck designated the creation of a "popular front" as the most important task. The Brussels Manifesto had this to say on the subject: "The German popular front is striving for a democratic republic; it is no mere maneuver in which partners are being switched at will."[21]

With respect to underground activity in Germany, the party should try, in spite of the fact that the Social Democratic executive committee unfortunately had declined the offer, to pave the road for a united front.

ESTABLISHING CONTACT WITH THE SOCIAL DEMOCRATIC EXECUTIVE COMMITTEE

As early as the beginning of 1935, the exile leadership of the German Communist Party had tried to initiate contacts with the Social Democratic executive committee. The Social Democratic party had been publicly approached to join forces in the underground groups in Germany for shop stewards' elections or similar local events. The executive committee had turned down these offers with the explanation that their groups at home did not favor collaboration with the Communist party.

The Communists also had been involved in the factional struggles shaking the Social Democrats since 1933. Close ties existed between the Communist representatives in Prague (Wilhelm Koenen and Walter Ulbricht) and the Social Democratic opposition group, the "Revolutionäre Sozialisten" (which included Siegfried Aufhauser, Karl Bochel, and Fritz Bieligk), as well as with another Socialist group, the exile headquarters of the movement "Neu Beginnen." The Communist press provided these groups with ample space for printing their resolutions and criticisms of the Social Democratic party.

In mid-November 1935, the central committee of the German Communist Party, which had recently been nominated in Moscow, wrote to the executive committee of the German Social Democratic party in Prague proposing that both party leaderships issue a joint declaration denouncing the Hitler dictatorship and calling for the reconquest of lost liberties. The Communists also sought an agreement on common measures in a series of current problems. The Communist leadership designated Walter Ulbricht and Franz Dahlem as their representatives and urged the Prague executive committee to select two representatives in turn, so that discussions could begin with respect to the proposals.

On November 23, 1935, a conference took place in Prague between the two Communists and the Social Democratic delegates Hans Vogel and Friedrich Stampfer. The Social Democrats turned down the idea of a joint declaration and an agreement on common measures. Instead, they proposed a nonaggression pact between the two parties as a first step, similar to the pact the French Socialists and Communists had concluded in July 1934. The Communists rejected such a pact because they were unwilling to commit themselves not to attack those Social Democrats who opposed a united front and insisted upon their demand that a joint declaration of a united front between Social Democrats and Communists be issued at once.

The Social Democratic leaders, in a memorandum to the negotiators, stated that the underground Social Democrats in the Reich were opposed to a united front with the Communists, because they put no faith in Communist assurances that they wished to restore democratic liberties. A joint declaration would propel Social Democratic sympathizers in Germany toward the right by creating the impression that the Socialists had joined the Communist fold. The executive committee itself had grave doubts about the earnestness of the Communists' new affirmative approach toward democratic rights and liberties.[22] This espousal of democratic beliefs by the Communist International was deemed a mere tactical maneuver, a new method of political warfare, and not a fundamental change in the Communist interpretation of means and objectives in the struggle to liberate the working class. All this, however, was no insuperable obstacle to *ad hoc* collaboration between the two parties, but Communists still would have to prove their good faith by deeds.

The meeting, held at the instigation of the Communists, brought no results. The Social Democrats proposed that the discussion be kept confidential and suggested that *ad hoc* collaboration could be undertaken. Later, when good faith was assured, a closer unity might evolve. The Communists declared they would publish a report, since they had already written about the impending discussion. With this, Communist initiative failed.[23]

THE GERMAN POPULAR-FRONT COMMITTEE IN PARIS

The ECCI had decided that Willi Münzenberg, too, within the framework of his Paris activities, should try to bring about a collaboration with the Social Democrats and bourgeois representatives of the German refugees. This was in line with his other political activities. The anti-Hitler German emigration, however, in contrast to the French Popular-Front movement, provided no mass basis. No more could be done than to establish contact with representatives of various parties and groups and with individual figures who in turn had ties with groups in the Third Reich or were publishing newspapers and periodicals attracting like-minded compatriots.

Münzenberg succeeded in winning over a group of émigrés who founded the Committee for the Creation of a German Popular Front on February 2, 1936, at the Hotel Lutetia in Paris. Among the 118 participants were several German writers, including Heinrich Mann, Emil Ludwig, Lion Feuchtwanger, Ernst Toller, Klaus Mann, and Ludwig Marcuse, as well as journalists Leopold Schwarzschild, Victor Schiff, and Georg Bernhard. Social Democrats Rudolf Breitscheid, Albert Grzesinski, Erich Kuttner, Alexander Schiffrin and Dr. Paul Hertz, as well as representatives of the Saar Socialists, also participated in the gathering, as did representatives of such other political groups as the Sozialistische Arbeiter Partei and the Internationaler Sozialistischer Kampfbund (ISK),[24] and certain independent intellectuals and professors. Franz Dahlem, Hermann Matern, Peter Maslowski, and Alexander Abusch were among the Communist functionaries present, aside from Münzenberg.

A committee was formed and a common manifesto formulated, approved and signed by those present. Heinrich Mann had an active part in drawing up this manifesto, which was worded as follows:

> The following resolution has been adopted by more than a hundred representatives of the liberal German bourgeoisie and the German working class of all political tendencies, who have gathered at this meeting abroad at the beginning of February 1936, three years after the establishment of the present regime.
>
> They ascertain that:
>
> 1) The present German government has raised havoc with economic and social conditions by wastefulness, armaments, destruction of foreign trade, and undermining of purchasing power. Under this regime, continued worsening is unavoidable.
>
> 2) By its un-German system of arbitrariness, of tyranny, of psychological coercion, of personal enrichment of those in power, the present German government has fostered a deep and uniform longing of nearly all Germans for an end to this terror and a restoration of the basic human rights.

They declare and demand:

1) The restoration of these elementary rights at present has priority over everything else. The individual parties and groups are called upon to join together and, while not relinquishing their stated goals, to direct all their energies toward the realization of the following generally valid and fundamental postulates:

Freedom of thought, freedom of speech, of research, and of teaching;

Freedom of belief and of worship;

Personal freedom;

Respect for the sanctity of human life, lawfulness and equality before the law, responsibility and removability of the highest government organs, control over public income and expenditure, eradication of corruption and parasitical party domination.

2) Any group or individual subscribing to these elementary demands is solemnly urged to become a comrade-in-arms and ally of any other group or individual sharing these demands. It is their duty to extend friendship to each other, disregarding class, group, or party barriers, to cultivate this friendship, and to lend assistance and protection to one another.

3) This attitude becomes a sacred duty at a moment when the German government is bringing its military, economic, moral, and political preparations for war to a head and the danger looms that the program for a war of annihilation and conquest—so clearly and carefully spelled out in "Mein Kampf," a book that remains as relevant as ever—is about to be carried out. In the face of this horror, which threatens Germany itself and the whole world with destruction, it must be emphasized that averting this doom may hinge on whether and to what extent resistance spreads among the German people and becomes organized. All groups and individuals heeding this appeal to ally themselves with us will do their share in saving the German fatherland and people, as well as the other countries and peoples, from annihilation in a new world war.

They resolve:

A subcommittee is entrusted with the task of working out a platform for uniting all opposition groups, with the help of the appropriate specialists. This committee shall elaborate a program that can serve as a basis for a Germany characterized by peace and freedom, morality, cleanliness and lawfulness, blessed with a strong, self-assured, and energetic democracy, capable of preventing abuse on the part of overpowerful economic forces, a democracy for workers in town and country.[25]

According to Kurt Kersten, this German popular-front committee constituted the "only large political committee uniting most political groups and personalities during the years of emigration. In a sense it could call itself for a time the spokesman for the political German emigration, even though the Social Democratic executive committee refused its official participation."[26]

Communists and Communist sympathizers, Social Democrats, members of the Sozialistische Arbeiter Partei, writers, artists, bourgeois journalists, representatives of the Catholic unions, intellectuals with or without party ties had come together in this committee. Under the impact of French developments, these heterogeneous elements believed themselves capable of setting aside their differences to speak as a solid opposition for the Germany which had been condemned to silence. The French Popular Front had become a reality. The leftist parties in Spain were about to join in a popular front and to win the majority in the Cortes elections. This fact helped to bring about an unduly optimistic estimate of the German possibilities.

COLLABORATION BETWEEN COMMUNISTS AND SOCIAL DEMOCRATS

Münzenberg welcomed the new line adopted by the Soviet foreign policy, since it coincided with the interests of the antifascist forces. He had experienced personally a great shock at the collapse of the Weimar Republic and the destruction of the German Communist Party, a shock which finally led to his break with communism. He had witnessed how Russian policy contributed to making not only the German Communist Party but the entire German labor movement victims of fascism. At that point he had not yet resolved to break with Moscow. He considered war imminent and unavoidable and felt that the political emigration made sense only if it united all forces against the impending catastrophe.

Under the impact of French Socialist policy, Rudolf Breitscheid and other men connected with the Social Democratic executive committee in Prague did participate in the popular-front committee and other united actions in Paris. Breitscheid was on intimate terms with Léon Blum and his group. He saw some value in attempting a limited collaboration with the Communists. He approved of the new Soviet policy of collective security. In Breitscheid's eyes the antifascist forces in all countries represented the proponents of peace. He believed that it was possible to agree with the Communists on a common program for preventing warlike adventures.

In the face of the new Communist tactic, the reaction of the Second International was equivocal and wavering. In a resolution of its executive committee, the Socialist parties were given a free hand in dealing with the Communist parties. The executive committee thus sanctioned the united-front policies of the French, Spanish, Austrian, and Italian Socialists. It is true that the most powerful parties of the Second International—the Scandinavian, the Belgian, the Dutch and the English—bluntly turned down any united-front policies with their Communist parties; the executive committee of the German Social Democrats followed suit.

Several common projects meanwhile were being tackled in Paris. A joint Social Democrat-Communist press service was established, the *Deutsche Informationen*; publishers and editors of this bilingual service were Heinrich Mann, Rudolf Breitscheid, Max Braun, and Bruno Frei. Under the leadership of the German Social Democrat Albert Grzesinski, a refugee committee was formed to give advice to all German émigrés and assist them in their relations with the French authorities.

The "Manifesto of the 118" expressed the deep-felt convictions of all émigrés. Each cherished the hope that his sad lot could be improved by joining forces with others, and that a united opposition would have more prestige abroad and at the same time inspire Hitler's opponents in Germany with new courage. German émigrés everywhere formed popular-front committees which published their own programs. In Buenos Aires the émigrés set up a popular-front committee on June 29, 1936. Another committee, in Uruguay, designated the popular front as a union of all Germans in Uruguay "opposed to Hitler."

Though there was unanimity about the advantage of collaboration of all émigrés in the framework of a popular front, the same was not true of their political programs. Except for the Social Democrats, the Communists, and the Sozialistische Arbeiter Partei, no German parties with exile leadership existed—only individual representatives of former parties in the Weimar Republic.

THE BOURGEOIS MEMBERS OF THE POPULAR-FRONT COMMITTEE

A group of progressive liberals gathered around Leopold Schwarzschild, publisher of the weekly *Das Neue Tagebuch* in Paris. In spite of his critical attitude toward the Social Democrats and his outspoken refusal to have anything to do with the Communists, Schwarzschild took part in the popular-front committee. Among his collaborators were Joachim Haniel, who worked out the economic section, Joseph Bornstein, who had left the Communist party together with Paul Levi, and Joseph Buttinger. Valeriu Marcu, like Bornstein a Communist from the days of the Russian Civil War and Lenin's personal courier, was in close touch with the group around Schwarzschild. This group believed that Münzenberg would be willing to serve the interests of antifascism even without close ties with the Communists, for his initiative was viewed in a favorable light; Hitler's war of aggression seemed imminent, and it was deemed necessary to prepare a platform of Hitler's opponents for the time following his overthrow, for the "Fourth Reich."

Das Neue Tagebuch thus conceived of the popular-front committee as a force which would one day serve to "replace the present regime by a new one without chaos or vacuum." It was hoped that this new regime would bring no new terror in its wake. That would happen only if "all classes—liberal, Stahlhelm, Communists, Catholics, artisans, workers, and farmers—worked together." The text of a leaflet distributed in Germany by the Communist party was printed in the paper with favorable comment. The leaflet stated, "We are willing to fight side by side with all antifascist elements for a democratic Germany, in which the German people chooses its government by self-determination." *Das Neue Tagebuch* gave this item the significant heading, "The German Communist Party brings these democratic tidings to its less well informed adherents at home."

Another representative of bourgeois, and particularly of Jewish, émigré circles, was Georg Bernhard, the publisher of the *Pariser Tageblatt*. He once had been sympathetic to the Social Democrats; as an émigré he had come into closer contact with the Communists. Like Schwarzschild, he had no understanding of Bolshevik ideology. In his eyes the Communists were undisciplined leftist Social Democratic deviationists, and he was under the illusion that the popular-front endeavors might restore the unity of the German working class. He had visions of "labor parties after the overthrow of the Hitler regime working shoulder to shoulder with all other wage earners to safeguard the civil liberties which constitute the basis for any civilization."[27] Inevitably, Georg Bernhard was taken in tow by the Communists more and more during the years of emigration.

Many writers, artists, and intellectuals suffered from similar illusions. They brushed aside as trivial the unbridgeable ideological oppositions between the German Communists and the Social Democrats. They felt attracted by the conspiratorial atmosphere of the Communist party, its willingness to make sacrifices, and its ties with a distant powerful state.

RESERVATIONS OF LEFTIST OPPOSITION GROUPS AGAINST THE COMMUNIST POPULAR-FRONT TACTICS

Heinrich Brandler's opposition group[28] and the Trotskyites were antagonistic from the beginning toward the reorientation of the Comintern. In their eyes the popular-front tactics constituted unprincipled opportunism; they reproached the Communists for having thrown overboard all revolutionary and Bolshevik principles, chided them as "social patriots," who had relinquished their political independence and betrayed the Leninist dogma of the function of the Party.

The Sozialistische Arbeiter Partei participated in the united- and popular-front committees, but had expressed reservations on political grounds from the start and criticized the popular-front tactics from the Marxist point of view. Their most prominent spokesman, Paul Frölich, expressed the view that the popular-front committee was not suited as "the general staff of the coming antifascist revolution."[29] It should limit itself instead to well-defined tasks, establish contact with the underground cadres in the Reich, collect and propagate information on a world-wide scale, and organize legal, material and moral aid for the persecuted. The Sozialistische Arbeiter Partei was to take part in the popular-front negotiations initiated by the German Communists "to the point where such a participation would compel it to make compromises in which the expected successes of the collaboration no longer compensated for the drawback of sacrificing the revolutionary standpoint."[30] In December 1936 the German popular-front committee published an appeal for "peace, freedom and bread," already clearly under the Communist imprint. It too, however, was still signed by all participants.

Relations between the Sozialistische Arbeiter Partei and the Communists deteriorated when the former publicly expressed its indignation at the Moscow trials and the shooting of old-guard Bolsheviks. Meanwhile, the Soviet secret police had extended its nefarious activities into Spain. Mark Rein, the son of the prominent Menshevik Rafael Abramovich, had been kidnapped in Spain by the GPU and never reappeared. At the second large meeting of the popular front, on April 10 and 11, 1937, the Sozialistische Arbeiter Partei attacked Communist terror in Spain.

The final breach between the two popular-front partners was not long in coming. The Communists wrote in July 1937 in the Prague *Deutsche Volkszeitung* that the Trotskyite Sozialistische Arbeiter Partei leaders had attempted to plan with the Spanish Trotskyists (Partido Obrero de Unificación Marxista—POUM) to bring about Hitler's and Mussolini's victory more effectively. Using the usual terminology, the Communists labeled the Sozialistische Arbeiter Partei a fifth column and an "agent of Franco."

THE GROUP AROUND SCHWARZSCHILD ABANDONS
THE POPULAR-FRONT COMMITTEE

Agreement upon a common platform in the popular-front committee hinged on an understanding with the group around Schwarzschild, through which the Communists hoped to establish more extensive ties in bourgeois circles in Germany. During the summer of 1936, several working sessions between Münzenberg and Schwarzschild took place, to elaborate a common program for the "Fourth Reich." Schwarzschild presented a draft for a program on the reorganization of the state after Hitler's fall, in which he laid down in great detail a constitution for the transitional period, as well as the bases for a definitive constitution. Additional paragraphs of the document dealt with the planned government and its branches, with this government's foreign policy and its military backing, and with the press. This program, imbued with a liberal-democratic spirit, was to be binding for all participants in the popular front during the transitional period. It soon became apparent that the drafts presented by Schwarzschild and his collaborators were unacceptable to the Communists.[31]

Schwarzschild in turn rejected the vague Communist proposals for a future economic program. He became conscious of the increasing pressure on the Paris popular-front committee by the Communist party, a pressure against which Münzenberg was defenseless. The negotiations were soon broken off without result. In October 1936, Schwarzschild defined the popular-front policy as one in which the Communists called a truce in their fight against the bourgeoisie. In his opinion, this Communist truce had borne no fruits, although the Soviet Union was working in the same direction through its Franco-Soviet alliance.

At the end of the year he summed up in these terms the achievements of the popular-front committee, from which he had irrevocably withdrawn:

> The most instructive result of the popular-front experiment in its German edition was in fact that the notion of adding together existing groups and hoping thereby to be more effective than the sum total of each group acting alone turned out to be an illusion. Adding the parts together produced less, rather than more, than each part acting alone. . . . There was no serious intention to attain a renovation of programs and unification. . . . No inspiring new program was brought forth, no objective planning for what was to be done in the Fourth Reich from its inception.[32]

THE GERMAN "FREIHEITSPARTEI"

Other bourgeois politicians had rejected from the start participation in the popular-front committees. Otto Klepper, the last minister of finance in the Prussian government, who had returned to Europe from China in 1936, urged that "a new movement be created, with the idea of freedom at its center."[33] He was in close touch with Dr. Karl Spiecker, former press chief of the Brüning Cabinet. Spieker's political friends included Peter Muckermann, who was publishing the weekly *Der Deutsche Weg* in Holland, and the prelate Poels. All these men maintained ties with their political friends in Germany.

These opposition circles suggested forming an émigré group and supporting friends at home by supplying them with information from abroad. The "Deutsche Freiheitspartei" was formed on a strictly conspiratorial basis and began to publish occasionally the so-called *Freiheitsbriefe*. The first letter, written by Otto Klepper, appeared in March 1937. It began: "What is the Deutsche Freiheitspartei and what does it hope to accomplish? It is a league of determined women and men whose only task it is to serve Germany, who know only one happiness in life, to serve the German people, and who have only one aim, to win freedom for it!"

When Münzenberg broke with the Communists in 1937, he was encouraged by Klepper and Spiecker to collaborate in the efforts of the Freiheitspartei. The initiators of the Freiheitspartei had made it their task to call on all democratic forces in Germany, excluding the Communists. The response from the Third Reich exceeded their expectations. The *Freiheitsbriefe* aroused such interest in the universities, the army and the youth organizations that the National Socialists were compelled to take a stand against them publicly.

Letters were delivered to Germany by couriers and by mail, at times even by balloons. The Gestapo assumed that transport planes were dropping the letters. In 1938 the group occasionally had a short-wave transmitter at its disposal, which operated from a fishing boat in the Strait of Dover, beyond the three-mile zone, until it had to halt its activity because of political difficulties with the host countries. The Gestapo hunted feverishly for the anonymous spiritual leaders of the Freiheitspartei. In the course of two years it confiscated forty-five different *Freiheitsbriefe*—all together about 10,000 copies. In January 1938 the Freiheitspartei issued the "Manifesto of German Freedom," the main purpose of which was to justify the right to rebel against the Hitler regime on religious, philosophical and constitutional grounds and to glorify this right as a moral duty. The published material implied that the group was aided by collaborators in influential positions among German officials, in universities, and in trade and industry.

The exile leadership of the German Communist Party was aware of the activity of the Freiheitspartei. It first attempted to make the nonpartisan popular-front committee condemn the Freiheitspartei, without success. A jury headed by Heinrich Mann declared that it saw no advantage in opposing the Freiheitspartei, and that it would be in line with the aims of the popular front to stir up opposition to Hitler inside Germany from all possible directions. The German Communist Party's central committee ignored these findings of the popular-front committee. In a circular to the party members of the committee, it stated that Münzenberg's conduct was being investigated because he had carried on discussions with rightist bourgeois circles without the Communists' authorization, and these dealings did not serve unification in the fight against Hitler. Another circular affirmed that some groups around Spiecker wished to work together with capitalist circles, rightist Catholic leaders, and Reichswehr generals and to exclude the Communists from the popular front. On October 27, all Communist Party members were finally informed that Münzenberg had been expelled.

THE COMMUNIST WOOING OF THE SOCIAL DEMOCRATIC EXECUTIVE COMMITTEE REMAINS FRUITLESS

The members of the Social Democratic executive committee remained aloof from the numerous Communist proposals for joint action, whether offered by Ulbricht or by Münzenberg through the

Social Democrats in Paris. Though no public reprimand was issued, Rudolf Breitscheid's, Rudolf Hilferding's, and Erich Kuttner's collaboration in the popular-front committee in Paris was viewed with disapproval by the Socialists in Prague. An argument that bore much weight with the Social Democratic executive committee was the fact that the party officials in the Third Reich did not wish any joint action with the Communists. The Communists in Germany had considerable funds at their disposal from Moscow and had greater freedom of movement. They deployed their Moscow-trained agents ruthlessly, and the Social Democrats feared that the Communists would infiltrate quickly their underground positions if Prague made the slightest concession. In September 1936, a Social Democrat official wrote to Prague: "Let us create a Socialist Germany on our own; we do not need Russian agents. We do not want to turn Germany one day into a colony of the Comintern."[34]

Curt Geyer,[35] who had had personal experience with Communist tactics, energetically opposed any attempt to collaborate with the Comintern. Friedrich Stampfer[36] rejected a united front, because it would hamper the Social Democrats' efforts to work with bourgeois and other non-Communist groups and thereby would delay Hitler's overthrow. The eighty-three-year-old Karl Kautsky was the most outspoken on this score among the Social Democratic leaders. In his preface to the new edition of the *Communist Manifesto* he wrote in December 1937:

> The Soviet Union's appeal for help to the democracies outside Russia, the Communist Party's advocacy of democracy and a united front with social democracy, hitherto opposed so bitterly—all this only represents a tactical about-face of the Communists. The Communists defend democracy only where they are in opposition; wherever they are in power, they wipe out any sort of popular front. . . . Should these rulers [the Russians] one day come to an understanding with Germany and Japan, Communists everywhere would become abettors of fascism.[37]

THE GROUP "DEUTSCHE VOLKSFRONT" IN BERLIN

The developments in Paris inspired a group of Berlin Social Democrats in 1935–36 to form a committee. On December 21, 1936, this group formulated the following ten-point program for a popular front in Germany:

> Brought together by the determination to overthrow the Hit-

ler dictatorship, to save democracy from destruction in a second world war and to restore liberty and equality as the tenets of political life for all Germans, the Liberal, Democratic, Socialist, and Communist groups in Germany have formed a popular front and proclaim the following demands as a program for the German people:

1) Overthrow and destruction of the dictatorship.

2) Rule of law and justice for all; liberation of political prisoners, abrogation of violence, amends for past crimes, compensation for past injustices.

3) Freedom of belief and of opinion; government protection of all religious worship, freedom of organization, assembly and press.

4) Full self-government and self-administration by the German people in a renewed country based on political, social and economic democracy.

5) Abandonment of the arms race and the war economy. Security through disarmament, shortening of military service.

6) Full reconciliation and complete understanding with France. Participation in the European political community, within the framework of a reorganized League of Nations. Peace and friendship with all lands.

7) Elimination of poverty and unemployment by restoring Germany's position in the world economy.

8) Safeguarding savings accounts and insurance policies from inflation. Free labor contracts. Forty-hour week.   -

9) Lifting of coercive measures with respect to agricultural lands (law on inherited property) and agricultural products (market regulation). Conversion of large estates to peasant settlements. Encouragement of agricultural cooperatives.

10) Nationalization of heavy industry, of chemical and power production, and of banking. Application of an economic policy aiming only at assuring Germany's livelihood.

Germans! The German popular front will not dissolve itself until its demands are realized. Join our ranks. Down with dictatorship! For a free, peace-loving and happy fatherland![38]

The leadership of this group was drawn from Social Democratic resistance circles, part of it recruited from the labor youth movement and former students at the Schloss Tinz (Thuringia) adult education center. Hermann Brill, leader of the group, was a teacher and, before 1933, permanent secretary in the Thuringian Ministry of the Interior. The ten-point program evoked a lively discussion in the resistance groups. The Communists immediately tried to win over the group for the creation of a united-front organization. A Berlin delegate traveled to Prague and presented the views of the group to the Social Democratic executive committee. He expressed the opinion that the mood inside Germany favored a united front and that steps should be taken to "organize a popular front in the face of outdated party squabbles."

The executive committee categorically rejected a united front with the Communists. Such a union was impossible because of the profound philosophical differences between the two parties. Communists were not able even to achieve unification with the Social Democratic splinter groups. In spite of grave misgivings about tying the group he represented to any émigré organization, Brill traveled to Brussels in December 1937 to confer with the Second International about approval of the group's popular-front program. There he met with Louis de Brouckère, Friedrich Adler, and Paul Hertz. The Second International, however, was equally unreceptive to united- or popular-front pacts with the Communists.

At the end of 1937 the popular-front policy was at the brink of collapse in the Western countries. In Spain the Communists had provoked the fall of Caballero's government in May 1937. The subsequent Negrin government still bore the popular-front label, but the decisive elements—Socialists and Anarchists—were hostile to the Negrin government and its Russian advisors.

In France Prime Minister Léon Blum, heading the popular front, had inquired what would be the attitude of the Soviet government if France were to send arms to the legitimate Spanish government and thereby incur an attack by Hitler. The Russians had replied that "the Franco-Soviet pact binds us to lend mutual assistance in case of an attack by a third power, but not if war is provoked by intervention of one of us into the affairs of another state."[39]

Stalin had feared since 1934 that Hitler would start a war, and his only objective was to keep Hitler away from the Russian borders. While Stalin was refusing to come to the assistance of the French popular-front government in case of war, the French Communist Party was campaigning for French intervention in Spain and raising the cry "Arms and airplanes for Spain" at meetings and demonstrations. As a result of these and other crises provoked by the Communists, the popular front in France was also on the verge of collapse.

On his return to Berlin, Brill deliberated at length with his group and issued in 1938 the programmatic text *Freedom* for the

Deutsche Volksfront.[40] The twenty-seven-page text, issued in one hundred copies, was couched in eloquent language and distributed to partisans in the Reich. The group continued its operations until the Gestapo in connection with other arrests, managed to seize the instigators of the Deutsche Volksfront in late summer and fall of 1938.

After a year-long investigation, the so-called Popular Front Trial against Brill was conducted before the People's Court in Berlin from July 14 to July 28, 1939. The leading Social Democratic members of the group were condemned to heavy penitentiary sentences for "attempted high treason," "illegal creation of a new political party," and other charges.

THE END OF THE POPULAR-FRONT COMMITTEE IN PARIS

During 1936 Ulbricht and the exile German Communist Party had involved themselves in the relations of the popular-front committee with its other partners. Münzenberg remained a member for some time, taking part in a second popular-front conference, completely dominated by Communists, which was held in a hall, Rue Cadet in Paris, on April 10 and 11, 1937. There were several hundred participants. Heinrich Mann spoke about the resistance movement "Zur Rettung des Friedens." Breitscheid discussed foreign policy, and Münzenberg spoke on the tasks of the popular front, which was to be forged into a politically active body. He urged the Communists in particular to act above-board, rebuking them for a policy of petty intrigues bound to undermine confidence. Heinrich Mann made a point of thanking Münzenberg of these honest words.

At the time of his last visit to Moscow in October 1936, Münzenberg had tried in vain to discourage a policy which was bound to be objectionable to the popular-front partners and prevent any united action with German anti-Hitler circles. Together with other Communist representatives of the Parisian group he had submitted a plan. The Comintern, however, was no longer interested in united action or popular-front tactics among German émigrés.

The activity of the committee was curtailed even further. In the fall of 1938 the Communists made one more attempt to revive the committee. The Social Democrats and numerous other personalities already had withdrawn. Heinrich Mann, who was by then completely in the Communist groove, once again was ready to participate, and he called for so-called popular-front discussions. Several bourgeois representatives of émigré organizations came as observers. Mann pre-

sided and nominated three well-known Communists for the leadership of the committee. When he asked the non-Communists to join
the committee, they refused on the ground that this was a Communist-
dominated organization. This meeting brought to a close the efforts
of the German Communists to establish a popular-front movement
among German émigrés.

COMMUNISM AND WAR

On August 23, 1939, Stalin concluded the pact with Hitler. With the
help of his new ally, Hitler smashed Poland and was then free to
attack the Western democracies. The Comintern responded "to the
changed situation with a changed tactic," as Dimitrov expressed it in
his speech "Communism and the War" delivered before the ECCI on
November 6, 1939. The Communists in the Western countries were
urged to break off any relations with the Socialists, who were supporting the war against Hitler. Dimitrov declared, "the Communists *can
have no united front whatsoever with those in a common front with
the imperialists and who support the criminal anti-people's war*
[against Hitler!]."[41] Thus the Comintern terminated the popular-
front era of the thirties.

Stalin's Massacre of the Foreign Communist Leaders

by

BRANKO LAZITCH

"The USSR grants the right of asylum to those foreign citizens who are being persecuted for defending the workers' interests or because of their scientific activity or their struggle for national liberation."—Article 129 of the Stalinist Constitution of 1936.

The non-Russian Communist leaders who became victims of the massacres ordered by Stalin during 1936–39 are almost completely condemned to oblivion. Their Russian colleagues who met the same fate at least were granted some publicity. At the time the Russian Bolsheviks were being executed, many people suspected the extent of the purges on the basis of the mock trials and the sudden disappearance of a great number of party dignitaries. Much later, de-Stalinization and the procedures of political or legal rehabilitation initiated by the twentieth congress of the Communist Party of the Soviet Union (February 1956) and since carried forward, placed them again in the limelight.

But the non-Russian Communist leaders were liquidated without public trials and without mention of their execution. Furthermore, they were accorded no posthumous rehabilitation, with the exception of Béla Kun, several Poles, and a few Yugoslavs. Thus, the silence which surrounded their fate after the period 1936–39 effectively has erased them from memory.

The extermination of the non-Russian Communists living in the USSR began at the very time that Stalin promulgated "the most democratic constitution in the world," which explicitly guaranteed the right of asylum to foreign Communists. And the massacres continued throughout the period of the "great purge."

The central apparatus of the Comintern had always been financially dependent upon the Russians and was operated under their orders. Moreover, with Stalin's final triumph the organization was thenceforth placed at the mercy of the GPU. Under the cloak of the Cadres Commission, the Comintern was studded with members of the Soviet police and their finger men. Stalin had the audacity to get N. I. Yezhov, member of the purge commission of the Russian Communist Party since 1933 and future head of the Soviet police, named to membership of the ECCI at the Seventh Congress in 1935. He went even further; from this time on, a certain M. A. Moskvin, whose name was entirely unknown at the Comintern, was included in the Presidium and the Secretariat. Moskvin was a fictitious name concealing the person of M. A. Trilisser, one of the GPU chiefs, who was made a leader of the Comintern and put in charge of its secret apparatus and its financial affairs, replacing Osip Piatnitsky upon the latter's removal.

Thus, when the great purge was launched in 1936, there already existed in the Comintern's central apparatus a well-oiled machinery, as well equipped in advance for the purge as any purely Soviet institution. Consonant with Stalinist practice, Trilisser and many other Cheka men on the Cadres Commission, after having set the purge in motion, themselves fell victims of it.

Only when the archives of the Soviet police are made public will the actual number of victims of Stalin's homicidal fury in the Comintern be known. This fury was directed against both leaders and Party militants, and even against simple workers who had come to settle in the Soviet Union. Moreover, though it is relatively easy to inquire into the fate of the leaders, who were known in their parties and in the Comintern hierarchy, it is impossible to do so for the militants and the workers who had taken refuge in the USSR.

The fact that the foreign Communist groupings were wiped out by Stalin can be confirmed, except for the details, in the rare disclosures of a few survivors. Arvo Tuominen, former chief of the Communist Party of Finland and alternate member of the Presidium of the Comintern Executive Committee until the end of 1939, wrote that "at least 20,000 Finns were taken to concentration camps, and a proportionate number must have been exterminated from among the

Communists of countries adjacent to the USSR."[1] Available evidence about the fate of Yugoslav Communist émigrés also indicates that leaders, workers, rank-and-file party members, and refugees were liquidated. Božidar Maslarić, who lived in the USSR at the beginning and end of the great purge, declared later: "Our [Yugoslav] émigrés suffered more cruelly than all others. Most of them were arrested in 1937–38 and their fate has remained completely unknown."[2] Alfred Burmeister (pen name of Wanda Pampuch-Bronska, daughter of an old Polish associate of Lenin's) cites another phase in this general purge: in 1936 the KUNMZ (Communist University for the National Minorities of the West), the first school for the training of Comintern cadres, was dissolved, and its entire teaching staff and nearly all its students were arrested, whereupon they vanished forever.[3]

Leaving aside the mass of rank and file party members seeking refuge in the USSR, the fate of the leaders can be summarized in the following categories:

1. All foreign Communists who had followed Lenin or had cooperated with him before October 1917, immediately after the victory and during the foundation of the Comintern in 1919, were exterminated.

2. The leaders of parties which had been outlawed in their own countries and who then sought refuge in the Soviet Union met the same fate. Djilas confirms this policy rule of Stalin's in his book *Conversations with Stalin*: "The purges were especially hard on the Communist émigrés, those members of illegal parties who had no one to turn to except the Soviet."[4]

3. The leaders who belonged to legal Communist parties in the European parliamentary democracies survived the massacres. Tuominen, discussing the Scandinavian countries, verifies this. "In the Scandinavian countries," he writes, "the Communist parties were legal; that is why their members were saved. The leaders did not reside in Moscow, and when they found themselves there, they had their nationalities and therefore did not live at the mercy of the Soviets."[5]

The application of these three guiding principles by Stalin's police accounts for the dissimilar fates that befell the Comintern's foreign staff.

The Polish Communist Party leaders fulfilled the conditions of the first and second categories. This party was the only one whose numerous founders had fought with Lenin before the revolution and had played an important role in the establishment of Soviet Russia and the Comintern. Because of this alone they were condemned by Stalin; in addition, they lived as refugees in the Soviet Union. All Polish leaders were exterminated (with two or three exceptions), while the Polish party itself was the only one to be dissolved at Stalin's orders.

The second category includes several Communist parties which had been outlawed by the dictatorial regimes in their own countries. Most of their leaders, living in refuge in the USSR, were arrested and killed by Stalin's police. This applied to those from Yugoslavia, Germany, Hungary, Rumania, the three Baltic countries, and Finland. Most of the leaders (not all) of only two parties in this category—the Bulgarian and the Italian—escaped the collective massacre.

The third category comprises parties from the "bourgeois democratic" countries, which played the role of protectors for foreign Communists, even in Moscow. This was true for Great Britain, France, Czechoslovakia, and the Scandinavian countries (Sweden, Norway and Denmark).

THE EXTERMINATION OF THE ZIMMERWALD LEFT

During the First World War, Lenin, as a refugee in Switzerland, attempted for the first time to go beyond the strictly Russian framework and to form a political organization on an international scale. At the International Conferences of Socialists Opposed to War, held at Zimmerwald (1915) and Kienthal (1916), the "Zimmerwald Left" was founded as a faction within the Zimmerwald movement, with Lenin as its guiding force. Although this faction was far from dominating—and at times even from influencing—the Zimmerwald movement, a number of Socialist party workers and leaders from several countries rallied under its program.

Besides Zinoviev, who was a member of the central committee of the Bolshevik party, many of the non-Russian Socialist leaders from Eastern and Central Europe attending these two conferences associated themselves with the Zimmerwald Left. The Polish Socialists were the most strongly represented. They included the following:

MIECZYSLAW BROŃSKI, like Lenin, lived in Zurich during the First World War, attended the Kienthal Conference as the Polish delegate, and was a member of the Zimmerwald Left. It was he who informed Lenin in February 1917 that the revolution had just broken out: "One day after dinner," wrote Krupskaya, "just as Ilitch was getting ready to go to the library, as I finished the dishes, Broński came to see us. 'You don't know?' he exclaimed, 'the revolution has broken out in Russia!' And he related to us the contents of the news dispatches which had just appeared in a special edition."[6] Bronski himself went to Russia in 1917 and after the Communist victory exercised important functions both in the Soviet regime and in the initial apparatus of the Comintern. He was arrested during the great purge and perished without trial. His wife too was arrested (her further fate is unknown), and his daughter Wanda was interned in a concentration camp where she remained until the end of the Second World War.

KAROL SOBELSON (*pseud.* Karl Radek)[7]—for his biography see pp. 305–07.

ADOLF WARSZAWSKI (*pseud.* Warski) was a member of the central committee of the Social Democratic Workers' Party of Russia from the time of the Stockholm congress (1906), participated in the Zimmerwald and Kienthal conferences, joined the Zimmerwald Left at that movement, was a member of the central committee of the Polish Communist Party from its founding, attended several congresses of the Comintern and was a member of its Executive Committee. A refugee in the USSR from 1929 and already in political retirement, he was arrested and, according to recent Soviet sources, died soon thereafter, on August 21, 1937.[8]

MAKSYMILIAN HORWITZ (*pseud.* Henryk Walecki), another ill-fated founder of the Polish Communist Party and prominent participant in Comintern activities, was executed by the Soviet police in 1937. The principal details of his political background are presented on pp. 375–76.

JAKUB FÜRSTENBERG (*pseud.* Hanecki) was a member of the central committee of the Social Democratic Workers' Party of Russia in 1907 (while the Russian Bolsheviks still belonged to it), aligning himself with the Zimmerwald Left during the First World War. After the October Revolution, he was engaged in the financial operations of the Soviets, both in internal financing and in the initial subsidizing of the Comintern. He disappeared in the great purge. According to the formula now in vogue, "In 1937, he became a victim of enemy calumny and was later rehabilitated."[9]

WŁADYSŁAW STEIN-KRAJEWSKIA a member of the Polish delegation (with Radek and Bronski) at the conference of Kienthal, was also a member of the central committee of the Polish Communist Party, participated in the Comintern congresses and was one of the functionaries of the cadre section in its central apparatus. A refugee in the USSR, elected to the control commission at the last Comintern congress in 1935, he was expelled from the Party as a Trotskyite and arrested in 1938. His fate is unknown.

PAWEL LEWINSON (*pseud.* Stanislaw Łapiński) took part in the Zimmerwald and Kienthal conferences, was a member of the central committee of the Polish Communist Party, but was arrested in 1938 and thereafter disappeared.

In addition to the Poles, other adherents of the Zimmerwald Left suffered similar fates, with two significant variations: the Swedish and the Dutch, both important elements in this group, broke with the Comintern at an early stage, thus avoiding dealings with Stalin's police; as for the remaining Zimmerwaldians, their number was very small. However, they did not escape extermination by Stalin if they had chosen to settle in the USSR (even if they had abandoned all political activity). Such was the fate of the following:

FRITZ PLATTEN, Swiss Socialist militant, who later became secretary of the party, was as well known in the Zimmerwald Left, as was Robert Grimm in the entire Zimmerwald movement; both were Swiss representatives, and their activities were concentrated essentially in Switzerland. It was Platten who negotiated for Lenin and a number of other Russian revolutionaries the famous passage across Germany in March 1917 and who was subsequently responsible for this convoy. It also was he who saved Lenin's life under dramatic circumstances, as recalled in an authoritative Soviet source: "In January 1918, Platten foiled an attempt on Lenin's life, suffering a slight injury as a result."[10]

Platten presided over the First Congress of the Comintern (jointly with Lenin and Hugo Eberlein) and later, in July 1923, came to settle in the USSR, where he vanished in the great purge. In 1956 his relatives addressed inquiries to the Soviet authorities and learned that his wife, Bertha Zimmerman, formerly employed in the Comintern, had been arrested in 1937, that Platten himself had been arrested in 1938 and sentenced to five years of forced labor, and that he had died of a heart attack in 1942.[11]

EDMONDO PELUSO, militant Italian Socialist, lived in the United States before 1914, and for an even longer period in Spain and Portugal. He was delegated to represent the Portuguese international

Socialists to the Kienthal conference, where he took a position close to that of the Zimmerwald Left. In 1918–19 he participated in the Communist revolutionary agitation in Germany.

He addressed the Fourth Comintern Congress, was the representative of the Italian party on the ECCI in 1923–24, and for several years was a contributor to *International Press Correspondence*, moving back and forth between Italy and Russia. Fascism finally drove him to seek refuge in the Soviet Union in 1927, where he too was arrested in the great purge. He died in 1942.

FRANZ KORITSCHONER, representative of the Austrian international Socialists at the Kienthal conference, was one of the founders of the Austrian Communist Party. He participated in the Third Comintern Congress, became a member of the ECCI, and settled in the USSR about 1929–30 as a functionary of the Profintern. Arrested in 1937 and, together with his wife, placed in detention at the time of the great purge, Koritschoner, like many German Communists, was turned over to the Gestapo in the wake of the Hitler-Stalin pact. Imprisoned in Vienna, he died there during the war in 1942.

WILLI MÜNZENBERG was the initiator of the International Socialist Youth Conference held in Berne in April 1915—a prelude to the conferences of Zimmerwald and Kienthal. He attended the Kienthal conference, where he drew close to Lenin. It was in Münzenberg's Zurich apartment that the representatives of the Zimmerwald Left held probably their last meeting before Lenin's departure for Russia.[12]

Münzenberg was the founder of the Communist Youth International (KIM) and later exercised important functions in the German Communist Party as well as in the central apparatus of the Comintern. He was expelled from the German party in May 1938; the expulsion was confirmed by the Comintern control commission in January–February, 1939.[13] He met death in France in 1940, under circumstances which lead to the conclusion that he was murdered by one of Stalin's agents.

YAN BERZIN (*pseud.* Winter), one of the leaders of the Latvian Socialist movement within the framework of the Social Democratic Workers' Party of Russia, also participated in the Zimmerwald conference, where he was one of the signatories of the Declaration of the Left. Upon departing for the United States, he turned his vote over to Zinoviev for the Kienthal conference. The first Soviet diplomatic representative in Switzerland in 1918 and secretary of the Communist International in its first year of existence, 1919–20, Berzin lost all his posts in both Party and state after 1927, from then on supervising the archives in Moscow until his arrest in 1937. He died in 1941.[14]

THE FATE OF SOME NON-RUSSIANS, HIGH SOVIET OFFICIALS

A militant Polish Socialist, JÓZEF UNSZLICHT (*pseud.* Jurowski), although he was not a participant in the Zimmerwald conference, belongs to a special category worth mentioning. Deported to Siberia during the First World War, he was not able to join forces with the Bolsheviks until April 1917. During the fateful days of October he was a member of the Military Revolutionary Committee in Petrograd. He was the only Polish representative to attend the founding congress of the Comintern in 1919, but actually he belonged to the ruling hierarchy of the Soviet party and state. During 1920–30, he was one of the heads of the political police and afterward assistant commissioner of the Soviet armed forces. One more victim of Stalin, he died on July 28, 1938, a date recently revealed by the Soviets.[15]

An identical fate was reserved for some other foreign revolutionaries who, after October 1917, had become high officials in the Soviet party and state. Among these were CHRISTIAN RAKOVSKY, head of the Socialist movement in Rumania, who later became president of the Soviet government in the Ukraine and ambassador to London and Paris (incidentally, Rakovsky's wife and only daughter also died in a prison or concentration camp); JAN ERNESTOVICH RUDZUTAK, a Latvian party worker, promoted through Stalin's patronage to membership in the politburo of the Soviet Communist Party in 1926 and liquidated in the great purge by order of that same Stalin; V. G. KNORIN, another Latvian and prominent participant in the Socialist movement in his native land, who after 1917 first engaged in revolutionary activity in Belorussia and then was called upon to assume high posts in Moscow as member of the central committee of the Bolshevik party from 1927 and head of the Central European secretariat of the Comintern from 1929 to 1936. He was arrested in June of 1937, replaced in his functions by Palmiro Togliatti, and executed by a firing squad in 1939.

THE ANNIHILATION OF THE POLISH COMMUNIST PARTY

When the fury of Stalin descended upon the Polish Communists who had taken refuge in the USSR, not a hint of what was happening to them appeared in the Comintern press. It is impossible to find in official publications the slightest information on the liquidation of the Polish party or the extermination of its leaders. There is only the accusation raised by Manuilsky, without any supporting evidence, at the eighteenth congress of the Soviet party in March 1939, after the liquidation had already been completed:

> In order to disrupt the Communist movement the Fascist-Trotskyite spies attempted to form artificial "factions" and "groups" in some of the Communist parties and to stir up a factional struggle. Most contaminated by hostile elements was the Communist Party of Poland, where agents of Polish fascism managed to gain positions of leadership. These scoundrels tried to get the party to support Pilsudski's fascist coup in May 1926. When this failed, they feigned repentance of their "May error," made a show of self-criticism, and deceived the Comintern just as Lovestone and the police "factionalists" of the Hungarian and Yugoslav parties once had done.[16]

Stalin had several personal reasons for sating his hatred of the Polish Communists in a blood bath unprecedented and unmatched in the annals of the Comintern. He detested all Poles, including Polish Communists; besides, a number of Polish Communist leaders had belonged to Lenin's entourage before October 1917, and were now living as refugees in the USSR, with no legal protection. The Poles were guilty of two additional sins in Stalin's eyes. In December 1923, one month before Lenin's death, when the struggle over his succession was being threshed out for the first time among the leadership of the Soviet party, only one party in the Comintern—the Polish Communist Party—undertook to defend Trotsky openly, pointing out to Stalin, Zinoviev and Kamenev the grave dangers which the elimination of Trotsky could entail. Just before Lenin died the Poles repeated their offense, as Stalin observed at the time: "For me," he stated, "it is clear that in the first period of the struggle waged by the majority of the Russian party, the leaders of the Polish party . . . sided with the opposition. . . .When the central committee of the Polish Communist Party forwarded this resolution to the central committee of the Russian Communist Party, it constituted without any doubt the Polish branch of the Russian Communist Party's opportunist opposition."[17]

Another sin of the Polish Communist leadership was the fact that they were Jewish, and Stalin disliked Jews. Thus, to be Jewish, Polish, refugees, former close associates of Lenin, and supporters of

Trotsky gave Stalin enough reasons to order the extermination. A number of Poles were "guilty" on all five counts, but even those whose culpability was reduced to one or two such charges did not escape liquidation, as, for example, in the case of JULIAN LESZCZYŃ-SKI (*pseud*. Leński; see below), who was neither a Jew nor a Trotsky-ite. To the contrary, he had been Stalin's principal agent in carrying out the operation directed against the Polish central committee in 1924.

At the time of Lenin's death the Polish Communist Party was in the hands of the "three W's"—Walecki, Warski, and MARIA KOSZUT-SKA (*pseud*. Wera Kostrzewa). A scant few months later, during the Fifth Congress of the Comintern in July 1924, Stalin found a way to seal the political fate of this leadership. A Polish commission was formed with himself at its head and Molotov as vice president. Its decision was clear: these leaders must be eliminated. The manner employed by Stalin—functioning for the first time as president of a commission at a Comintern congress and, moreover, for the first time active participant in any congress—must have been far from gentle, judging by Kostrzewa's remarks: "It is not those whose bones you may break for the same reasons that you are now breaking ours who constitute the principal danger for you, but rather those whose bones include no backbone at all."[18]

Wera Kostrzewa had been a member of the central committee of the Polish Communist Party from its founding. Active in the leader-ship of the Comintern during Lenin's lifetime, she delivered a report at the Fourth Congress, in conjunction with Eugen Varga, dealing with the agrarian question. She succeeded in retaining her position in the Comintern even after she was dropped from the directing hier-archy of the Polish party. She made a speech at the Sixth Congress in 1928, appearing as a member of the Presidium. In the summer of 1937, however, her time of grace ran out: she was arrested and died in the Lubianka prison.

JULIAN LESZCZYŃSKI (*pseud*. Leński), one of numerous Polish Communists who occupied posts in the Soviet government, was placed on November 28, 1917, in charge of Polish affairs in the com-missariat of nationalities, headed by Stalin. While in Stalin's service at the Comintern, he directed the campaign against the Polish party's leadership in 1924. As a reward he was admitted to the Politburo and later, from 1929 to 1937, served as secretary-general of the Polish Communist Party. He made speeches at the last three congresses held by the Comintern—the Fifth, Sixth, and Seventh—becoming a member of the ECCI after the 1928 congress, as well as member of the Presidium after the conclave of 1935. Nevertheless, the Soviet police finally arrested him. He died in 1939.

EDWARD PRÓCHNIAK (*pseud.* Sewer, Weber), the only Pole who had been a pupil in Lenin's school at Longjumeau (near Paris) in 1911, was a member of the politburo of the Polish Communist Party from its earliest years, and secretary of the "Provisional Polish Government" formed at Bialystok in 1920. He took an active part in the congresses and leadership of the Comintern. He was a representative of his party in the Comintern and a member of the ECCI at the Fourth Congress in 1922, was elected to the control commission after the Fifth Congress in 1924, given a seat in the Presidium of the ECCI from 1926 to 1928, and reelected to the ECCI at the Sixth Congress. At the Seventh Congress Próchniak was still an alternate member of this body. He worked in the central apparatus of the Comintern until his arrest in 1937; his two sisters and a younger brother also were arrested. His ultimate fate is unknown.[19]

HENRYK STEIN (*pseud.* L. Domski, H. Kamieński) was the editor of a Socialist journal at Krakow in 1912, the year Lenin moved to that city. He participated in Bolshevik publishing activities and, together with Hanecki, attended the restricted conference of Bolshevik leaders called together by Lenin at Poronino in the fall of 1913. A prominent leader of the Polish Communist Party from its founding, Domski was among the speakers at the Fourth Congress of the Comintern in 1922 and delivered a report at the second congress of the Polish party, which met near Moscow in 1923. The following year, he became one of the principal members of the new central committee of the party, after the old triumvirate of Warski, Walecki and Wera Kostrzewa had been ejected at Moscow's desire. Toward the end of the decade, however, Domski's own fortunes began ebbing: by stages, he was removed from the central committee, accused of "leftist deviationism," and expelled from the Party. He finally vanished during the great purge.

JERZY HERYNG (*pseud.* Ryng), another member of the Polish Communist Party politburo, participated in the debates of the Sixth Comintern Congress. He directed the clandestine Communist party in Poland and was among the leaders invited to Moscow for "consultation" at the end of 1937. Arrested soon afterward by the NKVD, he disappeared into Soviet jails. His name figured among the first five

Polish Communist leaders rehabilitated even before the twentieth congress of the Soviet Communist Party in February 1956 and Gomulka's return to power in October of the same year. In fact, on May 1, 1955, the official organ of the Polish party, the *Trybuna Ludu*, published photographs of the five Polish leaders liquidated in the USSR (without, of course, giving any details): Warski, Wera Kostrzewa, Próchniak, Leński and Ryng.

BRONISŁAW BORTNOWSKI (*pseud.* Bronkowski), a member of the politburo of the Polish Communist Party during the Stalinist period, was elected a member of the ECCI and alternate member of its Presidium at the last congress. Nevertheless, he too succumbed, sucked under by the great purge.

HENRYK LAUER (*pseud.* Brandt), a member of the Polish Communist Party's central committee from its earliest years and co-author (with Walecki) of *Communism in Poland*, was a spokesman for the Polish Communists at the Third and Sixth Comintern congresses. He was working on the Soviet planning commission when he was arrested in 1937.

SAUL AMSTERDAM (*pseud.* Henryk Henrykowski), a member of the politburo of the party, was one of its principal leaders from 1928. He took part in the debates of the Sixth Comintern Congress, returned secretly to Poland, and was subsequently included among the leaders invited to Moscow by the Comintern in 1937. Herbert Wehner, at that time a member of the central committee of the German Communist Party residing at Moscow's Hotel Luxe, describes in his memoirs the last days of this leader's life:

> The official of the Polish party, Henrykowski, had been occupying a room at the Luxe for six weeks. He had come from abroad to deliver a so-called report, but he must have realized before long that most of his Polish comrades no longer could be located. Leński, who like him had belonged for several years to the top ranks of the Polish leadership, had arrived in Moscow somewhat earlier, and had disappeared. Henrykowski left his room only at night to buy provisions. Those who were aware of his presence in Moscow expected any morning to find a seal attached to the door of his room, signifying that he had been taken by the NKVD during the night. Meanwhile, he "lived" alone, in the most terrifying isolation.[20]

He was soon arrested, and disappeared.

STEFAN KRÓLIKOWSKI had been a member of the central committee of the Polish Communist Party from its founding, and Communist deputy to the Polish parliament. He participated in the animated discussions about the Polish party at the Sixth Congress of the Comintern and later took refuge in the USSR. He was apprehended like the others.

TOMASZ DĄBAL [DOMBAL], another deputy to the Polish parliament, abandoned the leftist peasant party for the Communist movement. After imprisonment by the Polish authorities, he came to Moscow in 1923 with twenty-three other Communists just released from detention. *Inprecor* announced their arrival under the headlines "Dąbal in Moscow. Triumphal Welcome for 23 Polish Communists Exchanged by Soviet Russia."[21] Dąbal had already emerged at the founding of the Red Peasant International (Krestintern) as one of its principal leaders, and it was in this capacity that he addressed the Sixth Comintern Congress. But this did not prevent his liquidation.

STANISŁAW ŁAŃCUCKI was, with Dąbal, one of the first two Polish parliamentary deputies to join the Communist movement in 1920. He later sought asylum in the USSR and was swept away in the purge, like all his parliamentary colleagues.

JÓZEF CISZEWSKI, one of the founders of the Polish Communist Party in December 1918, and a member of its central committee; WACLAW WROBLEWSKI, an original and continuing member of this latter body; STANISLAW BOBINSKI, vice-director of the Communist University for National Minorities of the West (KUNMZ); and many other Polish leaders were liquidated by the Soviet police in Stalin's service. Also executed was JERZY SOCHACKI-CZESZEJKO, a member of the party's central committee, declared a "spy and provocateur working for Pilsudski."

THE EXTERMINATION OF THE LEADERS
OF THE YUGOSLAV PARTY

The Yugoslav Communist Party included neither former close associates of Lenin nor Jews in its leadership, but it came under condemnation by Stalin because its first chief, Sima Marković had opposed the Kremlin's new master in regard to the national question in 1925, and also because the Yugoslav party was outlawed in its own country and therefore its leaders who had fled to the USSR were at the mercy of the Soviet regime. Thus the Yugoslav party came very close to dissolution, as Tito later acknowledged: "In 1938, when I was in

Moscow . . . we were discussing whether to dissolve the Yugoslav Communist Party or not. All the Yugoslav leaders at that time in the Soviet Union had been arrested; I was alone, the party was weakened, without leadership; and I was there alone."[22]

The charges leveled against the Yugoslav leaders were presumably much the same as those used against the Poles and all other foreign Communist chiefs who had taken refuge in the USSR: they were termed hired agitators in the pay of capitalist espionage. Stalin had no need to give these foreign leaders a mock trial; it was enough to arrest them and then inform them of their sentence.

All top Yugoslav leaders—with the sole exception of Tito— were thus declared "enemies and spies" and met the fate reserved for such unfortunates. The following are the most important in this group:

SIMA MARKOVIĆ, party secretary after 1919, headed the first Yugoslav delegation in Soviet Russia at the Third Comintern Congress. The only Yugoslav speaker at this occasion, he had a fairly sharp exchange of words with Zinoviev, but nonetheless was named a member of the ECCI. Arrested soon after his return to Yugoslavia, he was elected in absentia at the Fifth Congress as an alternate member of the ECCI. He served out his sentence and again was appointed secretary-general of the party. After several vicissitudes he went to live in the USSR. Without exercising any functions in either the party or the Comintern, he confined himself to working in the Soviet Academy of Sciences. In July 1939 he was arrested, together with his wife, and sentenced to ten years of forced labor without the privilege of correspondence—as an "agent of imperialism."[23] He died in prison or in detention elsewhere.

FILIP FILIPOVIĆ, secretary of the party upon its establishment in 1919 and its president in 1920, emigrated to Russia in 1924. He gave a report at the Fifth Comintern Congress and was placed on the ECCI at the time. Subsequently, under the pseudonym of B. Bošković, he remained a member of the ECCI, in which capacity he was reconfirmed at the next congress in 1928, when he also was named to leadership in the Balkan Communist Federation. He was seen for the last time one evening in 1937, in Moscow, as he was being taken away by agents of the NKVD.[24]

MILAN GORKIĆ (Josip Čižinski), employed during the 1920's in the central apparatus of the Communist Youth International, was a delegate at the Sixth Comintern Congress. He also served on the

Comintern control commission as the representative of Youth International. Secretary-general of the Yugoslav party during 1932–37, he was made an alternate member of the ECCI at its final congress. In 1937, he was arrested and executed along with his former wife, Betty Glane, a Ukrainian who once had been secretary to Boris Souvarine at the Comintern, and then supervisor of the Maxim Gorki Park of Culture in Moscow. She was arrested as a "spy for the British intelligence service."

DJUKA CVIJIĆ, a member of the party's central committee from 1920, later assumed the post of its political secretary. While Marković led the rightist faction of the party, Cvijić was head of its leftists. Both died at the hands of Stalin's executioners.

ŠTEFAN CVIJIĆ (Djuka's brother), who had killed two policemen, fled his country as a fugitive from justice. In 1934 he became secretary of the Communist Youth International. He traveled in secret through nearly all countries of Western Europe, including Spain in 1937. The following year he was arrested in Moscow to die later in prison.

VOJA VUJOVIĆ was a revolutionary whose career unfolded not in the Yugoslav Communist Party, but in the French, and in the central apparatus of the Communist Youth International, where he served as secretary-general. He spoke in the name of the Youth International at the Fourth Comintern Congress and became a member of the ECCI in 1924. He was the only member of the latter body to align himself publicly with Trotsky in 1927; this earned him the penalty of expulsion from the ruling hierarchy, and, finally, deportation to Siberia and death. Two of Voja's brothers closely tied to the work of the Yugoslav party shared the same fate. Rada, a member of the central committee of the party, and Grgur, a member of the central committee of Yugoslav Communist Youth, both of whom had previously served prison terms in their own country, joined the general migration to the USSR and perished there.

VLADA ČOPIĆ, a Communist parliamentary deputy and organizational secretary of the party, went to the Soviet Union in 1925 after a term in a Yugoslav prison, was party representative at the Comintern, and a member of the Yugoslav party's politburo. He was a commander of the Fifteenth International Brigade in the Spanish Civil War and was recalled to Russia in 1938 and subsequently arrested. He disappeared.

JOVAN MALIŠIĆ-MARTINOVIĆ was among the first group of

Yugoslav Communists sent to Soviet Russia for training. Appointed as political secretary to the central committee in 1928, he kept this post until 1931, only to vanish later in the relentless sweep of Stalin's purge.

ANTON MAVRAK, likewise an "apparatchik" trained in the central lair of the Comintern, succeeded Martinović as secretary of the central committee of the Yugoslav party and finally followed his predecessor into the obscurity of death.

KOSTA NOVAKOVIĆ, Communist deputy, spokesman of the Yugoslav Communist left-wing opposition at the Fourth Congress of the Comintern in 1922 (using the assumed name "Stanić"), escaped from a Yugoslav prison in 1926, entered the Balkan apparatus of the Comintern and went to live in Moscow, where he was arrested in 1937 and disappeared.

KAMIL HORVATIN, a member of the central committee, left Yugoslavia for Russia in 1929 and became a member of the Yugoslav party's politburo, but was arrested with his wife, Jovanka, at the beginning of the purge in 1936 and disappeared.

IVO GRŽETIĆ-FLAJŠER, a member of the central committee, was the party's representative at the Comintern when he too fell victim to the purge in its earliest days.

PETKO MILETIĆ, a member of the central committee, was glorified as a "hero of the international proletariat" for his stance in the face of the Yugoslav police. "Petko Miletić," one reads, "heroically endured these tortures as only Bolsheviks are able to endure them."[25] In 1938 Miletić arrived in Moscow. A few days later he was arrested as an *agent provocateur* and shot.

SIMA MILJUŠ, a Communist deputy, sought refuge in the USSR, together with his wife. Both were taken into custody and never heard from again. They shared the fate of the other Yugoslav Communist leaders, to whom must further be added the names of MLADEN ČONIĆ and NIKOLA KOTUR.

The obscurity into which they vanished has remained largely unilluminated by the discriminatory rehabilitation indulged in by Tito's regime. It rehabilitated Filip Filipović, but left the "antiparty" label fixed to Sima Marković; it rehabilitated Rada Vujović, but has remained silent about his brother Voja; it rehabilitated Štefan Cvijić, but not his elder brother Djuka; Tito's own predecessor, Milan Gorkić, is still regarded not merely as "antiparty" but practically as a "suspicious figure," while Petko Miletić retains the stigma of "agent of the Yugoslav police."

THE MURDER OF THE GERMAN COMMUNIST LEADERS

Those of the German Communist Party who were opposed to the dictates of Moscow's leaders and, later, to those of Stalin himself, had almost fifteen years (from 1919 to 1933) to demonstrate their position at home and, ultimately, to draw the thunder of the Comintern. During this period the founders and the earliest leaders of the German party—Paul Frölich, Ernst Reuter (Friesland), Heinrich Brandler, August Thalheimer, Ruth Fischer, Arkadi Maslow, and others—had already been expelled from the Party by a decision of Moscow when they went into exile in 1933 (unlike the Polish and Yugoslav leaders, who still belonged to the Party, although they were often aloof from it, at the time of their emigration). Consequently, the German Communist émigrés who arrived in Moscow after 1933 were composed exclusively of leaders who had participated in the Stalinization of their party and of the Comintern.

HUGO EBERLEIN, a member of the central committee of the German party from its establishment in December 1918, was the only German Communist leader who could boast of having participated in the First Comintern Congress in 1919 and the last one in 1935. He was the only German representative at the founding congress, indeed the only genuine delegate from Western Europe. He shared the chairmanship of the gathering with Lenin and Platten. In 1922 he returned to Moscow, entered the Executive Committee and the Secretariat of the Comintern, and presented a report to the Fourth Congress. At the Sixth Congress he won election to the Comintern control commission and was reaffirmed in this capacity at the next congress. As late as 1937, *Inprecor* published an article by Eberlein entitled, "The Soviet Republic of Volga Germans—the Freest German Republic in the World." But a few days later, Eberlein was to lose his own fredom—just as the German Volga Republic itself soon was to be abolished. The suddenness of Eberlein's seizure by the Soviet police is described in this way by Herbert Wehner:

> The evening after Hugo Eberlein's arrest, Eva Sindermann, wife of Rudolf Lindau, who worked in the cadre section of the Comintern, expressed apprehension that she would doubtless encounter

difficulties. Very recently she had attended a party in celebration of Eberlein's birthday, which had been arranged by a small group that included Pieck. Pieck had even made a brief speech praising Eberlein's qualities and declaring that the moment was approaching when Eberlein would once more assume his position of leadership. She could not have had the slightest presentiment then that Eberlein was to be arrested soon afterwards.[26]

On the very eve of the arrest, Dimitrov himself had spoken with Eberlein concerning some budgetary matters.

HERMAN REMMELE, a member of the politburo of the German party for several years and a deputy in the Reichstag, also occupied seats on the ECCI and its Presidium from 1926 to 1928. He was reelected to the latter posts at the Sixth Congress, at which juncture Stalin was taking the Comintern firmly in hand. Remmele represented the German party in the Comintern until his arrest in 1937. His subsequent death was followed by the massacre of his entire family: his son Helmuth and his daughter-in-law, later his wife and daughter.

LEO FLIEG, who at the Sixth Comintern Congress was an elected member of the control commission, was an *éminence grise* of German communism. A member of the politburo, he was responsible for the party's secret apparatus—that is, its operations within the jurisdiction of Piatnitsky's OMS (relations with Moscow, funds from Moscow, false documents, and so on), and its activities aimed at subverting the German army. He was living in Paris in 1937 when he was summoned to Moscow. "He stepped off the train in Moscow right into the hands of the NKVD and was never heard of again."[27]

HANS KIPPENBERGER, head of the military intelligence service of the German party and a Communist deputy, arrived in Moscow in 1936 and was soon arrested, charged with being an agent of the Reichswehr, and executed.

HEINZ NEUMANN, member of the politburo and, with Remmele and Thälmann, one of the three leaders of the party during the first phase of Stalinization served as a Comintern emissary from China to Spain. Forced to take refuge in the USSR, he was arrested in April 1937 and disappeared in Soviet jails. His wife, Margarete Buber-Neumann, also was arrested and, in 1940, delivered to the Nazis.

FRITZ DAVID was not an important figure in the German Communist Party, but acquired notoriety as a victim of the great purge.

Editor of the party's daily newspaper, *Die Rote Fahne*, he fled to Russia upon Hitler's advent to power, arriving there in March 1933. He joined the Comintern's propaganda service (Agitprop) in the capacity of secretary, wrote for *Pravda*, and worked in close collaboration with Wilhelm Pieck. David attended the Seventh Comintern Congress as a delegate but was arrested shortly thereafter, charged with having planned to assassinate Stalin by order of Trotsky and of Trotsky's son, Sedov! Thrust together with Zinoviev and Kamenev into the hapless role of minor codefendant in the first great show trial of August 1936, David was sentenced to death—as, indeed, were all the other accused.

WERNER HIRSCH, secretary to Ernst Thälmann, fled to the Soviet Union and likewise was arrested and liquidated. The same fate lay in store for FRITZ SCHULTE and AUGUST CREUTZBURG, both members of the central committee; HEINRICH SÜSSKIND, editor-in-chief of *Die Rote Fahne*; WILLY LEOW, vice president of the party's shock troop organization (Roter Frontkämpferbund), and HEINRICH KURELLA, editor of *Inprecor,* which was published in German in Berlin until 1933. Among the few leaders who passed through the prisons without losing their lives were BERNARD KOENEN (released in 1939, but again arrested soon after) and ROBERTA GROPPER, former Reichstag deputy. Both returned to East Germany at the end of the Second World War, after the entry of the Red Army.

HERMANN SCHUBERT, a member of the central committee at the moment of Hitler's triumph in 1933, joined the fugitive party leadership in Paris (Auslandskomitee). Summoned to Moscow, he represented the German party in the Central European secretariat of the Comintern until his arrest, as related by Herbert Wehner:

> Hermann Schubert, who worked for the executive committee of Red Aid after being dropped from the party leadership, was preparing to take part in a debate organized by the Presidium of the ECCI, with a number of the organization's officials present, when Ercoli (Togliatti), chairman of the meeting, asked him whether it was true that he had expressed himself in the manner testified to in a letter written by Malke Schorr, Austrian official of Red Aid. In the letter, which Ercoli read aloud then and there, the woman described a brief conversation she had had with Schubert in a corridor of the Red Aid headquarters building. She had drawn Schubert's attention to the fact that Red Aid should take advantage of the Moscow trials in its international propaganda, in particular of Trotsky's relations

with the Nazis. Schubert had replied that this propaganda would be ineffective, because the enemy could retort that Lenin had crossed Germany in a sealed car with the permission of the Kaiser's militarists. Malke Schorr insisted that measures be taken against Schubert, who had dared put Lenin and Trotsky on an equal plane! Ercoli repeated his query and demanded that Schubert answer yes or no. Schubert wished to explain the circumstances of the conversation and the sense of his answer to Malke Schorr, but he was cut short. Soon afterward, he was arrested.[28]

GRETE WILDE, leader of the Communist Youth in Germany before Hitler's takeover, was the German Communist Party representative in the cadre section of the Comintern before her arrest and sentencing to ten years of forced labor at Karaganda, where she died.

To those arrested or murdered must be added the name of MAX HÖLZ, famous Communist *franc-tireur* of 1920–21 (that is to say of the Kapp-Lüttwitz putsch and the "March action"), who became a hero of the Comintern by being apprehended and convicted by the German authorities. At the Third Comintern Congress in 1921, Radek presented a resolution in favor of Hölz, and in 1927 *Inprecor* published an article demanding a judicial review of his trial. Released in 1928 and feted as a hero, Hölz left the following year for the USSR, where he soon lost his illusions: "With increasing vigor he demanded that he be allowed to return to Germany. He was counseled against it, denied a passport, and was prevented by every possible means from contacting the German ambassador."[29] This occurred before Hitler's rise to power and before the great purge. The Soviet police did not get around to ridding themselves of him until 1935, when he was found drowned in the Volga, near Nizhni-Novgorod. "Max Hölz, wearing his revolutionary decorations, was buried with full Soviet honors, with music and solemn orations, but not before the rumor had spread that NKVD agents had plied him with alcohol and then drowned him in the river like a mangy dog."[30] The facts surrounding this murder have been confirmed by a high official of the Soviet secret apparatus, W. G. Krivitsky: "Hölz was killed by the GPU because his glorious revolutionary past made him a potential leader of the revolutionary opposition to the Comintern."[31]

MAX LEVIN (or Levien) was another veteran of the German revolution who came to a tragic end. He even had been a participant in the 1905 revolution in Russia and had later met Lenin and other

Bolshevik leaders. He was active in the German Socialist movement and attended the founding congress of the German Communist Party (Spartakusbund) on December 30, 1918. Levin soon emerged as one of the Communist leaders in the final phase of the Bavarian Soviet republic set up in Munich. In flight after this regime's collapse, he was arrested in Vienna. He finally succeeded in reaching Soviet Russia in 1921, where he was to remain from then on. In 1934, just before the great purge, his name appeared in a published collection, dedicated to Lenin, of reminiscences by old revolutionaries, but later all trace of him was lost.

THE VICTIMS OF THE NKVD: FROM FINLAND TO GREECE

All Communist parties which were outlawed in their countries and whose leaders were refugees in Russia had to pay a blood tribute during Stalin's great purge. The Finns who had come to Russia after the failure of their 1918 revolution were not forgotten twenty years later. After 1936, they suffered the common fate Stalin had reserved for so many Communists, both Russian and foreign.

KULLERVO MANNER had been Socialist president of the Finnish parliament in 1917. In January 1918 he was named president of the fourteen-member People's Commissariat (one of the members of which was Otto Kuusinen) and sought refuge in Russia. On August 29, 1918, he directed the founding congress of the Finnish Communist Party in Petrograd, and the following year he participated in the founding congress of the Comintern. At its Second Congress, he was admitted to the ECCI, on which he was still seated before the Fourth Congress. He was reelected to the ruling body at the close of the Sixth Congress. Nevertheless, the Soviet police did not spare him: arrested and "judged," he was sentenced to death along with his wife; then his term was commuted to ten years in prison—that is, to a slower but equally certain death in Stalin's camps.

EDWARD GYLLING was finance minister in the Finnish revolutionary council of January 1918; it was he who signed the Soviet-Finnish treaty with Lenin, Trotsky and Stalin on March 1, 1918, in Petrograd. A fugitive in Russia, he participated in the leadership of the Finnish Communist Party until his arrest.

EERO HAAPALAINEN, commander of the Finnish Red Guard and minister of war in the revolutionary government, also became a victim in the USSR, along with JUKKA LETOSAR, like him a founder of the party, and several other leaders.

Since the Communist parties of the three Baltic countries also had been declared illegal, many of their leaders sought a haven in the USSR and occupied important posts in the Comintern's central apparatus. From the earliest years of the Comintern, several Baltic party workers had been associated closely either with the clandestine section (OMS) or with the police section (control commission) of the Comintern. Two noteworthy examples of this category were Anvelt, chief of the Estonian Communist Party and Angaretis, who headed the Lithuanian party.

JAN ANVELT was elected to membership on the control commission at the Sixth Comintern Congress and reelected at the Seventh Congress, during the period in which Stalin was eliminating from the Comintern leadership all those whose loyalty to himself personally he had any reason to question. Tuominen says of Anvelt,

> At the beginning of the 1930's, he held leading posts in the Comintern. He was at that time president of the control commission in effect the No. 1 man of the Communist International Tribunal, a domain in which Balts had long had priority. He could also be considered the chief of the Comintern GPU, since he had been asked to investigate the political deviationists in the various Communist parties and to expose violations of Party discipline, as well as espionage activities. His power was great because he had the right to bring against any party ominous accusations which could prove disastrous to them. . . . He was therefore a dangerous man in every respect. For this reason the question of doing away with him was debated during a session of the Comintern Presidium. It was simply decreed that he had participated in enterprises which were deleterious to the Soviets and that for twenty years he had caused a great deal of harm.[32]

Putting an end to Anvelt automatically menaced the entire central committee of the Estonian party with a purge, as Tuominen points out: "At the same time, it was declared that the entire central committee of the Estonian party also had been compromised. Anvelt's right-hand man, Alass, who had managed the financial affairs of the Estonian party, was arrested along with three or four other Estonian leaders."[33]

One of these leaders was HANS PÖGELMAN, the only Estonian present at the founding of the Comintern in 1919. He was first made a member of the ECCI and then served on the control commission for several years afterward, gaining reelection at the Sixth Congress.

Eventually arrested for "Estonian nationalist deviation," he was executed in 1938.[34]

The same fate was meted out to the leaders of the Lithuanian Communist Party, among whom ZIGMAS ALEKSA ANGARETIS is best known because he was, after October 1917, assistant commissar on Lithuanian affairs in the commissariat of nationalities directed by Stalin, and later Commissar of the interior in the Lithuanian Communist government during 1918–19. Angaretis was one of the principal "policemen" of the Comintern organization; he was regularly reelected to the control commission at the congresses of 1924, 1928 and 1935, and thus had a hand in all purges ordered by Stalin against "deviationists" in the Comintern. Once the great purge was under way, he was in the front ranks of the accusers. This fact is underlined in the reminiscences of a Yugoslav Communist living in Moscow during this period: "Presiding over the Yugoslav purge commission was Angaretis, chairman of the control commission."[35] But not even he was to be spared, and his ultimate liquidation carried the entire Lithuanian party leadership with it: "He was accused of espionage and arrested with all the other members of the central committee. The charge against them was that they were all working under the orders of Lithuania's semi-fascist dictator, Smetona."[36]

The Latvians were doomed to similar martyrdom—the leaders as well as the great number of active party members. Besides Berzin, already discussed (pp. 145–46), JAN KRUMINS should be mentioned. He was head of the Latvian section of the Comintern from 1931 until his arrest and execution in 1938. According to a written account by Bruno Kalnins (in the possession of the present author),

> After this arrest, the Latvian section was dissolved, the Latvian edition of *Prometheus* and the Latvian Communist journal *Krievijas Cina*, published in Moscow, were closed. Most of the 13,336 Latvian Communists organized within the framework of the Communist Party of the Soviet Union, including every single one of the leaders, were arrested and sent to forced labor camps or shot. Not one of the Latvian Communist leaders was able to return to his country after the forced annexation of Latvia to the Soviet Union in 1940.

The Hungarian Communist leaders chose the common path of self-exile after the downfall of their ephemeral Soviet republic in 1919. Like their Finnish colleagues, many of the people's commissars of this regime managed to escape the "White terror" only to fall victim to Stalin's "Red terror." The destiny of the most prominent among them BÉLA KUN, is described elsewhere in this book (pp. 302–04).

JÓZSEF POGÁNY (*pseud*. John Pepper, Lang, Strong) and several of his Socialist comrades joined Béla Kun's group on March 21, 1919, when the two parties concluded an agreement opening the way for proclamation of the Soviet Republic. He was a people's commissar until the regime was overthrown, whereupon he left Hungary and joined the Comintern's central apparatus. He was Béla Kun's lieutenant in the "March action," and the following year left for the United States, where he served as Moscow's emissary until 1929. A speaker at the Third, Fifth and Sixth Comintern congresses, he was attacked scathingly at the Sixth Congress by a young Stalinist, Lominadze, whose harangue was the unmistakable precursor of "Pepper's" imminent fall (a circumstance which did not preclude, however, the tragic end later of Lominadze himself).

BÉLA SZEKELY, people's deputy commissar of finance, and DEZSÖ BOKÁNYI, member of the central committee and a people's commissar of labor, both shared the fate of Béla Kun. At the trial of Russian Socialist-Revolutionaries in Moscow in 1922, Bokányi was delegated by the Comintern, together with Clara Zetkin, to be witness for the prosecution. For his behavior on that occasion, and for his general revolutionary past, he was praised in glowing terms by Karl Radek:

> Further were the S.R.'s indicted by the leader of the Hungarian workers, Bokányi. The appearance of this adored leader of the Hungarian workers revealed like a flash the historical significance of the S.R. trial. Bokányi has been fighting for thirty years among the Hungarian workers against the Hungarian capitalists and landowners. . . . He faced death in the prisons of the Hungarian White Terror, just as hundreds of other Hungarian workmen, who were murdered without a trial, before the eyes of civilized Europe. . . . The helping hand of Soviet Russia saved him from the hell of the Hungarian counterrevolution.[37]

After the downfall of the Soviet regime in Hungary, L. MAGYAR went to work for the Comintern's central apparatus and was active in Agitprop, where he published books and wrote for *Inprecor*. Before he and his wife, Alice, were arrested in the great purge, he undertook several secret missions abroad, including one in France during 1932–33. He died at Solovetski, but his wife survived fifteen years of detention and was able to return to East Germany in 1955. Several other leaders of the Hungarian Soviet Republic died under suspicious circumstances: JÓZSEF RABINOVICZ, former prisoner of war in Russia, who had embraced Bolshevism and returned with Béla Kun to establish the Hungarian Communist Party, in which he was a member of the central committee as well as party secretary in charge of Agitprop; BÉLA VÁGÓ, member of the central committee and commissar for internal affairs; JOSEPH HAUBRICHT, trade-union leader, commander-in-chief of the Budapest revolutionary troops, People's commissar of commerce, member of the control commission of the Communist-Socialist party unified under the Hungarian Soviet Republic; ISTVÁN BIERMANN, one of the leaders of the Budapest Soviet in 1919, who escaped to the Soviet Union and was promoted member of the central committee of the Ukrainian Communist Party, and who died in 1937 at the age of forty-seven; JÁNOS KOCSIS, member of the central committee of the Hungarian Communist Party, sentenced to two years of imprisonment by the Horthy regime, took refuge in the Soviet Union in 1929, died in 1938, thirty-nine years old; FERENC JANCSIK, supreme commander of Budapest's Red Guard, in Russia since 1922, died in 1938; EDE CHLEPKO, a member of the central committee of the Hungarian Communist Party since its foundation, political commissar of the Red Guard, escaped to the Soviet Union in 1923, died in 1938.

Among the many other leaders of the Hungarian Communist regime who were persecuted during the great purge and sent to concentration camps were ELEK BOLGÁR, former envoy of the Hungarian Soviets in Vienna, two brothers of Rákosi—ZOLTÁN and FERENC BIRÓ—as well as BÉLA SZÁNTÓ, a member of the central committee of the Hungarian party in 1919. A few managed to survive and return to Hungary in 1945.

The Rumanian Communist Party, also outlawed at home, had nearly its entire central committee in refuge in Moscow. Its principal figure was Anna Pauker's husband, MARCEL PAUKER, secretary-general of the party and its representative in the Comintern. Marcel and Anna both had been active in the Communist movement in Rumania from its beginning and had become hardened professional revolutionaries. When they participated in the Fourth Congress of the Comintern in 1922, Marcel spoke in the name of the Rumanian delegation. Anna was arrested in 1936 in Rumania while her husband was in the USSR, but he did not wait long for his own arrest there. Marcel was less fortunate than his wife, who was freed five years later from the "monarcho-fascist" jails of Rumania. Here is a comment on his death by Ivan Karaivanov, a Comintern functionary well acquainted with him: "The engineer Pauker was a well-trained Marxist and one of the best men in the Rumanian Communist Party. But he did not work for very long after his wife's arrest (1936); he was accused of collusion with the Zinoviev opposition, arrested, and liquidated following the trial of Zinoviev and Kamenev without being brought to trial himself."[38]

The same source lists several other members of the Rumanian central committee who, like Marcel Pauker, had remained in Moscow: MARIA CIOBAN, the representative of the Rumanian party in the Balkan secretariat of the Comintern in 1935, when Tito ("Walter") came to work there; Kodreanu, Joanu, Vanda, pseudonyms used at the time by one or another of the following leaders of the Rumanian party, all victims of the purge: CLARA SCHAIN, in the USSR since 1926; the engineer ALEXANDRU DOBROGEANU (son of the founder of the Rumanian Socialist movement), contributor to *Inprecor*; DR. ROZVANY, leader of the Communist movement in Transylvania; LENUȚA PHILIPOVICI, a worker who had escaped from prison, and who was glorified as a heroine of the proletariat before her arrest in Russia.

They have all become "unpersons" according to George Orwell's formula. They no longer are mentioned in the official writings of the party—a sure indication that they have been done away with. The only deviation from this systematic silence was the attack against Marcel Pauker at a plenary session of the Rumanian party's central committee in December 1961; he was posthumously accused of factional struggle, of class-against-class tactics and other "crimes," the true responsibility for which rests, of course, with the Comintern itself. All this has been said without revealing either his having been in the USSR or his tragic fate, which proves that Marcel Pauker's name is not only outside the "rehabilitated" category, but that he is still included among those who were "antiparty."

The Greek Communist Party, thanks to its geographical location, was less obliged to transfer its seat to Moscow than the other illegal parties in the countries bordering the USSR. Nevertheless, this party also lost two of its top leaders during the great purge. One of them was ANDRONIKOS HAITAS, a member of the central committee from the earliest years of the party, its representative to Moscow during 1924–26, and secretary-general of the party by election at the congresses of 1927 and 1928. Arrested in 1929 by the Greek police, he succeeded in fleeing in 1931 with another imprisoned leader, GEORGE KOLOZOV, secretary-general of the Greek Communist Youth and a member of the central committee of the party, who before his arrest had received his Communist training in Moscow at KUTV (Communist University of the Workers of the East).

In the USSR, Haitas was appointed professor of political economy at the University of Kuibyshev, but toward 1935 he was arrested on the charge of having taught the theories of Bukharin, and was shot. George Kolozov was assigned responsibility for the Greek minority in South Russia. Disillusioned with the Soviet regime, he succeeded in 1934 in sending his wife a letter through a sailor on a Greek ship. He concluded: "My ideals are dead. I am a man in despair, a doomed man."[39] Around 1935 or 1936, he was arrested, and it was later learned that he had been shot by "administrative decision" as a "traitor to socialism."

SOME SPECIAL CASES

If a Communist party was not prohibited in its own country but had a leader who had been compromised at home and then sought refuge in the USSR, Stalin's police did not forget him. In France, for example, the first two leaders of the Soviet spy ring were JOSEPH TOMMASI and JEAN CREMET. Both came under French police investigation, were forced to flee to the USSR, and subsequently died under suspicious circumstances—Tommasi of an "ulcer," quite suddenly, and Cremet "accidentally" during a mission to the Far East. Cremet since 1925 had been a member of the politburo of the French Communist Party and secretary of its central committee, and upon his arrival in the USSR was immediately named to the Presidium and the political secretariat of the ECCI. These latter assignments were effected at the end of 1926, but by 1927 he already had been dropped from the Comintern hierarchy. A young French Communist, in Moscow for the tenth anniversary of the Revolution, wrote about him in connection with a meeting of foreign Communists assembled to denounce Trotsky: "Cremet, a Frenchman in Moscow as a fugitive, was the only one to abstain publicly."[40] Henri Barbé, one of the French party leaders of the period, wrote of Cremet's demise:

> He knew some secrets which could be terribly compromising for the Soviet secret service. . . . It was at this time, at the beginning of 1929, that I learned in Moscow that Cremet would be given a mission. There was vague talk of a job which would be entrusted to him in the Far East. . . . I learned in Moscow several months later that Cremet had died as the result of an accident which had befallen him on the boat he was traveling on. Russian sources in the Comintern in Moscow secretly confided that Cremet had accidentally fallen overboard and that it had been impossible to rescue him. This more than strange disappearance took care of things all too well.[41]

GEORGE ANDREICHIN, of Bulgarian birth, was a militant member of the IWW (Industrial Workers of the World); he fled the United States just as he was slated to serve a sentence of several years in prison. Upon his arrival in Moscow, he was appointed a member of the Executive Committee of the International Red Trade Unions (Profintern, which had just been created in 1921) and chief of its Anglo-Saxon section. He later headed the Balkan and colonial sections but in 1927 did not hide his sympathies for Stalin's adversaries (Trotsky and the others), a political transgression which led to his arrest at the end of that year. Because of his fugitive status in the United States, the Soviet police felt exempted from the usual scruples observed in that period toward foreign Communists with legal and valid passports, who could invoke the protection of the embassies of their "bourgeois" countries and perhaps provoke a diplomatic scandal.[42] This, for example, was the reason that PIERRE CÉLOR, representative of the French Communist Party at the Comintern in 1931, was able to save his own life and that of his wife, after he had been "unmasked" as a "police agent" by the Comintern control commission: "A few days after the interrogation, Célor's wife, fearing for her husband's life, went to the French embassy and asked for its support and its help to enable her and Célor to return to France."[43]

But sometimes the Soviet police could act before the Communist leaders reached the decision to ask for embassy protection, as in the case of ARNE MÜNCH-PETERSON, a member of the central committee of the Danish Communist Party:

> Belonging to the Danish petty nobility, he had joined the Communist party and had become its representative in the Comintern. . . . Münch-Peterson was a Danish citizen, in Moscow in his

capacity as representative. Then one day he was placed under arrest by the GPU and nothing is known of what became of him after that. At one of the meetings of the control commission, there arose a question concerning him; the semi-official explanation of his arrest was that he had entertained relations with Axel Larsen, the official leader of the Danish party who around 1930 had been accused of being sympathetic to Trotsky.[44]

By the same token, if an alien female party member became a Soviet citizen by marriage, she lost her "bourgeois" protection and often followed her husband into prison or death. This was the fate of ROSE COHEN (wife of Petrovsky-Bennett), an Englishwoman who appeared as a speaker at the Sixth Congress of the Comintern. Petrovsky, of Polish-Jewish origin, was an alternate member of the Presidium of the Executive Committee and was in charge of the Anglo-Saxon section during 1928–30, while Stalin was engaged in harnessing the Comintern to his will. J. T. Murphy, English Communist leader, wrote of the woman, "I was not the only Englishman in the Hotel Luxe (1926). . . . Handsome Rose Cohen lived there too. Her love for Petrovsky, the one-time colleague of Trotsky in the days when the latter was Russia's commissar for war, landed her into a long spell in a Soviet prison."[45]

Finally, this fate was not reserved exclusively for European Communist leaders. Without doubt, they paid the highest price, since they formed the most numerous contingent in Moscow, but an Asiatic leader settling in the USSR might share the same lot, as was demonstrated in the case of the Iranian SULTAN ZADE. In Russia at the time of the Bolshevik revolution, he joined the Comintern and was elected at the close of the Second and Third congresses to membership on the ECCI, reappearing seven years later at the Sixth Congress of 1928. Stalin's purge was to take him too: "According to current Soviet historiography, Sultan Zade was a traitor."[46] He was liquidated in 1938.

TWO "EXCEPTIONS": THE ITALIAN AND BULGARIAN PARTIES

The Italian Communist movement, prohibited by Mussolini's regime, made the propitious decision to place most of its leaders and active party workers not in Soviet Russia, but in bourgeois France. Thus, almost all those among the hard core of Italian Communists who survived the Spanish Civil War, the French internment camps, and the Italian resistance struggle were able to preserve themselves. During

the great purge, few of the Italian leaders were in Moscow; nearly all
were in France or Spain. Some victims among the militant party
workers, however, had the bad luck to be in Russia, and of these,
some were arrested and brutally dealt with in prison. Among them
were PAOLO ROBOTTI (brother-in-law of Togliatti), who suffered
two broken ribs and spent more than two years in prison before he
was released, and EMILIO SERENI, director of the Italian Communist
journal in Paris, *La Voce Degli Italiani,* who was taken into custody
during a mission to Moscow at the time of the great purge, but later
regained his freedom.

There were other Italian Communist leaders who did not survive arrest and imprisonment—for example, VINCENZO BACCALA,
former secretary of the Roman Federation of the Italian Communist
Party. In addition, many rank-and-file party members came to Russia
seeking political asylum and work. They paid a heavy price during
the purge years, as testified by several Italian revolutionary trade
unionists who had been living as refugees in Soviet Russia from the
time of Lenin. One of them was FRANCESCO GHEZZI, who had fled
from Italy charged with killing a policeman during a "revolutionary"
strike. Arrested in Berlin in 1922, he was saved from extradition by a
campaign led by the Comintern and the Profintern. But no campaign
could save him when he was apprehended later in the USSR. By
1930, although suffering from tuberculosis, he had been in a Soviet
prison for eight months. An appeal was signed in his favor by Romain
Rolland, Panait Istrati, and Paul Langevin—the most glorious
names in the Communist cause in France at that time—but to no
avail: he was to remain in a prison camp and die.[47]

As for the relatively privileged lot of the Bulgarian Communist
leaders in the USSR, Djilas, recalling his conversations in Moscow in
1944, writes: "The Bulgarian émigrés were lucky that Dimitrov was
Secretary of the Comintern and a person with such authority. He
saved many of them."[48] Djilas also gives an example of a successful
intervention by Dimitrov: "I had already learned from Vlahović and
others that Chervenkov was the husband of Dimitrov's sister, that he
was to have been arrested at the time of the purges (the 'exposé' of
the political school where he was an instructor had already been published) but he took refuge with Dimitrov. Dimitrov intervened with
the NKVD and made everything in order."[49]

Wehner gives similar details: "Some of the Bulgarian Communists who were arrested were freed through Dimitrov's efforts. Among these were Vlahov, a veteran of the Macedonian Socialist movement, and Kabakchiev, one of the founders of the Bulgarian Communist Party and of the Communist International."[50]

But Dimitrov could not—or would not—save every Bulgarian Communist leader who fell into the hands of Stalin's police, as indicated by the fate of his codefendants in the Leipzig trial, BLAGOI POPOV[51] and VASIL TANEV. After having been feted as heroes in the Soviet Union and in the columns of the Comintern press, and after having had the honor of being received by Stalin personally and then photographed with the Soviet Politburo, they were soon presented with the other side of the coin. The same Comintern press published their self-criticism, and their fate was no different from that of the other victims.

It appears that the ultimate penalty was reserved for the "sectarian" leaders of the Bulgarian party, who before adoption of the popular-front tactics had been following a policy exactly contrary to it—a policy instigated and authorized by the Comintern itself, and which paralleled that of all other European parties. This group included PETER ISKROV, a member of the control commission and therefore active in police matters, who had been elected to this post at the Comintern congresses of 1928 and 1935. He was marked for purging at a plenary meeting of the Bulgarian central committee, held in Moscow during February–March, 1936. Among the other members of this "sectarian" leadership who were purged and never heard from again were BOJKOV and ROSSEN. They have not even earned the right to rehabilitation which was accorded, albeit posthumously, to one of their colleagues, KRUM GEKOV-BATCHVAROV, a Bulgarian delegate at the Fourth Comintern Congress in 1922 and, from 1925 to 1928, a student at the Lenin Military-Political Academy in Leningrad. Gekov-Batchvarov was serving as commissar of a Red Army brigade when he was arrested during the great purge.[52]

A similar fate lay in store for V. GANTCHEV-KOPRINKOV, who returned from Moscow to Bulgaria in 1927 in the double capacity of secretary of the central committee of the Communist Youth Organization and member of the Bulgarian Communist Party's central committee. In 1929 he was arrested in his home country and sentenced to prison, where he remained until his release in 1934. He then went back to the USSR, where he resumed his old post on the central committee of the Bulgarian party and was appointed director of the Bulgarian section in the Lenin School (under the pseudonym Ivan Nikolaevich Alexandrov). In time, however, he was arrested and lost his life—"during the period of the cult of personality," according to a recent report in the official journal of the Bulgarian Communist Party.[53]

THE REASON FOR THE MASSACRES

The staggering magnitude of this mass blood bath invariably led first the immediate victims, before their deaths, and then those who sought to investigate the grisly period, to try to comprehend its causes and rationale. Thus Herbert Wehner, a witness to these crimes, writes: "I could discern no system whatever in these abrupt and chaotic measures. . . . What was the line that was being followed with all these mass arrests, sentencings, executions, removals from official posts—in sum, all those measures which were creating a psychosis?"[54]

The only way to approach the truth is by applying the process of elimination. First, it is essential to remove from consideration all the indictments concocted by Stalin and his henchmen against the imagined infiltration into the Comintern of "enemy agents" and "foreign spies." Next, one should reject the fallacious explanations of some observers in the West who thought they were being "objective" in concluding that it was all merely a struggle for power between Stalin and the "Trotskyites," "Zinovievists," and "Bukharinists." There could not have been an internal power struggle involved in the massacres described here, because the victims were foreigners and therefore ineligible as potential rivals of Stalin (a charge which, strictly speaking, might have been made against the Russian Bolsheviks at the time of the great purge, but with only seeming validity). Nor does the explanation that the purpose of the massacre was to get rid of the remaining Trotskyite, Zinovievist, or Bukharinist elements suffice, for almost every foreign Communist leader arrested and killed by Stalin's police had in the past served Stalin against Trotsky, Zinoviev and Bukharin. The fact of the matter, far removed from the political-ideological clichés, is stark and chilling: the number of Communist leaders exterminated by Stalin far surpasses the total of their counterparts murdered by Hitler, Mussolini, and all other dictators and semi-dictators between the two wars; moreover—irony of ironies —Stalin sent to their deaths from the echelons of the Comintern more Stalinists than Trotskyites, Zinovievists, and Bukharinists combined.

In seeking the primary cause of Stalin's rage, it is also important to eschew explanations based either on the case of a single party within the Comintern or on an exclusively political rationalization. As an example of the first argument, the following explanation of the Polish massacres can be cited:

> The purge of the CPP's entire top strata and, finally, the complete dissolution of the party amounted to two things: first, the discarding of what Stalin must have regarded as an ineffective and unreliable instrument of policy, and second, the waging of preventive war against a potential opposition. Thus, it may be said that the CPP, one of the last major victims of the great purge, became one of the first victims of the Stalin-Hitler pact.[55]

This explanation, seemingly applicable to the fate of the Polish Communist leaders, is no help in any attempt to comprehend the massacre of the Balts, Finns, Germans, Yugoslavs, Rumanians and others, and the arrests and deaths of some of their wives and children.

A strictly political interpretation, even when extrapolated from the first argument, offers no more than an illusory key. In the words of a former member of the Comintern's central apparatus,

> I am convinced that Hitler's seizure of power and the tactics of the German Communists and the Soviet Union in the German question are directly tied up with the triumph of the Stalin "personality cult," and that the wave of terror against the Communists in the Soviet Union is linked with the consequences of the tactics from 1931 to 1933. This was also the conviction of many German and Russian Communists whom I met in the prisons and camps of the Soviet Union in the years of the terror.[56]

But neither does this explanation fit the tragic fate of the Baltic, Finnish, Yugoslav, Rumanian, and other leaders who did not have the remotest connection with Stalin's German policy before 1933. Some German Communist victims believed this to be the essential cause. It was neither the first nor the last time that victims failed to comprehend the reason for the evils befalling them. Captives of their own accustomed chain of thought, these Communists were unable to focus upon the nature of their situation because it did not figure in the context of their Leninist-Stalinist ABC.

The critical element was to be found in two determining factors: Stalin's personality and his impact on the political system he had been shaping since his accession to total power. Consequently, if we are to put our finger on the true reason for these massacres, we must avoid the mistake of restricting our scrutiny to specific victims, whether individuals or parties. The Comintern must be examined *in toto*, and, instead of a strictly political approach, we must seek a psychological, even psychopathological, approach, interwoven with the governmental structure at that juncture of Russian history.

Even before Stalin gave the order for the massacre, he felt contempt for the Comintern and its leaders. *"The Communist International represents nothing and only exists by our support,"* said Stalin before witnesses one day, as was disclosed later by Lominadze.[57] When Stalin, mesmerized by Hitler's meteoric rise and absorbed by his own foreign political maneuvers, decided to withdraw a substantial measure of his support from the Comintern, and then, bloodthirsty and cowardly, unleashed his storm of homicidal fury in 1936–39, he found an ideal arena to vent his frustrations: the mass of foreign Communist leaders, politically crushed in their own countries, stripped of all legal or diplomatic protection, totally at the mercy of Moscow.

No exclusively political interpretation could explain why it was necessary to murder, along with their wives and children, Comintern leaders who had been in Stalin's service for many years, some of whom had reached the age of seventy and had retired from all political activity. But once the paranoid traits of Stalin's personality are taken into account, the situation becomes more clear, and the genesis and pattern of Stalin's Comintern genocide become more comprehensible. Psychopathology plays a more important role here than in the massacres effected within the Bolshevik party, in which Stalin had to wage a power struggle against his competitors and opposition, whereas after 1929 only docile subjects, incapable of influencing Soviet domestic affairs, remained in the Comintern.

It was certainly not Stalin himself who made up lists of all foreign leaders in the Comintern doomed to die, but it was he who set the terrible machine in motion. Once the inexorable inertia of its forward movement was a fact, a collective psychosis was generated at all levels. The men of Stalin's entourage—the Party cadres, the police officials, the petty informers, the favor-curriers and sycophants—all displayed inordinate zeal in anticipating Stalin's wishes and plans for vengeance. The identical process took place in the Russian Communist Party and in the Comintern: from Manuilsky and Togliatti through the intermediate echelons down to the ordinary rank and file, each individual found himself cast as accomplice in this collective murder plot until his own turn might come (as it did for so many) to lay his own bewildered head on the common chopping block.

Just as the Molotovs, Kaganoviches, Zhdanovs, Mikoyans and Khrushchevs were able to play the game successfully for the sake of their personal careers and lives, so did some leaders in the Comintern manage to save their own skins while helping to dig the graves of former colleagues. Thus, Tuominen recounts the manner in which Manuilsky instituted charges against Béla Kun, while Wehner as a first-hand witness describes the denunciation of Hermann Schubert by Togliatti before a full session of the Presidium of the ECCI. But more often than not, the accomplices perished in their turn, as was true of thousands of Russian Chekists, beginning with Yagoda and Yezhov. Wehner summarizes the role and the final expiation of two German leaders in charge of the cadres section of the Comintern: "Grete Wilde and 'Cadre-Müller' were themselves arrested after having been instrumental either in the arrest of some thousands of German Communist Party members or in making trouble for them with their depositions."[58]

The ferocity of the process of mutual extermination in the Comintern was intensified by two factors: the existence of factions and rankling animosities inside the exiled parties, and the xenophobia of the Great Russians, to whom all foreigners were suspect. The members of hostile factions, or simply those among the ordinary party workers who had reason to despise one another, did not hesitate to act as informers to the Soviet police (in the guise of the control commission or the commission of inquiry) who duly took account of these denunciations, arresting first those against whom they were directed and then the denunciators themselves. All foreign leaders living as refugees in the USSR either had been subjected to confinement in "capitalist" prisons or had been forced to flee from the "capitalist" police; using this fact as a starting point, it was easy to concoct an exposé of their suspicious past and their alleged ties with the "capitalist" police. Stalin's system of justice needed nothing more: the foreign leaders were culpable not only because they had been politically defeated in their own countries, but also because they were *foreigners,* a category which had become especially suspect in the collective psychosis of the great purge.

Stalin basked confidently in the knowledge that he could order the extermination of the Comintern leaders with utter impunity, without encountering a single obstacle either in the execution of his plan or in its repercussions abroad. In fact, this blood bath, perhaps the most stunning in contemporary political history, was able to proceed in its relentless course almost unreported by the press and other communication media of the Western world. Furthermore, precisely at this time Stalin and Soviet communism were being adjudged by the West to be "undergoing a process of democratic evolution," and the Comintern was receiving a new impetus under the cover of the popular front from France and Spain to distant Chile, posing as the common man's champion in the struggle for humanity and democracy— at the very hour when the bloodiest terror was annihilating the leading cadres of this same Comintern in the land of the Soviets.

Comments on the Massacre

by

BORIS SOUVARINE

The whole truth probably never will be told about the massacre of the Communists carried out under Stalin. It falls upon the few survivors among those who participated in the leadership of the Third International in Lenin's time to contribute to establishing the truth—at least to the extent of their knowledge.

The socialists, syndicalists, anarchists, and pacifists who first heeded Lenin's appeals and became Communists in the years of turmoil following the First World War—these militants with diverse backgrounds and widely varied ideas—were far from sharing the coherent and systematic doctrine held by the International's founder. They were unaware even of its essential content, which had been elaborated in the course of the first twenty years of the century. They were inspired on the one hand by a feeling of humanitarian opposition to the European war, which they saw as a supreme form of homicidal violence, and on the other hand, paradoxically, by admiration for the Soviet revolution, which was no less cruel and inhuman, but about which they had only a vague idea. A number of conflicts, crises, and breakups were bound to arise from this initial confusion.

The original supporters, except for the handful of cynics or parasites who turn up in any political movement, were men of good will devoted to a cause worthy of respect. As a result, most of the early international Communist leaders became dissidents, either on their own or against their will, after Lenin's death. The ones who were willing or compelled to adapt themselves, for one reason or another, to second-generation "Marxism-Leninism" had to deal with Stalin when he began to turn the International into a mere instrument of his design, a tool of his foreign policy aimed at seeking an agreement with Hitler. By the late thirties, these men were no longer what they had been in the early twenties. They had adopted a line of conduct in which the means and the ends were not in harmony, and they had put themselves at the service of a state which had survived at the expense of its fundamental reasons for existing.

In the necrology of the preceding essay, the Polish Communists lead the sinister parade of their fellows to martyrdom, and they deserve special attention. The most important among them were considered an elite in the International, on an equal footing with Lenin and Trotsky, whose trials and tribulations they had shared under the tsars. They spoke French, German, and Russian with the same ease as their mother tongue; they were real Europeans, cultivated and knowledgeable men, who felt at home with both the Russian intelligentsia and their Western European brothers-in-arms. Stalin loathed them because of their evident intellectual and moral superiority and because he regarded them as an obstacle to a possible agreement with Hitler. After all, how could any normal Pole have sanctioned the splitting up of his country and the disappearance of Poland as a national entity as the price of an agreement aimed at destroying traditional civilization?

Among the Poles, I knew Warski and Broński best. They were friends of Dr. Jacques Goldenberg, who belonged to our party in France. I was also close to Walecki, who under Comintern instructions had become intimately concerned with French Communist affairs. These men came from the Russianized part of Poland and were in no way different from cosmopolitan Russians; their long residence in France and Switzerland had familiarized them with Western socialism. The appealing Dr. Goldenberg, who had been a resident of Paris for many years and had served in the French army as a medical officer, constituted the first link between his Polish friends and the young French Communists.

Warski was one of the founders of the Social Democratic party in Poland, a close friend of Rosa Luxemburg, a theoretician and spokesman of his party (which he frequently represented at Russian and international congresses), a highly respected and to all appearances invulnerable figure. When Stalin suddenly threw him in jail, he lost his sanity: there was cause enough. As for Walecki, he originally belonged to the Polish Socialist party, whose left wing, mainly under his influence, rallied to communism. He was a brilliant and talented man who enjoyed the company of Frenchmen, whose language he knew in all its subtleties. Like the unfortunate Warski, he perished without knowing the reason why, amidst the worst moral and physical agonies, as did many of his comrades. When one thinks of Soviet prisons under Stalin, one must compel one's imagination to visualize horrible conditions—conditions likely to break down the personality of any individual with the least bit of sensibility.

Under Stalin the words "prison" and "camp" were equivalent to terror and torture. I never can think without profound grief of the fate of Wera Kostrzewa and Henryk Brandt, both victims of GPU torturers, nor of the lot of so many other distinguished individuals. Though I do not wish to limit my compassion to those whom I happened to know more intimately, how can one avoid personalizing such collective misfortune? Wera Kostrzewa personified the finest fighters in this generation for the exploited and the oppressed; she combined the charm of intellectual brilliance with womanly refinement and manly courage. Brandt, a mathematician, was a sparkling conversationalist who had become enthusiastic about the rebirth of Soviet industry and was doing his share in promoting it, together with Piatakov. These persons spoke French and Russian so fluently we never thought of them as Poles. Anyway, national differences were ignored at that time among like-minded men devoted to the same ideal. It took Stalin to introduce odious nationalisms and chauvinisms in what used to be, before his days, the Communist International.

In the same way, neither Radek nor Unszlicht was regarded as Polish in our circles: they belonged body and soul to the Bolshevik party and the Soviet state. Together with Zinoviev and Bukharin, Radek belonged to the *troika* which was the permanent ruling group of the Comintern, by delegation from the Communist Party in power (Lenin and Trotsky kept in close touch with developments, but intervened directly only under certain circumstances). Radek spoke little French, so we conversed in Russian. He asked many questions, because his ideas of France were highly bookish, and he was always joking, in keeping with his well-earned reputation as a story teller and punster. His lamentable end hardly allows one to recall the lighter moments of his astonishing career, for his satirical zest and sometimes uncharitable sarcasm earned him much hostility which was translated into suspicious and malevolent rumors. To the extent that my modest opinion weighs in this matter, I would not confirm such hostile appraisals.

When I passed through Berlin in 1923, I talked with Radek, who told me of his worries about the conflict which had already broken out between the Moscow Politburo and Trotsky. He summarized the situation and expressed his own wishes in about these words: "Well, they are eight to one; let us hope this will make for a balance and they will continue to work together." This was not an attitude of opposition or of intrigue. When I was expelled from the Party by the Fifth Congress in 1924, Radek was the only one who thought of my financial predicament and, putting his hand in his pocket, inquired: "Don't you need some money?" I managed to get along without his help, but I never forgot the gesture. (Being excluded from the Party meant also that I lost my room, in the Moscow of 1924, at the height of a dramatic housing shortage, whose acuteness can hardly be imagined; but the Serebriakovs offered me their friendly hospitality, in the Russian tradition, as soon as winter came.) Trotsky and his supporters suspected Radek of having incited Blumkin, upon his return from Prinkipo where he had secretly met Trotsky, to make his confession to the GPU; he then was shot at once. But an equally plausible interpretation has it that Radek, on the contrary, tried to get Blumkin out of trouble by advising him to face the police and thereby prove his loyalty. Radek's role in the "witch trial" of January 1937 poses a thornier question; he was the first to pronounce Tukhachevsky's name from the bench of the accused. The only available source in this matter is the official record which, of course, is of no help in forming a judgment.

As to Unszlicht, he was in a way Radek's antithesis: cold, taciturn, reserved, committing himself as little as possible, as befit his role as head of the Cheka. I came into contact with him personally only at the Lubianka headquarters when I tried to intercede for political prisoners, which was very much frowned upon. His correct and icy reception hardly concealed his disdain for a sentimental comrade who was incapable, in his eyes, of understanding the cruel necessities of civil war. In my days he was seen at the Comintern only once, at the 1923 meeting of the enlarged Presidium at which it was decided to attempt a revolution in Germany. Stalin and Dzerzhinski also first participated in our deliberations at this meeting, for the apparatus of the Soviet state was about to throw its whole weight into the balance in a decisive move, and consequently the secret services were to play an essential role. But that story will have to occupy a separate page when the full history of the Comintern is written.

Having mentioned Broński, who was among the friends of Dr. Goldenberg that I had the good fortune to meet frequently, I should now devote a few words to him, although his work was not directly linked with the International. Broński completed his higher education in Germany. As a very young member of the Socialist Democratic Party of Poland and Lithuania, he fought in his country during the 1905 revolution and for this he spent long months imprisoned. Once released, he went to Switzerland and participated assiduously in the actions of the Socialist Party in Zurich, belonging at the same time to the Polish Social Democratic group. During the First World War, he joined Lenin in the Zimmerwald Left and was a delegate to the Kienthal Conference. In 1917 he returned to Russia. After the October Revolution, he assumed the highest function in the economic organization of the State, was "elected" to the Executive Committee of the Soviets, later appointed ambassador to Vienna, and finally became a member of the Communist Academy and professor of political economy at the University of Moscow. A man like Broński—cultured, polite, irreproachable—could not help but attract the murderous animadversion of the Despot.

I had only casual contacts with the other Poles of the Executive Committee or the Polish delegates at our congresses, except for my frequent business meetings with Edward Próchniak while he stayed in Moscow (he shuttled back and forth between Moscow and Warsaw). Of Próchniak, a serious and lusterless man, I can say nothing except that he typified his party to such an extent that his murder and the dissolution of the Polish party were responses to the same inexorable paranoic logic capable of decreeing both. Łapiński, an affable man and an economist of distinction, worked permanently in Berlin where he was in charge of an efficient documentation, information, and observation service, which was indispensable to the Soviet power. It seems indecent to speak up at all in defense of any of the annihilated Polish Communist leaders and militants, lest by so doing one would seem to admit that there could exist, in theory, a shadow of justification for the atrocious methods of their executioner.

The same applies to the other victims mentioned in the death roll. Christian Rakovsky, like Radek and Unszlicht, really should be put among the Russians and Ukrainians, although he was Rumanian and Bulgarian by origin and French-educated. As long as Lenin lived, Rakovsky was one of the main leaders of the International. Relegated later to diplomatic rank, he finally fell victim to the carnage whereby Stalin rid himself of Lenin's and Trotsky's collaborators to be free to make deals with Hitler undisturbed. In Rakovsky the early French Communists had a friend, a model of disinterested devotion and valor, and I cannot evoke his memory unmoved. Nor can I put into words my personal feeling of horror and disgust for the tyrant who threw to the wild beasts of the GPU Rakovsky's unfortunate wife and his charming, innocent daughter, whose vision often haunts me.

As for the three brothers Vujović, young Serbian Communists whose father was a blacksmith from Pojarevatz, I was on especially close terms with Voya and Rada, who were militants in France before they were drawn into the Comintern apparatus. Voya was ardent and single-minded to the point of fanaticism, while Rada was calm and smiling, but both were wholeheartedly devoted to the cause, and both blindly sacrificed themselves at the altar of Stalinism. Innumerable young men and women who were drawn to communism by an idealism which they naively mistook for materialism (no matter whether historical or dialectic) perished like the brothers Vujović for their failure to extricate themselves from the Communist apparatus after Lenin's death and for allowing themselves to be corrupted by the "professional revolutionaries" who subordinated their principles to a vulgar *Realpolitik*.

My relations with a number of Comintern colleagues were not very intimate for lack of time, for lack of a common language, or for lack of an occasion to work together. We exchanged greetings, smiles, handshakes, casual conversations in the corridors of the Kremlin, the dining hall of the Luxe Hotel, between sessions of the Executive Committee or of congresses. Thus after forty years Sima Marković and Kosta Novaković have faded in my mind, although I do remember them. I never met Milan Gorkić or any other militant of his generation, since I left Moscow in 1925, but I cannot forget the girl who became his mate, Betty Glane, who worked for some time as my close collaborator. This graceful and lighthearted young woman, naive in political matters, must have been bewildered by the fate she was to meet, and I dare not even think of the horror of her end.

Stalin owed it to himself to assassinate Hugo Eberlein, the delegate of the Spartacus League at the First Comintern Congress, the only authentic representative of an actually existing revolutionary organization at this meeting (aside from the Russians and their satellites from the former Russian Empire). This rather uncouth fellow, with narrow intellectual horizons, undoubtedly harbored no ideas that could offend Soviet laws, but this did not suffice to save his life. He had married Ina Armand, one of the daughters of Inessa Armand, who was Lenin's closest friend. Miraculously, Ina survived Stalin. Her memory (Ina Armand was my fellow worker after Betty Glane) still evokes for me our cordial friendship. She used to live at the Kremlin in the Lenins' home, where she was the object of great affection. She was a living link between Lenin and myself.

Eberlein spoke only German and had no regular contacts with Frenchmen, but I did have excellent relations with Clara Zetkin, who spoke French fluently and who died before she could witness the atrocities Stalin was to commit. I also knew well Brandler, Thalheimer, and Frölich, who were lucky enough to be excluded from the Party before the massacre. Heinz Neumann, who spoke French interlarded with Parisian slang, was not yet "Stalinized" at the time I knew him, and no one foresaw, even at the height of the conflict between Trotsky and the ruling *troika* (Zinoviev, Kamenev, Stalin) that things later would take such a horrifying turn. He paid with his life for the services he rendered Stalin, as did Münzenberg, although the latter decided—too late—to break with his master. There is no shadow of a doubt that Münzenberg was murdered in 1940 by the GPU, which then worked hand in glove with the Gestapo, for only the GPU did its killing on the spot; the Gestapo would have dragged its prey off to Germany, as in Hilferding's case. Dr. Fritz Brupbacher, who was a close friend of Münzenberg, also reached this conclusion and *a priori* eliminated the hypothesis of suicide, and I wholly agree with him.

The ruling circle of the International never stayed the same in Lenin's time, of which I am speaking, for the Communist parties lacked experienced personnel and could not leave their leaders in Moscow for extended stays. Personal contacts were established during congresses, sessions of the Executive Committee, and on special occasions, but during these first feverish and absorbing years many militants knew each other only by sight or superficially. The stable nucleus consisted of Russians and banished Poles, Hungarians, and others.

Having paid due respect to the sincerity, devotion, and good will of the majority of the people I knew then (I refer to the years before the 1924 "Bolshevization," which completely perverted the nature of the Communist movement), I now owe it to the truth to state that Béla Kun constituted an exception, in view of his unappealing character. Nobody liked or respected him, and people reported the most appalling stories about him. Lenin thought of him as a second-rater, but could not make up his mind to remove him completely; he simply relegated him to subordinate functions. At Stalin's behest, Kun carried out the most terrible tasks, until the day came when he himself fell victim to the same treatment he had inflicted on his many victims.

There are three more names on the obituary list that arouse moving memories in me: Andreichin, Peluso, and Koritschoner. Andreichin was an unsophisticated, generous, spontaneous young fellow, whose eclectic anarcho-syndicalist views were in sharp contrast to the dogmatism of the Social Democrats converted to communism. After being deported in the usual arbitrary manner, he did manage to survive and return to his native Bulgaria after the war. But he fell victim to the Stalinism rampant there and disappeared without a trace. Peluso and Koritschoner, so unlike in background and character, shared the passion for ideas, the conviction that they were serving a great cause and participating in a great task held by all the volunteers of the Socialist and Communist movement at that time when these two terms meant something, when essentially they meant the same thing. However, as a result of the withdrawals, the exclusions, the split-ups that later took place, I have been unable to trace, even from afar, the evolution of my former comrades or the road which led them to their graves: my comments apply only to the period of common experiences, my years of apprenticeship.

To avoid any risk of misunderstanding, these brief notes imply no apologia for the way things were under Lenin, by contrast to the way they turned out under Stalin. There is no need to emphasize Lenin's responsibility for the transformation of the Soviet revolution into its opposite, for the establishment of the regime of exploitation, of oppression of man by man, which emerged—the antithesis of that socialism or communism in whose name it was proclaimed in October of 1917. This responsibility necessarily extends to all those who consciously participated in this chimerical undertaking. It extends directly to Trotsky, to the Bukharins and Zinovievs of every shade, and consequently to the first adherents of the Third International who joined out of ignorance and youthful enthusiasm. But it would be a mistake to make no distinction between the time of the dreamers and the time of the profiteers, the time of utopia and the time of violence erected into the alpha and omega of a political system. No doubt some of the named victims of Stalin's massacre had been accomplices of their executioner, but before they were corrupted in Moscow by an absolute and absolutist power, they had had unselfish and respectable intentions. Many aspects of this vast tragedy remain obscure. For this reason our comments are meant only as a fragmentary contribution to this chapter of contemporary history.

The Comintern and the Insurrectional Activity of the Communist Party of Yugoslavia in 1941-1942

by

MILORAD M. DRACHKOVITCH

"Calling people to arms and securing its leading role in the people's uprising, our party has honorably paid its debt to the people, has justified the obligations assumed at the Seventh Congress of the Communist International"—Aleksandar Ranković, December 1942.

The victory of the Communist Party of Yugoslavia at the end of the Second World War was brought about by four decisive elements: specific features of the national crisis in Yugoslavia after its dismemberment by the Nazis and their allies in April 1941; activism of the party, a small but tightly knit group led by professional revolutionaries fanatically devoted to the Soviet Union and trained to implement Comintern directives; the impact of pro-Tito policies of the anti-Axis great powers during the war; and Tito's leadership of the Yugoslav party. None of these elements by itself would have determined the outcome of the war in Yugoslavia or is likely to have caused a different turn of events; taken all together, however, they sealed the destiny of the country.

The following pages attempt to analyze the second of these elements—to inquire to what extent the Comintern line, as established at the Seventh (and last) Comintern Congress in 1935 and complemented immediately after the German attack on the Soviet Union in 1941, affected the Yugoslav Communist Party's thrust for power during the war.

184

DIMITROV OFFERS PERSPECTIVE AND BLUEPRINT

The major report made at the Seventh Congress of the Communist International in Moscow on August 2, 1935 by Georgi Dimitrov, general secretary of the Comintern, was uneven in its significance and interest to his listeners. The report came as a welcome and refreshing change after years of the nonsensical sectarian phraseology inaugurated at the Sixth Comintern Congress in 1928. Still, Dimitrov's variations on Lenin's theme taken from *"Left-wing" Communism, an Infantile Disorder* (for this neo-Machiavellian book obviously was Dimitrov's source of inspiration) had only a limited impact on most delegates, who were unable to implement the Comintern's new course. On the other hand, one of the listless representatives of the Communist Party of Yugoslavia, aware that his party was at the bottom of the Comintern hierarchy and unworthy of Dimitrov's specific mention, found in the report just the elements needed to revitalize the party's inefficient performance in Yugoslavia.

Although the bulk of Dimitrov's report—devoted to Communist relations with Social Democrats and non-Communist trade unions—was of only theoretical importance to the Yugoslav Communists, they learned much from its general spirit and its tactical prescriptions. Above all, they gained an invaluable revolutionary blueprint for future actions from the Comintern's chief, who was incidentally one of their few friends in the international Communist hierarchy. Here, reduced to its essentials, is this blueprint as it emerged from Dimitrov's long and repetitious report.

The starting point is an enumeration of past mistakes not to be repeated and new initiatives to be taken without regard to former practice. Henceforth, at least in nonindustrialized countries, every Communist party should avoid the danger of isolation from the proletariat's natural allies: large masses of the peasantry and enthusiastic youth. The Party also should be sensitive to wounded national feelings existing in many countries by paying maximum attention to the national forms of the proletarian class struggle. In every country the Party should strive to create a broad, popular antifascist front; it should train hundreds and thousands of nonparty Bolsheviks, without, however, relaxing its own independent work of education, organization, and mobilization of the masses. This militant, deliberate proselytizing role of the Party was essential in the forthcoming political crises which would culminate in the establishment of Soviet power. But the task of the Party on the eve of the victory of the Soviet revolution was to form a government-in-readiness from the elements of an antifascist popular front. Such were the lessons of applied Leninism which, coupled with the experience of Russian Bolshevism serving as a model, would lead to proletarian victory.[1]

On the basis of these essentials of Dimitrov's report the congress adopted on August 20 the final resolution whose central and (for our study) most significant statement was formulated as follows: *"The establishment of the united front of the working class is the decisive link in the preparation of the toilers for the forthcoming great battles of the second round of proletarian revolutions."*[2]

JOSIP BROZ-TITO AND THE "BOLSHEVIZATION" OF THE COMMUNIST PARTY OF YUGOSLAVIA

The prospect of "forthcoming great battles of the second round of proletarian revolutions" was certainly appealing and comforting to the Yugoslav Communists, who had been among the worst losers of the first round, 1919–21. They were now barely emerging from the gloomy period of 1929–33 when, in Tito's words, "the work of the party had almost entirely come to a halt."[3] Slowly recovering under Milan Gorkić's leadership (1932–37), the Yugoslav party received a shot in the arm at the Seventh Comintern Congress, but it was essentially the follow-up of this congress which began to pay dividends.

The extent to which the Comintern's tactical reorientation affected the destinies of Yugoslav communism may be glimpsed from one supremely important instance. At a meeting held in Moscow immediately after the Seventh Congress, the politburo of the Yugoslav party decided to reverse its decade-old stand concerning Yugoslavia as a state. Previously, ever since the Fifth Comintern Congress in 1924 and despite resistance by the former party secretary Sima Marković, the Comintern had imposed as a mandatory political line for the Yugoslav party the dismemberment of the existing state, officially known as the Kingdom of Serbs, Croats and Slovenes. One paragraph of the Fifth Congress resolution on the national question in Yugoslavia reads, "The general slogan about the right of peoples to self-determination, on which the CPY insists, must express the demand for separation of Croatia, Slovenia, and Macedonia from Yugoslavia and their transformation into independent republics."[4]

This inept slogan which, among other things, contributed to the near extinction of the party in the late 1920's and early 1930's, was now replaced by an opposite consideration. Echoing the new Comintern course, the politburo of the party argued that under the present international circumstances and because of the necessity of creating an antifascist popular front, the claim to secession of any part of Yugoslavia now should be abandoned.[5] Compelled ten years earlier by the Comintern to work toward national dissolution, the Yugoslav Communist Party emerged from 1935 on—once more on Comintern initiative—as a party of national unity. This shift was to become a major asset six years later in the "people's liberation struggle" of the Yugoslav Communist Party.

In addition to this crucial change of tactics, the Comintern helped, directly and indirectly, in three ways to revive its moribund Yugoslav section.

First, some of its most prominent leaders (not to mention Tito) were trained at the Comintern's schools in Moscow. For example, Edvard Kardelj reached Moscow in November 1934, completed a course at the Lenin School, and later taught at that school and at the Communist University for the National Minorities of the West (KUNMZ). During his three years in the Soviet Union, Kardelj combined his teaching duties with practical work in various committees of the Comintern.[6]

Second, in August 1936 the central committee of the Yugoslav party systematically began to dispatch volunteers to the civil war in Spain. About 1,270 Yugoslav volunteers, 560 of them members of the Party, fought in the units of all international brigades.[7] About 670 Yugoslav volunteers fell on battlegrounds in Spain. Among them was Blagoje Parović-"Šmit," member of the central committee of the Yugoslav Communist Party and political commissar of the Thirteenth International Brigade. Practically all Yugoslav survivors of the civil war in Spain joined the ranks of the partisans in Yugoslavia after June 1941, thus enriching the Yugoslav party with the priceless fruits of their military and revolutionary experience in Spain:

> Of Yugoslav veterans from the Spanish war, 17 became commanders and political commissars in the Yugoslav People's Liberation War, 15 became commanders and commissars of unit groups, 7 brigade commanders and political commissars, 14 division commanders and commissars, and 8 corps commanders and political commissars. In the final operations of the Yugoslav Army, all 4 army commanders had taken part in the Spanish Civil War. During the war, 29 Yugoslav veterans from the Spanish war were promoted

to the rank of general. For their war service and service in the post-war reconstruction of the country 54 Spanish veterans were pro-claimed national heroes (the decoration National Hero is one of the highest war decorations in Yugoslavia) while many other Spanish veterans were awarded other high decorations.[8]

Finally, Georgi Dimitrov personally prevented the Comintern from carrying out its seriously considered plan to dissolve the Yugo-slav party. Instead, a last chance was given to Josip Broz—"Walter" as he was known at that time in Comintern circles—to try to revamp what seemed to be a hopelessly divided and inefficient party. The decision was undoubtedly fortunate for the future of Yugoslav com-munism, but its immediate significance merits a brief examination.

The mentioned listless delegation of the party at the Seventh Comintern Congress consisted of seven members, with Milan Gorkić as chairman and Josip Broz as secretary.[9] Two years later, in the summer of 1937, of all the members of this Yugoslav party dele-gation, whose destinies proved ironically divergent, Josip Broz was the only one to survive physically and politically.[10] The Comintern decision to put him at the helm of the Yugoslav party to replace Gor-kić, who had perished in the Moscow purges, was doubly characteris-tic. First, Broz was handpicked by the Comintern as the only trust-worthy Yugoslav Communist. Second, to merit such confidence and to emerge as the sole and thenceforth undisputed leader of the Yugo-slav Communist Party, "Walter" had to prove that he was the most fit in the deadly game which Milovan Djilas describes in the following graphic way: "There was no one to stand behind the Yugoslavs [dur-ing the NKVD purges]; rather, they dug graves for one another in their race for power in the Party and in their zeal to prove their devo-tion to Stalin and to Leninism."[11] In probably the most revealing—although understandably vague—description of the "most difficult days in my life" (meaning his stay in Moscow during the purges), Tito admits that he was asked by the Comintern to give his opinion about the imprisoned Yugoslav Communists. Although he asserts that he was careful in preparing these reports, he obviously took part, if only indirectly, in the liquidation of several scores of Yugoslav Communist leaders, including, with one exception, all former secre-taries of the Yugoslav party.[12]

The liquidation of the Yugoslav Communists in the Soviet Union was followed by a similar, though bloodless, cleansing process in Yugoslavia, where Tito was busily engaged in purging the old and shaping a new, "Bolshevik," Yugoslav party. He concentrated his energy between the end of 1937, when he replaced Gorkić, and July 1941, when the party launched the "people's liberation" campaign, to implement the directives of the Seventh Comintern Congress. Illegally circulated brochures containing reports delivered at the Seventh Congress by Dimitrov, Pieck, Manuilsky and Togliatti exerted, in Tito's words, "a tremendous influence on our party. This represented a real milestone in the work and development of the party organizations in the field. Only the decisions of the Seventh Congress of the Communist International indicated the path along which our party had to proceed and the manner in which it should link itself with the masses."[13] On many occasions (for example, in January 1939) the central committee of the Yugoslav party insisted on the necessity—with specific Comintern approval—of continuing to "cleanse the party even more energetically of all its alien and vacillating elements." All this was cogently expressed by Tito in an article written in the fall of 1939, in which he stressed that the Yugoslav party "is proceeding along the same road taken by the heroic Bolshevik party of the Soviet Union, learning from its experience as described in the *History of the All-Union Communist Party (Bolsheviks)*."[14]

This was the spirit in which the new cadres of the party were educated under Tito's prewar leadership. Milovan Djilas, who was the product of this atmosphere and training, describes the process of the ideological and political conditioning to which members of the party were subjected:

> The Yugoslav Communist Party was not only as ideologically unified as the Soviet, but faithfulness to Soviet leadership was one of the essential elements of its development and its activity. Stalin was not only the undisputed leader of genius, he was the incarnation of the very idea and dream of the new society. This idolatry of Stalin's personality, as well as of more or less everything in the Soviet Union, acquired irrational forms and proportions. Every action of the Soviet Government—for example, the attack on Finland—and every negative feature in the Soviet Union—for example, the trials and the purges—were defended and justified. What appears even stranger, Communists succeeded in convincing themselves of the propriety and suitability of such actions, and in banishing from their minds unpleasant facts.[15]

THE COMMUNIST PARTY OF YUGOSLAVIA
AND THE CRISES OF 1941

Hannah Arendt, in her recent masterly work, makes the following illuminating generalization about the relationship between revolutionary flareups and their beneficiaries:

> The outbreak of most revolutions has surprised the revolutionist groups and parties no less than all others, and there exists hardly a revolution whose outbreak could be blamed upon their activities. It usually was the other way around: revolution broke out and liberated, as it were, the professional revolutionists from wherever they happened to be—from jail, or from the coffee house, or from the library."[16]

This formulation fits admirably the case of Yugoslav Communists after 1937. The result of the process of Stalinist molding, as described above, was the emergence of strictly a cadre party, whose membership rose steadily,[17] but which still remained up to the outbreak of war in Yugoslavia more a militant sect than a powerful movement. Although officially illegal, the Yugoslav Communist Party was half tolerated by the authorities but was only moderately successful in gaining public acceptance. The party failed in its efforts to create the large antifascist popular front advocated by Dimitrov. With the exception of some left-wing non-Communist splinter groups without roots or influence in the country, none of the other political forces in opposition to Prince Paul's governments—including particularly the in-and-out-of-power Croatian Peasant party—were willing to become popular-front partners of the Communists. It is true that the Yugoslav party had achieved considerable success in organizing its cells in high schools and universities (the University of Belgrade was, so to speak, its stronghold), but this could not compensate for the party's lagging strength in the country at large. In his report delivered at the illegal fifth conference of the Yugoslav Communist Party in 1940, at Zagreb, Tito had acknowledged that the party's influence among the peasantry and in larger industrial centers was unsatisfactory. Moreover, despite all endeavors, the party had achieved only negligible results in infiltrating the army and the state administration.[18]

In fact, as long as the organized Yugoslav state existed, all Communist as well as fascist efforts to undermine it failed. The Communist Party could agitate, demonstrate and organize, but the forces of the established order were powerful enough to thwart any in-surrectionist bid for power. Communist chances for acceding to power in the foreseeable future seemed dim indeed; the government would easily checkmate any violent attempt on the part of the Com-munists; moreover, the opposition did not intend to let the party exploit the process of democratization of the country.

Then, suddenly, two crises, one national and the other inter-national, completely changed the existing situation, and, in Hannah Arendt's sense, "liberated" the Yugoslav revolutionists. The domes-tic cataclysm was the April 1941 invasion of Yugoslavia by the Axis forces. Occupation of the country by foreign troops meant the dis-integration of the existing order: instead of a single state authority with its institutional ramifications, improvised "authorities" of the occupiers or their puppets emerged; the fabric of political and civil life was destroyed; the military structure was demolished and largely discredited; tens of thousands of people became prisoners of war in Germany and Italy; internal ethnic antagonisms were inflamed by the genocidal policy of the Croatian Ustashis. In this general chaos, the only political organization whose cells remained operative through-out the country was the tiny Yugoslav Communist Party, caught no less unaware than everybody else by the catastrophic unfolding of events totally beyond its control.

The disintegration of monarchical Yugoslavia was, however, only one and even a minor precondition for action by the obedient Yugoslav section of the Comintern. The existence of the Hitler-Stalin pact which imposed a defeatist and anti-Western position upon the Yugoslav party, as it did upon loyal Communists everywhere, pre-vented the Yugoslav Communists from starting the antifascist strug-gle immediately. The party realized, however, that it had to be ready for any eventuality. On June 22, 1941, the German onslaught on the Soviet Union was the second and particularly welcome element of the party's "liberation": Adolph Hitler did the preparatory work of demolition for the Party on both Yugoslav and Soviet soil and at the same time brightened formerly dim prospects of actually implement-ing Dimitrov's antifascist precepts.

NEW COMINTERN DIRECTIVES AND THE RESPONSE OF YUGOSLAVIA'S COMMUNIST PARTY

Two documents, one private, the other destined for circulation, which were released on the same day—June 22, 1941—the first in the Soviet Union, the second in Yugoslavia, expressed the sudden turn in the Yugoslav party's passive attitude. Within hours after the German attack on the USSR, "Grandfather" (as the Comintern signed its communications to the Yugoslav Communists) sent the following telegram to the politburo of the party:

> Germany's treacherous attack upon the USSR is not only a blow directed against the country of socialism; it is also a blow against the freedom and independence of all peoples. The defense of the USSR is simultaneously the defense of the peoples occupied by Germany. An opportunity is offered to the peoples of Yugoslavia to develop a comprehensive liberating struggle against the German invader. It is vitally necessary to undertake all measures to support and facilitate the just struggle of the Soviet people. It is vitally necessary to develop a movement under the slogan of a united national front and the earlier united international front of struggle against the German and Italian fascist brigands, for the protection of the peoples subjugated by fascism. Such an exploit is indissolubly connected with the victory of the USSR. Bear in mind that at the present stage it is a matter of liberation from fascist subjugation, and not of Socialist revolution.[19]

As an indirect reply to this message, the central committee of the Yugoslav party on the same day issued a proclamation in which unconditional support of the Soviet Union was emphatically pledged:

> Proletarians of all parts of Yugoslavia, to your places, into the foremost fighting ranks. Close your ranks around your vanguard, the Communist Party of Yugoslavia. Everybody to his place! Without wavering and with discipline, fulfill your proletarian duty. Prepare yourselves without delay for the last and decisive battle. Do not allow the precious blood of the heroic Soviet peoples to be shed without your participation. . . . Mobilize all your strength to prevent our country from becoming a supply base for the fascist hordes, who like mad dogs assault the Soviet Union, our dear Socialist fatherland, our hope and beacon upon which the eyes of suffering working humanity throughout the world are fixed.[20]

This manifesto calling for a "decisive battle" contained no specific instruction about method and timing. Five days later, on June 27, at a meeting of the central committee of the party, it was decided in principle to prepare for partisan warfare, whereupon headquarters of the anticipated "People's Liberation Partisan Detachments" was established. On the same occasion it was resolved to dispatch about twelve of the most prominent members of the central committee to various regions of the country to conduct and supervise party activities on the spot. Still, since the meeting took place in Belgrade and the party emissaries were not as yet dispersed across the country, no detailed plan of action was drafted at the time, and no date was set for the official launching of the uprising. However, preparations by the party were precipitated when, on July 1, another telegram was received from "Grandfather." This time the instructions were more precise, calling for immediate action. The essential part of the telegram read,

> The hour has struck when Communists must launch an open fight against the invader. Organize, without wasting a single minute, partisan detachments and stir up in the enemy's rear a partisan war. Set fire to war factories, stores of inflammable material (petroleum, gasoline, and others), airports; destroy and demolish the railway, telegraph, and telephone network; do not allow the transportation of troops and munitions (of war materiel in general). Organize the peasantry to hide their grain and drive the livestock into the woods. It is indispensable to use all means to terrorize the enemy, to make him feel as if he were within a besieged fortress. Confirm receipt of these directives and communicate the facts to prove their fulfillment.[21]

The politburo of the Yugoslav party complied with this exhortation without, indeed, "wasting a single minute." At an expanded session of the politburo, which took place in Belgrade on July 4, a plan was worked out for the immediate creation of partisan detachments in all parts of Yugoslavia.[22] Three days later, on July 7, an incident occurred in the small village of Bela Crkva, in western Serbia, which later was designated and still officially is considered the beginning of the uprising in Serbia.[23] The incident took place after a public meeting at which a prominent local Communist, Žikica Jovanović —"Španac" ("Spaniard," so called because of his participation in the Spanish Civil War) harangued the people to join the incipient partisan detachments. A unit of local Serbian gendarmerie tried to disperse the assembled peasants. Jovanović intervened and killed two gendarmes.[24] Thus, rather symbolically, a former "Spaniard" dispatching two Serbian gendarmes initiated the "people's liberation struggle."

During the next months partisan detachments were established in several regions of Yugoslavia, and the partisan war in the enemy's rear was ignited according to the Comintern's directive of July 1. Thus, paradoxically enough, it was the same Yugoslav party that four years earlier had been on the verge of being dissolved by the Comintern as unworthy of existence which proved by its response to the Comintern's appeals to be a party whose fidelity and militant help to the Soviet Union were unmatched by any other Communist party in the world. Moreover, the unique response of Yugoslav Communists signified a Comintern (that is, Stalin's) initiative that at long last proved successful. In several earlier instances—China in 1927, Germany in 1933, Spain in 1936–39—attempts by local Communist parties to implement the political line dictated from Moscow had collapsed in defeat. Now, in the summer of 1941, when other Communist parties once again were showing themselves incapable of carrying out Moscow's instructions, the straggler became the leader; Stalin found in Tito his best executive agent.

Comintern appreciation of the stand of the Yugoslav Communists was manifested in two unusual instances. First, at the end of August 1941, in a conflict between the Yugoslav and Bulgarian parties over jurisdiction in Macedonia, occupied since April 1941 by Bulgarian troops, the Comintern decided that the Party organization in "Serbian Macedonia" (as the Comintern's telegram designated that part of Macedonia which in the interwar period had belonged to Yugoslavia) should remain within the framework of the Yugoslav Communist Party.[25] Second, with obvious Comintern blessings, the emissaries of the Yugoslav party during the second half of 1941 aided the organization of the Communist Party and its partisan movement in Albania. It was through the Yugoslav partisans' headquarters that the Comintern approved in May 1942 the convocation of the first conference of the Albanian Communist Party and confirmed its initial provisional leadership.[26]

HOW TO IMPLEMENT THE COMINTERN'S DIRECTIVES

The enthusiasm with which the Yugoslav Communists, liberated from the shackles of the Soviet-Nazi pact, took up arms to help their "dear Socialist fatherland," the Soviet Union, blinded them to discrepancies which existed between Dimitrov's 1935 blueprint and the new directives of June 22–July 1, 1941. In fact, Dimitrov's report at the Comintern's Seventh Congress had been a revolutionary document *par excellence*. Above all, its aim was to instruct the Communists on how to achieve the supreme goal—the seizure of power and the establishment of the Soviet system. The 1941 directives corrected the 1935 blueprint in several important ways. The Yugoslav Communists were advised that the "patriotic war" dictated an enlargement of the popular front and inclusion in it of all national and social elements, whereas the partisan struggle should de-emphasize for the time being any advocacy of social revolution. In essence, the Communists should forget temporarily their ultimate goal and behave solely as militant patriots, loyal initiators of an all-encompassing antifascist struggle. Class struggle and Socialist revolution should be put on ice pending victory over fascism.

If these discrepancies contributed to the misunderstandings which arose in 1942 and 1943 between the Comintern and the Yugoslav party, they did not embarrass Tito's party in the summer of 1941, when it was devising ways of combining the "class" and "national" tactical elements of the "popular" and "national" fronts.[27] Insensitive at that time to the implications of the 1941 directives, namely that its role should be predominantly that of helping the Soviet Union militarily rather than promoting communism in Yugoslavia, the Yugoslav party viewed the 1941 Comintern's appeals as a welcome complement to the decisions of the Seventh Comintern Congress. Was it not true that the war was laying open all the potential of revolution and that the time was ripe for vigorously applying the lessons of Lenin's teaching? It was therefore the understanding of Yugoslav Communists that the slogan of a "united national front," as recommended in "Grandfather's" telegram of June 22, was a condition for successful waging of a partisan struggle which could not have been foreseen in 1935. Likewise, the toning down of "Socialist revolutionism" under the conditions of the "patriotic war" was certainly not incompatible with preparing the ground for its ultimate triumph.

But the most important fact in the new situation after June 22 was that the total preoccupation of the Soviet leadership in waging its battle of survival against the advancing German armies prevented it from supervising the instructions given other Communist parties. Thus, for the first time in its history, the Yugoslav party was free to interpret the Comintern's line as it saw fit. In consequence, Tito was in a position not only to apply "Grandfather's" directives, but also to correct them in his own way. Indeed, the very zeal and militancy of his party were destined soon to go far beyond Moscow's intentions and guidelines.

At the very beginning of its military action, the leadership of the Yugoslav Communists clearly perceived that it had two fundamental tasks to accomplish. The international task was "to support through armed uprising the first country of socialism"; the domestic one was to transform the national war of liberation into Socialist revolution.[28] For the much more complex domestic task, Dimitrov's 1935 blueprint was invaluable. It suggested, when applied to the specific Yugoslav conditions, that a party based strictly on the cadre principle, such as the Yugoslav party, should above all try to mobilize the non-Communist peasant masses—the backbone of the country and certainly the most disoriented social stratum after the war and occupation.[29] To succeed in this endeavor, the party should appeal especially to the wounded national feelings of the Serbian peasantry, its hatred of the occupiers, and its resentment against the prewar regime, whose policies had led to the catastrophe of the April invasion. The masses, then, must be aroused in the name of nationalism and patriotism, and not in the name of Communism. A similar approach must be applied to the youth, among whom the party could score the greatest success, because youth "responds most readily to a call of battle."[30] The mobilization of peasantry and youth would, simultaneously, swell the partisan ranks, open new reservoirs of cadres to the party, and permit a systematic build-up of other organs of the nascent revolutionary power.

The following analysis will attempt to demonstrate how the domestic task was accomplished in the caldron of the partisan war, under difficulties both foreseen and unforeseen, and how and why at the moment of the Comintern's formal dissolution the victory of the Yugoslav Communist Party was assured.

A REVOLUTIONARY ARMY IS BORN

The Communist Party of Yugoslavia built its first partisan detachments with the utmost care. The party leadership was aware in July 1941 that another resistance movement—centered in the traditional region of Serbian struggles for independence, western Serbia, under the leadership of Colonel Draža Mihailović—was already active and increasingly popular, and that this rival could be outbid only by superior organization. An asset possessed by the Communist party in this respect was the existence of its so-called "military committees," created before the war and now ready for action. "The network of military committees was transformed into the leading center of the partisan detachments of National Liberation as the basic fighting force of the armed uprising."[31]

This hard core of party activists was to serve as the rallying center for all "patriots"; consequently it was instructed to build partisan unity in the name of a broad antifascist front, and not of the Communist party. To make this point unmistakably clear, the lead article in the first issue of the *Bulletin of the Headquarters of the People's Liberation Partisan Detachments* (as initially the entire partisan movement was called), bearing the date August 10, 1941, explained the genesis of these detachments and stated,

> they are not combat formations of any political party or group —including the Communist Party of Yugoslavia, regardless of the fact that the Communists are fighting in the front ranks—but the fighting detachments of the peoples of Yugoslavia in which all the patriots fit for the armed struggle should find their place, irrespective of their political convictions.[32]

This formulation, which conformed to the "united national front" directive of the Comintern's June 22 telegram, was reiterated in many variations during the war and still represents the official version of the origins of the partisan resistance movement in Yugoslavia.

But if the party leadership was anxious to invite all to join the partisans, it was nonetheless careful to keep the combat initiative under strict party control, and to subordinate every partisan unit to centralized discipline. Two of Tito's own statements concerning the earliest phase of the partisan struggle illustrate these points. In his July 1948 report to the fifth congress of the Communist Party of Yugoslavia in which he defended the "Bolshevik" purity of his party against the Cominform's charges, Tito declared that since its inception, on June 27, 1941, the first partisan headquarters,

> was composed of members of the politburo of the central committee, and later on it was extended to include some senior leading comrades and military men. The president of the military committee up to that time, that is, the secretary of the party, began to carry out the duty of military commander of the Partisan Detachments of Yugoslavia.[33]

The extent to which the politburo of the Yugoslav Communist Party, in its new official function as headquarters for the partisan detachments, was unwilling to tolerate any deviation in the process of building these new units and was insistent upon exclusive party command over them may be seen from the following letter sent by Tito on September 12, 1941 to Rade Končar, member of the politburo of the Communist Party of Yugoslavia and secretary of the central committee of the Communist Party of Croatia:

> Let everyone know immediately that the word "guerrilla" is abolished. For the entire country the popular word "partisan" is valid, as decided by headquarters; there cannot be several names for our people's partisans only because somebody in your province dislikes this word, although partisan and guerrilla mean the same in different languages. Our partisan detachments are under the central leadership of the headquarters and the central committee of the Communist Party of Yugoslavia, which is gradually transforming these scattered partisan detachments into one liberating army, which will be under our exclusive leadership and influence. Our task is to make our detachments as numerous and disciplined as possible, attempting at the same time to cooperate intimately with all those who want to fight for liberation from the yoke of the occupier.[34]

BUILDING OF REVOLUTIONARY POWER

The July 4 session of the politburo in Nazi-occupied Belgrade made final the plans and preparations for the immediate creation of partisan detachments and the launching of an armed uprising. Shortly thereafter, at the end of September 1941, another meeting of the Yugoslav party leadership took place in the western Serbian village of Stolice, near the town of Krupanj. Present were most members of the politburo (that is, of the partisans' supreme headquarters), members of the central committee, and the commandants of some of the larger military units from other regions of the country. In addition to reviewing the results of the three-month military struggle and discussing the political mistakes committed during this period, the participants decided to establish, in areas controlled by the partisans, "people's liberation committees" as organs of the new authority to replace all vestiges of the old one, or as Tito later stated, to serve as "guarantees of the success of the liberation of the Yugoslav peoples."[35]

In the first issue of *Borba*, organ of the Yugoslav party, which appeared after a twelve-year pause in the town of Užice in western Serbia on October 19, 1941, Edvard Kardelj published a much-quoted article entitled "The People's Liberation Committees Must

Become the Genuine Temporary Custodians of the People's Authority."[36] In this article, Kardelj tried to explain why all existing forms of local authority—*opštinske uprave, sreska načelstva* (community and district administrations respectively), *poreske uprave* (tax bureaus), *žandarmeriske stanice* (police stations), and so on—even if their representatives were people of undoubted integrity, should be replaced by the new committees. In Kardelj's interpretation, these new "people's liberation" bodies were indispensable as basic tools of the people's liberation struggle. Their functions would encompass all prerogatives of authority in a given territory, with the exception of strictly military affairs. In their activities, the committees would cooperate closely with the headquarters of the partisan detachments. At the same time Kardelj explained that the People's Liberation Committees should not be "organs of any party or any individual organization, but all political groups, organizations, and men standing on the front-line of the struggle against the occupiers should be represented in these committees." Twice in his article Kardelj emphasized the temporary nature of the committees' functions:

> They [committees] are today *effective* although *temporary* bearers of power. For their task is to exercise their functions in the interest of the people's liberation struggle, until the liberation of the country, until the moment when, following the expulsion of the occupier from our country, it will be possible to undertake the organization of the state's administration.[37]

The importance which the architects of the Communist party ascribed to the functions of the People's Liberation Committees may be seen from a statement of Moša Pijade, member of the party's central committee and the party functionary especially charged with developing the "people's authority":

> As soon as a territory, no matter how small, was liberated, the need arose to organize it as a focus of people's struggle, and this would unconditionally result in assumption of the functions of the organs of power by the people's liberation committees.[38]

As the partisan struggle evolved, the People's Liberation Committees became more elaborate. In February 1942, during its prolonged stay in the little town of Foča in eastern Bosnia, the partisans' supreme headquarters issued two documents dealing with the tasks and organization of the People's Liberation Committees. In these documents the committees were still defined as "temporary bearers of authority," but six months later it was decided to drop the qualification "temporary" and to consider them thenceforth as the sole, legal, and permanent organs of power. In a letter sent in September 1942 to partisan headquarters for Croatia, Tito was explicit:

> The character of the People's Liberation Committees is changed today. Although they still remain as a transitory form towards the future people's regime which the people will establish after final liberation, we must stress that this statement about transitory form does not mean that the question of the future form and character of the authority may be left to chance, that it cannot be yet perceived in the mist of the future and that this authority may be transformed into some other form. That phase we have left behind. Therefore, it does not make sense to emphasize today the temporary character of the People's Liberation Committees as an organ of power. This is valid even when we cannot retain a given territory and when our military force is transferred to some other territory. . . . In a word, stop stressing the temporary character of the power of the People's Liberation Committees, and stress these committees as *organs of authority* and as an embryo and basis of the future people's regime.[39]

Behind the facade of the People's Liberation Committees appears their real significance for the Yugoslav Communists. According to Jovan Marjanović,

> The best people, those most active in the people's liberation struggle, were chosen for the People's Liberation Committees. Such men were in the main Communists, candidates for membership in the party, members of the Young Communists League, or people in one way or another closely connected with the party. Through the Communists the Yugoslav Communist party directed the activities of the People's Liberation Committees.[40]

Similarly, the source and inspiration for the creation of these committees was bluntly identified by Moša Pijade after the war:

> The People's Liberation Committees were obviously based on the experience of the Soviets. Their name conformed to the concrete conditions of our uprising and war. The merit of our leadership was not only in adopting that form but also in the fact that it was aware that the struggle for liberation of the country could not be successful unless simultaneously with the struggle against the occupier the old apparatus of power were destroyed and replaced by a new revolutionary authority whose most suitable form was the People's Libera-

tion Committees, a form which today has been adopted by all the peoples' democracies from Czechoslovakia to Northern Korea.[41]

THE "PROLETARIAN BRIGADES" AND
THE CIVIL WAR DURING THE OCCUPATION

It was easier to conceive in theory than to implement in practice the fusing of "national" and revolutionary elements in the partisan struggle, and to instruct every party cell and local partisan command to concern itself with broadening the partisans' ranks while at the same time maintaining exclusive Communist control. In other words, it was one thing for the politburo of the Communist party to play the Leninist game of exploiting the war for national liberation in the interests of Communist seizure of power and quite a different thing to make party activists throughout the country fanatically militant and yet flexible. The failure of a large number of party organizations to achieve the desired political balance led to a severe crisis in the partisan movement which reached its climax between early winter of 1941 and early summer of 1942.

The crisis had many causes and aspects. First, the partisan movement had been unevenly dispersed across the country, and in some parts, such as Croatia and southern Serbia (Macedonia), it was still in an embryonic stage in 1941–42. Second, in regions where the Serbian population was in the majority, the Communist party had great difficulty in combining the patriotic and revolutionary elements. Although the party's anti-occupation slogans were usually welcomed by the Serbian peasants, other features of partisan behavior and propaganda engendered opposition: the unfamiliar name "partisan"; the red stars on partisan caps; the political indoctrination by the commissars in the detachments (again something new to the politically alert Serbian peasant); the burning of official buildings and documents in the villages and small towns, and the appointing of new "authorities"; the exaltation of everything Soviet Russian and, at the same time, silence on King Peter and the Western Allies.

In addition, popular distrust was precipitated by the fact that the partisans were late-comers, particularly in Serbia. Colonel Mihailović was already there in full swing, organizing national resistance in easily comprehended forms and terms. Enlisting the people on the basis of the traditional and famous Serbian "četnik" movement in the name of the highly popular young king in exile, and professing complete solidarity with the Western powers, allies of the First World

War, Mihailović was in a more favorable position to appeal to and be followed by the people. At the same time, however, his task was complicated because his organizational problems were formidable, his "cadre" material insufficient and unable to match the partisans' network in every area, and his fighting methods at loggerheads with the partisans' scorched-earth policy. Mihailović was aware of the political implications of the partisan struggle and was determined not to be the pawn in the Communist game. The short-lived alliance between the two resistance movements in occupied Yugoslavia fell apart on the fundamental issues of leadership and methods to be used in fighting the occupation forces, as well as on the political substance of their shared antifascism. Tragically enough, this problem of the postwar political order, which after 1945 brought the "cold war" contest to the fore, precipitated a civil war in occupied Yugoslavia between the pro-Western četniks and the pro-Soviet partisans.

The outbreak of this civil war, which began in Serbia in November 1941 and quickly spread to other regions, seriously complicated the political situation of the Communist party. The Russo-German war, which the party had expected to be a short and victorious Red Army operation, was developing disastrously for the Soviet Union; the "united national front" operation in Yugoslavia was being endangered by the Communists' failure to outmaneuver the četniks; German and Italian troops in Serbia and Montenegro had crushed the initial uprisings and, worst of all, many party organizations were guilty of tactical mistakes which alienated popular support for the partisans.[42]

Faced with the gravity of the situation, particularly after the retreat of supreme partisan headquarters from western Serbia in December 1941, the politburo of the Yugoslav party made a fateful decision to reorganize the partisan manner of action. Up to that time, the individual partisan units had had an essentially territorial character; they were not accustomed to mobile warfare, to leaving their own territories, and to fighting in other parts of the country. Now, after the withdrawal of partisan headquarters from Serbia, with many detachments dispersed and for all practical purposes lost, the politburo decided to fuse the remnants of these detachments and to build around the supreme headquarters itself a "proletarian shock brigade."

Established on Stalin's birthday, December 21, 1941, and called by Tito "our glory and pride, our real Red Army,"[43] the First

Proletarian Brigade was a desperate answer to a desperate situation. It was also an effective answer to the incipient civil war between the četniks and the partisans. In several orders and letters written either in the name of the supreme commander of the People's Liberation Partisan Detachments or of the central committee of the Communist party, Tito explained the decision to establish the proletarian brigade. In his letter to Milovan Djilas dated December 28, 1941, Tito wrote:

> The situation here [in eastern Bosnia] has improved since our arrival [from Serbia]. Before our arrival there was a large-scale desertion of Bosnian partisans to the četniks. It was due, on the one hand, to our party's neglect of political work among the Bosnian partisan units. It is often difficult to distinguish a četnik from a partisan, not only because of their garments, but also because of their mentality and political ideas. Consequently, we arrived here at the eleventh hour. The proletarian brigade will play a tremendous role here, not only in the fight against the occupiers and the ustashis, but also in the strengthening and political development of our Bosnian partisan units.[44]

Successful in its immediate task of preventing complete disintegration of the original local partisan units in eastern Bosnia, the First Proletarian Brigade became the model for reorganization of the partisan army, its iron first in the civil war against the četniks. Between December 21, 1941 and June 22, 1942, when supreme partisan headquarters made another momentous decision—namely, to undertake its own "Yenan march" in the direction of western Bosnia —four other proletarian shock brigades, numbering 800 to 1,100 fighters each, were created. They also were composed of the hard core of partisan detachments forced out of Montenegro, Herzegovina and the Sanjak.

The praetorian character of the proletarian brigades was outlined in Article 1 of their statute:

> The proletarian people's liberation shock brigades are the military shock formations of the peoples of Yugoslavia under the leadership of the Communist Party. Their fighters are forged in the ranks of our heroic partisan detachments in the process of combat against the occupiers and their valets.[45]

Later articles of the statute enumerated other tasks and distinctive features of the proletarian brigades: they were designed as the "embryo of the future people's army," with an "iron discipline"; brigade commanders were called "heads" of the units, and political commissars their "souls"; every brigade was to have its own red flag, with the hammer and sickle in the upper right corner and the five-pointed star in the center, together with the name of the brigade; they were to be mobile units, prepared whenever necessary to be split up into smaller units (battalions, companies, platoons). The statute was to serve as a model for the formation and organization of new partisan detachments whose territorial character would remain intact.

The radicalization of the Communist Party's tactics, as reflected in the establishment of the proletarian brigades, amounted to a violation of the Comintern's war instructions: although these tactics did not mean rejection of the "popular" or "national" front tactics in further political work with non-Communists, they did mean that glorification of the "patriotic war" was to be much more closely linked with the Communist Party's revolutionary aims. At a time when Tito's wireless communication with the Comintern was indirect and unsatisfactory, he had decided to act on his own. He was aware that the Yugoslav party was fighting for its existence, and that only a total fanatical commitment of its best members—5,000 cadrists—to the undiluted and undisguised Communist objectives could enable the party to survive its darkest moment.

The creation of proletarian brigades posed the crucial problem of their military employment. In mid-June 1942, the harassed supreme partisan headquarters and the five proletarian brigades were concentrated in the mountainous area of four regions (Montenegro, Herzegovina, the Sanjak, southeastern Bosnia). The area was arid and sparsely populated; the fighters, their ammunition low, were exhausted, practically starving. Many of the leaders (including Djilas and Dedijer) dreamed of returning to Serbia. Tito resolved otherwise:

> It was proposed that with the five [proletarian] brigades we move on toward Serbia [in June 1942]. I was then decidedly against that and the comrades immediately agreed. I said that in Serbia we did not have the conditions for making war with five brigades, that circumstances were unfavorable, and that we would melt away. Our elite would perish—five brigades full of politically highly conscientious and mature men. I said that we should go where they would find a mass base, where there existed the hearth of the partisan movement in its greatest scope, that is, western Bosnia.[46]

This partisan "long march," two hundred miles to the northwest, ended in a territory belonging partly to western Bosnia and partly to Croatia—one under Italian and the other under ustashi control. It proved to be the promised land for the shock troops of the Communist Party. Indeed in that chaotic part of the "Independent Croatian State," the party elite found the most favorable ground for its military and political actions. The Serbian population, decimated by the ustashi-led pogroms, lived in the mountains ready and itching for a desperate fight (while the local četnik as well as partisan units were much less expertly led than elsewhere). It was among the western Bosnian peasant youth that the party found new reservoirs of partisan fighters and prospective members. New, shifting, "free territories" under partisan control were established there and in adjacent regions. They served as experimental terrain for the forthcoming political trials and as attractive rallying points, particularly after the capitulation of Italy, for the Croatian *domobrans*, ideologically noncommitted soldiers who wanted to abandon the sinking ship of Pavelić-Hitler.

Still, for the time being, the strong "proletarian" medicine used by Tito in treating the infirmities of the partisan movement aroused alarm where least expected—on the part of "Grandfather."

TITO'S REVOLUTIONARY INITIATIVES AND THE COMINTERN'S MODERATING COUNSEL

After the conquest and dismemberment of Yugoslavia in April 1941, the Yugoslav party maintained wireless contact with the Comintern from an illegal post at Stenjevac, in the vicinity of Zagreb. Contact was difficult and irregular because of the hundreds of miles that separated the perpetually moving Yugoslav politburo (partisan headquarters) from Stenjevac, and because of the necessity of entrusting delicate messages to couriers exposed to the risk of capture by Nazis, Italians, or other enemies. Worse, the person in charge of radio communication (referred to in intraparty correspondence only as N. N.) was suspected of being hostile to Tito and the Communist leadership.[47] This awkward situation changed on February 9, 1942 when, to Tito's great satisfaction, radio contact was established directly from his headquarters to "Grandfather." "I must tell you some very cheerful news," wrote Tito to Edvard Kardelj and Ivo Ribar, Jr., on February 23, 1942. "For the past fourteen days we have had direct contact with Grandfather. This contact is magnificent, and one could not imagine it to be any better. It is no longer a catch-as-catch-can contact, but every day I send long 'sausages' [telegraphic messages], something that would have been simply impossible formerly [in Stenjevac]. Paja and Veljko [radio telegraphists] are actually jumping with delight."[48]

In some of these "sausages," Tito informed Moscow about his latest moves, the flaring up of civil war with the četniks, and his charges that the now General Mihailović and the entire Yugoslav government-in-exile in London (of which Mihailović had been minister of war since December 1941) were collaborating with the enemies.

Fearing that the Yugoslav Communist Party's brawl with the rival London-connected resistance movement might cast a shadow on British-Soviet relations, "Grandfather" sent the following telegram of inquiry to Tito on March 5, 1942:

> Study of all the information you give leads one to the impression that the adherents of Great Britain and the Yugoslav Government have some justification in suspecting the partisan movement of acquiring a Communist character, and aiming at the Sovietization of Yugoslavia. Why, for example, did you need to form a special proletarian brigade? Surely, at the moment the basic, immediate task is to unite all anti-Nazi currents, smash the invaders and achieve national liberation.
>
> How is one to explain the fact that supporters of Great Britain are succeeding in forming armed units against the partisan detachments? Are there really no other Yugoslav patriots—apart from the Communists and Communist sympathisers—with whom you could join in the common struggle against the invaders?
>
> It is difficult to agree that London and the Yugoslav Government are siding with the invaders. There must be some great misunderstanding here. We earnestly request you to give your tactics and your actions most serious thought and make sure that you have really done all you could on your part to achieve a true united national front of all enemies of Hitler and Mussolini in Yugoslavia in order to attain the common aim—the expulsion of the invader and would-be conquerors.[49]

Five days later, another telegram from the Comintern amended a draft of the proclamation the Yugoslav party had prepared for dissemination among the Western European resistance movements. Moscow's version deleted all mention of the Yugoslav party as organizer of the partisan action, as well as all passages hailing the Soviet Union exclusively. Instead, a paragraph was added saluting "the powerful coalition of America, Great Britain, and the USSR, around which all freedom-loving peoples are rallying."[50]

"Grandfather's" main concern at that time was to avoid anything that could complicate the Soviet Union's relations with the United States and Great Britain. This point was underlined in another telegram sent to Tito early in March of 1942:

> Take into account that the Soviet Union has treaty relations with the Yugoslav King and the Government, and that taking an open stand against these would create new difficulties in the joint war efforts and the relations between the Soviet Union on the one hand and Britain and America on the other. Do not view the issues of your fight only from your own national standpoint, but also from the international standpoint of the British-American-Soviet coalition. While doing all you can to consolidate positions won in the national liberation struggle, at the same time do show political elasticity and some ability to maneuver. We are all full of enthusiasm at your heroic fight and wholeheartedly delighted by your success. We are trying to make your cause widely popular in all countries, and it justifiably excites the enthusiasm of the peoples fighting against fascism, and among public workers, and serves as a fine example for popular resistance in other occupied countries. It is our wish to see you courageously come through all the trials ahead of you and win further great successes. We firmly grip your plucky hands.[51]

The text of these two Comintern telegrams,[52] viewed against the background of the radical measures taken by the Yugoslav party to assure its survival, point up the pattern of relations between Moscow and the Yugoslav Communists during the period here under review. There existed, to be sure, a discrepancy in Soviet and Yugoslav attitudes at the beginning of 1942, in the sense that while Moscow was insisting on the importance of the alliance with the West, Tito had already given priority—in fact, if not openly—to waging civil war against a Western ally in Yugoslavia. "Ćaća" (colloquial Serbo-Croatian for "father," as the Yugoslav Communist Party was called in the exchanges with the Comintern) and "Grandfather" were at tactical odds, in particular during the period of malfunctioning radio contact, as aptly summarized by a Yugoslav scholar:

> The Comintern based its attitude toward the People's Liberation Struggle (as witness its telegrams) on a theoretical concep-

tion of a struggle by stages. In its opinion, the year 1942 represented the stage at which the People's Liberation Movement should have been engaging its forces exclusively in the fight against the occupier, while the settling of accounts with the četniks, in the judgment of the Comintern, should be left to the second stage, that is, following liberation of the country. For that reason the Comintern was convinced that the Yugoslav party was forcing the struggle against the četniks primarily because it wanted to solve the problem of the revolution (the problem of the second stage) through the struggle for national liberation.[53]

These early tactical misunderstandings (which left their scars, and which were used in 1948 as the basis for mutual recriminations in the wake of the conflict between the Cominform and the Yugoslav party) did not seriously impair the relations between the Yugoslav partisans and Moscow during the war. Both sides were anxious thenceforth to justify every new move: "Grandfather" advised his obstreperous "son" to be cautious and to proceed step by step,[54] all the while assuring him that he enjoyed "our complete, unbreakable confidence."[55] The "son" in his replies to "Grandfather's" paternalistic messages painstakingly explained the reasons for his behavior, protested his undiluted loyalty, and in his subsequent moves always took into account "Grandfather's" earlier communications or tried to anticipate his reactions. Tito proved in the end that he was a better Bolshevik than anyone else in "Grandfather's" family, and this explains why the first official mission of the Yugoslav partisans, which reached the Soviet Union in March 1944, was received "with extraordinary geniality and consideration."[56]

A brief analysis of an initiative by the Yugoslav party's politburo, which at Comintern instigation had changed in form but not in substance, will illustrate the preceding points.

A "SUPREME SOVIET" THAT HIDES ITS NAME

After the politburo of the Yugoslav party had recovered from its "long march," it intensified its political work toward a threefold objective: to strengthen the military units of the partisans; to enlarge the network of People's Liberation Committees and make their functioning more efficient; to take a qualitative step forward and create a supreme political body for the entire country, one which would encompass all local People's Liberation Committees and challenge the authority of the legal royal Yugoslav government in exile, a government officially recognized by all Allied Powers. In this way, a sharp blow would be dealt to the only important contender for postwar power,[57] General Mihailović, minister of that government and then (latter half of 1942) at the pinnacle of his domestic and international popularity.

When preparations for this latest venture were sufficiently advanced, Tito informed Moscow, on November 12, 1942, about his intention: "We shall now set up something like a government, which is to be called the National Liberation Committee of Yugoslavia. This committee will include representatives of all the nationalities of Yugoslavia, drawn from various previous parties."[58]

In reply to this telegram came the following message from Moscow:

> *The creation of a national liberation committee of Yugoslavia is very necessary and of exceptional importance.* You must not fail to give the committee an all-national Yugoslav and all-party antifascist character, both in personnel and in programme of work. Do not look upon the committee as a sort of government, but as the political arm of the national liberation fight.
>
> Do not put it in opposition to the Yugoslav government in London. At the present stage, do not raise the question of abolition of the monarchy. Do not put forward any slogan of a republic. The question of the regime of Yugoslavia, as you understand it, will come up for settlement after the German-Italian coalition has been smashed and the country freed from the invaders.[59]

Tito complied with every item of this directive, encouraged by the Comintern's comment on the "exceptional importance" of the step he was about to take. This consisted in organizing a meeting on November 26 and 27, 1942, in the little Bosnian town of Bihać, recently taken from its ustashi garrison; the purpose was to establish the "Anti-Fascist Council of the People's Liberation of Yugoslavia" (hereafter referred to as AVNOJ, according to the initials of the Council in Serbo-Croatian). A special "preparatory committee" was selected to organize the gathering and to prepare the drafts of resolutions, decisions and manifestos to be submitted.[60]

This committee was composed of five persons: one a member of the Yugoslav party's Politburo (Ivan Milutinović); two members of the Party's central committee (Moša Pijade and Ivo-Lola Ribar); the fourth a prominent Communist intellectual (Veselin Masleša) who even before the war, as a newspaperman in Belgrade, had served as liaison man between the Comintern and the Yugoslav party; the fifth (Ivan Ribar, Sr.) a prewar "bourgeois" and earlier even an anti-Communist politician, now swayed to the Communist side by the influence of his two sons, both high functionaries in the Alliance of the Communist Youth of Yugoslavia.

While this "preparatory committee" was arranging the Bihać meeting, Tito himself, over the signature of "Commandant Tito," addressed letters of invitation to seventy-one "prominent fighters and patriots" who had taken part in the "people's liberation struggle" since its inception. Appealing to their devotion and loyalty, Tito asked them to accept membership in the AVNOJ and to attend its founding session in person.[61] Fifty-four of these invited managed to reach Bihać on time, but the committee on credentials decided to consider as present all those to whom Tito's invitation had been extended.

This first session of AVNOJ took place without any deviation from plan. It was opened on the evening of November 26 by Tito's address, a "most emotionally stirring moment of the Bihać session."[62] Tito extolled the valor of the partisans in the process of being transformed into a "powerful people's liberation army." He declared that under the present circumstances and the existing state of international relations, it was not possible to create a legal government, but that the supreme headquarters of the People's Liberation Army and the People's Liberation Committees had every right to build a new supreme political body with the power to supervise both military and political mobilization. He also stressed favorable developments in the international military situation, with particular mention of the Red Army's offensive at Stalingrad. His most glowing words were addressed to the Soviet Union:

> Comrades, in concluding I would like to emphasize that the results of all of our struggles achieved up to now are for the most part due to our great Slavic brothers, the Russians, and to all the peoples of the Soviet Union. Only faith, profound faith in the strength and might of the Soviet Union, in the strength and might of the Red Army, sustained us while we were overcoming all the difficulties we endured during these past eighteen months.[63]

Three other members of the central committee of the Yugoslav party, Sreten Žujović, Cana Babović, and Ivo-Lola Ribar, speaking respectively in the name of the party, antifascist women, and antifascist youth, followed Tito on the rostrum with appropriately militant speeches.

The next day the meeting had the character of a working session. Two basic reports were read—one by Veselin Masleša on the people's liberation struggle and the foundation of AVNOJ, the other by Moša Pijade on AVNOJ's organization. Masleša's report was a review of the antifascist struggle in Yugoslavia since 1935. A large part of the report was a settling of accounts with all prewar political parties, which were without exception accused of open collaboration with or nonresistance to Hitler ("None of the leadership of any political party in Yugoslavia," he declared, had been willing to join the people's liberation struggle—only some of their honest former adherents). Speaking of AVNOJ, Masleša admitted that its members had not been elected, but he argued that they were nonetheless fairly representative of the people's will because of their participation in the people's liberation struggle.[64] Pijade's report dealt with the organizational structure of AVNOJ and its threefold division: plenum, presidium and executive committee.

The discussions that followed Masleša's and Pijade's reports had a genuine "national front" character. On the rostrum, succeeding one another with enthusiastic speeches hailing the partisans and "Mother Russia" were, among others, a former deputy of Maček's Croatian Peasant party from Dalmatia, a wealthy peasant from Serbia, an orthodox priest from Montenegro, a prewar senator from a reactionary Muslim party in Bosnia, and so on. Both reports and the corresponding resolutions, as well as AVNOJ's manifesto to the peoples of Yugoslavia,[65] were then adopted unanimously. And, although nobody pronounced the word or compared the institution, everybody present was aware that "there was being formed in a new way a government which was in essence identical with the Soviet."[66]

Two days after the creation of AVNOJ, on November 29, Tito reported to "Grandfather" what had been achieved:

> We agree to the advice you gave in your telegram and shall observe it. But I must inform you precisely that the active civilians of the council, and the whole body of the people present, condemned the Yugoslav government as traitorous. Although we do not look on this executive committee as a sort of government, it will nonetheless have to look after all state business and occupy itself with the war, in which it will have the support of the People's Liberation Committees which have been set up in nearly all districts on both

liberated and unliberated territory. There are no other public authorities in Yugoslavia outside these committees and the military authority conducting the struggle. The session was summoned by the
supreme staff of the National Liberation Army and Partisan Detachments of Yugoslavia, who enjoy immense authority throughout
Yugoslavia.[67]

A LESSON IN APPLIED LENINISM

With the establishment of AVNOJ, the Yugoslav Communist Party
achieved what Dimitrov in 1935 had visualized in purely theoretical,
speculative terms: *the creation of an antifascist popular front government on the eve of a victorious Soviet-style revolution.* In November
1942, partisan forces were still meager and the Communist party
faced enormous domestic and international problems along its road
to power. However, already at that time the party had succeeded in
establishing the rudiments of a microcosmic partisan state on the
shifting "free territory" of western Bosnia and parts of adjacent
regions. At the end of the war this structure was extended to all
Yugoslavia.

Thus, six months before the official dissolution of the Comintern, its Yugoslav section had put its cards on the table. A year later,
in November 1943, the second session of AVNOJ took place in
another small Bosnia town, Jajce. This time, without restraining influence from abroad, the Communist party enlarged the scope of its
performance at Bihać. It established a formal government, openly
challenging the one in London, and acted with increasing confidence
as the self-appointed master of a still-occupied country whose small
and ever-changing patches of peripheral territory it managed to keep
under its control.

After this was accomplished, it was international rather than
domestic conditions which later determined that "a victorious Soviet-
style revolution" eventuated in Yugoslavia. The destiny of the country, particularly during the second phase of the war, rested more and
more in the hands of the great powers. This last point merits emphasis: the entire postwar situation in Yugoslavia could have been
different had the Western allies been as alert to the final aims of the
partisans as "Grandfather's" apprehensions had led him to believe
they would be. In other words, if Great Britain had viewed the situation in Yugoslavia as it did in Greece, and if it had actually pressed
for the "fifty-fifty" solution agreed to in writing by Stalin and Church-

ill in October 1944, the partisans would not have been the *sole* beneficiaries of the huge inpouring of Western military and political aid. It was this aid, beginning in the second half of 1943, together with the entrance of the Red Army into Yugoslavia a year later, which ultimately assured the Communists their victory in the civil war. This consideration is included here to stress the initial premise—namely, that even the most skillful implementation of Comintern directives and the Yugoslav party's talent for improvisation would not have sufficed in themselves to achieve the party's final victory. The paradoxical fact was that the Communists benefited not only from the blessings and help accorded them by their "dear Socialist fatherland," but also by their class enemy, the Western "imperialists."

In his *History of the Russian Revolution*, Trotsky wrote that "in order to conquer the power, the proletariat needs more than a spontaneous insurrection. It needs a suitable organization; it needs a plan; it needs a conspiracy. Such is the Leninist view on this question."[68] Paraphrasing this statement on revolutionary tactics and viewing it in the light of the Yugoslav experience, one could say that the partisan insurrection and seizure of power were the best planned such enterprises in the history of the Communist International. An organization of professional revolutionaries was there to transmit Dimitrov's blueprint into reality, making alterations where necessary. It was in keeping with the dictates of conspiracy that the real aims and methods of the "people's liberation struggle" be concealed, both at home and abroad. Whether dealing with unsophisticated peasant youths in Yugoslavia or with the oversophisticated chancelleries of the West, the Yugoslav Communists indeed demonstrated their shrewd ability to put into practice the well-learned lessons of applied Leninism.

Recollections

Stalin and the "Rebellion" of Tasca and Humbert-Droz

by

HENRI BARBÉ

EDITORS' INTRODUCTION—The year 1928 was a landmark in the history of the Third International. Its Sixth Congress celebrated the victory over the "social-democratic deviation of Trotskyism," but at the same time earmarked the new internal enemy: "The main deviation is to the right of the correct political line," according to the theses on the international situation and the tasks of the Communist International, as spelled out by the congress. In fact, a few months after the Sixth Congress, the Comintern's official head, Bukharin, and his followers among the Russian Communists and in various Comintern sections learned the practical meaning of that sentence. When they fell away politically, nobody in the Comintern's ranks dared to challenge publicly Stalin's total dominance over Lenin's 1919 creation.

These facts are well known. Not so well known are some dramatic circumstances which had preceded Stalin's triumph. The following, therefore, is a chapter from the unpublished memoirs of Henri Barbé, who had watched on the spot (without realizing at the time its meaning) the disappearance, at the end of 1928, of the last traces of open disagreements in ruling Comintern circles.

Henri Barbé was born in 1902. He began his apprenticeship as a mechanic, joined the organization of Socialist Youth at the end of the First World War, and later became a member of the Communist Youth. As early as 1924, he was a member of the French Communist Party delegation to the Fifth Congress of the Communist International.

In 1926 he was promoted to the post of secretary-general of the

217

*Communist Youth in France, and in 1928 he was sent to Moscow as
a delegate of the French Communist Party and the French Communist Youth. There he advanced rapidly to membership in the
Comintern's Executive Committee, Presidium, and political secretariat of the Executive Committee. He delivered a report at the Sixth
Comintern Congress and performed his three functions in 1929–30.
At the same time he was one of the secretaries of the central committee of the French Communist Party.*

*As chief of the group of the "young," he was pushed to the first
rank by the Comintern's apparatus, by Manuilsky in particular. This
position began to be withdrawn from him in 1931. His group at the
head of the French Communist Party was disjointed: two members
who denounced him, Raymond Guyot and François Billoux, were
promoted (they still are, in 1966, members of the politburo of the
French Communist Party) and another, Pierre Célor, was expelled
as "enemy agent." Barbé himself was sent back to the "base."*

*Closely associated with Jacques Doriot, Barbé largely shared
his political destiny: both were expelled from the French party in
1934 and together they established the Parti Populaire Français
(PPF). Although Barbé dissociated himself from Doriot in 1939, his
violent anticommunism led him into collaboration with the Germans,
during their occupation of France, as a member of Marcel Déat's
movement. He died on May 24, 1966.*

*Barbé wrote his memoirs, "Souvenirs de militant et de dirigeant
communiste," in 1949–50. The original manuscript is now in possession of the Hoover Institution. The chapter below begins with Barbé's description of the political atmosphere in Moscow when he
arrived there in October 1928. The notes were supplied by the
editors.**

During this time . . . the crisis between Stalin and the Bukharin
group was developing. People were beginning to talk about it cautiously in the upper circles of the Hotel Luxe. But the crisis did not
break out. Bukharin and his group were tough. Stalin was putting
everything off by liquidating friends and men of secondary importance who sympathized with the Bukharinists.

In the Comintern, a slow and secret force was at work aimed at
discrediting Bukharin by presenting him as a hazy ideologist and an
intellectual of bourgeois origin. Rykov was said to do nothing except

---

* Notes follow this chapter.

get continually drunk. Tomsky was accused both of labor demagogy and of petty-bourgeois deviations. Stalin's bureaucrats, secretaries and propagandists outdid themselves. All this activity and idle talk bewildered me. I felt inside me disgust and sickness, but I could not understand clearly what was happening. My loyalty to the Communist International, the prestige of Moscow and the Russian Revolution were stronger than my anxieties and confusion.

At this time a discussion of the "German question" began in Moscow within the committees, the secretariats, and the head of the Comintern.[1]

Two former leaders of the German Communist Party, Heinrich Brandler and August Thalheimer, had been relieved of their positions at the head of the party and sent to Moscow where they worked in scientific institutions. But both continued to maintain close political contact with German militants. Besides, they commanded great authority in the German Communist Party.

Brandler and Thalheimer had been disgraced because of their disagreements with the Comintern and the heads of the left wing of the German Communist Party. Basically, they were opposed to rigid tactics against German social democracy. But at the same time, they were just as hostile to measures taken in the Comintern and in the Russian party against Trotsky, Zinoviev and other opponents. In short, they were anti-Stalinists. That is why their position in Moscow became insecure and their close ties with Germany a source of danger; before long, the Brandler-Thalheimer case was in the making.

The Communist party in Germany, as in France, was applying the new tactics of "class against class," which meant a more relentless struggle against the old social democracy and complete independence of the Communist party from the Socialists and reformist trade-union leaders.

On this basis the discussion opened which, *a priori*, aimed at the liquidation of right-wing deviations and their principal representatives, Brandler and Thalheimer.

At this time one of the leaders of the Italian Communist Party, Angelo Tasca,[2] arrived in Moscow, as his party's representative,[3] going by the name of Serra. (He is known presently in Paris under the name of Rossi). He worked at the Latin secretariat of the Comintern and seemed to me to be on close terms with Jules Humbert-Droz.[4] I did not know Tasca personally, but I knew the reputation of the group of Italian leaders. We French militants liked the Italian Communist leaders—Bordiga, Ercoli (Togliatti), Tasca, and Grieco (Garlandi)—who were living in exile and underground, fighting against Mussolini's fascism.

I often passed Tasca, either in the Hotel Luxe where we were living, or in the Latin secretariat where we were working, but we rarely had the opportunity or desire to speak with each other. I myself was quite timid, and I think that Tasca did not care to get involved in discussions. He impressed me as being an intellectual, a little on the bookworm side. I would never have guessed that he would one day provoke the greatest outburst ever experienced within the Comintern leadership.

It began in connection with the discussion on union tactics in Germany. That day at the Presidium of the ECCI a report was presented by S. I. Gusev, an old Russian militant, on the necessity of adopting in Germany a labor-union policy which was more independent of the labor-union leadership.

There had been no split in the German unions. The old German labor federation, which was called the Allgemeiner Deutscher Gewerkschaftsbund (A.D.G.B.), was composed of a majority of Socialist-reformist workers and a minority of Communist and Communist-sympathizing workers designated by the name of Red opposition, Rote Gewerkschafts-Opposition (R.G.O.).

In concluding his report, Gusev, supported by Solomon A. Lozovsky, head of the Red Trade Union International, asked the R.G.O. to leave the A.D.G.B. and to found a new independent, revolutionary union organization.

I saw nothing objectionable in this especially since we had done this in France by creating the C.G.T.U. But Tasca stated that in his opinion Gusev's conclusions were erroneous and that he intended to declare himself against the union split in Germany and for keeping the opposition within the German A.D.G.B.

This outburst provoked some amazement. In the Comintern one was not used to seeing differences expressed so categorically. Tasca began to become conspicuous. He was an Italian and had a spontaneous and somewhat naive way of stating his convictions, which made an appealing impression.

Tasca had stated his differences of opinion in regard to union tactics in Germany, but the fact that he harbored deeper and more fundamental disagreements became apparent in further debates on the internal situation of the German Communist Party in the various secretariats and committees of the Comintern. Several times Tasca had occasion to express his views on the policy of the Comintern with regard to the German Communist Party.[5] He opposed measures concerning some former so-called right-wing leaders of the party and protested against the sectarian tactics and outlook that the Comintern wished to impose on this party, as it had already done with respect to the French Communist Party.

These controversies about the "German question" were important and desperate because they were a testing ground and extension of the "Russian question" and, more precisely, of the ferocious battle which Stalin waged against the Bukharin group. In this whole series of intrigues, controversies, maneuvers, purges and debates carried on behind a politically objective façade, Stalin and his men were not concerned with the real makeup of the parties and their leadership. But they were determined to eliminate all elements likely to show any independence in the upper ranks of the parties, especially in the German Communist Party, and, even more so, all who had been connected with Bukharin and showed sympathy toward him.

In retrospect, I am convinced that these considerations determined the discussion on the German Communist Party. Tasca certainly must have recognized it, although I, the young neophyte, was almost completely in the dark. One day Tasca and I walked from the Hotel Luxe to the offices of the Comintern. I asked him, "Why are you so stubborn about your differences with the leadership of the International?" He repeated his arguments on the situation in Germany and on the faulty judgments of the Comintern and its erroneous tactics in regard to social democracy. My perspective as a young militant, who had been slightly overawed by the prestige of the Comintern's leadership, was not so easily changed. I still believed in the infallibility of the Bolshevik "giants" and in blind and formal discipline under them. For me the Comintern was at the same time a marvelous school and a High Command which one was to respect and not to question. Although Tasca had denounced the flaws in the methods and practices of the Comintern, I found him appealing and a little crazy for daring to launch such a battle. I told him, however, that I could not agree with him.

Tasca did not stand alone. The head of the Latin secretariat, Humbert-Droz, basically went along with him in his disagreements on the German question.[6] It was known that Humbert-Droz had been on close terms with Bukharin and continued to support him. No one, however, wanted to bring up the two problems together in the discussions.

The disagreements publicly expressed by both Angelo Tasca, a respected Italian leader, and Humbert-Droz were becoming serious matters for the head of the Communist International and for Stalin and his men. As a result, one day the secretariat of the Comintern announced that a meeting of the ECCI had been called to settle the differences on the German problem. This meeting was to include the various collaborators of the Comintern's political apparatus and a few students of the Lenin School. The students of the school had been invited because the disagreement had become known to them.

This meeting, then, was to be a full-scale assembly of the Comintern leadership. Besides, we were informed that Stalin himself would attend it and would take the floor to answer Tasca and Humbert-Droz.

If my memory does not fail me, the meeting was postponed one day, which aggravated the tension in the house. Some were anxious and uneasy. Others felt a suspicious, almost sadistic thrill at the idea of attending a circus. The calmest and most surprised at all this was certainly Tasca, who did not seem aware of the excitement.

Finally the meeting opened.[7] Tasca was seated almost in the middle of the room, not far from Humbert-Droz. I was seated behind him. But the two were already looked upon as men struck by the plague, who must not be approached too closely. The seats beside them were empty.

Tasca was all smiles, but Humbert-Droz was very pale, nervous and ill at ease.[8]

We were all awaiting Stalin's arrival. There was a long delay. Finally he appeared, surrounded and escorted by about twenty men whom we did not know, but whose behavior, clothing and manner fooled no one. The GPU had done things well: Stalin was not alone, but strongly protected.

Immediately the secretary-general of the Bolshevik party went to the front of the room and took a seat to the right of the table and platform. Piatnitsky opened the meeting. I do not recall what he said during the first part of this meeting. But I clearly remember Stalin.

As was his custom, he gave a report in the calm and sometimes caustic tone of which he was particularly fond. When I had listened to Stalin before, on two occasions, I had noticed that he did his utmost to make his speeches seem logical and of impeccable construction. They abounded in "firstly's," "secondly's," and "thirdly's." But it was shocking to hear Stalin from time to time present crude assertions as proved facts.

That day Stalin intended to prove that Tasca and Humbert-Droz were questioning the foundation of the Communist International and the world revolution. But at the same time he was putting on his most seductive airs and apparently playing the role of the good leader who wanted to save the unfortunate ones who were going astray.[9]

However, an extraordinary incident occurred which raised havoc with Stalin's subtleties and wiles. We must remember that Stalin seldom attended these meetings, but when he did it was a great event; because of the enormous prestige of the Bolshevik party and the skilled publicity which was beginning to raise him on a pedestal, he was listened to as one listens to an oracle; no one would ever have taken it into his head to interrupt Stalin while he was speaking.

No one except Tasca. At a particular moment, when Stalin was addressing Tasca, asserting that certainly he was mistaken and was bound to recognize it, Tasca stood up, interrupting the speech to reply that he [Tasca] was certainly not going to recognize that he was wrong. Keeping up this astounding interruption, Tasca held up a resolution of the Red Trade Union International which put Stalin in contradiction with earlier decisions on the problems of union tactics.[10] We were dumbfounded by the daring of the Italian delegate. Stalin himself, little accustomed to being treated that way, was disconcerted and did not manage to pick up the thread of his talk.

For several minutes, we had the impression that the meeting of the Presidium would fall apart. But Stalin concluded the meeting by asking the opponents to recognize that they were wrong, stressing that the leaders of the Communist International and of the German Communist Party should take all political and organizational measures for the strict application of the Comintern line. The end of this speech was a mixture of appeals and threats, particularly in regard to Humbert-Droz. Tasca did not seem to realize the extraordinary experience he had provided for us.

I seem to recall that a resolution was then adopted by the Presidium approving Stalin's conclusions.[11]

Tasca went on for several months thereafter participating in the work of the Comintern, but was expelled from the Party in 1930.[12]

Humbert-Droz also remained for some time in the Latin secretariat;[13] then he was unofficially replaced by Stepanov.[14]

In addition to myself, who was [in Moscow] as a representative of the French Communist Party, there were Billoux (representing the Communist Youth organizations) and several French students attending the Lenin School, among them Paul Marion (who later was to become minister of information in the Vichy regime of Marshal Pétain) and André Parsal (former Communist deputy, now heading the Independent Trade Union Federation; after the Hitler-Stalin pact he left the Party). The C.G.T.U. delegate to the Red International of Trade Unions, Marceau Delobelle, was also on hand.

Tasca's attitude made a deep impression on all of us. We were uneasy and felt a mixture of admiration for his pluck and anxiety for his fate. I drew up, at the time, a report for the French party's politburo which expressed these sentiments.

Then I left again for Belgium and France to prepare the discussions for the party's forthcoming national congress. I profited by the occasion to bring the members of the "Youth Circle" and the politburo up-to-date on the session of the Presidium and Tasca's attitude. I alluded for the first time to a possible tie-up between these discussions and the internal developments in the Bolshevik party leadership. I was acting only on my personal initiative; I had no Comintern directive on that score. But such was the force of habit that all members of the politburo assumed my statements to be the result of a mission undertaken for the Comintern's leadership.

However, the opposite would have come closer to the truth, because my statements were favorable rather than hostile to Tasca and Humbert-Droz. In fact, most members of the politburo would have been reluctant if they had been asked to take a clear stand against the two "rebels."

I remember a lengthy meeting with Doriot in Brussels.[15] Since he was well informed on the internal situation of the Bolshevik party, he made me realize that all these discussions in the Comintern were only a side product of the Russian situation, and that all measures set in motion were meant mainly to isolate Bukharin and his group and to strengthen Stalin's position.

We were being tossed about in this network of intrigues, half-baked information, and mystery. Thus, Doriot, considered an opponent of the Comintern's policies, was (because of his connections and flair) better informed than we on the Comintern's and the Bolshevik party's internal struggles. The same was true of Tasca. But my comrades and I were, basically, mere pawns in a terrible game of chess. The less we knew, the better this served the realization of Stalin's objectives. We were ignorant of the degree of the Comintern's fanaticism and failed to recognize the gravity of the internal situation in the international Communist movement.

Notes

1. For a background of the "German question," see Jane Degras, *The Communist International, 1919–1943: Documents* (London-New York-Toronto: Oxford University Press, 1960) I, 564–67; also Ruth Fischer, *Stalin and German Communism* (Cambridge: Harvard University Press, 1948). Although Fischer's book does not analyze the events of 1928, it contains a list of about ten German Communist groups, in and out of the Party, which in 1927–28 confronted each other and competed for Party leadership and Comintern confidence, 603–04. In one article of a series devoted to analyzing the first decade of the existence and work of the Italian Communist Party, Angelo Tasca described the situation existing in the Comintern in 1928–29, and offered some interesting comments on the "German question." "La nuova politica," *Il Mondo*, September 22, 1953.

2. Born in November 1892 in a small town in Piedmont, son of a railway worker, Tasca was able to win a doctoral degree at the University of Turin. The subject of his dissertation was Leopardi and the French philosophy of the eighteenth century.

   As a young man he was associated with the Italian Socialist Youth, and was close to Mussolini during the latter's radical, Socialist period. At the end of the First World War, Tasca, along with Gramsci, Togliatti, and Terracini, became a founder of the *Ordine Nuovo*, the first Italian publication with Communist leanings. With the split in the Italian Socialist party in January 1921, Tasca became one of the leaders of its Communist wing.

   Until the Fascist victory in 1922, Tasca was in the first ranks of the political, trade-union, and cooperative activities, holding several top posts in these fields. In 1922, he attended the Fourth Comintern Congress in Moscow as one of eight delegates of the Italian Communist Party. Since the congress took place immediately after Mussolini's "March on Rome," Tasca remained for several months in the Soviet Union. He returned clandestinely to Italy in 1923 and worked in the secretariat of the Italian Communist Party until December 1926, when the executive committee of his party sent him to France. He reached the summit of his political career as a Communist at the Comintern's Sixth Congress, when he was elected to membership in the Executive Committee, Presidium, and Political Secretariat. (Under the pseudonym of Serra, he was, together with Bukharin, Jules Humbert-Droz and Henri Barbé, one of the eleven members of the Political Secretariat.)

   Tasca's eminence in the Comintern's hierarchy was short-lived. His falling in disgrace—described in note 12 below—was a direct consequence of his agreement and solidarity with Bukharin's ideas. On his return to France in 1929 (the year of his expulsion from the Italian Communist Party), Tasca adopted the pen name of "A. Rossi," under which name he continued his prolific work as publicist and historian until his death in March 1960. In 1934, under another pen name—"A. Leroux"—he became foreign political editor of the French Socialist newspaper *Populaire*—a post which he held until 1939. He became a French citizen in 1936. Between 1937 and 1940, he was in charge of the Italian program over the French radio.

In 1938 he published an outstanding volume, *The Rise of Italian Fascism* (London: Methuen & Co.), which was translated into several languages. After the war he pursued a productive career centered particularly on the study of the French Communist Party and Soviet foreign relations. His major works of that period include *Physiologie du Parti communiste français* (Paris: Editions Self, 1948); *Deux ans d'alliance germano-soviétique* (Paris: Arthème Fayard, 1949); *Les Communistes français pendant la drôle de guerre* (Paris: Les Iles d'Or, 1951); *Les Cahiers du Bolchévisme pendant la campagne 1939–1940* (Paris: Dominique Wapler, 1951); *Le pacte germano-soviétique, l'Histoire et le Mythe* (Paris: Ed. "Preuves," 1954); *La Guerre de papillons. Quatre ans de politique communiste* (Paris: Les Iles d'Or, 1954).

3. According to Ignazio Silone, in his essay included in the French edition of *The God That Failed*, entitled *Le Dieu des Ténèbres* (Paris: Calmann-Levy, 1950), 124, Palmiro Togliatti had "the perfidy to induce Angelo Tasca, whom he loathed and of whom he was jealous, to accept the role of permanent delegate of the Italian

Communist Party in Moscow, which meant acceptance of being exposed to inevitable ruin." This passage is omitted from the British and American editions of the same book.

4. Swiss by origin and originally a Protestant minister, Jules Humbert-Droz began to espouse pacifist and revolutionary ideas during the First World War. He joined the left wing of the Socialist party and was among the founders of the Swiss Communist Party, established in March 1921, after he had been a speaker a year earlier at the Second Comintern Congress. He attended the Third Congress in the summer of 1921, and, along with Rakósi, Kuusinen, Safarov and Souvarine, was elected later to membership on the ECCI and its Secretariat. He was reconfirmed in these posts at the next three congresses. In addition, for nearly a decade he was the head of the Latin secretariat, which was in charge of all Communist activity in Belgium, France, Italy, Spain, Portugal and Latin America. During this period he was often sent as emissary of the Comintern to several countries: France, in 1922 (see p. 347); Italy, in 1923; Spain, in 1924; Holland, in 1931. In 1929 he represented the Comintern at the founding congress of the Federation of Red Trade Unions in Montevideo. He also directed the first gathering, at Buenos Aires, of all existing Communist parties of South America. His duties as secretary of the ECCI included presiding over the British and American commissions and supervising the information section of the Comintern. For several years he served as liaison official between the Comintern and the Red Trade Union International, and was chairman of the Comintern Trade-Union Commission.

After Zinoviev had been replaced by Bukharin, Jules Humbert-Droz became the new Comintern president's closest collaborator, as well as his personal friend. This explains his political viewpoint during 1928–29, as described above by Henri Barbé. For an account of his demotion, see note 13.

5. In a sharply worded document, dated November 2, 1928, Tasca expressed his firm disagreement with the organizational policy of the German Communist Party under Thälmann's leadership, a policy approved by the majority of the Comintern Presidium. Attacking Thälmann's leadership as "factionalist," in "radical contradiction" with the decisions of the Sixth Comintern Congress, and "detrimental to the interests of the German Communist movement," Tasca declared he would abstain thenceforth from voting in favor of any measure concerning the internal situation of the German Communist Party. For the complete text of his declaration, see Jules Humbert-Droz's unpublished "Archives" (a microfilm copy is in the possession of the Hoover Institution), No. 0310.

6. On the basis of available documents in Humbert-Droz's "Archives," one gets the impression that Humbert-Droz's opposition to the policy of the Stalinist majority in the Presidium on the "German question" was even stronger than Tasca's. An undated document in his "Archives," No. 0311, contains the text of a long speech in German on the German question which he made at a Presidium meeting, probably at the end of November 1928. Like Tasca, he insisted in his speech that the leadership of the German Communist Party had revised the decisions of the Sixth Congress by anticipating a more rapid disintegration of capitalism than outlined in the Sixth Congress. He favored also the establishment of internal democracy, and the use of persuasion in the fight against the "right" within the German Communist Party.

7. The meeting took place on December 19, 1928. Its main task was to discuss the drafts of an "open letter" of the Presidium to the central committee of the German Communist Party and of a confidential communication to the same body, prepared by the two commissions set up by the Presidium. According to a Humbert-Droz letter, he, Angelo Tasca, and Klara Zetkin voted against the texts of these two documents. Bukharin was absent, but, to quote Humbert-Droz, "He was naturally against it too." "Archives," No. 0324. In his article quoted in note 1, Angelo Tasca described that meeting and explained that in order to fight successfully his "rightist" rivals in the Russian Communist Party, Stalin needed to have his way on the German question.

8. The December 19 meeting had two sessions, probably separated by an intermission. During the first session Humbert-Droz read a three-page declaration ("Archives," No. 0320) concerning the mentioned drafts. As he explained in a long letter to the politburo of the Swiss Communist Party (No. 0324), his declaration was "rather sharp in form and substance" in its criticism of the Presidium's open and confidential letters to the German party. He criticized in the same manner "the methods of the Comintern's leadership." No wonder he was "very pale, nervous and ill at ease," awaiting Stalin's reply.

9. That Stalin in fact wanted to humiliate and condemn Tasca and Humbert-Droz without calling for their political liquidation at that time may be seen from his December 19 speech before the Presidium, entitled, "On the Danger of Rightist Deviation in the German Communist Party," printed in the official Comintern organ, *Komunisticheskii Internatsional*, December 28, 1928, No. 52 (178), 14–20. In his speech Stalin gave his views on the three interrelated questions: capitalist stabilization, class battles of the proletariat in connection with the allegedly disrupting capitalist stabilization, and

the German Communist Party. Here are some excerpts from the speech in which he attacked Humbert-Droz and Tasca: "I must unfortunately state that on all these three questions comrade Humbert-Droz and comrade Serra [Tasca], both of them, sank into the swamp of cowardly opportunism.... What does that mean? It means that in addition to open opportunism there exists also concealed opportunism, afraid to show its true face. And this is precisely the opportunism of conciliators with respect to the Right deviation" (p. 14). "Whom does comrade Humbert-Droz ridicule? It is clear that he ridicules the decisions of the Sixth Congress" (p. 15). "What do these facts show and what do they signalize? They indicate that a new revolutionary upswing of the workers' movement is taking place in capitalist countries. That 'something new' is what comrades Humbert-Droz and Serra do not see and what as a rule comrades accustomed to look backward instead of forward will never see" (p. 16). "These comrades [Humbert-Droz and Tasca] are ready to support the rightists and the conciliators, even at the cost of total disintegration of the German Communist Party" (p. 17). "The position of comrades Humbert-Droz and Serra on the question of the German Communist Party is the position of a cowardly, lawyer's defense of the right wingers against the German Communist Party and the Comintern" (p. 19).

10. Here is the point of Stalin's speech to which Tasca took exception: "He [Tasca] does not approve that the German Communists in their struggle for the organization of the locked-out metalists went beyond bounds of the existing trade unions and disrupted them. He sees in this a violation of the resolutions of the Fourth Congress of the Profintern. He asserts that the Profintern instructed the Communists to work only inside the trade unions. This is nonsense, comrades. The Profintern gave no

such instructions (Lozovsky: 'Right!')." *Ibid.*, 16. It is understandable, then, that Tasca's interruption must have been embarrassing to Stalin (and to Lozovsky, who as Profintern head must have known better), for the resolutions of the Fourth Profintern Congress, which took place in Moscow between March 17 and April 3, 1928, clearly contradicted Stalin's assertions. Thus, the resolution on the report of the Profintern's executive committee stated: "Under these conditions, the central objective of the partisans of the Red International of Trade Unions in these countries [Germany, England] is the conquest of reformist trade unions." Likewise, a detailed resolution on the objectives of the Profintern's partisans in Germany urged them as well as all nonaffiliated workers "to adhere to the [existing] trade unions, and to strengthen there, as active trade-union militants, the local and regional cadres of the [trade-union] opposition." *Thèses et Résolutions du IVe Congrès de l'I.S.R.* (Paris: Imprimerie de la Maison des Syndicats, 1928), 18 and 112.

Stalin declared in his December 19 speech what the Profintern decided at its Fifth Congress, held in Moscow in August 1930. At that congress a resolution on the "questions of organization for the revolutionary trade-union movement" instructed the Profintern adherents that "the creation of consolidated and permanently functioning organizations of the trade-union opposition is one of the most important tasks of the Red International of Labor Unions supporters in the countries where there are no independent revolutionary trade unions (Germany, England, Poland, the Scandinavian countries, and others)." *Resolutions of the Fifth Congress of the R.I.L.U.* Published in London in January 1931, for the Red International of Labor Unions by the Minority Movement, 82.

11. In fact, a motion was voted by the

majority of the Comintern Presidium, on the very day—December 19, 1928—when the "conciliatory-opportunistic declarations of Comrade Humbert-Droz" were "categorically condemned." The motion accused Humbert-Droz of supporting the rightist elements in the German Communist Party and stigmatized his declaration as a "shameful pre-attack against the Comintern." Twelve members of the Presidium voted in favor of the motion; Tasca abstained, and Klara Zetkin voted against it. For the text of the motion and the voting score, see Jules Humbert-Droz, "Archives," No. 0321.

In a letter to Bukharin, dated February 11, 1929, Humbert-Droz confirmed that during the December 19 Presidium meeting, Stalin told him "go to the devil," and Molotov treated him as a "hypocrite." "Archives," No. 0327. Droz compared this rude behavior toward a foreign Communist leader with Lenin's invariably friendly treatment of foreign leaders.

12. Stalin's attack on Tasca in his December 19, 1928 speech bode ill for Tasca's future Comintern career. In fact, it very soon came to an end, precipitated by Tasca's own conduct. His memoranda to the central committee of the Italian Communist Party and the Comintern Executive Committee (never printed in their entirety in official Comintern publications, but often alluded to as proof of his errors) became sharper and broader in their criticism of the Comintern line in general and of Stalin's policies in particular.

In a recent article, Ignazio Silone makes the following comment regarding Tasca's situation at this juncture: "Tasca, on the other hand, faced the storm with unbelievable candor. He carried on a strange and audacious correspondence in code with the foreign center of the Italian Communist Party. Somewhat ingenuously, he forecast some important abrupt changes in Russia, and he was awaiting such developments

in order to protest against the exiling of Trotsky to Alma-Ata; he said all kinds of things about the new Genghis Khan. Was it possible for this correspondence, entrusted to Russian couriers, to escape the hands of Stalin's police? It is obvious that Tasca was convinced this was so. What about Togliatti? That is improbable. There could be doubts as to efficiency of the Russian peasants under the new regime, but not as to the pedantic punctiliousness of its police. The police did intercept these sacrilegious messages, decoded them without difficulty, and then always allowed them to proceed to their destination." Ignazio Silone, "A. Rossi, historien du fascisme," *Preuves* (Paris, November 1963), 48.

Tasca's oppositional attitude at the session of the central committee of the Italian Communist Party held on March 1, 1929 provoked a declaration of the central committee, condemning in five specific points his "serious opportunist deviations." While four out of five points followed closely Stalin's arguments in his December 19 speech, the fifth point criticized Tasca's views on the "Russian question," that is his denial of the existence in the Russian party of a "rightist" danger, and his demand for a revision of the line laid down by the fifteenth congress of the Russian Communist Party concerning the struggle against the growth of the capitalist elements in the village. (The complete text of this declaration is printed in *Inprecor*, March 15, 1929, pp. 267–68). In spite of the sharpness of these attacks on Tasca, no punitive measure against him was taken. Moreover, his own offer to resign from his post in the party's politburo was rejected by the central committee.

Four months later, in July 1929, at the Tenth Plenum of the ECCI in Moscow, Tasca was the target (more thoroughly than Humbert-Droz) of severe and detailed criticism by all emerging Stalinist

Comintern leaders. Manuilsky, Molotov, Kuusinen, Thälmann, Ulbricht and Togliatti vied with each other in exposing Tasca's political sins. Manuilsky called him a "Zarathustra of conciliators"; Molotov forced the note and declared that Tasca was not a conciliator but a full-fledged "rightist," whose ideas contradicted those of the Comintern; Kuusinen gave Tasca the alternative either to accept without reservation all Comintern decisions or to leave the Communist Party; other speakers followed suit. Togliatti, whose stand and even loyalty were questioned by some at the same plenum, hastened in a long speech to explain and condemn the Italian party's leniency in Tasca's case. Hinting that there were people (himself?) who knew Tasca from the beginning and always had fought against him, he gave reasons for the attempt to save Tasca for the Party; since it was a mistake, Togliatti promised that in the future no weakness would be shown toward "opportunists" and "revisionists," because, as Stalin puts it, "at sharp curves there is always somebody who falls from the carriage and remains prone." Finally, the plenum took a unanimous decision to remove Tasca (together with Bukharin, Humbert-Droz and Gitlow) from the Presidium. *Protokoll des 10. Plenums des Exekutivkomitees der kommunistischen Internationale* (Berlin: Verlag Carl Hoym Nachf., 1928), *passim.*

The central committee of the Italian Communist Party met early in September 1929 to examine the results of the Tenth Plenum. Tasca took part in the discussions and developed, according to the official version, a series of views which would mean "a complete and thorough break with the ideology, program, and political line of the Communist world movement." As a result, the central committee decided to expel him from the ranks of the Party. In May 1930, the enlarged Pre-

sidium of the ECCI endorsed the central committee's decision to expel Tasca, "the renegade." Cf. *Inprecor,* September 20, 1929, pp. 1127–28, and May 28, 1930, p. 459.

To quote once again from the article by Ignazio Silone, "The honor of expelling Tasca from the ranks of communism was left to the leadership of the Italian Communist Party. The time was the spring of 1929. Those among us who were soon due to follow along the same road committed the error of not leaping immediately to his defense. This was not opportunism. We encountered great difficulty in the fact that Tasca's political program contained no reference to the Italian situation. How could we explain to the small clandestine groups engaged in the antifascist struggle a personal break motivated by disagreement over certain German and Russian questions? Once again, Tasca had to suffer the bitterness of standing alone."

13. Humbert-Droz's relationship with the Comintern followed a course different from that of Tasca. A day after Stalin's speech, on December 20, 1928, he requested in a letter to Piatnitsky to be relieved of his duties in the Comintern and to be placed at the disposal of the Swiss Communist Party. "Archives," No. 0323. This petition was not approved; instead, he soon was sent on an official mission to Latin America. Unlike Tasca, Humbert-Droz gave up his opposition to the Comintern official line, and soon after his removal from the Presidium at the Tenth Plenum of the ECCI, he surrendered unconditionally. On October 19, 1930, in Moscow, he made a public declaration in which he acknowledged his erroneous position with respect to the policy of the Comintern and affirmed that the Presidium had been entirely correct in censuring him on December 19, 1928. He admitted having shared in essence the political views of Bukharin,

Rykov and Tomsky. He also confessed his "error of waiting two years before recognizing my mistakes openly and frankly," and promised to cease forthwith all ideological opposition. (His declaration appeared in *Inprecor,* November 6, 1930, p. 1043.) On the bottom of the second page of his personal copy of the "Declaration" ("Archives," No. 0333) he has made—undoubtedly as an afterthought—the following handwritten notation: "Declaration required by Manuilsky on threat of expulsion, made by me for reasons of discipline and not by conviction."

During the next several years his attitude toward the Comintern wavered. At the end of 1931, he returned to Switzerland and was designated secretary of the Swiss Communist Party. Since he continued, however, to express nonorthodox views, the Twelfth Plenum of the ECCI in September 1932 suspended him from the leadership of the Swiss party, without expelling him from the Party. He again represented the Swiss party at ECCI's Thirteenth Plenum, held in Moscow in December 1933, and attempted to clarify his position. The Comintern's turn to the "right" at its Seventh Congress of July–August, 1935, met with his enthusiastic approval. "Nothing separates me any more," he declared, "from the ECCI and the central committee of the Communist Party of the Soviet Union." His zeal for the popular front (he spent some time in Spain during the Civil War) even outlasted the Hitler-Stalin pact of August 1939. Although in conflict with the official leadership of the Swiss party, he was involved, at Dimitrov's own insistence, in Soviet intelligence operations in Switzerland after the outbreak of the war. His mission consisted in setting up a courier service among the people crossing the German frontier daily in the course of their normal work, in order to keep in touch with Ger-

man Communists and pick up every available bit of information. Cf. Alexander Foote, *Handbook for Spies* (London: Museum Press, 1949), 78–79, and 101–03.

During a later phase of the war, early in 1943, Humbert-Droz finally was expelled from the Communist Party and soon joined the Swiss Socialist party, serving as its secretary-general until the end of the 1950's.

14. This was one of the many pseudonyms used by the Bulgarian, Mineff. A left-wing Socialist who lived in Switzerland during the First World War, he joined the Bolshevik cause and began working in the central apparatus of the Comintern soon after its formation. Under the pseudonyms of Lorenzo Vanini and Chavaroche, he appeared as an active figure in Western Europe and later turned up in Stalin's secretariat, this time bearing the name of Lebedev. He next emerged as Stepanov, in his new role as head of the Comintern's Latin secretariat, replacing Humbert-Droz upon the latter's removal from this post. Some time later, "Stepanov" served as one of the Comintern's chief emissaries during the Spanish Civil War, rejoining the central apparatus of the Comintern after the victory of Franco.

15. Jacques Doriot was born in 1898 in Bresles, a small town in the department of Oise, in a peasant-worker family. He left home at the age of seventeen and established himself at Saint-Denis, a workers' suburb of Paris. In 1916 he joined the Metal Workers' Union, the Socialist Youth Movement, and the Socialist party. Mobilized in 1917, he had a rich war experience and returned to France only in 1920. After acting for some time as secretary of the Socialist Youth of France, he joined the Communist party and was sent as representative of the French Communist Youth to the Third Congress of the Comintern (June–July, 1921). He spent fourteen months in Russia (returning

to France at brief intervals), learned German, and early in 1923 was sent to Germany for six months on a Comintern assignment. Later in the same year he was appointed secretary-general of the Communist Youth of France. Under the pen name "Guilleau," he was highly successful as a youth organizer, but the violence of his antimilitarist propaganda caused his first arrest. He was still in jail when, as the result of the general election of May 1924, he was elected to the National Assembly as the Communist deputy for Saint-Denis.

The months that followed represented probably the climax of his popularity in the party. His violent anti-imperialist speeches in the Assembly — particularly those on the question of war in Morocco — in February, May and June, 1925, "were and remain," in the words of an official historian of the French Communist Party, "an example of the revolutionary utilization of the bourgeois parliamentarianism." A. Ferrat, *Histoire du parti Communiste français* (Paris: Bureau d'Editions, 1931), 146.

After a bitter controversy with Doriot, Aristide Briand reportedly declared, "One day this man will govern France. One day he will understand." Reginald J. Dingle, *Russia's Work in France* (London: Robert Hale, 1938), 55. At several points in his memoirs, Henri Barbé speaks about Doriot's extraordinary political ability and popularity at that time: "He was a young idol of the militants."

The Comintern also had its eyes on Doriot. At the end of 1925, after Manuilsky's visit to France, Doriot was summoned to Moscow. In the Stalin-Trotsky struggle his sympathies were on the side of Trotsky, but he soon was sent to China on another Comintern mission. A year later he was again back in Paris and in the forefront of the Communist party, but his integrity began to pale. Here is how Ignazio Silone describes that evolution: "Year by year, he became an increasingly important figure in the hierarchy of International Communism, and, year by year, each time I came across him, I found him changed for the worse, skeptical, cynical, unscrupulous, and rapidly becoming Fascist in his political attitude toward men and the State. If I could triumph over my natural repugnance and write a biography of Jacques Doriot, my theme would be: 'Militant Communist into Fascist.'" *The God that Failed* (New York: Harper, 1949), 104–05.

Albert Vassart refers to another paradoxical element in Doriot's career (see pp. 243 ff. of this volume). A partisan of the popular front when the Comintern opposed it, he misread Moscow's change of line in 1934, and missed the opportunity of becoming the leader, instead of Maurice Thorez, of the French party. Expelled from the Party in June 1934, he followed a unique and in the final analysis catastrophic political career. In June 1936 he founded the *Parti Populaire Français,* claiming six months later that it had a hundred thousand members. "Nothing," he boasted at that time, "will arrest our progress to power." In fact, he and his party remained only one of several movements of the French extreme right at that time, probably the closest French copy of fascism or nazism. And it was only natural that Doriot became collaborator par excellence with the German occupiers during the war. Perhaps his last great political compliment came from Adolf Hitler himself. After a meeting in Germany in December 1944, and in the presence of Ribbentrop and Himmler, Hitler declared: "Doriot, I know that you are a courageous soldier; you are also, I think, a real political revolutionary. I want to believe in your success." The Führer had in mind a French government in collaboration with Germany which Doriot had then just been requested to establish. Robert Aron, *Histoire de Vichy, 1940–1944* (Paris: Arthème Fayard, 1954), 723. Two months later, on February 22, 1945, Doriot was killed in his car by shells dropped by an American or British plane in action over German roads.

The Moscow Origin of the French "Popular Front"

by

CÉLIE AND ALBERT VASSART

EDITORS' INTRODUCTION—*Albert Vassart, born in 1898, was caught up in the revolutionary trade-union current of the period immediately following the First World War and drawn to communism. He was active at first in his own region (France-Est), and after his ability as an organizer had been recognized, he was sent to Paris and became one of the first graduates (1924) of the Party school which had been founded at Bobigny. He then was assigned to the Party apparatus as a permanent member, and in 1926, at the Congress of Lille, was promoted to membership in the central committee, on which he served almost fifteen years.*

In 1932, together with Maurice Thorez and two other leaders, he became a member of the secretariat of the central committee. He made a trip to Moscow in 1933 and the following year was named representative of the French Communist Party at the Comintern. From April 1934 to April 1935, when the strategy of the popular front was worked out, he and his wife were in Moscow.

Vassart was married to the former Cilly Geisenberg, who had been an early active member of the German Communist Party, but who had been expelled in 1929 after being pilloried, together with the group's leaders, for her membership in the Brandler-Thalheimer faction. After her marriage to Vassart, she was permitted to join the French Communist Party.

Upon the return of the couple to Paris from Moscow, the Communist party named Albert Vassart to head the list of candidates in the municipal election of Maisons-Alfort, where he became mayor.

234

At the time of the Hitler-Stalin pact he broke with the Party, followed by his wife, because of his disagreement with its official policy, but he was arrested soon after by the police and spent more than a year in prison. Upon his release he resumed his office as mayor of Maisons-Alfort. His continued outspoken disagreement with the Communist party resulted in an attempt on his life, organized by the Party, at the time of the Liberation.

From this moment, he became one of the most active and militant anti-Communists in France, particularly in the area of trade unionism and in the publication of literature on communism, then an enormous task inasmuch as the Communist party in France at the time was maintaining silence on many aspects of its past and current activities.

Albert Vassart died in February 1958 without having published anything about his life as an active Party member; his widow, Célie, passed away in 1963.

The following text is part of an unpublished, typewritten manuscript (in possession of the Hoover Institution) entitled "Le Front Populaire en France," written by Célie Vassart on the basis of notes left by her husband. Complementing this text are some notations by Branko Lazitch and the French historian Claude Harmel, based on their conversations with Albert Vassart during 1955–57. These notations appear below in italics.

According to one widely publicized version of events, the popular front in France was the result of fear by French leftists, especially Communists, of the possible establishment in France of a regime similar to the one in Germany and Italy—a fear evidently engendered by the nationalist revolt of February 6, 1934, in Paris. The Vassarts repudiated this version, and here propose their own, based on personal experience.

The part of the manuscript preceding the one below ended with quotations from the French Communist press, including some by Maurice Thorez (dating to the middle of April 1934) attacking the Socialists ("social fascists"). Then the tone suddenly changed, and a conciliatory hand was extended to the enemies of yesterday.

CHANGE IN TACTICS

This abrupt change can be understood only by taking into account the requirements of USSR foreign policy at that time.

At the end of 1933, the Soviet Union was in need of closer diplomatic ties with the democracies; at the same time it wanted to enable the Communist parties in the respective countries to put pressure on their governments to pursue a pro-Soviet policy.

However, even though the Comintern was a tool in the hands of the Soviet government and was at its service in advancing its foreign policy, the Communist leaders in other countries not only failed to realize this fact but would have rejected scornfully an assertion to this effect. They sincerely believed that they were serving the working class by carrying out the required Comintern policies.

For this reason Thorez adhered rigidly until May 1934 to his policies of "class against class" and "united front from below," for such had been the Comintern's line during the preceding years. The obedient servant Thorez insisted on adhering to theses of the congresses and to the resolutions of the Executive Committee of the Comintern until these were replaced by new ones. And he called Doriot an oppositionist and an opportunist because Doriot, who felt that this policy was leading the Communist party into isolation, was urging a rapprochement with the Socialist party.

From Lenin through Stalin to Khrushchev, the foreign policy of the Soviet Union revolved around Germany. This was the country upon which Soviet Russia wished to exert its greatest influence, regarding it—as it does today—as the key to Russia's influence on Europe as a whole. The Soviet Union kept a sharp eye on German political developments, would tolerate no opposition, and kept replacing the leadership of the German Communist Party until it found a tractable, if mediocre, instrument in Ernst Thälmann, who followed instructions to the letter.

But, simultaneously, the Soviet Union maintained a strong trade mission in Germany—which was not only concerned with trade —and direct contacts with the Reichswehr.

The Rapallo treaty and the contacts maintained by von Seeckt with the Red Army should be recalled here, as should Tukhachevsky's mission in Germany, which cost him his life when it became Hitler's interest to weaken the Red Army.

The objective of Soviet foreign policy was and is* to get a foothold in Germany, either by agreements or through the intermediary of a strong Communist party.

---

*The Soviet Union partly achieved these ends in 1945. Through its satellite, the German Democratic Republic under Ulbricht's leadership, it has reached the Elbe. It would like to be at the Rhine, and its policy is oriented toward this goal. In this, it is merely continuing its policy of the past.

However, in the period before 1932 the Comintern made one miscalculation: it underestimated the strength of the National Socialist movement. The economic debacles in Germany prior to 1924 and following 1929, the dispossession of the middle class as a result of the 1923–24 inflation, which put it on the same footing as the proletariat, appeared to the Comintern as the basis for a stronger German Communist Party and the road to eventual power in Germany.

The only obstacle to this goal was the existence and the genuine influence of German Social Democracy, which was barring the way to Communism.

The Communists therefore considered Social Democracy as their prime enemy, not only in Germany but everywhere, because it was competing with them for the allegiance of the workers. Its numerical strength was greater, and its ideological influence extended over wide strata of the working class; but it was also the ideology of salaried employees, civil servants, and other workers who had no desire for a Russian-style revolution, and who considered as adequate the trade-union struggle and such peaceful means as demonstrations for attaining a higher standard of living.

The Comintern's strategy of a "united front from below" (that is, unite with the Socialist rank and file but fight against the Socialist leadership) was determined by this situation. In Germany this strategy bore no fruits; it was equally unsuccessful in France.

What about Hitler's threat?

At the Eleventh Executive Session of the Communist International in Moscow in April 1931, Manuilsky said, "Fascism, à la Hitler, may decline, and is probably already on the wane thanks to the influence of our party." And Ernst Thälmann, in December 1931, wrote in *Internationale* (the periodical whose role was similar to that of the French *Cahiers du Bolchévisme*): "By raising the spectre of Hitler's fascism, Social Democracy is attempting to sidetrack the masses from vigorous action against the dictatorship of finance capital. . . . There are some people who fail to see the Social Democratic forest for the National Socialist trees."

The German Communist Party, as a result, concentrated its artillery on the German Social Democratic party.

On July 20, 1932, von Papen threw the Prussian Socialist ministers out of office. He could do this because the National Socialists had demanded and obtained a referendum with this objective in view. The German Communist Party backed this referendum, which thereby was approved by a majority of the voters. It should be noted in passing that Prussia was the last stronghold of the Social Democratic party at the time.

In December 1932, Thälmann came to Paris to take part in a large rally organized in Bullier Hall by the French Communist Party. He had been compelled to enter France illegally and was to leave in the same manner.

Albert Vassart had been entrusted with Thälmann's safety. Vassart, who spoke a little German, received Thälmann and brought him to the meeting. Few people were aware of Thälmann's arrival. So when he took the floor—with all the doors of the hall closed—the enthusiasm was great.

He gave his speech, the translation of which had been prepared in advance, and left the hall as soon as he had finished while attention was focused on Thorez, who was reading the translation. Vassart led Thälmann toward a waiting car a short distance beyond the police who surrounded Bullier Hall and who paid no attention to these two men who left far in advance of the others.

During this short walk, Vassart asked Thälmann what he thought of the German situation and the Hitler movement. Thälmann replied (and Vassart knew enough German and was familiar enough with the Communist vocabulary to understand him correctly) that Hitler was on the decline, and that the Social Democrats remained the principal foe of the German Communist Party.

All this happened on December 1, 1932. Two months later, on January 30, 1933, Hitler was in power in Germany.

But even this event was not yet taken seriously by the Comintern. It felt that Hitler's accession to power had the advantage of destroying the German population's democratic illusions, which had been fostered by the Social Democrats; this might be useful to the Communist party when its turn came to take the place of a "worn-out" Hitler.

That this was indeed the Comintern's evaluation of the situation in Germany is apparent from the pronouncements of the Communist International in those days. *L'Humanité* of April 1, 1933 contains the text of a resolution adopted by the Presidium of the Executive Committee of the Communist International at the end of March 1933. It appeals to Communists everywhere to close their ranks, to continue a united front with the Socialist workers (at the grass-roots but in opposition to the Social Democratic leadership) in order to overthrow the Fascist dictatorships by armed insurrection, and then it specifically appeals to the German Communist Party in these terms:

> The establishment of an undisguised Fascist dictatorship, by dispelling the democratic illusions of the masses and freeing them from the influence of Social Democracy, is accelerating Germany's march toward a proletarian revolution. The Communists' task must be to explain to the masses that Hitler's government is leading the country to disaster. The masses must now be counseled more energetically than ever that the workers can escape growing misery and avoid catastrophe only by a proletarian revolution and the dictatorship of the proletariat.

One could hardly have been farther from the mark!

But the year 1933 proved that Hitler's position was firmly established. He had deployed the techniques used by the Bolsheviks in 1917–18 and thereafter: one-party rule, political police, destruction of all opposition within the party and of all adversaries. Then he turned abroad for assistance. Ribbentrop, the Minister of Foreign Affairs, was making overtures to various governments, then paying visits abroad, and he made the mistake of hinting that Hitler's Germany wished to live in harmony with all its neighbors but was planning to fight against the Soviet Union.

The Soviet government paid close attention. Of course, the words of this former wine salesman and apprentice diplomat were received coolly by those democratic countries which had diplomatic and trade relations with the Soviet Union. But the latter had been warned. One never could tell; this incipient threat might some day become reality.

After some time, Hitler made friendly overtures to Pilsudski, then Polish head of state, and his gestures did not go unheeded. The danger was drawing near the Soviet border.

The master of the Kremlin therefore decided to launch a "diplomatic offensive." He had a much abler diplomat than Ribbentrop at his disposal—Litvinov, an appealing figure, multilingual, familiar with the Western world.

He drew up nonaggression pacts with some states between February and April, 1934, negotiated the "Eastern Locarno" pact, and prepared the ground for Soviet Russia's entry into the League of Nations, aided in this step by the French minister of foreign affairs, Barthou.

Meanwhile, the Comintern, in line with the policy of establishing closer ties with the democratic forces and in order to weaken Hitler's fascism, wanted the support of strong Communist parties.

But there was hardly a Communist party in existence other than the French.

Although great international congresses, such as the Amsterdam Congress against War in 1932 and the Anti-Fascist Congress held in Paris in Pleyel Hall the following year, were conspicuous and served a useful propaganda purpose, they increased Communist influence only in some intellectual circles without denting the Socialist parties, whose members participated in small numbers and on a strictly personal basis in these congresses.

The French Communist Party, at the end of 1933, was practically isolated. It represented no major base of support for the Soviet Union. Its strategy of "class against class" and "united front from below" did not secure it a significant influence in the country.

The Russian leaders had grasped the reasons for this isolation and decided to find a different strategy to strengthen Communist influence abroad. If they succeeded in achieving a greater influence for the Communists, this would have repercussions in the other democratic countries and would make it easier for the Soviet Union to find support against Hitler.

This was the situation when the Thirteenth Plenary Session of the ECCI was held at Moscow in December 1933. The French delegation was headed by Thorez, whose conscience was untroubled because he had implemented all earlier decisions of the Comintern.

Moreover, the French Communist Party had slightly improved its position, had taken part in the preparation of the Anti-Fascist Congress in Pleyel Hall, had reorganized its districts, and had registered a slight gain in membership and in the sale of *L'Humanité*.

Thorez, however, became the object of strong criticism at this session. He had expected, if not praise, at least less harsh criticism of the French Communist Party. He did not understand why the Comintern was so severe toward his party.

The leaders of the Comintern were playing a subtle game. They hoped that the French Communist leaders would give them a lead in changing their policy in France. But Thorez never had been an astute person. He felt his party had been unfairly accused; he was sure of having followed the correct line, the one expressed in all theses and resolutions. His mistake was that he never questioned that line itself. The Comintern hoped that he would condemn the strategy applied so far as ineffective, but he did nothing of the sort. What he did was to attack Doriot, who was beginning to create an opposition within the Communist party and to advocate an understanding with the Socialists.

Manuilsky, then one of the secretaries of the Communist International, was so exasperated by Thorez' attitude that he told him, "You are too subservient to be a real leader!" This was a painful utterance to hear but should have given Thorez pause: he should have realized that Manuilsky was blaming him precisely for his blind obedience to the old theses. But he did not have enough subtlety for that. He was only deeply irritated by this utterance, which had been addressed to him in the presence of other French comrades.

But Vassart, who could put two and two together, took these words to convey not so much an insult to Thorez as a suggestion to discard the old theses and to propose a new policy.

Since Thorez had been unable to interpret the words properly, the leaders of the Comintern realized that Thorez would not propose anything new and decided to take steps to attain their ends.

No sanction was applied against Doriot, and it was decided that Vassart would be summoned to Moscow as the representative of the French Communist Party to the Comintern. This implied that Vassart had been relieved of his functions as secretary in the French Communist Party organization.

The ties between the national Communist parties and the Comintern were established by two procedures: the International sent an emissary to each of the parties, and each party sent a representative to the Communist International. (See pp. 45 ff. of this volume.) The latter post happened to be vacant for the French party at the time the ECCI was meeting, in December 1933, because Marty, who had held it, had returned to France and was now editor-in-chief of *L'Humanité*.

In France Thorez gave his own account of the decisions reached by the Thirteenth Session of the Executive Committee with respect to the French Communist Party.

He related the harsh criticism which had been leveled against him and announced that Vassart had been relieved of his functions for "a tour of duty in Moscow." This made everybody—including Vassart—think that Vassart was to be the scapegoat. He therefore asked Thorez in what capacity he was to go to Moscow. The latter only replied, "Just go ahead, we shall see!"

At heart Vassart was convinced that the policy in force was not a good one, and he took the decision relieving him of his secretarial post philosophically, feeling that only a good policy could produce good results for the organization. But he was hardly pleased by the prospect of being cast into the wilderness burdened with the sins of the party. He asked numerous questions of Thorez, who only replied: "We shall see."

In retrospect, it seems possible that Thorez was not eager to have Vassart in the post of representative and that Thorez hoped that Vassart might refuse to be "victimized."

This was indeed Vassart's first reaction, but the Comintern's representative in Paris (who also was unaware that a shift of policy was in the offing) discussed the matter with Vassart, appealed to his sense of discipline, and persuaded him to go to Moscow.

He was set to leave at the beginning of February 1934, but the mounting political tension anchored him in Paris, and he continued to exercise his functions as secretary of the organization until the eve of his departure. This gave him a chance to have his say in the Communist party's decision to participate in the general strike and the demonstration of February 12, 1934.

Vassart had not yet reached Moscow when, at the seventeenth congress of the Bolshevik party (January 26 to February 10, 1934) Stalin made his "Fascism Means War" speech, on which Thorez commented (in 1937!) in his *Fils du Peuple*: "Fascism means war. Our struggle against war thus became a struggle against fascism, for the defense of democratic liberties. Any threat to democratic rights represented a step toward fascism" (p. 90).

But as late as April 1934, Thorez was excoriating anyone who proposed a rapprochement with the Socialist party for the sake of defending democratic liberties.

After February 12, 1934, Doriot and Barbé, along with several other comrades, advanced arguments in favor of a rapprochement with the Socialist party, thereby incurring Thorez' wrath. Doriot composed an "open letter to the Communist International" which he published in the local Saint-Denis newspaper, *L'Emancipation,* simultaneously with, or even before, dispatching it to its destination—a serious breach of discipline.

Shortly before his departure Vassart was given the task of arguing against Doriot in Doriot's party cell, but failed to obtain a vote against him. After the meeting, Vassart told Doriot he was leaving for Moscow in a few days and offered to get Doriot invited by the Comintern. But Doriot was skeptical. He believed that such an invitation would be of no avail and stated in a disillusioned tone that he expected nothing of such a trip. He gave the impression of a man who, considering his efforts futile, was expecting reprisals by the Comintern.

Vassart left for Moscow in the second half of April 1934, accompanied by his wife.

He was very warmly received and immediately recognized as the representative of the French Communist Party. This came to him as a surprise after his conversations with Thorez, but the first talks with the Comintern leaders made clear to him that he was expected to help change the tactics of the French Communist Party.

He was delighted by this, for he saw in this the Comintern's readiness to help the French Communist Party shed its isolation and assume a greater importance in one of the few countries where it had not yet been outlawed. He too was unaware that the new foreign policy of the USSR was alone responsible for the shift in France, and saw in it only the Comintern's keen understanding of what should be the proper policy of the French Communist Party.

"You will make us a report," Manuilsky told Vassart, "about what the French Communist Party wants the International to know."

Vassart then made an orthodox report before half a dozen Russian professors of the Lenin school, after which Manuilsky said: "It is a good official report. But since the official ceremony is over, you will agree that I should ask the question: 'What does Comrade Vassart think?' "

And since Vassart was trying to get away, Manuilsky cut short: "I shall see you tomorrow morning. I want to know what you think. And bear in mind that I have certain information which you do not have. I don't believe the French Communist Party fibs. February 12 marked a great Party victory. There are other forces which should join in the struggle with the French party."

Vassart therefore spoke at a restricted meeting of the political commission of the Comintern. He pointed out that Doriot was correct in thinking that the French party could not succeed by following the line fixed by the Executive.

"What do you propose?"

"I propose that you invite Doriot." (Violent opposition.) "I have spoken to Doriot."

Feigned surprise: "What kind of methods are these?"

"I said to Doriot in Paris, if I were he I would ask that my point of view be explained to the Comintern. This would be the beginning of a change.—'You don't know the Russians,' replied Doriot. 'I will not go to Moscow. If I go, it would be only if forty per cent of the party were behind me.'—'The way the party is organized, this is impossible,' said Vassart. 'And what if I get you an invitation?'— 'Keep trying,' was Doriot's reply."

Manuilsky was among those who objected most vigorously, but he was soon won over by Vassart's suggestion. He told him several days later: "Send a telegram, but invite both Thorez and Doriot."

By inviting both Thorez and Doriot, the Comintern put them on an equal footing. It is true that Thorez at that time was not yet secretary-general of the Communist party. He was one of the three party secretaries, but he was the one who was responsible for party policy. Nevertheless, by addressing an invitation to both Thorez and Doriot, the Comintern indicated its desire to choose between the two views and to approve the better one. Of course there was nothing in the invitation hinting that a decision had already been made, but the fact that there existed a "desire to choose" implied at least that Thorez' views were not being accepted *a priori* and that Doriot was to get a hearing.

THE INVITATION TO MOSCOW AND ITS CONSEQUENCES

This summons was published in the April 27 and 28, 1934, issues of *L'Humanité*. It was addressed to the French politburo, of which both Thorez and Doriot were members, as well as to each of them personally. It stated:

"We consider it necessary to put an end to the party's internal battle. Send Doriot and Thorez here. The Comintern will look into the factional disagreement in the French party. Let us know when they will leave."

Thorez packed his bags and left at once.

Doriot did not leave and made no reply.

If Thorez had shown lack of perspicacity at the beginning of 1934, it was now Doriot's turn. He should have realized that the expression "look into the disagreement" with respect to him meant that his opinion would be listened to! This lack of insight just when it was needed most determined the future course of his development.

Twice more Doriot was asked to leave—by the politburo of the French Communist Party on April 30 and by a message from the Comintern on May 10. But he failed to reply and did not leave.

During his two weeks' stay in Moscow, Thorez was at loose ends. No deliberations took place; in reply to his requests for interviews with the leaders of the Comintern, he was told that the deliberations would begin upon Doriot's arrival.

Thorez left toward the middle of May without having had any discussions with a responsible organ of the Comintern. Did he realize that he and his policy had been rejected, that the Comintern was relying on Doriot to make a successful switch, and that by such a change in the Communist party leadership, the will of the Party to seek a rapprochement with the Socialist party would find more natural expression and would be more easily carried out?

But Doriot did not come to Moscow, did not even reply, and this was too serious for the Comintern to forgive and forget. Still, it spared him to the utmost, and even when it finally decided to authorize the French Communist Party to expel him, it wrapped this decision in unusually indulgent terminology, hoping that Doriot would come to his senses. But he did nothing of the sort, making his expulsion irrevocable.

Thorez did not conceal his jubilation. He compared Doriot to Trotsky and blamed him above all for having wanted to follow the policy which he, Thorez, was to launch a few weeks later. This took place on May 23, 1934, at a meeting of party militants, to whom Thorez gave the reasons for Doriot's expulsion.

THE POLICY SHIFT

It should be recalled that during March and April the Socialist party had made several proposals for joint actions to the Communist party, of which nothing came because the Communist party had set impossible conditions. Upon returning to France, Thorez was preoccupied by his triumph over Doriot and did nothing to alter his policy.

Between May 20 and 23, 1934, a minority at the Socialist congress proposed unity of action with the Communists on a revolutionary basis. A motion proposing "action for the conquest of power through unified proletarian action" received majority approval.

In Moscow at the Comintern it became clear that the time was ripe for action and that the motion voted by the majority could serve as a basis for a rapprochement. It was also evident that the French Communist Party had not changed its tactics and that its political secretary had not understood the Comintern's intentions. These intentions would have to be spelled out more explicitly.

Sometime in May, Manuilsky declared to Vassart, "For the June French Communist Party conference, a new policy must be worked out." At this moment, Manuilsky was the only one to think thus, and Vassart did not know the reasons for his sudden about-face.

There were long discussions between Manuilsky and Vassart, in which Ercoli (Togliatti) and Gerö were invited to participate. The subject was the need for finding ways of banding together the greatest possible number of people in France to rally against fascism. Even in the army, for instance, there were officers who were good republicans. The problem was how to isolate the fascist officers from the republican officers.

Then one day Manuilsky asked Vassart and Révai to see him.

"Good day, Comrade Vassart," he said in a very officious tone. "Sit over there," he said to Révai. "You, Vassart, are the French ambassador in the Comintern. I am going to tell you, Révai, just what I think of the French situation. A few days ago, Ramette [a French Communist leader] made a speech in the French Chamber of Deputies on the subject 'There is no difference between the left bourgeoisie and Social Democracy.' This is an example of political cretinism. The fundamental difference between the right and the left must be understood. There is no difference from the standpoint of principle, but there is a fundamental difference if this is considered from the point of view of tactics. It is as simple as ABC. We need a vast rallying together. We cannot stop with Socialists."

This was Manuilsky's way of letting Vassart know that the game had been won. Stalin had approved the change of Party line. This had not been done with difficulty. One day when Vassart found Manuilsky particularly gloomy and commented on this, Manuilsky replied, "I am risking my neck for the sake of your affairs."

During this entire discussion, Vassart did not once see Stalin, or any other leader of the Soviet Communist Party.

Therefore, shortly after the congress of the French Socialist party, Vassart was entrusted by the Secretariat of the Comintern with the task of drawing up a document to be sent to the French Communist Party to serve as a foundation for the national conference of the Communist party planned for June 23 and 24, 1934, at Ivry. This document expounded the theses that the bourgeoisie must no longer be regarded as a single bloc, that the Communist party must learn to exploit the differences in the enemy camp, work more closely with the Socialists, and consider the struggle against fascism as the prime objective. The Communist party therefore should put all its energies into enlisting all those who wanted to fight against fascism and create a broad united front.

This sounded the death knell for the policy of "class against class" and "united front from below." The document contained the main bases for the future work of the Communist party, including the principle of the popular front, though the term itself did not appear in it as yet. The document was sent to the Communist party and arrived in time to bring about the change in policy at the Ivry conference.

Drawing up this declaration required some time, and the approval of the Secretariat of the Comintern still had to be obtained. But it was in the hands of the Communist party leadership shortly before the national conference—not soon enough, however, to prevent the French Communist Party's leadership from making another blunder.

The people connected with the Comintern were at the time concerned about the dangers to which Thälmann, head of the German Communist Party, was exposed, having been arrested by the Nazis. A sentence was about to be handed down against him and three comrades, and it was feared that he would be condemned to death. The Comintern thereupon sent a message to the French Communist Party, asking it to wage a campaign to save Thälmann by organizing rallies, demonstrations, and so on in his favor. This appeal appeared in the May 31, 1934, issue of *L'Humanité*. The Comintern also asked the French Communist Party to appeal directly to the Socialists, which it did. The Socialist leadership accepted on June 5, and a meeting between the delegates of the two parties took place on June 11. The Socialist party delegates expressed their willingness to undertake a joint campaign, under the sole condition that the Communist party call a halt to its attacks against the Socialist leaders. The Communist delegates declined this condition, and the negotiations were broken off (see *Le Populaire* of June 6 and 12, 1934).

It is hard to imagine the reaction produced in Moscow by this attitude of the Communist leaders; such complete lack of understanding was simply too stupid to believe.

But that was not all. The Socialists had voted against the military budget in the Chamber of Deputies. Thorez suggested that they wage a joint nationwide campaign against militarism (June 15, 1934). Again, the Socialists were willing and negotiations resumed, only to be broken off two days later because of insults in *L'Humanité* and the *Cahiers du Bolchévisme* against the Socialist leaders.

The reaction of Socialist leaders was natural. How could there be a common action with a partner who attacked those with whom it negotiated? It was probably at this point that the Socialist leaders decided they had had enough. The Communists' desisting in attacking the Socialist leaders was a *conditio sine qua non.*

The organ of the Northern Socialist Federation in Lille, *La Bataille Ouvrière,* was the first to publish a proposal of a "nonaggression pact" in its June 22, 1934 issue. This proposal, which probably had been drafted by Lebas, was presented by the Socialist party to the Communist party as a basis for collaboration.

Le Populaire of June 23, 1934, again took up the proposal that the Socialist party was to submit to the Communist party. Léon Blum, commenting on the proposal in this issue of the paper, declared that he wholly agreed with it and stated that it faithfully reflected the spirit pervading the whole Socialist party.

The issue of *Le Populaire* containing this proposal arrived in Moscow on the next day (the Comintern received the newspaper daily by air). Vassart took note of it. He realized that here was a chance, perhaps the last, to reach an accord with the Socialists. Manuilsky was of the same opinion. He even remarked that the Communist party leadership must not be given time to "make a mess of things" again! Vassart suggested to him that a counter-proposal be drafted, which not only would accept the idea of "nonaggression" but would go even further and lead to "unity of action."

Manuilsky also had read Le Populaire and had the same reaction as Vassart. He suggested sending an uncoded telegram to the French Communist Party.

"Impossible," replied Vassart.

"But if we lose forty-eight hours they will do something stupid.

I'll send word to Piatnitsky. It should be sent within three hours."

This first telegram was worded as follows: "Wait before reply-ing. Proposals follow."

Several days later (about July 1), Fried arrived and Manuilsky rudely insulted him. Fried tried to defend himself: "My tasks are stag-gering. I have not been able to isolate Doriot. What is the main thing required of me?"

"Do you think that a Comintern delegate should ask such a question? You will not return to Paris."

Vassart took up Fried's defense.

Manuilsky asked him to be quiet. "You are not qualified to talk about it," said Manuilsky. "We know our own personnel better than you do."

"Personnel? He is the Executive delegate!"

The text of the Socialist proposal, as it appeared in *Le Populaire* of June 23, 1934, was as follows:

PROPOSAL OF A SOCIALIST-COMMUNIST NONAGGRESSION PACT

Spurred by the desire to defeat fascism, convinced that it is in the interests of the working class to improve and make more broth-erly the relations between the two parties, in the absence of an organic unity for which conditions are perhaps not ripe, the con-tracting parties, in the face of the fascist danger which confronts the world of labor and realizing the need of undertaking definite actions with the agreement of both parties, are resolved to conclude a pact containing the following provisions:

1. Each of the contracting parties promises to put an end to attacks, insults, and criticism leveled against the organizations and the responsible and elected militants of the other party. This prom-ise is binding for the regional and local organizations.

2. If, in the course of meetings or demonstrations, militants belonging to one or the other party are locked in struggle with fascist adversaries, the members of the contracting parties must render each other mutual aid and assistance in repelling aggression.

3. The obligations stipulated in articles 1. and 2. above shall not in any way limit or prohibit the right of each party to carry on its own propaganda and recruitment.

4. Disputes over points of doctrine and tactics, far from being proscribed, are desirable to the extent that they raise the intel-

lectual level of the masses and are carried on in a fair and equitable manner.

5. Each of the contracting parties promises to respect in every way the sovereignty and authority of the supervisory organs of the other party and not to interfere in any way in its internal affairs, particularly abstaining from any action which might give rise to or encourage any splintering tendencies.

This is the counterproposal worked out by Vassart, as printed in the July 2, 1934, issue of *L'Humanité*:

The Central Committee of the Communist party and the Permanent Administrative Commission of the Socialist party are impelled by the desire to defeat fascism.

It is obvious that this aim can be attained only by the joint action of the working classes coming together for specific battle goals. It is in the interest of the working class that the Communist party and the Socialist party organize this common action against fascism. Faced with the danger which fascism represents for the working class and with organized onslaughts by armed bands against the proletariat, the Communist party and the Socialist party recognize the necessity for undertaking this specific action by common agreement, under these terms and conditions:

1. Each of the parties promises to organize jointly and to participate with all the means at its disposal (organization, press, elected leaders, party militants, etc.) in a nationwide campaign with the following aims:

    a. To mobilize the entire working population against the fascist organizations in France in order to bring about their disarmament and dissolution;

    b. To oppose laws by decree;

    c. To oppose the Hitler terror and to fight for the release of Thälmann and all other antifascists.

2. This antifascist campaign shall be waged by means of joint rallies in the largest possible number of places and plants, and by means of antifascist street demonstrations. The campaign against laws by decree shall be similarly waged, supplemented by the use of methods of agitation and organization suitable for achieving a broad strike action against such laws.

If members of one or the other party should, in the course of this common action, find themselves in conflict with fascist opponents, the members of the other party shall aid and assist them in repelling the fascists.

3. During this period of common action, the two parties

shall abstain from reciprocal attacks, insults, and criticism against the organizations and party militants loyally participating in the action.

However, each party will maintain complete independence in working out its own propaganda and carrying on its own recruitment program.

4. Disputes over doctrine and tactics, far from being outlawed as a result of our unity of action, remain essential for raising the political level of the masses and for developing the class consciousness of the proletariat.

5. In the interest of successful common action, each party reserves to itself the right to denounce those who, after accepting specific obligations, try to evade their implementation as well as those who adopt positions or commit acts which might be deleterious to the success of action in progress.

The sleight of hand consisted in changing just a few sentences in order to convert a negative document "against mutual aggression" into a positive proposal "for unity of action."

Vassart's text was approved at once by the Secretariat of the Comintern and was cabled to the French Communist Party for submission to the Socialists on June 25, 1934.

The permanent administrative commission of the Socialist party replied that the Communist party's proposal would be submitted to the national council of the Socialist party, which was to meet on July 15, 1934.

Reinforced by the document of the Comintern and the proposed pact for united action which he had received from Moscow, Thorez brought about the shift in the party line at the national conference of the Communist party in Ivry, June 23–26.

Then, on July 1, 1934, Thorez published an article in the *Cahiers du Bolchévisme* in which he explained the change in position of the Communist party by blaming the old policy on all those expelled from the Party, Doriot in particular.

Naturally, the Socialist party leadership was somewhat astonished by the sudden about-face. Léon Blum tried to make sense of it and, indeed, he was one of the few men who grasped the essence of the situation. In an article published in *Le Populaire* of July 13, 1934, he wrote:

> Hitler's accession to power . . . confronted the Russian Revolution with the most serious danger it had faced in thirteen or fourteen

years. This danger has increased now that Hitler, after establishing closer ties with Pilsudski, is preparing a German-Polish coalition to attack Russia. There is no need to go farther afield in seeking the cause for this diplomatic N.E.P. and for Russia's impending entry into the League of Nations.

He then explained that, in his opinion, the Soviet Union wanted to safeguard its European front by a system of international guarantees. Furthermore, in the course of making overtures to the French government, it sought the support of the masses of the French people by rallying them behind the idea of an antifascist struggle. Léon Blum obviously knew what it was all about. But among the ranks of the workers there was nothing but jubilation at the fact that the great day of unity was dawning.

The Communist party leadership suddenly had become all sugar and honey.

The Founding of the Cominform

by

EUGENIO REALE

The wheel of history—an expression commonly used and abused by the Communists—spun full turn for the eighteen Communist leaders from Eastern and Western Europe who took part in the founding of the Cominform in September 1947. Only one member of the team from Eastern Europe can boast of having kept his position intact without a break: G. Dej, the secretary-general of the Rumanian Communist Party.* Another, W. Gomulka, succeeded in regaining his position after some vicissitudes, including disfavor and prison. A third member occupies a special place: Edvard Kardelj, who was labeled "traitor," "revisionist," or "comrade," depending on fluctuations in policy with respect to Yugoslavia. The other leaders from Eastern Europe all have been eliminated, either politically by purge, in most cases entailing their expulsion from the Party—like G. Malenkov, V. Chervenkov, H. Minc, Anna Pauker, M. Farkas, and J. Révai—or physically—like A. Zhdanov, V. Poptomov, R. Slansky, St. Bastovansky—by death from natural causes or by judicial murder.

On the other hand, the Communist leaders of Western Europe who were present at this historic event—J. Duclos, E. Fajon, and L. Longo—were able to maintain their positions, since the so-called bourgeois democracies offered greater personal and political safety. I am the only Westerner to have quit the Party; indeed, among the founders of the Cominform, Djilas and I are the only ones to have broken definitively and irrevocably with communism—with both the doctrine and the movement.

---

*G. Dej died on March 19, 1965, after this article had been written.—EDs.

253

Djilas is now in prison, after having published his memoirs on Stalin, in which he but briefly mentions the founding of the Cominform. Consequently, I am the sole witness able to relate what happened at Szklarska Poreba between September 2 and 27, 1947. I have given an account of these events in my book on the establishment of the Cominform.[1] But these personal notes, jotted down during sessions at that Polish castle and introduced by a long preface of my own, warrant some comments and clarifications in the light of today's historical perspective.

I have read the articles about the founding of the Cominform written at the time of the event and the studies that have appeared since dealing with this institution, and then asked myself two questions.

First: Do the other texts, resolutions, and declarations of Communist-Stalinist origin deviate as widely from facts as they do in this case? For there is a marked discrepancy between what I saw and heard at Szklarska Poreba, and what was published later in official documents on the founding of the Cominform.

Second: Why did the news commentators and later the historians never question the accuracy of these official texts, but base their analyses and hypotheses on them? These surely would have been different if the Stalinist versions had been taken with a grain of salt.

In examining the documentation on the conference published by the official organ of the Cominform, I fail to discern in the text of the speeches (with the exception of some statistical data) any resemblance to my personal notes, which constitute a kind of abbreviated report. I have in mind not only the understandable omissions on the crucial issue (the strategy for seizing power) and the disputes which arose among the representatives of the different parties, but even questions of secondary importance, whose disclosure certainly would have had no harmful consequences. Even these have been distorted or made unrecognizable. One gets the impression that an alien hand must have kneaded the material according to a recipe into the desired distorted shape.

A fundamental issue on which the official documents maintain silence is the question of interparty differences. The conference served largely as a platform from which issued forth vigorous, scathing criticism of opportunism, legalism, bourgeois parliamentarianism, and other such ailments with which the French and Italian Communist parties were said to be afflicted.

The official documents also say nothing about the revealing reports presented by Communist leaders from countries about to be sovietized. The Chervenkov report does not mention sentences hinting at new arrests and exterminations of the non-Communist opposition, which I transcribed in my notes, such as: "We intend to shut up all opposition. There are still some imperialist agents among us, but we are determined to put an end to that." Nor is there any trace of the threat contained in the speech of the Hungarian delegate Révai, a threat soon to be carried out: "The destruction of Pfeiffer's party[2] is indispensable; we shall use the police to carry it out." The same holds true of Slansky's warning: "As far as we are concerned, our task is to deal a death blow to reaction in Slovakia."

Another point left unmentioned by the official documents is that the Communist leaders from Eastern Europe cynically admitted having succeeded in penetrating the non-Communist parties belonging to the "National Front," foreshadowing the so-called peaceful conquest of power. This is how Kardelj characterized the position of the Communists vis-à-vis the other parties in the National Front of Yugoslavia: "The Communist party is the only one that counts in the National Front. The others are nothing but figureheads. . . . The secretaries of all the National Front committees are simultaneously Communist party secretaries. . . . Of the twenty-four ministers in the central government, sixteen are Communists, and the others are closely affiliated with our party. All assistant ministers are Communists." Here is how Révai described the role of the National Peasant party (not to be confused with the Smallholders' party) in Hungary: "It acts under our guidance. The secretary is a Communist; one of the two ministers representing it in the government is a Communist. Fifteen of its thirty-two deputies are Communists; eight are sympathizers." Dej gave the following bizarre interpretation of the election outcome in the Rumanian parliamentary elections: "Election results show that the Party is the strongest in the country: 180 Communists were elected out of 340, although officially there were no more than 70."

As I cite these statements, I still can recall vividly my reaction to these revelations. I was floored when I heard Révai make the foregoing statement without compunction. How could the secretary of one party belong to another? My reasoning was evidently out of touch with bolshevik or, at least, Stalinist logic. And when Révai added that out of thirteen ministers, four were Socialists, four Smallholders, two representatives of the National Peasant party—and *seven* Communists—which added up to seventeen, instead of thirteen ministers—I was certainly astonished.

Finally, nothing is said in the official Communist documents about the presence of an entire auxiliary apparatus largely composed of "apparatchiks" formerly on the staff of the Comintern. Among them was Vitavski-Geminder, a member of the Czechoslovak delegation because of his position as head of the foreign section of his party secretariat. He had belonged to the central apparatus of the Comintern until its dissolution in 1943. Returning to Czechoslovakia, he played an important behind-the-scenes role until he was arrested and shot together with Slansky and others in December 1952. (From his cell in the Prague jail Vitavski-Geminder addressed an anguished and moving letter to his old friend Togliatti, with whom he had enjoyed close relations during their several years together in Moscow, who knew him better than anyone and therefore could have testified in his favor and affirmed his innocence. But Togliatti did not lift a finger to help his old friend and co-worker.)

The Soviet delegation included D. Shevliagin, a Communist bureaucrat responsible for keeping watch over the French and Italian Communist parties, particularly the latter. He retained this function through the upheaval following Stalin's death and continues to exercise it even now. The former Comintern "apparatchik" in the Yugoslav delegation was V. Vlahović, a veteran of the International Brigades in Spain, later the representative of the Communist Party of Yugoslavia at the Comintern and one of the secretaries of the Communist Youth International on the eve of its dissolution. Vlahović was head of the foreign section of the secretariat of the Yugoslav party's central committee in 1947. His opposite number in the Polish Communist Party was also present in Szklarska Poreba, as were several other Polish Communist leaders. The auxiliary personnel, however, were not entitled to attend the meetings, a privilege limited to the eighteen delegates.

THE COMINFORM WAS NO NEW COMINTERN

The founding of a new international Communist organ known as the Cominform did not necessarily signify revival, pure and simple, of the old Comintern. Nevertheless, this was the inference drawn by nearly all Western commentators.

In assessing the differences between the two organiza
remember two significant circumstances.

The first was the absence in all delegations of those old v
of the Comintern who in 1947 headed most of the parties in\
Szklarska Poreba. The most notable Soviet leader of the last period of
the Comintern was Manuilsky, who had worked in the Comintern
apparatus since its "heroic" period under Lenin and Zinoviev, and
who during the final ten years had held more actual power than Dimitrov, the titular secretary-general. Manuilsky was removed from the
arena of international communism shortly after dissolution of the
Comintern in 1943. It was Zhdanov who appeared in the role of
master of ceremonies at the founding session of the Cominform; yet,
although elected a member of the ECCI at the 1935 congress, he had
never participated actively in the work of the Comintern before
1939, and even afterward his function in the organization had been
limited to signing its dissolution decree in 1943. He was seconded in
his performance at the conference by Malenkov, who himself had
never played any part in the international Communist movement.

The situation was even more clear-cut for Bulgaria. Two of Bulgaria's party leaders, Kolarov and Dimitrov, had participated in the
work of the Comintern since the time of Lenin, and both had held the
highest positions in the Presidium and the Executive Committee of
the Comintern, as well as in its Secretariat. Still, neither of them was
present at Szklarska Poreba.

As for Czechoslovakia, only one national leader had played an
important Comintern role in the past—Klement Gottwald. His
counterpart in Hungary was Mátiás Rákosi, who had served as secretary of the Comintern while Lenin was alive. Both stayed away from
the conference. Rumania was represented by G. Dej, who never had
exercised any function in the Comintern, and by Anna Pauker,
whose husband had once occupied a position of some importance in
the Comintern's central apparatus but had been executed by Stalin
ten years earlier. Anna Pauker's name figured only once in the upper
echelon of the Comintern—on the occasion of its dissolution in May
1943. The French Communist Party had three leaders who had held
high honorary or actual posts in the Comintern: Thorez, Marty and
Cachin. They had been elected to the Presidium of the ECCI at the
last Comintern congress in 1935. Yet all three were replaced by Duclos, who had been named in 1935 to the Executive Committee only,

and by Fajon, who had never had any connection with the Comintern.

I know that Togliatti had been asked to go to Poland and had succeeded in backing out, yet it hardly seems credible to me that ten former Comintern leaders—especially those on the other side of the iron curtain—could possibly have emulated Togliatti by refusing to attend the conference. Only one other hypothesis remains: they were not invited, deliberately not associated with this undertaking, in accordance with instructions from Stalin.

There was another intriguing omission. During the entire six days of our meetings, the word "Comintern" was never mentioned—clearly an intentional taboo. Needless to say, the Stalinist training of the participants saved them from the blunder of raising the question of the Communist International or even of alluding to it by a word.

In contrast to the way the Comintern had prepared its statutes at the beginning, we were left in the dark about the basic machinery of the organism we were supposed to be creating. Thus the question of our next meeting or of the frequency of our meetings was never raised in our discussions, nor was it said which parties were to be members of the organization. Why, for instance, had Albania not been invited to this meeting, considering that its Communist party had seized power with considerably less outside aid than practically any other Communist party of Eastern Europe, where Communist regimes had been imposed from the outside? Why was East Germany, whose party one year earlier had fused with the Socialists, not represented, although this kind of fusion was soon to be carried out in Czechoslovakia, Bulgaria, Hungary, Rumania? Why, finally, were Asian Communist parties excluded, such as the Chinese Communist Party, already marching to final victory? What about North Korea, where Russian soldiers already had helped place the Communist party in control, as they had done previously in Eastern Europe? These pertinent questions never were raised openly in Szklarska Poreba.

There was one decisive point, however, in which the new Cominform bore a fraternal resemblance to the final stage of the old Comintern: Stalin was its absolute master, without even condescending to put in an appearance. We were made conscious of this fact in the course of our debates by the existence of a direct telephone line between our Szklarska Poreba castle and the Kremlin. Zhdanov was at our end of the line (or sometimes Malenkov), and from the other end came orders from Stalin personally, as I was to learn during a brief conversation with Zhdanov.

I had objected to the title proposed by Zhdanov for the Cominform newspaper, *For a Lasting Peace, For a People's Democracy,* as being too long and complicated. "I cannot visualize," I said, "an Italian worker saying to the vendor: *'For a Lasting Peace, For a People's Democracy.'* Let's pick a shorter title." Zhdanov gave me a crushing look: "Titles are neither long nor short. The title must express an idea, a program. In any case, if you must know, it was Stalin who thought up this name and communicated it to me over the telephone this morning."

Stalin's idea of choosing such an absurd title to "express a program" was an accurate gauge of his level of intelligence and the caliber of his reasoning. I failed to realize this at the time, as I should have, and Zhdanov was justified, from his standpoint, in bringing me to heel, in impressing on my memory Stalin's personal role in concocting this title. Djilas, who was much more familiar at the time with the secrets of the Soviet pantheon than we Italians, also recalled this episode and mentioned it in his book, *Conversations with Stalin*: "I might mention as a curiosity that it was Stalin who thought up the name of the Cominform's organ *For a Lasting Peace, For a People's Democracy,* with the idea that the Western press would have to repeat the slogan each time it quoted something from it. But Stalin's expectation was not fulfilled: because of the length and transparent propaganda nature of its name, the newspaper was—as though for spite—most frequently referred to simply as 'the organ of the Cominform.' "[3]

THE COMINFORM'S AIM

We Italians were not kept informed of preparations for the establishment of the Cominform. We had been invited to the founding conference, but no one had told us what it was all about or what goals had been set. Stalin's disdain was evidenced, as usual, in varying degrees. Most foreign parties were not considered important enough to be invited to this conference; among the nine that were invited, some were apprised as to what was going on well before September 1947, whereas others, notably the French and Italian parties, were given notice just a week before the meeting.

When Longo and I arrived at the conference site, we learned

that nearly all delegates of the other parties had already arrived, some of them several days earlier. Only later did I realize with what care preparations had been made: everything had been arranged with minute precision and consummate skill. The work was to begin upon arrival of the French representatives. Stalin's two envoys already were conferring with the members of the other delegations, and I was conscious of some embarrassment on the part of our colleagues when we appeared on the scene.

The Yugoslavs were most privy to the secrets of the Kremlin gods, I observed. I heard that they had spent three or four days deliberating with the Soviet delegates on the spot.

Only later, when reading V. Dedijer's book, *Tito Speaks*, did I learn that as early as June 1946 Stalin had spoken with Dimitrov and Tito about the need of establishing an Information Bureau (the Cominform's official name) rather than of simply reviving the Comintern, on which Stalin heaped a torrent of insults and abuse which caused Dimitrov to become alternately pale and flushed with repressed anger.

During our discussions at Szklarska Poreba, I was made aware of one objective that Stalin had set for the new organization. From what the Communist leaders of Eastern Europe were saying, it became apparent that the communization of these countries, still only partial and uneven (Yugoslavia's was nearly complete, while Hungary's and Czechoslovakia's were far behind schedule), was now to be carried out at top speed.

While we were waiting for the report of the representative of the Bulgarian Communist Party, V. Chervenkov, the real aims of our conference began to emerge in sharper focus. The purpose was not so much to tighten the bonds between the different Communist parties as above all to apply the final touches to a general plan for easing the "National Front" allies out of power and establishing a Communist dictatorship in all countries of Eastern Europe, just as was being done in Bulgaria.

As our work progressed, this aim became more and more apparent. Herein lies the significance of the Szklarska Poreba conference, but the historian would seek in vain for any hint of it in the documentation from Communist sources, prolific though it is.

Indeed, the political and police measures taken in the Eastern European countries during the months following our conference, particularly the Prague coup in February 1948, furnished ample evidence, even to the uninitiated, that the Cominform was carrying out its assigned task.

In ensuing months another of Stalin's objectives for the Cominform of which nothing was said during our meeting—and for good reason—became apparent: the groundwork had been laid for Stalin's move against Tito.

On the surface nothing was said or done at the conference to arouse the least suspicion of Soviet intentions vis-à-vis Yugoslavia. On the contrary, the Yugoslavs alone gave the impression of having assumed the role of Soviet partners, while the others were being treated as more or less negligible quantities. Two special honors were accorded the Yugoslavs: Djilas and Kardelj shared the distinction of opening fire on the "opportunism" of the French and Italian parties; and Belgrade was selected as the capital of the Cominform.

However, Stalin's diabolical brain had hatched an entirely different scheme.

The Soviets had come well supplied with material suitable for denouncing French and Italian "opportunism," and had put it at Kardelj's and Djilas' disposal at the preliminary meetings just before the conference. Thus the Yugoslavs were amply provided with ammunition to attack us, as they had been ready to do anyway.

But Stalin had other worries than the ideological purity of Marxism-Leninism. He wanted to widen the gulf between the two main Communist parties of Western Europe and the most important Eastern European party (aside from that of the USSR, of course), according to the ancient principle: *divide et impera*. Many years after our Szklarska Poreba conference, Kardelj told me that his violent and basically unfair attack had been prepared with Zhdanov's and Malenkov's assent, that they had assigned the stellar role to the Yugoslav delegates and then scrupulously distributed lesser parts to others among the different delegations. This was the reason for the later arrival of the French and Italian delegations, the Russians having arranged it this way to allow sufficient time for determining the proper attitude to be adopted toward us. In Kardelj's opinion, the plan was based on an ulterior motive: Stalin, the omnipotent though invisible stage-setter at the conference, already harbored a grudge against Tito and the Yugoslavs, a grudge which was to burst forth so spectacularly into the open the following year. An important preliminary step in the dictator's scheme of vengeance was his casting of the Yugoslav delegates in the unsavory role of accusers.

Considering Stalin's political behavior in the years before the conference, the validity of these conclusions hardly can be doubted. In any case, such was the sequence of events. At the second conference of the Information Bureau, Togliatti emerged as the most uncompromising enemy of the Yugoslavs, anxious to avenge the previous year's insults by a frontal assault upon the Yugoslav Communist Party. The French Communist Party acted similarly. Etienne Fajon, the second-place French delegate at Szklarska Poreba, was given the task of drawing up the indictment against the Yugoslavs at the plenary session of his party. He pointed out that those who had attacked the French and Italians last year as deviationists had just been unmasked themselves, and with good reason.

A second outgrowth of our conference—the choice of Belgrade as the Cominform capital—also had a deeper significance in terms of Stalin's plans against Tito. At the time, comments on the eastern side of the iron curtain about this choice suggested this was a special honor conferred on the Yugoslavs by Moscow, while the free world surmised that the choice was the result of an alliance between Zhdanov and Tito, two "hard-liners," as opposed to such "soft-liners" as Malenkov, the Czechs, and others. Both interpretations were wide of the mark. Stalin, to "honor" the Yugoslavs with a special token of his favor, had prepared a poisoned chalice for them by choosing Belgrade; as to the presumed alliance between Zhdanov and Tito, Zhdanov possessed no power of decision on this score but simply had the privilege of passing on Stalin's orders. Stalin was the one who decided to base the Cominform at Belgrade, as Djilas very usefully recalls in his book:

> Stalin also decided in the end where the seat of the Cominform was to be. The delegates had agreed on Prague. The Czech representative, Slansky, hurried to Prague by car that evening to consult Gottwald about this. But that night Zhdanov and Malenkov talked with Stalin (for not even in that remote pension and distant location did they fail to have a direct telephone connection with Moscow), and though Gottwald was reluctant to agree, Stalin ordained that the seat should be in Belgrade.[4]

In all likelihood, Stalin's choice of Belgrade was part of his plan to infiltrate the Yugoslav regime more effectively, to surround it, under pretext of intra-Cominform cooperation, with Soviet and international personnel subject to Moscow's orders, and thus to prepare the ground for the decisive test of strength with Tito. In any event, if this was Stalin's intention, it did not crystallize into action when the crisis with Tito finally occurred.

Nonetheless, Stalin had at his disposal an international Communist organism, an "established name" on which to base his denunciation of Tito and which provided a tactical advantage of some formal significance (especially if compared with the clumsy way in which Khrushchev proceeded against the Albanians and the Chinese).

"MONOLITHISM" AND THE ATTACKS UPON
THE FRENCH AND ITALIANS

When Stalin was all-powerful, the term "monolithic unity" invariably appeared in every Communist declaration, whether a single party or the entire international movement was under discussion. By repeating it incessantly for twenty years, Stalin achieved one undeniable result: many people (above all Westerners) eventually belived in this "monolithic unity," just as they were taken in by such myths as Stalin's genius in military affairs, theoretical thought or linguistics. In truth, Stalin's world was no more monolithic than Stalin was a Marxist genius.

Stalin had been eminently successful in constructing a monolithic façade by his methods of lies and terror. He had massacred a large number of militant Communists, both Soviet and foreign, proclaiming the reign of "monolithism" over their dead bodies. He then transformed the Communist movement by turning it into a robot blindly obedient to him alone, and into a hermetically closed society to which only the ruling elite had access. Thus he created the impression of "monolithism." This façade crumbled into dust at his death, revealing the truth: the Communist world bore more resemblance to a basket of crabs than to a monolithic bloc.

Stalin reached his zenith between 1945 and 1948 as victor in the war, communizer of Eastern Europe, and all-powerful leader, glorified in both the Communist and the Western world. During these years I was a member of the central committee (enlarged politburo) of the Italian Communist Party and head of the central committee's foreign section. Even in my daily work I had occasion to observe that my own party was certainly not monolithic—no more so than was the French Communist Party—and that the leaders continued to like or dislike one another and to carry on intrigues. The same was true for

relations among all the major Communist parties. Only Stalin's omni-
presence prevented a public airing of these differences or any open
defiance of Moscow's orders; this happened only after Stalin's death.

The following is a brief, incomplete recapitulation of the points
of dissension among the Communist parties during the period of
"Stalinist monolithism."

In the Balkans, the Yugoslav and Bulgarian Communist parties
each included a faction for and a faction against cooperation in the
crucial Macedonian question. The Albanian Communist Party was
divided into Titoist and non-Titoist factions. Nor did unanimity reign
within the Greek Communist Party; moreover, while Soviet interest
in the Communist insurrection in Greece—in full swing during the
conference—seemed relatively secondary, the Yugoslavs responded
differently, giving it their unreserved support. (The Yugoslav-Soviet
disagreement on this point was conspicuous to us at Szklarska Poreba
when Kardelj, in contrast to Zhdanov and Malenkov, hailed this
rebellion as a positive event and prophesied a victorious conclusion.
When the Yugoslavs proposed that the Cominform's founding declaration pay a special tribute to the Greek insurrection, their suggestion was rejected by Zhdanov and Malenkov, well informed as they
were on the current state of Stalin's mind.)

The situation in Central Europe was hardly better, as Imre
Nagy was to confirm later in a manuscript submitted to the central
committee of the Hungarian Communist Party.[5] Disagreements
arose in this period between Nagy and Rákosi. At the same time,
relations between the Hungarian Communist Party and the fraternal
parties of Czechoslovakia and Rumania were far from cordial. When
I served as Italian ambassador to Warsaw from August 1945 to January 1947, I had the opportunity to learn about the "solidarity" of
Polish Communists with the Czech and East German Communists—
not to mention their feelings toward the Russians. (The memory of
the dissolution of the Polish Communist Party and the murder of almost all its leaders by Stalin's police was still very vivid.)

As for Moscow's relations with the Chinese Communist Party
during 1945–48, Stalin himself had laid down a clear line to follow.
According to Dedijer,[6] the Kremlin was anxious to cooperate with
Chiang Kai-shek and called in a delegation of the Chinese Communist Party to prevail upon it to support this line. The Chinese
feigned acceptance, did exactly the opposite when they returned
home, and ultimately won the war against Chiang Kai-shek.

The conference at Szklarska Poreba—especially the sessions of September 25 and 26—provided a classic illustration, deeply engraved in my memory, of the discrepancy between the monolithic unity proclaimed to the outside world (including the mass of Communists themselves) and the real state of affairs.

At the September 25 session Kardelj delivered his indictment of the Italian Communist Party. He said that Togliatti's fundamental mistake had been to stake everything on an impossible act of collaboration with de Gasperi just as the latter was preparing to eject Togliatti from the government. The Italian Communists always had asserted that de Gasperi was an honest man and never had ceased to consider his party a mass party, instead of unmasking it as the party of reaction and of the Vatican. A people's democracy—as the Italian and French comrades should have borne in mind—could never be initiated by Communist participation in a bourgeois government. Furthermore, Kardelj asserted, the Italian Communist Party had realized too late the real meaning of American policies and had coined the opportunist slogan, "Neither London, nor Washington, nor Moscow!" when it was obvious that liberty could not be secured without Moscow.

After criticizing the Italian Communists for their errors in the postwar period, Kardelj went on to recall their mistakes during the partisan war, their hesitancy, their reluctance to follow the Yugoslav example and turn to insurrection. Refuting Togliatti's claim that such a policy would have transformed Italy into another Greece, Kardelj retorted sarcastically that in his opinion the situation in Greece was better than that of either France or Italy. He then once more scathingly denounced the opportunism of the Italian Communists, who, regarding the game as already lost, had not lifted a finger to aid the Greek people in its struggle.

The attack by Djilas was even more aggressive and violent than Kardelj's. He began by asserting that the French and Italian Communists had placed their countries at the mercy of American imperialism, first by permitting the resistance forces to be dissolved, then by making one concession after another to the forces of reaction, and finally by tolerating their own exclusion from the government. The two parties had committed their major error when they declared that they would never sway from the path of parliamentarism. According to Djilas, the French Communist Party was completely undisciplined; anyone could join or quit it at will; the party members did not feel themselves bound by any pledge. There was only one guiding principle: increase the membership at any price. The defeats suffered by the two Western parties could be accounted for, above all, by this "political and ideological liberalism" of the leaders, by their fear of assuming responsibilities, and by the absence of genuine revolutionary vigilance. The French Communists should have realized that the bourgeoisie was in the saddle and that the parliament was one of the facets of its power. They should have prepared the party to deal with this situation. This they failed to do, and the enemy exploited this failure. Therein lay Djilas' principal argument in his unrelenting battery of charges. Communist policy toward Blum and Ramadier had been weak, naive and mistaken in both form and content. Moreover, the French Communists had underestimated the Gaullist danger, the threat posed by a man who during the war had done nothing but act as an agent for Churchill, a sort of French Mihailović, getting ready to take over from Blum and Ramadier as soon as they had done all expected of them.

The next day Longo spoke briefly, admitting the validity of the criticisms leveled against the Italian party, and promising that they would be taken into account. He was able to maintain a dignified bearing. Then Duclos replied to the criticisms and accusations of the "fraternal" parties. I have never witnessed such a revolting performance. The secretary of the French Communist Party behaved like a small shopkeeper caught in a swindle: he humiliated himself, admitted his mistakes, made innumerable excuses and promises. His voice trembling, his fists clenched, Duclos spewed forth an undistinguished and depressing shower of self-criticism.

He was interrupted repeatedly by Zhdanov ("Do you not believe, Comrade Duclos, that the people would have understood the situation better if you had said that the Communist party was an opposition party? This expression has not occurred in either Thorez' or your speeches since May. If the Communist party observes that it has taken the wrong road, it must openly confess its mistake; this you have not done!"). Malenkov urged him to give a precise account of his errors ("We would like Duclos to state his conclusions clearly, to tell us just what errors were committed by the leadership of the French Communist Party"). Duclos hastened to follow orders and started off on a minute analysis of all his mistakes, past and present. Viewed from today's perspective, the Soviet-supported Yugoslav denunciation of Franco-Italian "opportunism" stemmed from the same principles as do the attacks now being launched by the Chinese not only against Togliatti and the Yugoslavs (those former hardliners), but against the Soviets themselves.

ANOTHER HUSHED SUBJECT AT THE CONFERENCE: FINANCIAL AID TO THE COMMUNIST PARTIES

During our nearly week-long discussions, the problem of financing the international Communist movement was another point never raised—except in casual conversations, where it cropped up frequently. For example, we Italian delegates informed D. Shevliagin, the Soviet emissary responsible for the Italian Communist Party, that we urgently needed more newsprint for the proper functioning of our newspaper *L'Unità*. Shevliagin passed the request on to Zhdanov, who informed Stalin accordingly in one of his regular nightly telephone conversations. A scheme was quickly worked out: 20,000 tons of lemons and oranges stored by a firm run by Italian Communists were shipped to the USSR, payment for which was then used to buy the necessary paper.

Generally speaking, however, there was inadequate coordination of the Communist movement in Europe—a defect that the founding of the Cominform was intended to remedy. One of the areas in which this lack of coordination found its expression was in financing, and here it led to some odd occurrences. Rakosi cited an example to me during a conversation in Budapest: Hertta Kuusinen came to Rakosi to ask for funds to purchase a Communist printing press; Rakosi (who had served in the secretariat of the Comintern alongside Hertta's father in the days of Lenin) undertook to raise the money. But when he arrived in Moscow shortly thereafter, he heard that another Finnish Communist leader had arrived there with the identical request and had been granted the funds.

On the other hand, the transfer of money from Communist countries was greatly facilitated until 1947 by the presence of Communists within western European countries' governments; as members of a coalition they were in a position to thwart police control. For instance, in 1945–46 money was transferred to the Italian Communist Party through the Yugoslav embassy in Rome, a task assigned to a Slovene Communist serving as counselor at the embassy under the name of Yakuba. The money was always in United States dollars, carried discreetly in a suitcase to a safe place selected for the rendezvous by a Yugoslav emissary and a trusted Italian Communist working under P. Robotti (Togliatti's brother-in-law), who was then responsible for these delicate operations.

With the centralization of financial assistance to the Communist movement in the capitalist world and the exclusion of Communists from the coalition government, more systematic and conspiratorial methods had to be devised. The situation required rapid development of a plan then in its fledging stage—namely, the establishment of legal commercial enterprises which would enable the Party to fill its coffers without flagrant violation of the law. Some months after the Cominform was founded, I left the politburo of the Italian Communist Party to take charge of all so-called legal economic and commercial activities of the Italian Communist Party, a function I was to fulfill until the eve of my rupture with communism in 1956.

Documents

Documents

Paul Levi and Moscow

EDITORS' INTRODUCTION—*Paul Levi, president of the German Communist Party—the most important section of the Communist International after the Russian Communist Party—was the first to become embroiled in a conflict with Moscow and to incur its wrath. The deterioration of his relations with the Comintern leadership is best illustrated by two dates, which are very close together: in July–August 1920, he was one of the presidents of the Communist International's Second Congress (and confirmed president of the German Communist Party by December of that same year) and in April 1921, he was excommunicated by the Comintern's Executive Committee.*

During this period of less than a year, Paul Levi was involved in a number of quarrels with the Comintern leadership, several of which had public repercussions. In January 1921 he wrote an article in the German Communist Party organ Die Rote Fahne *expressing his opinion on what had happened at the congress of the Italian Socialist Party in Leghorn, which he had just attended (thereby provoking a three-article reply, written by Karl Radek, but signed with the initials P. B.); in February, his disagreements were discussed by the German Communist Party's executive committee (and he was in a minority position); in March, he opposed the "March action" instigated in Germany by Béla Kun and his team.*

These three events gave rise to open polemics which, however, did not go to the heart of the issues that put Levi at odds with the maneuvers of the Executive Committee or, more precisely, with the maneuvers of the Russians inside the Comintern. The Bolshevik leadership had reasons for concealing what was happening behind the scene, and Levi in turn felt restrained by Communist discipline, which deprived him of some of his best arguments in his controversy with Moscow. These restraints apply particularly to the problems which arose between him and Moscow in January 1921, before the disagreements became more serious and degenerated into a public conflict.

The following two confidential documents, published for the first time, provide—after forty years—some valuable insights into the relations between Moscow and the German Communist Party.

DOCUMENT No. 1:

REPORT OF COMRADE LEVI TO THE EXECUTIVE COMMITTEE OF THE
THIRD INTERNATIONAL ON THE ITALIAN PARTY CONGRESS,
BERLIN, JANUARY 20, 1921

EDITORS' INTRODUCTION—*Like any political organization, the Communist International had a public face and one reserved for the initiates. But in the Comintern the clandestine, undercover part constituted its essence. Hence the revelation of the Comintern's secret documents is particularly important. Stalin, whom Khrushchev accused of "personality cult," has had his share of truths told about him. But while Stalin was "unmasked" by his heirs, Lenin has been more and more deified. Thus historical research is confronted by two different situations: while the "negative sides" of the Stalinist years are admitted today in the Soviet Union, no "negative sides" are acknowledged for the "heroic" Leninist period of the Comintern.*

This report by Paul Levi to the Executive Committee of the Comintern on January 20, 1921 lifts part of the veil which covered the events at the 1921 Leghorn congress of the Italian Socialist party, whose split gave birth to the Italian Communist Party. Although this split took place on January 21, Levi's report, drafted in Berlin the day before, after his return from Leghorn, gives a complete account of the event, as though it had been written in retrospect, rather than before the split. The report shows political clear-sightedness and intellectual honesty—two qualities with which Paul Levi was endowed to a much higher degree than the other Communist leaders in Europe at that time.

Paul Levi grasped from the beginning that the Leghorn affair was not purely an Italian concern but had implications for the Comintern as a whole. His interventions at Leghorn, his strong reactions upon his return to Berlin, and his speech on the same subject the following month (February 1921) before the German Communist Party's "Zentrale," can be understood only in this light. The methods used and the goal set (and attained) in Leghorn must have made a deep impression on Levi, particularly in relation to the French Social-

ist party congress in Tours twenty days earlier and the Congress of the German Independent Socialists in Halle in October 1920.

Levi subscribed to the Comintern's aim at both of these congresses—to provoke a split in two parties that were not Comintern members and to attract their majorities into the Comintern (an aim which was achieved in both cases). But the aim at Leghorn was to provoke a split in a party that had belonged to the Comintern since 1919 and, besides, to attract only a minority to the Comintern and lose the large mass of adherents, who had previously been in the Comintern. This tactical error seemed unforgivable to Levi, because he was aware that the accusation raised by the Comintern delegates Kabakchiev and Rákosi (especially the latter)—that Serrati had refused to break with the reformist Turati faction—had no foundation. Serrati's position, as Levi had found out from the Italian leader himself, was that this break was premature since the fermentation among Italian Socialists was still in process. Serrati's entire subsequent conduct, despite the accusation by the Comintern that he had been a "renegade" since the time of the Leghorn congress, only confirmed Levi's judgment: after Leghorn and despite the Comintern's hostile attitude, Serrati separated from the reformists, came to Moscow as early as November 1922, during the Fourth Congress of the Comintern, and shortly thereafter joined the Italian Communist Party.

During his three or four days' stay in Leghorn, Levi was able to draw other conclusions which went counter to the fixed ideas prevailing in Moscow. Thus, in this report, when he quoted Serrati's statement about the cordial conduct of two Italian Communist leaders, Bombacci and Graziadei, toward Turati, he was trying to demonstrate that in Italy, among Italians, things did not happen the way the Bolsheviks imagined. He observed also that inside the Italian Communist Party, which was about to be formed, violently hostile factions already existed, since the iron Bolshevik discipline did not manifest itself in the same way under the Moscow skies as on the Mediterranean. Finally—and this was most important at that moment—Levi recognized that the majority of the Socialist proletariat would not follow the Communist dissidents, while in Moscow the notion was that all that was needed to gain the allegiance of the proletarian masses was to speak over the heads of the leaders and condemn them.

But Levi's report is important not only because of his assessment of what happened in Leghorn but because of his opinion of

Moscow's role in this event. Of course Paul Levi was addressing himself to this same Moscow forum, and he was the victim of the classic illusion of all non-Russian Communist leaders: knowing that he was right on this particular point and that Moscow was wrong, he believed that he could make the Bolsheviks understand this mistake and change their minds. At that moment Levi was not addressing the Executive Committee as an opponent, even less as a dissident, but as the leader of the German Communist Party and as a member of this same Executive Committee, to which he had been elected by the Second Comintern Congress. For this reason he was much more implicit than explicit in his criticism of the Comintern's conduct.

After Levi had left Berlin for Italy following the publication of the January 8, 1921 letter in which the proposition to form a united front was first made to the Socialists (with Radek's direct participation), and after Levi had discussed with Radek what attitude to take in Leghorn, he discovered that not only was his position at variance with that of the two emissaries from Moscow, but that even Radek switched sides and attacked Levi for his attitude in Leghorn. Once more Levi displayed the typical opposition attitude, at least in what he wrote, although it is likely that deep down he had already lost all his illusions: he proceeded to blame not so much the real head, that is, Zinoviev (and Lenin himself), but Zinoviev's emissaries.

Thus Levi revealed two characteristic Comintern methods in this report. The first concerned the tactic against Serrati engineered in Moscow: at the Second Congress, in the summer of 1920, Serrati was still a member of its Presidium and had been elected at the end of the congress a member of its Executive Committee, but by January 1921, two obscure Comintern emissaries, neither of them even elected members of the Comintern's Executive Committee, had arrived to "liquidate" Serrati. This they proceeded to do on the basis of a decision taken in Moscow, while Serrati did not know—even after the opening of the proceedings of the Leghorn congress—that a Moscow delegation was present in the hall. The second revelation made by Levi concerns the role of a Comintern secret emissary who appeared in Italy before the Leghorn congress under the cover name of "Comrade Carlo." This emissary (he was, in fact, a Russian Communist, Liubarsky, who later joined the diplomatic service of the Soviet Union), behind Serrati's back, sent to Moscow reports whose contents the Italian leader discovered during his stay in Moscow during the Second Congress, July–August, 1920. Levi added dis-

creetly by a parenthetical remark that "this had also happened to other comrades," thinking doubtless of himself and of reports by Moscow's emissary in Berlin (one "Comrade Thomas") of which reports Levi learned by chance in Moscow during the Second Congress.

THE REPORT

Dear Comrades,

As you surely know, I went to Leghorn as representative of the German party and do not want to be remiss in giving you a report on my impressions there. When I arrived in Leghorn, the first thing that struck me was that the relations between the Communist and the Serrati factions were exceedingly strained—so strained that there existed no political or even personal contact between the two groups. As soon as I arrived, I first had a conference with Comrade Bombacci and then with Kabakchiev. Bombacci was of the opinion that, as matters now stood, a split in the party, in Serrati's direction, was unavoidable. If I understood him correctly, Bombacci felt that the split at this point would be regrettable, but that it was too late to avert it. Comrade Kabakchiev, with whom I talked next, went even further and believed that the split in Serrati's direction was a desirable objective at the Congress for the Third International. With the agreement of the two comrades, I then asked Serrati for a conference the following morning. I started this conference by saying that I had talked matters over in Germany with Comrade Klara [Zetkin] and your friend. The three of us might not be properly informed about the party situation in Italy, and I asked him to give me his interpretation. This is what Serrati told me: He and his parliamentary group were determined to eliminate the reformists. However, as things now stood in Italy, it would be extremely difficult to do this presently and abruptly. The conflicts between the two wings of the Italian party had not come to a head sufficiently for that, and he felt that the required steps had not yet been taken by everyone to make these conflicts apparent. By way of example, Serrati described a scene during a parliamentary debate about a shooting incident in Bologna between the Fascists and the Communists. When this matter was discussed, the Communist wing itself had asked Comrade Turati[1] to act as spokesman for the parliamentary group. Turati had done this in a manner which he, Serrati, did not approve. Turati had even advocated a collaboration between parties. After Turati's speech, Bombacci and

Graziadei had jumped to their feet and—I presume this is an Italian custom—embraced Turati in parliament and congratulated him openly and publicly for his speech. Serrati said he only related this to prove that the differences between the reformists and the left wing had not as yet come to a head. In this connection he also referred to the letter of the Executive of January 9 which mentioned that because the situation in Italy was extremely revolutionary, even the reformists took a relatively leftist position there. Serrati's opinion was that this was not correct. The reformists in the party were relatively leftist in Italy because the most blatant reformists had already been excluded in Regio Emilia in 1912. He stated with due firmness that he was determined to exclude the reformists from his parliamentary group, but that this had to be done in such a way that the masses would understand the reasons for this exclusion. He would favor and support the exclusion of any member of the reformist wing who gave expression to his reformist views.

For my part, I insisted to Serrati that I agreed with the Executive Committee and considered the exclusion of the reformist wing absolutely indispensable, and that I did not go along with his envisaged method of eliminating the right wing, because it did not serve the purpose. Particularly in the light of its impact on the masses, the break with the right wing should be made in a public, clear and, if necessary, brutal form.

After taking leave of Serrati, I had another discussion with Comrades Kabakchiev and Rákosi. I described my conversation with Serrati to both of them and explained to them my impression that there was an extremely strained relationship between Serrati and the Communists, and that I had not succeeded in obtaining any positive proposal from Serrati: to that extent the conference had been unsuccessful. We tackled the question of what to do under the circumstances. I proposed to make no concessions in demanding the immediate exclusion of the reformists, but to leave open the possibility of altering the resolution asking for this exclusion. The Bordiga resolution stated that all those who took part in the Regio Emilia conference should be excluded. My proposal was that if the Serrati followers and the Communists could not get together on the basis of this resolution, a different wording should be drawn up. I thereby wanted to avoid creating the impression in the Serrati camp that the Bordiga resolution represented in some way a stinging humiliation, and that as a result they would lose face by accepting this resolution, with which they actually agreed in principle. This method, of course, would make sense only if the splitting off of the Serrati camp was not precisely the object of the party congress.

My efforts were furthered by a suggestion on the part of Comrade Graziadei. He proposed that the resolution be phrased as follows (I do not have the draft at my disposal, but I remember it well enough to quote nearly verbatim): "Exclude from the Party those who, either out of conviction or by their votes or action, do not place their allegiance with the Third International." Comrade Kabakchiev raised the objection that such a resolution could be equally acceptable to the Turati camp, so that it would misfire. I expressed the opinion that the Turati camp could not possibly go along with such a resolution. There was no denying that not only the Third International but also the Second International was making efforts to rally the proletarian camp to its side. If the Turati group accepted this resolution, they would, on the one hand, sooner or later be misfits in the Communist party, and, on the other, they would no longer be fit allies for the Second International. I therefore did not share this apprehension. Comrade Graziadei, whose proposal also had the object of keeping the Serrati camp within the Third International, left after a lengthy discussion without having accomplished his purpose. Comrade Bordiga then joined our subsequent conversation; Comrade Kabakchiev formally assured him that the representatives of the Communist International approved of Bordiga's intransigence toward Serrati and fully supported it, and that they proposed to adhere unalterably to Bordiga's resolution as it now stood. For my part, I declared that, as I had made clear at the beginning of the conversation, I was merely the representative of the German party, and that, although I personally judged this rigid adherence to the wording of the Bordiga resolution unwise, the Executive Committee and its representatives had the final responsibility for making the decision and that I would of course go along with it.

After the discussion was concluded, the following incident occurred. Comrade Serrati appeared and declared that he had informed his comrades of his conversation with me. His comrades also wished to talk to me, if I were willing. I replied that I would be glad to do so, but wished to know whether they desired that a representative of the Executive Committee also should attend; I personally favored his presence. Comrade Serrati expressed surprise at the presence of a representative from the Executive Committee. I was taken aback by this reaction and did not know whether I had been hasty in revealing the presence of a representative of the Executive to Comrade Serrati, and therefore gave an evasive reply. Serrati stated that in any case it did not matter to him. I then gave this information to Comrades Kabakchiev and Rákosi. These two suggested that a member of the Bombacci-Bordiga group also should be present. Serrati was willing to let them attend as well, but only reluctantly, so that we finally gave up this idea. The conference took place that evening. The comrades accompanying Serrati expressed a point of view similar to Serrati's. They too insisted on the exclusion of the reformists, but believed that the proper preconditions had to be created, and that these preconditions surely did not exist at the moment. The conference, which lasted one and a half hours, was ineffective in terms of the decisions made by the representatives of the Executive Committee that morning, since neither side made any proposal to which both sides could agree. After this conference, there was a meeting later in the evening of the two representatives of the Executive Committee, the steering committee of the Bombacci-Bordiga group, and myself. I once more exposed my own views in the light of the experience in Germany and said nearly verbatim that the exclusion of the Turati group should be made crystal clear, and that we must be absolutely resolute on that point, but I advised that we be more conciliatory as to the wording in order to create the basis for agreement on that score. I drew the comrades' attention to the fact that they should not underestimate to such an extent the value of a party organization. While party cohesiveness in Italy was admittedly not as strong as in Germany, the organization as such had an inherent strength which was not negligible; the comrades would complicate their task immeasurably if, under the conditions prevailing in Italy, they excluded not only the reformists but also the Serrati camp. I believe I made some impression with my remarks, since the steering committee of the parliamentary group resolved to adhere to their intransigent stand but, if the Serrati group's statement showed any evidence of assent, the question of the wording might be viewed in a new light.

The next morning Kabakchiev made his statement in the name of the Executive Committee. I feel compelled to say that this statement was unfavorably received, if only for purely external reasons. It covered twenty-six typewritten pages and was too long to be effective when read before a congress, and an Italian one at that. Another negative aspect was that this long declaration was directed almost exclusively against Serrati. This fact aroused extremely bad feeling in a party congress where this group represented by far the majority of the gathering, and the Serrati camp surely comprised numerically a three-quarter majority of the delegates. I myself had made up my mind to intervene in the discussion and to defend, as agreed with Kabakchiev, our thesis that the reformists must be excluded at once, giving our reasons for this decision. I was forced, however, to end my stay before that time, since the time I had been allotted for this Italian trip had been extremely brief and had run out already. Under the impression of the unfavorable effect of Comrade Kabakchiev's statement, I did request another conference with Comrade Serrati and gave him word for word the following explanation: I still believed the separation should be carried out at once and in the form of an open break. However, neither I nor Klara Zetkin nor other friends in Germany shared other aspects of Kabakchiev's views. Without giving Serrati further details as to what I meant, I wanted to convey that I had in mind the hostile attitude displayed by Kabakchiev toward Serrati's group. I proceeded to explain to Serrati that after my return to Germany I would draw up a report on my interpretation of the Italian situation. I also asked him to postpone any decision with respect to his position toward the Third International until the Executive Committee in Moscow had had time to reconsider its stand. Serrati thereupon reiterated what he had already declared when I first spoke to him—namely, that the thought did not even enter his mind to make contact with the Second-and-a-Half International in Vienna: he and his group were Communists, and Communists they would remain. If the Third International excluded them, he would remain at the doorstep of the Third International, even on his knees, but under no condition would he go to the Second International. I replied that in the long run this situation would be untenable, and that one way or another he ultimately would be compelled to take a stand. In this final conference I once more assured him of the necessity of excluding the reformists at once and explained to him that even though I admitted that on the basis of past developments an immediate break would be hard to explain and that there were some flaws in the declaration of the Third International read by Kabakchiev, because it wished to prove that the need for an immediate break with the reformists could be adduced from past development, I was still convinced that in the interest of the future an immediate break was indispensable. Nobody could foresee when a revolutionary movement would set in in Italy, and it would be fatal if at such a time struggles and differences should arise within the leadership of the Communist party. Such struggles should be concluded beforehand. I had the feeling that this last argument made some impression on Serrati, and I broke off the conference at that point.

It is unfortunate that I had to leave the congress at that time and before the Serrati group had taken a definitive stand. Now that I have made this detailed report, I would still like to assess briefly conditions in Italy as I see them. The conference made an excellent overall impression. Not only the Italian temperament was responsible for some very powerful scenes; they were due as well to the genuine proletarian element assembled there. As to the composition of the different groups, I was assured by various of our close Italian friends that the Serrati group is composed overwhelmingly of radical and revolutionary men and comprises the same element as the left wing of the Independents in Germany. Our friends have the fond hope that these elements will switch over shortly (they envisage a period of two months) to their group. I spoke up against this view and this optimism. I drew their attention to our experiences in Germany and the significance of party limits, even where the views of the mass of the Party members are in harmony. Our relations with the left-wing Independents in particular, before the break, served as a pertinent example. I pointed out to them that their relations with the Serrati group would be much less favorable than ours with the left-wing Independents. For there never arose any split or sharp struggle between us and the mass of the left-wing Independents, whereas they were just now separating themselves from this mass after a sharp conflict and a sharp disagreement, a fact which would influence their relations with the revolutionary masses for quite some time, certainly more than two months. I also explained to our comrades, in reply to their statement that it was better to be few in number but firm in principles rather than the reverse, that in order to be a party capable of leading a large movement, both elements were needed; principles without followers constitute a party no more than followers without principles. My opinion is that our people, when they view their chances, err in their optimism, and that Serrati's speculation—one could say unfortunately—will be vindicated. For Serrati says that if the split now takes place on that basis—Serrati's people versus the Communists—the former then would make a break with the reformists, and thereby they would be the wing around which the Italian proletariat would rally. In this Serrati is clearly and obviously speculating on the inner dissensions of the Communist wing.

As I said, I am afraid that Serrati's speculation will be vindicated. Bordiga seems to be extremely resolute, energetic, and purposeful, but the Communist wing comprises a large number of groups, tendencies, and so on. My answer to the question whether a party without a clear and firm core resting only on these diverse tendencies, directions, and views can be viable is more likely to be negative than affirmative. I am firmly convinced that without the left wing of the Serrati group the party will lack a core and am also convinced that if this left wing can be won only by paying the price of accepting Serrati, Serrati must be taken in the bargain, even if one views his person with more distaste than I do.

My judgment is not colored by moods aroused in the heat of battle, which I know diminish the value of such judgments. This could not apply to me, since I am not involved in the struggles. In this connection, and in order to contribute to a proper assessment of the Serrati group and Serrati as a person, I would like to add that there is an extremely sharp personal antagonism between Serrati and Comrade Carlo. The antagonism stems from the fact that Comrade Serrati, like some other comrades, happened to come across some reports in Moscow which had been sent by Comrade Carlo from Italy to Moscow, and which Serrati asserts showed the grossest abuse of the political and personal trust which existed between Serrati and Comrade Carlo before Serrati's trip to Russia. My purpose in bringing up this matter is not to act as an informer (far be it from me to judge, let alone to identify myself with Comrade Serrati's judgment in a matter about which I know nothing). I am mentioning this matter just in case you might want to take it into account in reaching an unbiased opinion.

All in all, I think that we will greatly weaken our position in Italy for a long time to come if we now and under these circumstances carry out a break with Serrati, and that we will almost perforce hand a victory to the Vienna International. For there unfortunately can be no doubt that no matter how often Serrati vows that he is not thinking of going to Vienna and is even, as I assume, perfectly sincere at the moment, if we forcibly knock him to the right, he will gradually have no choice but to go to the right. I am not referring here to Serrati personally but to the large masses of revolutionary proletarians, who will remain estranged from us for many years. I will even be so bold as to point out to you what effect this split will have in other countries, where we already must bear the onus of splitting the proletariat. Without wishing to anticipate the judgment of the Executive Committee, I am of the opinion that it would be most sensible on the part of the Executive Committee, which now, after the Communists have split from Serrati and the latter still claims that he wishes to remain within the Communist International, will have to reach a new decision, to send to Italy a special emissary with special authority—of course no one belonging to the German party—to make an on-the-spot decision. Serrati is quite right that we have lost important power centers by this split. Serrati pointed out, for example, that in Italy 2,500 out of 8,000 communities have a Socialist mayor. Serrati rightly says that this fact implies an immense opportunity for bringing in arms and doing undercover work. These 2,500 mayors have police powers in their localities. The mayors are decisive when it comes to hiring armed Carabinieri, storing arms, and so on. Something I read in the newspaper during my stay in Italy proves that these mayors do not look at their position in the same way as the German Social Democratic mayors, who only think of hanging on to their jobs. The mayor of Ferrara together with another comrade was arrested at the station as he was about to leave for the Leghorn party congress because they were suspected of having favored or actively encouraged the elimination of several Fascists in Ferrara. This one example points up the opportunities which the Serrati group fully realizes, and which it will exploit. But there would be nothing gained in losing these positions, and it would do us no little harm in the eyes of the proletariat if it looked as though we were to blame for this loss.

DOCUMENT No. 2:

A CONTROVERSY BETWEEN RADEK AND LEVI
BEHIND CLOSED DOORS

EDITORS' INTRODUCTION—*The second document on Levi's relations with the Comintern leadership is even more confidential than the first. In the Leghorn affair Levi had written an article in the German Communist Party newspaper and Radek had made his reply in a series of three articles, which implied that their controversy was at least partly public. But secrecy was complete with respect to this second document: not only was it kept from the press, but Radek's presence itself was not divulged.*

This controversy behind closed doors between Levi, the leader of the German Communist Party, and Radek, Comintern representative for German affairs, took place, as the title of the document indicates, in the presence of the Zentrale *of the German Communist Party, that is, of the leadership elected after the unification of the Communists—Spartakists and the left wing of the German Independent Socialist party. The* Zentrale *consisted of the following members: presidents Paul Levi and Ernst Däumig; members Heinrich Brandler, Otto Brass, Wilhelm Koenen, Wilhelm Pieck, Hermann Remmele, Walter Stoecker and Klara Zetkin; alternates Otto Gäbel, Curt Geyer, Fritz Heckert, Adolf Hoffmann and August Thalheimer. One of these fourteen members was certainly absent: Curt Geyer, sent to Moscow as a representative of the party to the ECCI.*

The document, drawn up in a telegraphic style not meant for publication, includes a series of admissions and revelations on Radek's part, generally in contradiction to the Comintern's public stand on various questions of that moment. The Comintern had greeted the Leghorn split and the founding of the Italian Communist Party as a success, but Radek was closer to reality in Berlin than his colleagues in Moscow: "It is an illusion to believe that we have a Communist party in Italy." Radek characterized the German Communist Party, the best organized party in the entire Comintern (except the Russian Communist Party) at the time with the categorical remark: "The party does not yet exist as a working machine." (This observation did not prevent Zinoviev from hurling this same party into the "March action" two months later.)

Radek makes other interesting statements. He describes the intentions, the state of mind, and the illusions prevailing in Moscow at the time of the Russian-Polish war of 1920 when he puts his faith in the contradictions of capitalism and when he reiterates Moscow's firm confidence in a political offensive against the capitalist world.

The remarks on the Comintern's internal situation are also interesting: Radek tells of his quarrels with Levi (and admits that after he had accused Levi of telling "deliberate untruth," he had been compelled to retract before the Zentrale*); Levi tells about his strained relations with Zinoviev. This oratorical duel shows in dispute two ranking members of the Comintern who, though in general agreement in their assessment of the political events in Germany during 1919–20, were about to cross swords and thenceforth go their separate ways. As human beings, they were already worlds apart.*

Levi was a skeptical intellectual with strong artistic interests; Radek was a journalist absorbed by politics. Levi was guided by a rare moral rectitude; Radek, as everyone knew, was morally indifferent. Levi had doubts and apprehensions on the manner in which the Russian Bolsheviks were running the Comintern; Radek already definitely had thrown in his lot with Moscow and chosen Soviet Russia as his adopted country.

Different though they were, both debaters had the political insight not to overlook the basic issue—the relations between the German Communist Party and the ECCI. Radek said bluntly: "What mostly instigated my sharp polemics against Levi was not the disagreement on the Italian question, but rather the relation with the Communist International." And Levi stated: "We are confronted with a certain mistrust, and any attempt on our part to criticize mistakes will be interpreted only as opposition against the Communist International."

This central issue was of historic importance and had symbolic character. For ever since then, nearly all conflicts between Western Communist leaders and Moscow have stemmed from Moscow's ceaseless ambition to dominate and the refusal on the part of foreign Communist leaders to obey unconditionally. This is largely the reason for Levi's defense of Serrati, who was not completely willing in 1920–21 to bow to Moscow's dictates, and for Levi's own break with Moscow several months later.

From the very beginning of the Comintern, foreign Communist leaders did not have enough prestige and power to take the entire Party with them into opposition. Ultimately Moscow won out, and these rebels were reduced to leadership of a dissident minority. The Bolsheviks transplanted into the Comintern two techniques they had mastered before the October Revolution: the splitting technique, which was tested at the Halle and Leghorn congresses, and the factionist technique, which was applied to defeat Paul Levi. Radek had not been sent to Berlin by Moscow to discuss the matter before the Zentrale; he had only one mission—to prepare Levi's elimination whenever the need arose. There was thus nothing accidental about the formation of an anti-Levi faction within the Zentrale, a faction with which Radek was to keep in touch by circumventing the official governing body of the party. Nor was it accidental that the "left wing" faction, including Ernst Reuter (Friesland), Ruth Fischer, and Arkadi Maslow, became active at that time and began its attacks on Levi in Die Rote Fahne. *Levi's case was soon settled, but the same fate was to befall first the Radek and then the "left-wing" factions which came to the helm of the German Communist Party one after the other. The reason was identical: such was Moscow's will.*

The document, probably written in haste by someone who wanted to capture the essentials, has a few passages which were difficult to translate because of the unclear meaning in the German original. These passages are followed by [sic].

THE TEXT

Session of the *Zentrale* with the Representative of the
Executive Committee for Germany
Friday, January 28, 1921

After a lengthy debate on whether or not a concrete discussion should be part of the agenda the decision is reached to ask Comrade Max [Radek] to give an analysis of the political situation.

COMRADE MAX: I believe that we pay too little attention to concrete facts in Western Europe. Besides tactical and organizational questions, we should not forget that the Red Army is now one of the most important power factors. We must not disregard its existence in our assessment of the situation. That would be a mistake which would prevent our viewing the mistakes of the Executive in the light of the true facts. In 1919 our position was much weaker and different from what it is today. During the Polish war, the Executive believed that the revolutionary movements were maturing in Western Europe, that in the drive toward the West the aim was not to impose Bolshevism at bayonet point, but only to break through the crust of the military might of the ruling classes, since there were already sufficient internal forces unleashed in Germany to keep things under control. The second cornerstone of the policy of the Executive was its assessment of the concrete situation in Germany. The Executive believed that in Germany things were already ripening for the seizure of political power. It was believed that if we held Warsaw, there would be no further need to advance all the way to Germany. By occupying the Corridor, the German government would find itself at loggerheads with the Entente. Kopp[2] came to Moscow at that time with a treaty draft of the German government. However, that crafty Mr. Simon managed to pull his neck out of the noose in the nick of time [*sic*]. There was another school of thought in the Executive Committee— the so-called South-Eastern tendency, which held that the break- through must be attempted not in Germany but somewhere else altogether, in countries with an inflammatory agricultural setup, [such as in] East Galicia, Rumania, Hungary, and which was convinced that if we stood at the Drava and Sava [rivers], the revolution in the Balkan states would be accelerated and the requisite agrarian hinter- land would be created for the Italian revolution. The creation of an agrarian hinterland is as crucial for the Italian revolution as for the German revolution.

The Serrati group did not consider the situation revolutionary and still does not. First, there is the danger of a blockade. Serrati did not believe that it could be carried out; we were more skeptical. But everyone agreed that the establishment of an agrarian hinterland was essential. Our conversations with Serrati on that score continued and then concerned themselves with the implementation of the revolu- tion. The entire democratic-illusionist section remained in the Party —particularly hundreds of union leaders. For Serrati the trade- union bureaucracy was a sacred cow. For him it was important to leave the whole apparatus intact rather than to clear out the re- formists. He admitted that they were reformists, but he said that they would submit to discipline. He could not be persuaded to tighten his grip on the Party. The Congress decided to send the Italian party a letter. Its purpose was to further the immediate preparation of the revolution. The letter was not published until three months later. No attempts were made to reach an understanding of how the resolution could be implemented. On the contrary, Serrati's agitation in defense of the reformists began. I have already quoted the letter, which is bound to dispel all doubts. We are convinced that the underlying assumption of Serrati's policy is that he does not think the time is ripe for a revolution. He says: In Italy we have favorable conditions for fighting the bourgeoisie. At the same time, like Hilferding,[3] point by point, he describes the consolidation of the bourgeoisie on a world- wide scale. The situation in the Balkan countries is important for the assessment of his perspective. Therein lies the paradox; thereby one can explain Serrati's stand. He says: If I were convinced that it is only a matter of the leaders . . . and so on. In assessing the situation, there are no moral issues involved. There would thus be no sin against com- munism if he asserted that revolution is not possible. But his conclusion shows that it is not his assessment which is different. If revolution is not imminent, there is still the gradual advance of communism, for which separation from the reformists is required. His relation to the reformists is very peculiar.

Half of the things we may expect in the near future hinge on developments here in Italy and in the Balkans. We will not tilt at windmills. The Red Army will not be demobilized; it will be made more flexible and brought to the southwestern and western borders. We will not wage war in winter. With a nation the size of Germany, a direct, aggressive intervention would in any case be a blunder. It would strengthen nationalism and the bourgeoisie to such an extent that the workers would be rebuffed. But if we occupy the Corridor and stand at the border, this creates a different and much more favorable condition for the struggle. I must admit that at this point we have a stronger inclination toward an aggressive foreign policy than before. We are skeptical about the commercial treaty negotiations with England. But everything hinges on whether independent large-scale movements will take shape in Western European countries, and whether they will have a firm core.

I am convinced the split in Italy has greatly impaired the chances for a revolution in the near future. It is an illusion to believe we have a Communist party in Italy. The objective now is to shape the Communist wing of the workers in such a way that it is capable of exerting some influence on the masses. The situation is more favorable in Poland. It is true that there are 7,000 comrades in jail. But there are strikes everywhere. Pilsudski has gone to Paris to seek help. It is a fact that we have no Communist party in Bohemia. But if a strike there could break out spontaneously with 900,000 participants, conditions would lean very strongly in our favor. The wild wave of persecutions in Yugoslavia, which came not in the wake of a revolution but [comes] now, two years after the end of the war, against a strong Party, proves that this Party is indeed strong and that the government fears it. In Croatia the Radić party is creating an agrarian revolutionary movement.

This is how I see the German situation: leaving out of account the effects of our own action, everything depends on whether compromise is reached between the Entente and Germany. If it is reached, the question still remains whether the bourgeoisie will receive economic help sufficiently fast to contain the revolutionary movement. But by then prospects for the German bourgeoisie will be so favorable that they will attack us with ten times as much determination even before they are economically consolidated. If the Entente pursues a hostile policy, the radicalization of the working class must go forward. But here, unfortunately, a basic difference exists on our part. In a country with such strong trade-union organizations, it is unlikely that spontaneous movements will break out and toss the leadership into our hands. The organizations act as the breakwaters of this movement. I therefore feel it is most important to bring in other parties. The Party's activation is still very slight. Just look at this simple technical matter: the *Reichsausschuss* did not bother even to discuss the most important step in the drive for a united front—the open letter[4]—and its agenda did not even include organizational measures to make the letter effective. As matters stand now, I believe that the conscious will of the Party to bring about a revolution is a much less crucial factor for the future than the question whether the Entente will come to an agreement with the German bourgeoisie or not. The Party as a machine is still nonexistent.

It is too early to say today whether we will be involved in conflicts. All we can say is whether we want to bring them about or to avoid them. And the Executive says: We do want to bring them about! History must be driven forward.

I am convinced that because of the internal situation in Russia, we will have great difficulties with the peasants, but we will stand firm. Our motive for activation does not lie in the internal Russian situation; the reason for it is that the longer it takes us to attain power in Western Europe the more serious will be the disintegration. Power would then be in our hands, but we would lack the barest essentials to give to the workers. That is the guiding motive for our insisting on activation.

This leads to the following conclusion for Germany: in the eyes of the Executive, relations with the KAPD[5] must take into account the fact that in spite of the KAPD's immature elements, its core still contains a discontented proletarian segment which will be willing to fight whenever there is an active conflict. And that is why the Executive did not want to create an abyss between itself and these people. If we foresaw a tranquil evolution, we would say: Let us thrash them until they see the light. But since the Executive thinks that things ought to be speeded up it says: We cannot take them into our fold, because they will not submit, but we must not let the thread be broken. Shortly before I left, our people read what the KAPD press was writing about Russia. Everyone realizes that our material situation is terrible. But the important criterion is whether one is repelled by it. An additional consideration is the fact that Rühle and Wolffheim[6] were kicked out, which proves that these people have a sound core.

On an international scale, the relation with the syndicalists is clear. We cannot make out without ties with the French and American syndicalists and shop-stewards. The English Communists are completely out of touch with the masses. This Left really must be drawn into the fold. But because these unions do not yet see things clearly, our idea was to found a Zimmerwald-like trade union which is not yet the Communist International, but a transitional stage. On the strength of my 1919 views. I opposed the admission of the KAPD; I do not believe that we will assimilate this party. If the Executive now does its duty, if it now calls attention to the conditions for admission and raises its voice in the KAPD press, it may meet with considerable success. It will surely have some impact on some of the KAPD members.

Now for the situation in the trade unions. I have not yet been able to obtain an analysis. When we passed out the watchword "Infiltrate the Unions," all of us believed that this would entail splitting. That possibility was always kept in mind. It was obvious the union bureaucracy would kick us out; that is why we indicated in the resolution at which point the splitting was appropriate. The conduct of the bureaucracy proves we are now a power factor in the unions, and they do not wish to give us enough time to organize. It would be stupid if we now got out of the unions. We will have to fight for each position. We will have to consider carefully the possible spots where we will be followed by a large part of the union members when we are expelled, and then the job will be to pull together these unions and to carry out a process of concentration. We must take care to safeguard what we have already achieved in the unions, but on the other hand, we must not take an anti-union stand. If we are accused of splitting, we must insist that we are actually doing this in order to bring workers to the unions.

Now for the Italian question. I am convinced that Levi has not grasped the heart of the matter. I have said Levi told a deliberate untruth. I already have written him that I would take this back expressly before the *Zentrale,* and I will repeat this statement. It seemed incredible to me that a man as clever as Levi would not grasp the meaning of these two facts: Serrati declared on the one hand that he would get rid of the reformists only gradually, and Serrati was willing on the other hand to risk a break with the International. So it is my well-considered opinion that the conflict with respect to the Italian matter signifies a sort of interlude. It can be traced back to inadequate information on the part of the German *Zentrale*. Thalheimer said, when I was reading him Serrati's letter, "It is perfectly obvious that this is straight Hilferding." I believe that the matter will become perfectly plain: Serrati does not wish to make a break with the reformists, and since that is the case, he must be fought. We will have to make our way over Serrati's political corpse to get Turati's scalp. I believe there are no miracles in politics. If [there are] 89,000 members of the Italian party—new members admittedly—after these differences of opinion (for the entire last half year the party has been torn by conflict), how can it be due to chance that they do not want it [*sic*]? The majority of the workers in the Italian movement are not yet Communists. The overwhelming majority favor the Third International insofar as they equate it with the Soviet Star. But in terms of concrete policies, they still have a long way to go. Is there any possibility of winning these masses by negotiations? Zetkin claims that we must make contact with the masses. The only way to do that is through their representatives. Serrati is not willing—and you can reach the masses only through an open and bitter struggle. Does that mean that we should not try it at the moment? Of course not. We must tell them: You turned the thing down. We must say to them: What is it that you actually want? I told Levi before his trip to Italy that the masses will come to us in this manner. Today we must form a small Communist party. And then Levi said a few times: "We have Bordiga, and the others are not entitled to criticize" [*sic*].

What did you [German Communists] propose in the matter of the seizure of the factories? When we were all stuck in the mud, they [Italian Communists] did not manage to unite as a party group. It is not a matter of doctrinal unification. Serrati will fail when the time for action comes. But you must not fail now. I am far from delighted with the tactics of the Italian Communists. The Executive was hesitating whether to send a telegram. Zinoviev was inclined to wait a little, but the telegram was sent off anyway under the influence of Lenin, who shared Thalheimer's conviction after reading the letter. We must reckon that we will have a weak party in Italy for some time. In Germany the Italian business may provoke some difficulties in the fight against the centrists, but it may have great impact in France. The French party is rough-hewn; it includes many heterogeneous elements. Lafont's[7] entering the party proves that things are still unclear. Here in Germany it is possible that some elements will switch over to the right; in France it is probable. As to the other points at issue, I am to tell you that the Executive, after having read your letter, completely agrees with the official answer that I gave you on the KAPD matter. You have to live with things as they are. Now it is a matter of urging on the Executive to do its duty and of working on the KAPD and to show that we are trying to reach the left-wing workers. As for the unions, the problem is that some of the old USP [Independent Socialists] comrades are unwilling to submit to the general directives and to accept the line of approach to the trade unions. You must clean up this mess. I am making no personal attacks. If the comrades are disciplined, individuals should not be singled out. But it is clear that the Party should say explicitly what needs to be done and transfer to other positions [comrades who] disregard directives.

Activation requires an altogether different attitude on the part of the press. Your press is anything but an action press. The central organ is incapable of conducting a single concrete drive for even one week. Then other special matters must be considered, such as the M.P. affair.[8]

Now as to external organizational matters. What mostly instigated my sharp polemics against Levi was not the disagreement on the Italian question, but rather the relation with the Communist International, which came to the surface not so much in what was printed as in the actual discussions. Needless to say, I have no blind allegiance to the Executive Committee. I have dealt out and received my share of blows. But there is criticism and criticism.

First question: Is the general political line of the Executive correct? If in individual discussions things come up which make one draw the conclusion that one must continue to fight against the left, to postpone conflict against the right, would Levi go along with the policy of the Executive? But even that is not the whole story. A finer differentiation must be made. A left wing and a right wing will spring up. But the second question is the most crucial.

Second question: If Levi were to put the disagreements in these terms: "The Executive favors a rigid tactic; I favor a flexible one," that would be acceptable. But if he says "a large and healthy

Party was destroyed"; and if in reply to my question "How do you visualize relations of the Executive with Europe," he says, "It is no use; you cannot make yourself heard," then I say that this constitutes an inadmissible relationship.

The Communist International is not a single act, but rather a continuous process. In 1919 it was merely a rallying cry; today it is backed up by a German party of half a million members; there is progress in Bulgaria, in Serbia. The French Socialist Party is evolving in a favorable direction, since it is seeking for the first time to establish closer ties with a large segment of the trade unions. Under these circumstances, it is inadmissible to assume that the Executive cannot be brought to correct political mistakes with an open, clear and unequivocal policy, with the words "We disagree." It is still worse to believe that we cannot even change its organizational setup. To that there could never be an answer, because that answer would amount to a negation of the Communist International. If the German party sends two men, not great geniuses but two workers from the ranks, why should that be ineffective? Or the Executive might be asked to send four members to Western Europe. These are feasible things which would alleviate many difficulties. In my opinion the trouble afflicting the Executive is that it is situated in a state involved in revolutionary action. One should blame it not for issuing ukases, but for failing to intervene. It only intervenes when there is an acute crisis. The matter of the open letter is typical. If I were in Moscow, this idea would never even come to me. Let us insist that the Executive have representatives, experienced comrades, in Europe, and then we will have an Executive which is ten times as effective. Such a concrete and positive attitude is what is lacking. I know it is difficult to put through any changes, but there is no alternative. Either we say that we will soothe our consciences from time to time and then pull them out of our pockets at the congress and display them publicly, or we must put aside any sort of skepticism and send responsible comrades—though they should not stay there [in Moscow] too long and should be rotated frequently so that they are not cut off too much from the party. The disagreement lies in the fact that I believe that we are dooming our Communist efforts if we further tolerate skepticism of this sort. We must voice criticism and we must express our opinion positively. These questions must be resolved organizationally. Next to the Russian party, you are the strongest Communist party. You bear the same amount of responsibility as the Russian party. You must find people to send to Moscow. You must take active measures.

PAUL LEVI: My letter contains a very concrete question: Does the Executive favor my removal from the post of chairman? I am in general agreement with Max's views. We held these views when we were in Moscow. The Red Army must be counted as an important factor. I reject the idea of transferring the seat of the Executive from Moscow because for me the pursuit of proletarian international policy is of overriding importance. The Executive should have its seat not in a place where there is merely the best general orientation, but rather in that place where international proletarian political leadership is really centered.

I also agree with the remarks about the deployment of the Red Army. The succinct formula—the revolution cannot be advanced at bayonet point—originated at a time of hardship. The other formula also originated in a special situation last summer in Moscow: the Red Army could be deployed, not in a mechanical fashion and without link to the masses in other countries, but only as an organic instrument. In that way it can be a decisive factor in Germany. It can crack the cover by military means. Taken in this light, the remarks just made are absolutely correct in my opinion. In this way we would be safeguarded against a totally nationalist attitude, and at the same time we would be assured that the Red Army would not be deployed purely in the military interests of the Soviet Republic.

Now as to the special disagreements which have arisen in Germany. Comrade Max blames me for viewing the mistakes of the Communist International with a certain skepticism. That there are such mistakes we both agree; I am not sure that we agree on what they are. For my part, I deny any skepticism. I do diagnose each illness individually. I have seen illnesses to which I applied remedies. But I also have seen illnesses for which I thought waiting seemed necessary. My relations with Zinoviev have improved slightly since his stay in Germany, but still I must reiterate: We are confronted with a certain mistrust, and any attempt on our part to criticize mistakes will be interpreted only as opposition against the Communist International. That is not in the least my intention. The Third International must keep its center in Moscow. What I say is this: This discussion has been an eye-opener for me. Comrade Max let his horse get away from under him, and there re-emerged trains of thought which are strong and alive in Moscow. In the light of all these facts, I believe that we would aggravate the malady instead of fostering the healing process by voicing any so-called active criticism and making positive proposals on specific questions in a more outspoken manner. Not all illnesses require operations. There are illnesses which heal much faster. After the last session, I was more certain than ever that it would make matters even worse if we took up this other attitude toward the Executive. I think that we should maintain essentially our present attitude toward the Executive. I think that we should instruct our representative in Moscow not to get involved in sharp discussions under any condition. He should state our views emphatically, note the divergence, but desist from sharp discussions.

The queston is raised: Do we deviate from the line of the Executive or not? Max himself said that if I had called the alternatives rigid or flexible, he would have had no objections, but I said that a strong Party had been destroyed. But does that not amount to the same thing? I said that the rigid method did nothing to prevent this result.

Now the general question: Does our stand differ from the overall behavior [of the Executive]? Max tried to prove that this was the case. On the one side there is a sharp struggle to the left, on the other the desire to keep doors open to the right. I am not sure whether any basic disagreement exists between me and the Executive if I say I have learned one thing from the appalling collapse of the first act of the German revolution, and that is that a resolute Communist Party is absolutely indispensable and is the most precious thing with which one can endow a proletariat for making a revolution. If we had had a resolute Communist party in Germany, even if it had been numerically weak, the first act of the revolution would have taken a different course. In all my thoughts, on the national and international plane, my overriding concern is this: How can we shape a proletarian organization that is distinct and Communist? The Executive of the Communist International does not adhere to this line intransigently enough to suit me. I have expressed this point of view already in Moscow. In Germany, we had to initiate our campaign to set up militant Communist groups after Rosa's [Luxemburg] death. First of all, we had to lead the struggle toward the left. The fact that our struggle, in which our unit organized itself, was directed primarily toward the left, not against the leftist USP [Independent Socialists], was not due to any forethought or clear plan on our part: it resulted rather from the backwash of the revolutionary tide. This objective situation brought us up most sharply against leftist elements, and our party was shaped by this struggle. And now I know that Moscow firmly believes that I waged this struggle for a lark. I can only state once more I did not, for our part, let it come to an exacerbated conflict at all. The fight was carried out in Heidelberg[9] without insults. The organizational threads were not severed in Heidelberg but elsewhere, without my participation. We never once conducted ourselves in a manner which could be interpreted as a total rejection of the left. The others were always the aggressive party. There always remained the possibility for cooperation.

What kind of relation should we establish with [the left]? Should it be one which facilitates cooperation in concrete situations? We were in the process of establishing such a relation, since the proper people were again being drawn into our orbit. The Executive by its action did not eliminate the best solution for the KAPD question, but it did delay it. But a further point is this: Should our relation with these leftist elements, with whom, as I say, there should be no conflict, immediately be converted into an organizational one? I do not think so, because if the relation becomes organizational rather than purely political, the building up of a Communist party, which I consider the prime objective, will be impeded. Its most important function is not the issuing of resolutions and ukases; its most potent influence lies in its mere existence and in Russia's influence. The mere fact that it exists and how it exists—that Russia is fighting on, etc.—these are its major contributions. And by admitting into this unified Communist party elements that are not Communist, we are disturbing this process. The comrades from the Executive realize this danger and seek to avert it by recognizing these people only as sympathizers, or else they recognize them as members and then pass resolutions against them. But in my opinion this deflection by means of resolutions, theoretically, does not counterbalance the fact that they have established an organizational link, which covers up everything else in the eyes of the masses. These are my main considerations with respect to Germany, Italy, and so on.

My considerations are the same regarding agreements with the syndicalists and the unionists. In Western Europe the relation of the Communists with the organized masses is much more significant than their relation with the unorganized masses (although the importance of the latter should not be underestimated either), much more so than in other countries. In countries with less highly developed capitalism the readiness of the proletariat for revolution hinges on the relationship between the Communists and the unorganized masses. In Germany the relationship to the organized masses is much greater and more important. In Germany, too, the unorganized play a certain role. They are an important factor, but their significance is not as overwhelming as in other countries. In Germany we are now engaged in a bitter struggle for the masses in the trade unions. We are at a particularly difficult juncture, and if we do not exploit it shrewdly, we may be heading straight toward a catastrophe. And it is exactly this moment that the Communist International picks for accepting the syndicalists and the unionists into the Trade Union International on the premise, it is said, that the Red Trade Union International is really only like Zimmerwald. That is a point of view which can be justified theoretically, but which is completely irrelevant for purposes of agitation in the masses. The fact which strikes the German proletarian is that syndicalists and unionists have been admitted to the Trade Union International which we are asked to join. Now for us Communists, there is no need to fear syndicalists and unionists. But if we want to fight for the masses whom we want to win over, we are terribly handicapped by having an organizational relationship with them. It is the most powerful weapon the Majority Socialists and the Independents have in attacking us. One might well say, "This is all petty-bourgeois nonsense." But in a treacherous situation this may be the most dangerous slogan. Let me say one thing: Moscow is not at the root of this but rather these commissions which are sent to Europe and which are inevitably busybodies; they are very much inclined to be satisfied with a common sparrow if they fail to catch the dove. That is why they take steps which they certainly could not take if they saw things from a larger perspective. If Belinky[10] had a broader perspective, he would not put us into such a dangerous situation for the sake of 100,000 unionists. In short, we are faced with a difficult situation, which arises from the fact that the Executive gives priority to establishing organizational ties with non-Communist elements rather than trying to reach some sort of political accord with them.

Now to the matter of accepting things as they are. I am convinced that the resolution in the KAPD matter and in the union matter cannot be brushed aside. But as things now stand, with the eyes of all Germany on us, we have been compelled to emphasize our stand against the KAPD. We had to do so, in order to avoid being thrown into one pot with the KAPD, even if this rejection meant a more strained relation with the KAPD. This second step followed inevitably from the first, whether we wanted it or not. I believe that Moscow should take the initiative in correcting these mistakes. We did not become aggressive against the KAPD. Now that things stand as they do, it is the Executive's duty to take the consequences and face the KAPD leaders with the question: Which way are they heading in such a hurry? I am not saying that we did anything to counteract this development, which was inevitable. We had to save face in the eyes of the German workers.

Now to come back once more to the Italian question. I repeat: I do not have the least intention of identifying myself with and uniting with Serrati. I told him emphatically that I considered it imperative that the exclusion take place at once, and I believe that the reasons that I gave him for this step impressed him more strongly than Kabakchiev's. But I am convinced that the nucleus which in Germany constitutes the left-wing USP remained loyal to the Serrati group. I consider it a serious mistake for the Communist International to knock this nucleus forcibly and obstinately toward the right. And what is more, the best hope for retaining this nucleus was forfeited by the way things were done at the Italian congress. The Executive gave up trying to retain this nucleus. Max said that Serrati would have to give his consent. The congress did offer the possibility of talking with these people. I remember how Graziadei came and said, "The left wing might be pried loose from the Serrati group if one makes concessions in the formulation." And the representatives of the Communist International there just said no, they wanted to fight for it, and that is how the business miscarried. I insist that this was a mistake and remain convinced that undoing this mischief will be much harder, but that the possibility still exists and that it should be exploited. Quite possibly, if one were to present the Serrati group with the kind of resolution Graziadei proposed, Serrati might make an about-face and cross over with his followers. Kabakchiev remained adamant about the wording; I do not know whether that was the plan, since the plan was to drive off Serrati. I think that if winning over the left wing really hinges on having Serrati come along too, he should be taken in the bargain. In my opinion, Serrati's person is not too high a price to pay for the left wing. Then one still has opportunities to come to an understanding with him. Max and I agree on how seriously the development of the Italian Communist Party is now endangered. He himself says that the revolutionary strength in Italy and the growth of the Communist Party have received a setback for some time to come. Nobody can deny that. And I anticipate even more serious troubles than Max, because I expect that in the Bombacci-Bordiga group no real nucleus will emerge and the International will not be able to exert such a strong influence because Borgi is in the Party, and the syndicalists and anarchists, who abound in Italy, belong to the old school and will be intractable. These people will not become Communists merely by belonging to the Party. There is a third consideration. In Italy tactical rigidity has put a large share of the onus of the split on us. That was the consequence of clumsy tactics. And the onus will be even greater when the consequences of the split make themselves felt. Some very bright people in the communal administrations, and elsewhere, will be lost to the Communist Party. For all these reasons I am absolutely in favor, now as before, of using any means and paying any price except that of the exclusion of the reformists to retain the Serrati wing in the Communist fold.

KOENEN: I think that there are no further disagreements regarding our perspectives on world policies. That is essential. It is also obvious with respect to the trade-union question that the German syndicalist movement must be evaluated differently from that in other countries. There is no possibility of negotiating with German syndicalists. To create a Zimmerwald from Moscow is itself nonsense. The way it looks now, the matter must be handled quite differently. There is no Zimmerwald but rather there are two Internationals. If some comrades are willing to go along, that is fine; I am not intransigent in the union question either. I want to say this to Paul: I cannot approve of the tendency to let illnesses run their course. We must do all in our power to make our influence felt regularly in Moscow by means of a more energetic delegation. We also must see to it that such illnesses do not break out.

COMRADE MAX: I only wish to reply to the question whether in the opinion of the Executive or my own, Levi's stand makes it desirable for him to give up his post as chairman. The Executive will never try to influence the choice of leaders in the Communist parties, as long as the party does not transgress against the tactics of the International. I have spoken up only to give Levi some food for thought on these matters. But I am certain that Levi can retain his chairmanship as long as he does not differ from the Party on essential matters. I personally consider it very expedient that he continue as chairman, but I do think it is harmful if he writes articles on the basis of incorrect facts and impressions.

BRANDLER: I do not share either Max's or Levi's point of view. I completely agree with Paul about his assessment of the syndicalist and the union movements. But there is absolutely no point any more in deploring and bemoaning these things. I have urged that we hit the KAPD on the head three times a day and that we do the same with the unions. I do not believe that we will succeed in altering the stand of the Executive by means of a delegation. And since I cannot alter that stand, I am taking it as a point of departure for working.

With Comrade Max's consent, it was decided to inform the joint *Zentrale* of Comrade Max's presence and identity and to pass resolutions only in the session of the joint *Zentrale*.

BIOGRAPHICAL NOTES

To make the preceding documents more meaningful, the editors have prepared biographical data (alphabetically arranged) about key persons in the documents.

NICOLA BOMBACCI. Schoolteacher, secretary of the chamber of labor before the First World War, radical Socialist ("Maximalist") during the war, elected Socialist deputy in 1919 and subsequently named secretary of the Socialist party. In this twofold party capacity, he was sent as a member of the Italian Socialist delegation to take part at the Second Comintern Congress in 1920. He and Graziadei were the two leaders won over by Moscow to implement its anti-Serrati strategy. He played an important role at the Leghorn congress of the Italian Socialist party in January 1921, was elected to the central committee of the newly established Italian Communist Party in which initially he was the second most prominent leader, after Bordiga. He was reelected to the same post at the next party congress in Rome, in March 1922. After Mussolini's victory and the establishment of diplomatic relations between Moscow and Rome, Bombacci began to speak of "two revolutions": the Bolshevik and the Fascist. As a consequence he was censured on several occasions by both the Italian Communist Party and the Comintern: in March 1924 the ECCI passed a resolution aimed specifically at Bombacci. In 1926 he was asked by the party to emigrate; he refused and finally in 1928 was expelled from the party because of his ambiguous attitude toward fascism. Afterward, his rapprochement with fascism went all the way: he remained loyal to Mussolini even when fascism was over-thrown in Rome in 1943, served as a leader of Mussolini's "Social Republic," and was fatally shot on April 28, 1945, in Dongo, where Mussolini was hanged on the same day.

HEINRICH BRANDLER. Born in 1881, a construction worker by trade, he was active in the German Social Democratic and trade-union movements before 1914, took a leftist stand during the war, and was the organizer of the Communist party in Chemnitz imme-diately after the German Communist Party was founded. He was elected to the central committee in 1920, identified himself with the anti-Levi group formed by Radek in early 1921, and was Levi's suc-cessor as president of the German Communist Party, only to be arrested shortly thereafter as a result of the "March action" in April 1921. Thrown into jail and convicted, he was named one of the honorary presidents *in absentia* of the Third Comintern Congress. After his release, he left for Moscow at the end of 1921 as a repre-sentative of the German Communist Party and was elected a member of the Presidium of the Executive Committee in March 1922, at the close of the First Enlarged Plenum of the Comintern. He returned to Germany in August 1922 and became political secretary of the Ger-man party's central committee. He remained titular head of the German Communist Party until after the abortive insurrection of autumn 1923, the failure of which the Comintern leadership decided to blame on Brandler, Radek and Thalheimer. Brandler was stripped of all his functions, and called to Moscow, where he was given the opportunity to address the Fifth Comintern Congress. He then was retained in Moscow, together with Thalheimer, as an official of the Comintern's central apparatus. He was a target of Comintern attacks at the Fifth Plenum in 1925 and the Seventh Plenum in 1926, but was not excluded from the German Communist Party until 1929.

ANTONIO GRAZIADEI (1873–1953). Professor of political economy, deputy of the Italian Socialist party, he belonged to the right wing of that party until the outbreak of the First World War. In the wake of the October Revolution, he went along with his party in joining the Comintern. He was a member of his party delegation and a speaker at the Second Comintern Congress in 1920. He was one of the men entrusted by Moscow with the task of creating a Communist and anti-Serrati group.

Graziadei was closely linked with the splitting operation which took place at the Leghorn congress, although he did not become one of the fifteen members of the central committee elected when the Italian Communist Party was constituted. At the party congress in Rome in March 1922, he again did not number among the members of the central committee. He did, however, participate in the delegation sent to the Fourth Comintern Congress, where he was one of the speakers. He was criticized for relapsing into rightist deviation, particularly in his analysis of the Comintern's tactical instructions regarding the workers's government. This tactical revisionism was added to his theoretical revisionism; in his writings, Grazaidei proposed revising certain basic Marxist concepts, such as the theory of value. He was excluded from the Italian Communist Party in 1929. Later, however, he made his "self-criticism" and was readmitted to the Party. He remained a member until his death.

CHRISTO KABAKCHIEV (1878–1940). A militant of the Bulgarian Socialist party from early youth, Kabakchiev came into contact with Socialist ideas and leaders in Europe as a student in Geneva. When the Bulgarian Social Democratic party split up, he became a leader of the "Tesniaks" (narrow ones) and served as a member of the central committee, editor-in-chief of the party organ, and deputy in parliament.

He joined the Comintern along with all the other "Tesniaks," and attended the Second Comintern Congress in 1920 in Moscow, where he presented the report on the statutes of the Communist International. In October 1920 he was a member of the Comintern delegation at the Halle congress of the German Independent Socialist party, and in January 1921 he was the Comintern spokesman at the Leghorn congress. In November 1922, at the Fourth Comintern Congress, he was one of the three reporters on the program of the Communist International. In January 1923 he became political secretary of the Bulgarian Communist Party. He was arrested immediately after the September 1923 insurrection. Released in 1926, he became a political refugee and remained in this status for the rest of his life. After a brief stay in Vienna, he returned to Moscow, where he was first active as a member of the International Control Commission, to which he had been elected *in absentia* during the Fifth Comintern Congress in 1924. He then held a professorship at the Lenin School and was a "scientific worker" at the Marx-Engels-

Lenin Institute, the Historical Institute, and elsewhere. His book on the birth and development of the Comintern, published on the occasion of the organization's tenth anniversary, dates from this period. In 1937, at the time of the "big purge," he was thrown into prison once more, but escaped a prolonged prison term only to fall seriously ill in 1938.

WILHELM KOENEN (1886–1963). Starting out as a member of the German Social Democratic party, Wilhelm Koenen (not to be confused with his brother Bernard Koenen, who was also a high Party and Comintern official) joined the Independent Socialist party in 1917 and became a member of the German Communist Party's central committee at the time of the fusion of the Communist-Spartakists with the left wing of the Independent Socialists. Early in 1921, he went to Moscow as a representative of the new anti-Levi majority, became one of the presidents of the Third Comintern Congress and was even promoted to membership in the "Little Bureau" (the future Presidium) of the ECCI before the opening of the congress. After the Third Congress, he was named a member of the International Control Commission, but soon thereafter was dropped as a member of the German party's central committee. He reappeared later, in 1927, as a Communist deputy at the Reichstag. Koenen emigrated from Hitler Germany, reached London via Prague and Paris, and took part in the activities of the Communist emigration (such as the 1937 appeal for a German popular front which he signed for the German Communist Party). He returned to East Germany in 1945 and held various posts, serving at the same time as member of the central committee of the Socialist Unity party.

BÉLA KUN (1886–1939). Born in a small town in Transylvania, Kun was attracted to Socialist ideas early in his youth, became a Socialist while studying law, and continued his Socialist militancy until the outbreak of the First World War, when he was mobilized and sent to the Russian front. He had attained the rank of junior lieutenant in the Austro-Hungarian army when he was captured and interned in a camp near Tomsk. After the Revolution of February 1917, he got in touch with a nearby Bolshevik organization, and after the Bolshevik victory in Petrograd he went there, became personally acquainted with Lenin and other revolutionary leaders and was put in charge of organizing foreign communists (mostly former prisoners of war) who espoused the Bolshevik cause. In March 1918 he founded the Hungarian Federation attached to the Russian Bolshevik party and was elected its president; a month later he was promoted to chairmanship of the Confederation of Foreign Communist Groups with the Bolshevik party. He also took an active part in a Bolshevik action to crush a mutiny of Socialist-Revolutionaries in Moscow in the summer of 1918.

In November 1918 he returned to Budapest and became head of the Hungarian Communist Party when it was established on November 25. February 20, 1919, he was arrested together with a group of Communist leaders. On March 21, however, after a delegation of the Hungarian Social Democratic party visited him in prison and established with him a political accord, Kun was released from prison and the Hungarian Soviet Republic was proclaimed. Béla Kun immediately assumed the actual leadership of the Republic, although he was officially only a people's commissar of foreign affairs.

The Republic lasted only 133 days. After its collapse Kun escaped to Austria, where he was interned until the summer of 1920. He reached the Soviet Union shortly after the conclusion of the Second Comintern Congress (1920), and in the fall of the same year, he took part in the liquidation of General Wrangel's troops in the Crimea (he distinguished himself by his brutality toward the prisoners, which provoked protest even among the Russian Bolsheviks).

At the end of February 1921, Kun was co-opted to the Little Bureau (Presidium) of the ECCI and was sent to Germany where he was in charge of the famous "March action." At the Third Comintern Congress in the summer of 1921, his behavior in Germany was severely criticized by Lenin. As a consequence, Kun was dispatched to work on the regional Bolshevik committee in the Urals. In February 1922, the First Enlarged Plenum of the ECCI was about to establish a commission of inquiry to examine the accusations against Kun made by certain Hungarian Communists, but the matter was dropped.

As early as at the Fourth Comintern Congress, in November 1922, Kun resumed his place in the Comintern hierarchy; he was chosen as rapporteur on the same point of the agenda—the Fifth Anniversary of the Bolshevik Revolution and the Prospects of World Revolution—as Lenin, Trotsky, and Klara Zetkin. Thereafter, Kun took an active part in all the congresses and in nearly all the enlarged plenums of the Comintern from 1924 to 1935. He was at various times member or deputy member of the ECCI, deputy member of its

Presidium, member of the organizational bureau (Org-Bureau) of the Comintern, head of the Comintern's secretariat for the Balkans, head of the Agitprop section of the Comintern, and speaker on innumerable occasions at various Comintern meetings (congresses, enlarged plenums, committees, etc.). During the same period he wrote numerous pamphlets, from the one on Soviet Hungary, published in 1920 under the pseudonym "B. Koloszvary," to the one on unity of action which appeared in 1934.

Béla Kun followed faithfully and promptly every turn in Soviet policies and hailed the downfall of each Soviet leader who lost favor during that period. He assailed Trotsky from 1924 on, disassociated himself from Zinoviev after 1926, survived Bukharin, and became a member of the Stalinist leadership of the Comintern. All this, however, could not save him during the great purge. He was elected a member of the ECCI at the last Comintern congress in 1935, but in 1937 he was summoned before a Party tribunal composed of his colleagues (Manuilsky, Dimitrov, Togliatti, etc.) as a prelude to his delivery into the hands of Stalin's police. When Kun fell victim on November 30, 1939, the Second World War had already begun and the German-Soviet pact was in full force.

He was rehabilitated in an article signed "E. Varga," published in *Pravda,* February 21, 1956.

PAUL LEVI (1883–1930). A lawyer by profession, Levi was active in the German Social Democratic Party, belonged to the Spartacus League during the First World War, and came into contact with Lenin and the Zimmerwald Left during his stays in Switzerland in 1915–17. He happened to be there at the time that Lenin and other Russian revolutionaries started out on their journey through Germany and was among the ten European Socialists Internationalists to sign under the assumed name of Paul Hartstein the text underwriting this trip. As a leading member of the Spartacus League in the final phase of the war, on very close terms with Rosa Luxemburg and Leo Jogiches, Levi automatically belonged to the central committee of the German Communist Party from its founding. After Rosa Luxemburg, Karl Liebknecht, and Leo Jogiches were assassinated, Levi became the effective head of the party and was in charge of the German delegation to the Second Congress of the Comintern in July–August, 1920. At this congress he was a member of the Presidium and was elected a substitute member of the Executive Committee. At the congress of October 1920 at Halle, where the fusion of the left wing of the Independent Socialist party and the German Communist Party took place, he was elected one of the two presidents of the unified party.

Having inherited Rosa Luxemburg's and Leo Jogiches' ideas—including their distrust of Bolshevik methods of operation—he soon came into conflict with Moscow on a series of issues. The breaking point came in the wake of the "March action" of 1921, of which he strongly disapproved. On April 15, 1921, the *Zentrale* of the German Communist Party expelled Levi from the Party, and eleven days later the ECCI's confirmation of that decision finally put Levi out of every connection with the Comintern.

At first, he and his political friends formed a Communist opposition group; he then joined the Independent Socialist party (the group which had refused to become part of the German Communist Party in 1920); and finally, along with the Independent Socialists, he rejoined the German Social Democratic party. He was a parliamentary deputy from 1920 on (he and Klara Zetkin had been elected that year, the only two Communist deputies to the Reichstag), and retained his mandate as a Social Democrat until his death in 1930. As a member of the left wing of the Social Democratic party, he was one of the editors of the periodical *Der Klassenkampf*.

KARL RADEK (1885–1939). (His real name was K. Sobelsohn; his other pseudonyms: Parabellum, Paul Bremer, A. Struthahn.) Born in L'vov, Galicia, Radek took part from his early youth in the Socialist movement, first within the Social Democratic party of Poland and Lithuania, then in the German Socialist party, and finally in the Russian revolutionary movement. He was a political journalist and a gifted analyst and polemicist, but became a target of political and moral attacks in all three of these workers' movements. When he was expelled in 1912 from the Social Democratic party of Poland and Lithuania following an internal split, he was accused of having mismanaged the funds of the party. In 1913, at the Yena Congress, the German Socialists also denounced him; his case ultimately was brought before a special committee composed of different factions of Russian Social Democracy which met in Paris (Lenin himself in a letter published for the first time in 1930 confirmed this fact).

In Switzerland, where he lived after the outbreak of the First World War, Radek adopted an internationalist attitude and took part in the Zimmerwald and Kienthal conferences. At this time he joined the Zimmerwald Left, although he did not adhere to the Bolshevik party until 1917. Because the Provisional Government (established after the Russian revolution of February 1917) refused to grant him permission to enter Russia, Radek established himself in Stockholm as a member of the foreign delegation of the Bolshevik central committee. He went to Petrograd after the Bolshevik victory early in 1918 and entered the commissariat of foreign affairs dealing with Central Europe. He joined the left-wing Communists during discussions concerning the conclusion of Brest-Litovsk peace treaty.

Shortly after the November 1918 revolution in Germany, Radek entered Germany clandestinely and took part in the congress at which the German Communist Party (Spartakists) was founded, late in December 1918. After the revolutionary days of January 1919, a warrant for his arrest was issued by the police. He was apprehended in February and held first in prison, then under house arrest (first in the home of a baron and then in the house of a policeman) before being deported to the Soviet Union in January 1920.

In March 1919 he had been appointed *in absentia* to the central committee of the Russian Bolshevik party, and after his return from Germany he was named secretary of the Executive Committee of the Comintern. From that time until the beginning of 1924, Radek occupied a prominent place in the Comintern hierarchy—particularly in his role as its representative in charge of affairs of the German Communist Party, which was the most important section of the Comintern. He was speaker and rapporteur at the Second, Third, and Fourth Comintern congresses and at the first three enlarged plenums. In April 1922, with Bukharin, he headed the Comintern delegation during negotiations with the Socialist internationals in Berlin.

In October 1923, Radek was representative of the Comintern during the unsuccessful attempt to provoke a revolution in Germany. Since he opted for Trotsky at the beginning of Kremlin's internal strife, Radek was accused by the "troika" (Zinoviev, Kamenev, Stalin) of failure in his mission in Germany and of "rightist deviation." At the beginning of 1924 he lost at the same time his high function within the Comintern and his post in the Bolshevik central committee.

In 1926 he became rector of the Sun Yat-sen Communist University for Chinese and other Oriental students in Moscow, but was dismissed from that post a year later. At the Fifteenth Congress of the Bolshevik Party in December 1927, he was expelled from the Party;

in January 1928, he was deported (Trotsky was deported at the same time). In 1929, however, he broke with Trotsky, made public his self-criticism, and was readmitted to the Bolshevik Party in 1930. Although he was not reinstated into high Comintern or Party positions, he did become chief foreign affairs commentator in the leading Soviet papers. In 1935 he was a member of the commission charged with the preparation of a new, "Stalinist," constitution, and at the beginning of 1936 he publicly approved the preparations for the first trial of Zinoviev and Kamenev. But in the same year he again was expelled from the Party, and in January 1937 he appeared among the defendants charged with adherence to the "Anti-Soviet Trotskyite Center" at the second Great Purge Trial. There he played the role assigned to him by Stalin and Vyshinsky: he incriminated Marshal Tukhachevsky, who was arrested soon afterward and executed in June 1937. Of the group of seventeen accused in the trial of the "Anti-Soviet Trotskyite Center," thirteen were sentenced to death and executed. Radek, however, received a relatively mild sentence: ten years in prison, where he died in 1939.

Radek was the author of numerous pamphlets. His articles on the Comintern were published in two volumes entitled *Piat' Let Cominterna*, and his articles on the German Communist movement appeared in three volumes entitled *Germanskaia Revoliutsia*.

MÁTYÁS RÁKOSI. Born in 1892, Rákosi joined the Socialist youth movement in 1911 and studied in Budapest, and in Germany and England. He was mobilized in 1914, captured on the Russian front, and imprisoned until 1917. In autumn 1917, he was among a group of Hungarian prisoners of war who, under Béla Kun's leadership, rallied to Bolshevism. At the beginning of 1918 he returned to Hungary. After that country had been proclaimed a Soviet republic, he was named assistant commissar for commerce and communications, and later commissar for production.

When the Soviet Republic collapsed, Rákosi followed Béla Kun into exile in Vienna, and from there reached Moscow. He attended the Second, Third, and Fourth congresses of the Communist International. At the Third Congress, in 1921, and the Fourth Congress in 1922, he was named to the secretariat of the Communist International's Executive Committee. On one of his several trips as a Comintern emissary, he attended the Leghorn congress of 1921 in Italy, at which the Italian Communist Party was constituted.

In 1925, on orders from Moscow, Rákosi was sent to Hungary

to reorganize the Communist party which had been outlawed in
1919. In Hungary he was arrested in September 1925 and condemned to nine years of prison; on the eve of his release he was sentenced once more—this time for life. The Communist International
thereupon turned Rákosi into one of the heroes of the world proletariat, alongside Dimitrov. The Hungarian Communist batallion in
the International Brigades in Spain carried his name. In 1940, however (at the time of the Hitler-Stalin pact), he was exchanged for
some old Hungarian flags dating back to the Revolution of 1848,
which the Soviets handed over to the Hungarian government.

From 1940 to December 1944, Rákosi, who had become a
Soviet citizen, resided in the USSR. His signature appears on the
act of dissolution of the Communist International.

Rákosi was named secretary-general of the central committee of
the Communist party when he returned to Hungary along with the
Soviet troops. Subsequently, on November 15, 1945, he became vice
president of the government, and in that capacity he accompanied
the prime minister, Ferenc Nagy, on his visit to the United States in
1946. Rákosi attended the second and third meetings of the Cominform in 1948 and 1949. He also was head of his party's delegation at
the Nineteenth Congress of the Russian Communist Party in 1952.
On August 14, 1952, he became head of the Hungarian government,
a post he retained until July 4, 1953, when he turned over the pres-
idency to Imre Nagy in line with the principle of "collective leadership" newly proclaimed in Moscow. He did, however, retain his
position in the secretariat of the central committee, and he was reelected to this post at the third congress of the Hungarian Communist
Party in 1954. On July 18, 1956, after a trip to Moscow, he resigned
as party secretary. His resignation was understood to be a gesture to
appease popular dissatisfaction with his rule. After the Hungarian
October 1956 revolution, Rákosi took up permanent residence in the
Soviet Union. On August 19, 1962, he was expelled from the Hungarian Socialist Workers' (Communist) party on the ground that he
was chiefly responsible for "the unlawful trials conducted in the
years of the personality cult against personages of the workers' movement on trumped-up accusations."

OTTO RÜHLE. Born in 1874, Rühle was a political and literary
figure first active in the German Social Democratic party. He was
elected a deputy in 1912, and was the second deputy (after Karl

Liebknecht) to vote against military credits in the Reichstag. He joined the German Communist Party early in 1919, soon opted for its left wing, and became one of the founders of the Kommunistische Arbeiterpartei Deutschlands (KAPD) after the Heidelberg congress of the German Communist Party in October 1919. In 1920, he made a trip to Moscow in the name of the KAPD and took part in the Second Comintern Congress. He maintained, however, a critical attitude toward Moscow's policies, especially in regard to German problems. In 1921 Rühle came into conflict with the KAPD leadership because of his opposition to rigidity in the organization of the party. Later he devoted his time and interest to research in pedagogy and history and published a well-known biography of Marx. Rühle escaped to Mexico after Hitler's rise to power. He died there during the Second World War, and his widow committed suicide a few hours after his death.

GIACINTO MENOTTI SERRATI (1874–1926). A militant Socialist from his youth, Serrati became one of the leaders of the "Maximalist" left wing of the Socialist party during the First World War. In 1915 he became editor-in-chief of the party organ *Avanti* and was a delegate of his party to the international Zimmerwald and Kienthal conferences. Arrested in 1917 on charges of "anti-militarist propaganda," he then became an ardent proponent of his party's withdrawal from the Second International and of its joining the Third International in 1919. At the Second Congress of the Comintern, July–August 1920, he was elected a member of the Executive Committee and served on the Presidium. From the start, however, he expressed such disagreement with certain ideas and methods of the Russian Bolsheviks in the Comintern administration that by the autumn of 1920 he had become the object of a full-scale attack in which Lenin and Zinoviev personally participated.

At the Socialist congress in Leghorn, in January 1921, when the Italian party split into three factions, the largest portion of the members remained loyal to Serrati. The Serrati group refused to join either the Second or the Second-and-a-Half International, in order to leave open the way for a reconciliation with the Communists which was accomplished in the period between the Fourth Congress (which he attended) and the Fifth Congress of the Comintern. He joined the Communist party, was appointed to its central committee, and remained an active member of the Party until his death.

KLARA ZETKIN (1857–1933) was born in a village in Saxony, daughter of a schoolteacher. Attracted to Socialist ideas in her youth, she married a Russian revolutionary, Ossip Zetkin. During the period of illegality of the German Socialist party, she lived abroad and took part in the Socialist movements of France, Austria and Italy. She was well acquainted with Engels and participated in the preparation and work of the founding congress of the Second International in Paris in 1889. She attended all congresses of the International before 1914, and belonged to its left wing. In March 1915, she organized in Bern an international Socialist women's conference against the war. On her return to Germany she was arrested and briefly imprisoned. In later phases of the war she was militant in both the Spartacus League and the Independent Social Democratic party. In 1919 she joined the German Communist Party and was elected a member of its central committee, a post she held until the end of her life. On several occasions, however, she was close to those in the German party who were critical of Moscow's leadership of the Comintern (she agreed initially with Paul Levi's attitude), but she never decided to break officially.

Klara Zetkin was elected delegate of the German party at the Second Comintern Congress but reached the Soviet Union for the first time in September 1920. Beginning with the Third Comintern Congress, she was a member of the ECCI and of its Presidium. She also headed the international women's secretariat of the Comintern and was active for many years in the organization of the International Worker's Red Aid.

From 1920 on, Klara Zetkin was a Communist deputy in the Reichstag. In August 1932, while living in Moscow, she fell gravely ill, but recovered enough strength to return to Berlin to open the session of the newly elected Reichstag, in which she was the oldest deputy. She died on an estate near Moscow on June 30, 1933. She had received highest Soviet decorations, and the urn with her ashes is immured within the Kremlin wall.

Interference by the Comintern in the Affairs of the French Communist Party (1921-1923)

"The Executive Committee of the Communist International considers it not only permissible but even obligatory to 'intervene' in the affairs of the parties that belong to, or wish to belong to, the Communist International"—From G. Zinoviev's report on behalf of the ECCI at the Second Congress of the Comintern.

EDITORS' INTRODUCTION—*Moscow's direct intervention in the internal affairs of the parties adhering to the Comintern stemmed from two sources: the nature of Leninist concepts and the statutes approved in accordance with them at the Second Comintern Congress in 1920. This intervention touched upon all essential aspects of the parties' existence: the ruling organs, tactics, organization, finances, propaganda, and so on. It is hardly surprising, therefore, that the titular and at the same time actual leaders in the three large Western European parties—Serrati (Italy), Levi (Germany), and Frossard (France)—who had joined the Third International as early as 1919 and 1920, all got into conflict with the Comintern and broke with it (although Serrati soon thereafter rejoined its ranks).*

The French Communist Party was subjected to particularly vigorous intervention by the Comintern at the time of the party congresses. In December 1920, at the Tours congress marking the founding of the Communist Party, Moscow's intervention assumed an open and public character, as was poignantly illustrated by the telegram (later called "Zinoviev's pistol shot") against Jean Longuet and his friends. Notwithstanding the wishes of the majority of the Communist-voting delegates, who certainly wanted to see Longuet join the new party, the cable from Moscow slammed the door in the face of *this grandson of Karl Marx: "The draft resolution signed by Longuet** *and Paul Faure proves that Longuet and his group do not wish to dissociate themselves from the reformist camp. They have been and still remain determined agents of bourgeois influence on the proletariat. . . . The Communist International can have nothing in common with the authors of such resolutions."*

The Comintern had its way, but the Bolshevik rulers (Lenin in particular) who paid close attention to questions of tactics and efficacy soon realized that sometimes these public missives could provoke much commotion and gratuitous reaction, and that it would be wiser to act covertly thereafter. Thus evolved the practice of sending from Moscow emissaries equipped with precise directives, or of forwarding directives by reliable couriers for the use of such emissaries. These texts no longer were communicated to the congress as a whole or to the press, but were confided to a restricted number of leaders; the meetings themselves were held in closed session, with no press coverage.

Following are four documents of this type. Though originating at the apex of the hierarchy (one of them bears Zinoviev's signature and another Bukharin's), they are not "sensational" in the journalistic sense of the word, but they reveal the method used by Moscow for harnessing the foreign Communist parties as Lenin intended and as Stalin later fully succeeded in doing. The four documents are these:

1) A report by Albert Treint on the joint session held in Marseille, December 27, 1921, during the first congress of the French Communist Party, between representatives of the subcommittee on general policy of this congress and the delegation from the Communist International, consisting of Amadeo Bordiga and Henryk Walecki. The original minutes bear the title "For the Communist International," which indicates the destination of the document. The document consists of twenty-seven unbound sheets, 21x27 cm., in blue mimeograph ink. It seems to have been run off rather hastily, for it contains a large number of typographical errors and omitted and misplaced words. These mistakes have been corrected in the version presented below.

2) A circular entitled, "Supplemental Instructions to the Delegates of the Communist International to the French Communist Party Congress in Paris," dated at Moscow September 20, 1922, with

---

*For biographical notes, see pp. 358 ff.

*the seal of the Executive Committee of the Communist International
and the written signature "G. Zinoviev." The document consists of
five sheets, 21x33 cm., written in purple ink.*

*3) A photocopy of a letter in French signed by N. Bukharin,
written in the name of the Presidium on the letterhead of the Executive Committee of the Third International, dated Janunary 15, 1923,
and addressed to the left wing of the French party.*

*4) A photocopy of a typewritten letter on plain paper and
dated March 18, 1923, in which Albert Treint, then secretary-
general of the French Communist Party, informed his fellow members of the Politburo of his intention to resign his post.*

DOCUMENT No. 1:

MINUTES FROM A SECRET MEETING BETWEEN
SOME REPRESENTATIVES OF THE FIRST CONGRESS OF THE
FRENCH COMMUNIST PARTY AND COMINTERN DELEGATES,
MARSEILLE, 1921*

EDITORS' INTRODUCTION—*The congress of the French Socialist
party held in Tours (December 1920) put the party apparatus and the
party newspaper into the hands of a heterogeneous majority of party
members who claimed to favor adherence to the Third International,
but who had the most varied reasons for this stand and were not really
Communists in the sense that the word was to take from then on; they
were not Bolsheviks, as one would have said at that time, or Marxist-
Leninists, as one was to say later.*

*Conflicts were inevitable among the groups constituting the
majority at Tours. Having remained below the surface throughout
1921, they broke out into the open at the first congress of the party.
The latter, meanwhile had changed its name to Communist Party in
accordance with the twenty-one conditions of admission to the Communist International adopted at the Second Comintern Congress.*

*The first French Communist Party congress was held in Mar-
seille December 25–30, 1921 (as reported in L'Humanité, December
26–31, 1921). The meeting with which the following document deals
took place, therefore, during this congress.*

The congress discussed and adopted three resolutions defining

---

*Excerpts from this document were published in March 1922 in *Populaire*, the
organ of the French Socialist party.

the party's position on the following vital issues: national defense, relations between the party and the trade unions, and agricultural policy.

But three controversial and irritating questions arose to provoke the crisis: the question of the united front, the question of reorganization of the party leadership, and the problem of personalities.

The Question of the United Front

The united-front tactics were worked out by Lenin, Trotsky and Zinoviev during the fall of 1921. At the meeting of the ECCI, February–March, 1922, Willi Münzenberg explained that, upon learning of the catastrophic harvest in Russia as a result of drought in the summer of 1921, the ECCI had decided upon an international proletarian rescue action with the participation of all workers, regardless of their political or trade-union affiliation. "This was the first practical attempt to set up a united front," the speaker declared;[1] it would have been more accurate, however, had he said that this attempt spurred the leaders of the Communist International on toward new tactics.

It was on December 4, 1921, that the ECCI, through an appeal to the workers of all countries to aid the Russian proletariat, inaugurated the tactic of the "united front." A few days later, on December 18, the ECCI adopted detailed directives "on the United Front of the workers and on the attitude toward workers belonging to the Second, Two-and-a-Half, and Amsterdam Internationals, and to those who support anarcho-syndicalist organizations."[2]

The Marseille congress opened a week later. The French Communist Party's sections thus had no time to discuss the new tactics; most of them did not even know of their existence. Moreover, to many party members, including the leaders, the idea of a "united front" appeared to aim at a reconciliation with the Socialist party, and thus was contradictory to the basic line of the Tours congress which had enjoined the total break with the Socialists. On the other hand, the question of the united front was not completely unfamiliar to the leaders and better-informed militants of the French Communist Party. They had received word of it through Antoine Ker, a prominent activist, who had just returned from a trip to Germany, where he probably had been in touch with the Comintern's permanent representatives operating in and from Berlin. Ker therefore had been in a good position to inform his French comrades about the existence and political consequences of the "open letter" of the German Communist Party (which will be referred to in the document that follows). This letter, published in the official organ of the German party, Die Rote Fahne, on January 8, 1921, appealed to a number of German labor organizations, political as well as professional, to participate in common action for the protection of the immediate interests of the proletariat. "The letter, which [Paul] Levi had drafted with [Karl] Radek's blessing, if not Radek's assistance, was an appeal for working-class solidarity and as such foreshadowed the united-front tactics of the future."[3] The failure of the letter to influence political events in Germany, and Paul Levi's expulsion from the German Communist Party in April of the same year, could only have increased the reluctance of the French Communists to follow the united-front line. By the same token, they were not yet aware that the Third Congress of the Comintern which convened in Moscow (June 20–July 12, 1921) already had indicated the switch toward the united front without spelling out the terms.

Reorganization of the Party Leadership

The Third Congress of the Comintern adopted a long text entitled "The Theses on the Structure of Communist Parties and on the Methods and Content of their Work." The organization and discipline of the Party were summarized in fifty-nine theses which conflicted with the ideas that had always been nurtured in France on these matters in Socialist circles.

Thesis 46 proclaimed that "the party as a whole is under the leadership of the Communist International" and stated that "directives and decisions of the International are binding on the party, and of course on every individual party member," but thesis 47 went even further, imposing on all parties an organization of the ruling apparatus which effectively put them at the mercy of the International. The aim was to concentrate all control over the party in a "close-knit leadership" removed from the influence of the party and subjected to that of Moscow.

The wording of these directives in thesis 47 is rather confused, but the intention is clear. This is the text: "The central leadership of the party (central committee and advisory council or committee) is responsible to the party congress and to the leadership of the Communist *International. The smaller committee as well as the larger committee and advisory council is, as a rule, elected by the party congress. If the congress considers it expedient it may instruct the central committee to elect from its own membership a smaller committee consisting of the members of the political and organizational bureaus. The policy and current activities of the party are directed by the smaller committee through these two bureaus.*"[4]

These concepts were alien to most of the French "Communists." To be sure, they had adopted at the Tours congress a resolution (based on the "twenty-one conditions") on "democratic centralism," but they had little faith in it. They tended therefore to delay the implementation of the Comintern's directives and to alter their sense when applying them. For its part, the ECCI made matters even worse by using the word "presidium" (that is the "smaller committee" or bureau of the mentioned Thesis 47), a term unknown in the French political language, the familiar French term being "bureau exécutif."

The decisions of the Third Comintern Congress were severely criticized by Henri Fabre in the Journal du Peuple. *He ridiculed the rules proposed at the congress and spoke about "Moscow's ukases." These open attacks annoyed the comité directeur of the French party, but it took only some mild measures against Fabre.*[5] *The commission on disputes of the party merely reprimanded him. In October, after a discussion with Jules Humbert-Droz, delegate of the Comintern, the comité directeur approved the proposal to create a presidium. But this approval was neither unqualified nor deeprooted.*

The reluctance of the French Communists to implement the Comitern directives was manifested at the Marseille congress. On the second day of the congress, its subcommittee on general policy adopted a resolution proposed by Frossard, according to which the party was to have an executive bureau (presidium). It was to be restricted, however, to dealing with administrative and minor political matters between sessions of the comité directeur.

This concession to the Comintern directives was accepted only after long discussion. To the delegates of the Comintern it seemed inadequate.

The Problem of Personalities

It is usually considered that the Marseille congress was dominated by the problem of personalities, or rather by the issue posed by one per-

son: Boris Souvarine. This is erroneous; as already indicated, the divergencies were purely political. The problem of personalities was in fact closely bound up with the then threefold division of the French party. Its right wing and center made certain accusations against Souvarine, representative of the left wing. For the Comintern, the main danger was from the prominent rightists—Brizon, Fabre, Verfeuil; and later, Victor Meric and Georges Pioch. It may be said, therefore, that the "affair Souvarine" was, to some extent at least, a response to the "affairs Brizon, Fabre and Verfeuil."

Boris Souvarine's prominent role in the establishment of the French Communist Party is discussed in the notes on contributors. His "affair" occurred when, after the Third Comintern Congress, he remained in Moscow as the representative of the French Communist Party to the ECCI.

The directives addressed by the Comintern to the leadership of the French party, as well as all critical comments, were relayed by Souvarine. These letters exasperated the leaders of the French party. But instead of examining their substance and comprehending that Souvarine was transmitting not his own opinions but those of the Comintern, they accused Souvarine of misinforming the Comintern and of imparting a personal, harsh and offensive tone to its criticism. Some ten years later, still acutely indignant, Frossard wrote: "From Moscow Souvarine bombarded the comité directeur with sharp barbs of criticism: we were not a true Communist party; we were tolerating monstrous heresies; we were accomplishing nothing."[6]

In fact, Souvarine's expressions of disapproval, if sometimes formally excessive, were certainly justified from the Comintern's point of view: the party, with Frossard as secretary-general, was not inactive, but it certainly was not a true Communist party; it tolerated in its ranks people whose ideas had nothing in common with Bolshevism. Frossard himself corroborates this by asking an introspective question: "Have I ever been a Communist? As I recall the atmosphere of the congress of Tours, I feel that I can emphatically reply to this question in the negative."[7]

Trotsky, at that time especially interested in the affairs of the French Communist Party, defended Souvarine, notably in a speech made on May 19, 1922, at a meeting of the ECCI. He spoke sarcastically about the leaders in France who wanted to create the impression that Souvarine was a sort of "apocalyptic phenomenon . . . possessing insurmountable mysterious influence, who dominates and *deceives the Executive, and all this to attain his personal goals." At this point, Bukharin interrupted Trotsky by exclaiming: "Souvarine, Rasputin!"*[8]

However, these personal accusations and recriminations, simmering below the surface, erupted at the Marseille congress and raged during the ensuing months. Charles Rappoport, who, even before the congress, had submitted a motion to the comité directeur concerning the "powers of the delegate to the Comintern," attacked Souvarine (still in Moscow) on the floor of the congress for his allegedly malicious interpretation of Rappoport's article in Journal du Peuple *in connection with Rappoport's "good friend Serrati." Bestel replied immediately, declaring that the ECCI was against Rappoport's motion and asking the congress not to adopt it. As will be seen from the document that follows, the motion was finally rejected after the intervention by Comintern delegates.*

Still, the "affair" was not settled. When, at the closing session of the congress, Frossard communicated the results of the vote to the comité directeur, Souvarine's name was not among those who had been reelected. Immediately afterwards, Loriot, Treint, Vaillant-Couturier, and Dunois, the most prominent representatives of the left wing of the party, resigned amidst clamor and turmoil.

The crisis in the leadership of the party had now broken into the open.

A Closed Meeting Between Two Comintern Emissaries and the Leaders of the French Communist Party

At the time this meeting convened (December 27, 1921), the Marseille congress had been in session for three days and was proceeding in a direction contrary to the desires of the Comintern delegates. This was especially true with regard to the question of the united front, for the congress overwhelmingly approved Frossard's repudiation of it; his argument was that it would lead to an agreement with the "dissidents"—that is, with the Socialists who refused to adhere to the Comintern or were denied membership in it. A subcommittee on general policy also had adopted almost unanimously, with Treint alone demurring, a resolution drawn up by Frossard which in effect synthesized the main centrist views on the mentioned controversial three questions.

At that moment the two delegates of the Comintern went into action. H. Walecki (whose name Treint had erroneously spelled

Walewsky in the document that follows) and Amadeo Bordiga insisted on a closed meeting with the delegation of the subcommittee on general policy of the French Communist Party. The latter was composed of five members: Treint, Rappoport, Renoult, Brodel and Soutif. By meeting separately, away from the turmoil of the congress, the Comintern delegates hoped to prevent a formal censure of the united-front tactic by the congress; to strengthen and enlarge the functions of the executive bureau (already affirmed in principle by Frossard) beyond the scope of mere administrative and minor political matters, particularly in cases of emergency; and to eliminate any mention of personality problems in the final resolutions of the congress.

After this closed meeting, two more days of discussion were necessary to overcome the opposition of the congress and to put through a motion which, in Treint's words, "was sufficiently satisfactory to both the Treint-Souvarine faction and to the International."

The Minutes

To understand the Congress of Marseille fully, one needs not only to follow its public proceedings, but also to be acquainted with the main work accomplished by its committees.

The most important committee session was unquestionably the joint meeting held in Marseille on December 27 between the subcommittee on general policy and the delegation from the International.

I noted, during the session, all the remarks point by point. Since that time, I have had the opportunity to read my analytical report to Renoult of the tenth Paris section. Renoult does not agree that the motion mentioned in the beginning was formulated by Frossard. I am certain that on December 26 Renoult had declared before the plenary session that Frossard was the author of this motion. In any case, this is an unimportant detail.

Before I began reading, Renoult made the remark that this report was my personal construction. He held fast to this reservation after hearing the report; however, when I urged him to specify in what way the report was incomplete or inaccurate, he remained silent.

Besides, if the accuracy of this report were questioned, Walecki or Bordiga could always be called in as witnesses.

For my part, I declare that I took down the utterances if not verbatim at least point by point. Moreover, the successive remarks are so closely interrelated, that I could not, even unintentionally, have changed a single one without changing the whole report.

After much opposition indeed, a motion finally was adopted on the 29th which was satisfactory to our group and the International.

However, on the basis of past experience and in the light of the composition of the new comité directeur (to which Souvarine was not reelected while others were elected who had firmly opposed the International in numerous newspaper articles), there is reason to think that the concessions were purely verbal and were meant only to conceal before the party the deep divergencies existing between the current leadership of the party and the International.

It will be easy to see, upon reading this report, whether personal or political differences were at stake at the Marseille congress.

If one knows the frame of mind of the various people, one will be in a better position to judge the assertions of some who profess agreement with the Executive Committee of the International.

May this modest effort contribute to the clarification of the votes cast that night in Marseille and help our Party proceed along the road which leads to the Communist Revolution.

January 19, 1922　　　　　　　　　　　　　　　　　　　Albert Treint

Session of December 27, 1921
Joint Session Held in Marseille
between the Subcommittee on General Policy
and the Delegation from the International

Chairman of Session: Treint

Renoult reads the motion adopted by the subcommittee with the approval of all but Treint. This motion (which Renoult had stated at the plenary session of the committee on resolutions on December 26 had been drawn up by Frossard) included among other points:

1) A condemnation in principle of the united-front tactics.

2) An organization of the party's executive bureau whereby this bureau would be responsible for minor administrative and political matters in the interval between the sessions of the comité direc-

teur. (This represented the outcome of a long dispute after which Renoult had agreed to insert the word "political.")

3) References to earlier polemics which obviously were aimed at Souvarine in particular.

This motion did not contain any condemnation of the *Journal du Peuple*'s opportunist policy.

The discussion begins after this reading.

BORDIGA: I could raise the preliminary question in connection with the part of the motion which concerns the united front. The party has not yet taken a stand on this question. However, I do not want to evade the heart of the matter. Let me say at once that this motion contains a poor definition of the united-front tactics—a poor definition which presents these tactics as a step toward reunification and rapprochement with the dissidents. This way of representing the matter distorts the thinking of the national sections applying these tactics, as well as the thinking of the International.

WALECKI: Above all, let me say that approval of the motion concerning the united front would put the French party into opposition with nearly the entire International. For many sections, for the International itself, the united front is not a matter of pure theory. Everywhere, and notably in Germany and Italy, the proletarian battle against capitalism is being waged according to the united-front formula. The French party, which has not yet joined the battle exactly along these lines, must beware of not hampering in the name of pure theory the action of the International which is in the process of applying the united-front tactics through several of its sections.

I would like to note, moreover, that the French party would put itself into opposition to the resolutions of the Third Moscow Congress by taking such a radical stand against the united front.

(Walecki reads paragraph 34 of the Theses, on the organization of Communist parties. This paragraph states:

> Should the Communist party make the attempt to take over the leadership of the masses at a time of political and economic tension which promises to lead to the outbreak of new movements and struggles, special demands need not be put forward but appeals can be made directly to the members of Socialist parties and trade unions in simple and popular language not to shrink from the struggles which their needs and the increasing oppression of the employers make necessary, even if this should be opposed by their bureaucratic leaders; otherwise they will be driven into complete

ruin. The Party press, and, in particular, its daily newspapers, must in these circumstances emphasize and demonstrate every day that the Communists are ready to intervene as leaders in the present and forthcoming struggles of the impoverished proletariat, that they are whenever possible prepared to come to the help of all the oppressed in the present tense situation. It must be proved every day that without these struggles the condition of the working class will become impossible and that nevertheless the old organizations avoid these struggles and try to prevent them. . . .)

Without specifically mentioning the words "united front," we have here a complex of ideas which perfectly correspond to the united-front tactics.

The International has been preparing the Marseille congress for weeks, and so have the neighboring sections. Men like Lenin, Trotsky, Bukharin, have given deep thought to the problems brought up in Marseille, despite the other tasks which claim their attention. For weeks the German party has been devoting itself to this task. The Italian party postponed its own congress to a later date in order to partake in the Marseille congress. Under these circumstances, the French party cannot possibly take a casual stand on the basis of a misleadingly phrased question. There certainly is a misunderstanding between the International and the French party. And one must surely wonder how a misunderstanding could have arisen on such an important question.

In any case, the International has troops fighting everywhere under the united-front slogan. The entire French party, with all its sections and federations, after having studied the question on the basis of precise information, must have the final say.

RAPPOPORT: Is the united front an appeal to the troops or to the reformist or opportunist leaders?

WALECKI: Here is my answer. Let me first indicate simply that if in France the words "united front" give rise to a misunderstanding, we don't insist on the words, but for what they stand.

At this juncture an employers' offensive is being combined with reactionary governmental measures. We are faced with an attempt to reduce wages, with an unemployment crisis, with a threat to the eight-hour day; we are even faced with a legal or administrative or armed struggle against the very existence of our organizations (as is the case with fascism in Italy).

According to Communist doctrine, when the vital needs of the proletariat are threatened, it must defend itself spontaneously, biologically. That much is within the grasp of all workers.

Such a situation makes feasible at this time the united front. By appealing to all workers to defend themselves against the bourgeoisie, we shall break the stranglehold of nefarious organizations on the proletariat. We will push to the wall all those opportunist or reformist leaders who do not want a class struggle.

Rappoport's question is a purely secondary, formal one. Is it better strategy to address these appeals directly to the masses in order to drive the leaders to the wall and unmask them, or to address the appeals simultaneously to the local or central organizations through their responsible leaders? This depends on a large number of local or national circumstances.

Depending on whether the Communists have the majority or are in the minority among the politically organized proletariat and whether the trade unions are split or not, depending on the traditions of the labor movement, these methods of applying the united-front tactics may vary.

Unquestionably the "open letter" addressed by the German party to all organizations was an excellent thing.

In Italy, for certain reasons, the Communist party addressed itself only to the trade unions.

We only ask you not to denounce the tactics of unity of the proletarian front and to express this as best as you can according to the French dictionary.

TREINT: If an example from French experience need be drawn upon, it is that of the textile strikes in Roubaix and Tourcoing. It undeniably militates in favor of the united front. Comrade Brodel, by the way, as secretary of the Fédération du Nord, could well supply us with valuable information.

BRODEL: Indeed, large strikes took place in the Fédération du Nord, and trade-union organizations and Communists were fighting economic battles side by side. These movements failed, however. The working class did not in the least improve its lot. Since this battle ended in defeat, the poorly informed masses could well deduce from it an argument against the united front and say, "The alliance with evil partners did not succeed." For us the defeat serves as an argument against the reformists, but for the masses it speaks against the united front.

BORDIGA: All this shows that after the battle the Communist

organization must not stay inactive. It must criticize operations. It must show responsibilities of the reformist leaders. Having drawn the proper lessons from the struggle, it must make use of the experience gained in it to win over to communism the reformist Labor Exchange of Roubaix. Obviously such a result may not be achieved in a day.

BRODEL: This is how we try to interpret the lessons of the experiment and to discredit the reformists. But we operate by going over the heads of the leaders.

BORDIGA: With what program are you approaching the masses?

RENOULT: With a revolutionary program!

BORDIGA: That is not specific enough for arousing the enthusiasm of the large masses. What characterizes our time is that the bourgeoisie can save its own neck only by worsening the lot of the working class. At such a time, the most modest claim is revolutionary, because the bourgeoisie cannot satisfy it. Consequently, concrete claims can lead to mass action of the proletariat.

RENOULT: Agreed. But we are now dealing with the question of the united front. It is our right as well as our duty to have our say on the subject. We are free to act this way. Far be it for us of course to interfere with the freedom of other national sections. Whether you like it or not, the united front implies a certain rapprochement with the dissidents. This is unacceptable to us. When Frossard in his speech took a stand against the united front, the congress expressed its overwhelming approval. The Communist party is thus informed to a certain degree and can make a decision.

WALECKI: The united front does not mean a rapprochement with the dissidents. Quite the contrary.

RENOULT: Our working class is feeling an increasing irritation toward the reformists. The need for issuing concrete slogans is not connected with the tactics of the united front. Moreover, by conceiving the problem as they do and by proposing a joint government with the Socialists, the German Communist comrades have confirmed our opposition to the united front.

BORDIGA: This is altogether a different matter. The way the Germans are applying the united front, which the next International congress will examine, is a specific problem which must not be confused with the essence of the problem.

RENOULT: Souvarine was speaking in our name when he raised objections to a common action with the Second, the Second-and-a-Half and the Trade Union International in Amsterdam, as far as aid to Russia and steps for an international proletarian loan are concerned.

BORDIGA: As far as aid to Russia is concerned, this is a question neither of principle nor of tactics.

RENOULT: In any case, we are well aware of what is at stake; there is no misunderstanding. Our minds are made up, quite made up. What we say is: mass movements, yes—united front, no.

BORDIGA: Belonging, as I do, to a party sometimes accused of extreme intransigence, I am delighted to see this manifestation of intransigence among our French comrades. But intransigence is not synonymous with oversimplification. We must confront our intransigence with reality. We must be intransigent and still penetrate the masses.

RAPPOPORT: In short, stay virtuous in the midst of temptations!

BORDIGA: We must pull the rug out from under the reformists. If the tactical approach considered by the German party has its dangers, this danger can be averted only if we demonstrate the possibility of staying intransigent amidst reality.

You say: Mass actions, yes! But you must take a stand before the masses. A campaign cannot be waged only through the press and rallies. You must also attend all workers' and peasants' meetings and rouse them against the reformists. In Italy, we voted for a united general strike at the General Federation of Labor (CGT) and simultaneously attacked the reformists vigorously, which proves that one can advocate united action and attack reformist leaders at the same time.

Say if you will that the French party is incapable of rapprochement with the dissidents, but do not disavow the united-front method; that is another matter altogether.

The French party must at least reserve for itself the possibility of deriving from its own experiences suitable formulas for keeping out of its ivory tower, and turning its intransigence into something fruitful. The question must be left open and pure negation avoided.

RAPPOPORT: I would like to outline the historical account of the united front question as far as France is concerned.

When Ker returned from Germany, I did not agree with Renoult about condemning the united-front tactics. I had reservations only about the specific slogan: Seizure of the Gold Stock.

Then Souvarine's letter arrived. Like all the rest of us, he said that in France he opposed the united front for aid to Russia.

As far as the German party's "open letter" is concerned, I expressed a favorable opinion toward it in *L'Humanité*. I approved this strategy of appealing to the masses over the heads of their leaders.

Aside from these questions, which were debated in limited circles and in a superficial way, it must be admitted that the question of a united front has not been submitted to French Communist opinion.

BORDIGA: In Italy, we are in favor of the united front. But we reserve the right to choose suitable methods. Recently one organization had called together all the others. We turned down this appeal. For this particular question we preferred to see the united front materialize around Communist committees.

RAPPOPORT: When Moscow approaches us with the question of the united front, we are inclined to view these new tactics as a result of the historical necessity stemming from Lenin's opportunism.

WALECKI: You say *We*! You are authorized to take this stand. Has the French party made up its mind on this subject?

RAPPOPORT: No. I am expressing a state of mind which actually exists in the French party. Now that the Russians are in power, they find themselves in a moderate zone, while we are in a tropical zone. The cold air seems to be coming from Russia.

I personally do not share this state of mind. I can remember old articles in *Iskra* hinting at that time at the strategy of grouping all the leaders for common action in order to expose those who betray the interests of the working class.

I therefore believe that the united front is not just the latest Russian fad. It is down-to-earth revolutionism. I am willing to accept the principle.

But you must remember that Frenchmen are inclined to apply simplified logics and fail to grasp all these points.

BORDIGA: But it should be easy enough to explain: if we approach the reformist leaders it is to quarrel with them.

RAPPOPORT: Two years ago we did something along these lines. We had a meeting at Bonvalet's place with the C.G.T. for the defense of the Russian Revolution. Merrheim was there. . . . The question never has been raised in the French party since.

WALECKI: In any case, the question of the united front is not new. All the ideas suggested by the words "united front" turn up in the international theses of the Third Congress. The "open letter" of February was also discussed there. Well, not a single French delegate expressed the least reservation on this part of the theses and tactics either in committee or at the plenary session.

Besides, the worldwide state of mind must be taken into account. An employers' offensive is in the air. This is what determines the tactics, and not more or less valid emotional considerations.

If this question comes up—in case of violent agitation, what will you do about Renaudel?—you join us in saying: We will hang him. That is not the real problem. The real problem is this: How will you deal with the Roubaix working class? Is this split forever? No doubt Roubaix has reformist leaders. Well! Do unmask them.

Brodel was saying that the working class is disillusioned. After these failures, it is against any new struggle. It is up to you to counteract. The workers must not believe that they would have been immediately successful, even if the Roubaix reformists did not exist. The Roubaix experience should help the Communists conquer Roubaix.

BRODEL: Agreed, one is defeated only when one admits defeat. For us Communists from the North, the battle continues. But we have to acknowledge that presently the local working class is sick and tired of all struggle.

WALECKI: It is a period of discouragement which will give way to a period of new struggles under the impetus of Communist action.

As to the committee's resolution, it is unacceptable for the congress and for yourselves too. You must change it.

Right after having mentioned in your resolution the split in the trade unions, you use the expression "along the same lines" to introduce your conclusion regarding the united front. It seems thus that you are accepting the trade-union split quite casually. In a way, you are providing ammunition to those who always go around picturing us as promoters of splits.

And then with respect to the united front, which is not a principle but only a suitable tactic for a given situation, all you see in it is a rapprochement with the dissidents. You seem to be saying that

Moscow is advising this rapprochement. This may not be what you mean. However, if your text stands, many in the Party will understand it that way. And that will not be right.

What is to be done?

You might draw up a separate motion on the united front. But do not forget that since the Third Congress the parties no longer have much leeway. This is not just a German-Italian question. Steps toward a united front were already taken at the Third Congress.

If you are advocating a revision of the decisions of the Third Congress, you must make sure that you use proper channels for revising the decisions of the International.

At any rate, the question cannot be settled by wiping it off the slate with a single sentence. A polemic statement cannot resolve such a problem; the committee's text is unacceptable.

Or else you might decide that the question has not been sufficiently considered. Then you will put it on your party's agenda, on the agenda of your comité directeur, and that of the federations. You will request the International itself to participate in the discussion.

RENOULT: I agree to a new consideration. We might ask all prominent members of the party to serve on the committee.

We do not feel that we are bound by the Third Congress, where the united front was not mentioned. We consider that the question is settled and that the party has taken a stand. Frossard was highly applauded when he spoke against the united front.

BORDIGA: This is no question merely to be touched upon and settled on the basis of applause.

BRODEL: Besides, the main reason for the applause was that Frossard emphasized the abyss between the dissidents and ourselves.

BORDIGA: Put that at the beginning of your motion. But do not confuse the united front and the irrevocable break with the dissidents.

RENOULT: Our aim is to take a stand and make our opinion known before the whole International.

BORDIGA: In that case you should present a text that does justice to the scope and importance of the question.

TREINT: Renoult's opinions are not unanimously shared by the party. That is why I did not vote in favor of Renoult's motion. I think the united-front tactics are valid and suit the global international situation. Doubtless the finer points of these tactics in France must take into account the weakness of the dissidents, whose tarnished escutcheon must not be regilded at any price. That is certainly not the aim of the International.

One must admit that our propaganda at rallies always reaches the same public of sympathizers and we limit ourselves to a theoretical demonstration in favor of communism before an unchanging audience.

By rousing the proletariat to common battles on a united front, with specific slogans and for well-defined actions, we will compel the reformist leaders either to wash their hands of the struggles or else to betray the workers' interests. In either case they can be exposed by Communist criticism. Theoretical demonstrations before limited audiences thus would be replaced by an experimental proof of the reformist leaders' betrayal of the workers' interests. This experimental proof will reach not only limited audiences but the entire working class which is participating in the struggle.

BORDIGA: Let us not say substitution of experimental proof for theoretical demonstration. There is room for both.

TREINT: You are quite right.

I would like to add that to the extent that the split is final, irrevocable, and to the extent that the Communists are in control of their organization and are free to criticize the reformist leaders, can the united-front tactics be envisaged.

Solid Communist organizations, sure of their criticism, are essential for effective united-front tactics.

Far from implying a reunification, the united front is feasible only because of the existence of distinct Communist parties. Far from being a return to the old unity, the united front is a concrete method of enlightening the masses led astray by reformist movements and of leading them to communism. Bordiga spoke a moment ago of renewing contacts with the reformist leaders for the purpose of coming to blows with them, and—one might add—in such a way that the masses side with communism in the fray.

BORDIGA: You are perfectly right. (Turning to Renoult): By the way, you attacked the project for reorganizing the comité directeur presented by Loriot by saying that the federations have not been consulted. And yet nothing beyond the organization of the internal work of your party was involved. Why is this argument not valid for a much more important question like that of the united front?

RENOULT: Because the reorganization of the comité directeur requires a change of statutes.

WALECKI: That is another matter, which we will examine shortly.

BRODEL: Besides, we had some notion about the presidium, whereas I realize now that we were completely in the dark about the united front. We cannot take a stand without presenting the matter before the federations.

WALECKI: No matter what text you approve, this will open rather than close the debate. The International will have to intervene and expose its views publicly. It would be very awkward to vote first and debate afterwards.

RENOULT: Agreed. We will resume our deliberations, but I do not think that the point of view of the majority, of the near-unanimity of the committee, can be affected.

WALECKI: All this demonstrates that something needs to be changed with respect to international relations. I am amazed that such a misunderstanding could have arisen with the French party on a question of this importance. Let us now broach the other questions.

You speak favorably of democratic centralism, contrasting it with oligarchic centralism, which you denounce. There are different degrees of centralism depending on the circumstances of the struggle. But no matter how concentrated the centralism, it remains democratic in the sense that even the most closely knit leadership of the Party accounts for its actions whenever possible.

We ask you to omit your passage on oligarchic centralism because it seems to be coming to grips with an existing tendency, while, to the best of my knowledge, such a tendency never existed.

RENOULT: The Seine [federation] insisted on having this distinction between the two sorts of centralism appear in the motion. We are determined to uphold it. This does not mean that there were instances of oligarchic centralism.

WALECKI: I do not like to quibble about words. I am speaking of things and texts. Whether you meant it that way or not, your motion proclaims to the whole world that in the French party or the International two currents confront each other, one favoring democratic centralism, the other oligarchic centralism. In all sections of

the International your texts will be scrutinized and will provoke
excitement which is all the more useless since there is no basis for the
implicit assertion that there is a tendency toward oligarchic centralism, as you well know.

The problem under discussion was the reorganization of the
comité directeur. That is an important question. You speak of a small
bureau capable of making decisions on minor political and administrative matters between the sessions of the comité directeur.

TREINT: And at that, the word "political" was added as a result
of a long discussion.

WALECKI: Well, there is something hypocritical about this text.
If five comrades devote eighty hours a week to the Party, they cannot
help becoming administrative specialists and carrying weight in the
leadership and the whole life of the party. They cannot actually be
relegated to secondary tasks.

The small bureau has its own role, which is to make even important decisions. The comité directeur, in turn, has the function of
scrutinizing the decisions which were taken by the small bureau,
which is responsible to it, and can change these decisions at will.
I do not believe that this division into major and minor matters
is a good method of organization.

Let us now look into the question of the control of the press.
Your motion refers to the deplorable conduct of some journalists. If
such is the case, with an energetic leadership, you should either have
prevented or criticized it. But all these polemics which you say aim at
personalities also have their political side. Perhaps there is a conflict
of tendencies. You do not say a word about it.

There are papers owned by members of the party. There are
also some comrades who thus express opinions they could not otherwise express publicly. In the *Journal du Peuple,* last month, there
were violent criticisms against the International, criticisms associated
with the policies of the "bloc des gauches." Such a political problem
surely merits closer attention than the undesirable conduct of some
journalists.

The fact that party members are contributors to private newspapers surely has a well-defined color and flavor. It is the color and
flavor of rightist opportunism. I do not deal in personalities. I am
concerned about the phenomenon as such. In a party which has just
gone through the split in Tours, it is small wonder that there is some

inclination to return to the past. Your motion does not say a word about that. But that is certainly more important than the coarseness of a journalist.

The truth is you are criticizing a single comrade. Well, if Souvarine is coarse in private, pull his ears; if he is coarse in public, criticize him.

But you speak of a faultfinder. Will you curtail Souvarine's right to express his opinion on the political actions of certain Party members?

Actually, by attacking Souvarine in your motion you have hit out against the left. You forgot to strike against the right. You said nothing about the content of Fabre's articles.

RAPPOPORT: Nobody takes Fabre seriously.

WALECKI: One always says that, and in this way evil takes root and grows. And even if you are right to say that it does not matter, think of the repercussion of such articles abroad. Spare the sensibilities of the men in Moscow. They have other fish to fry. Now that the time has come to expose Serrati, there is no need for Rappoport to hold out a hand to him.

Cut out all these things. Of what interest are they to the working class?

BORDIGA: One should say in the motion that measures will be taken against the polemicists, particularly against the political conduct of the right wing, which is at odds with the decisions of the International.

RENOULT: But still, don't forget Souvarine's polemics.

WALECKI: Beg your pardon! Who started it all? And the World War? Who will ever know who started it?

RAPPOPORT: I would like to say a few words about Serrati and the Italian question.

The Italian Communists did not see things my way. They said that Treint was the one who had properly understood the situation. Before the Milan congress, Serrati wrote to me. I still have the letter.

WALECKI: Show me the letter.

RAPPOPORT: I replied to Serrati: If you think Lenin is wrong, you better make sure that you are not alone in being right.

At the time I wrote this, the decision to exclude the Italian Socialist party had not yet been made.

TREINT: But your reply was subsequent to the Milan congress. There Walecki, speaking for the International, had already let the

Italian Socialist party know that it was being excluded from the International. The Executive Committee of the International had not yet formally ratified this decision. But you were sufficiently familiar with the Italian situation to know this ratification was a mere formality.

By criticizing the International in your article just when Serrati was being excluded, you hampered the Italian Communists.

BORDIGA (ironically, turning to Rappoport): Your reproach that we did not sufficiently take into account Serrati's mass following was really a compliment for us. We had been doing what you proposed for a whole year.

WALECKI (to Rappoport): And then, you know, it is politically unwise to give lessons on tact and tactics to Moscow in the *Journal du Peuple*.

RAPPOPORT: That was not my intention. I should certainly have been more restrained. Souvarine blamed Rappoport on this score because he could find nothing else for which to blame him.

WALECKI: Well, do you refuse to alter the text of your resolution?

RENOULT: We want to let it stand; it faithfully reflects the feelings of the committee. The congress has been degraded by personal polemics.

As to *La Vague* and the *Journal du Peuple,* we all agree.

But it was stated in the *Bulletin Communiste* that Paul Louis nauseates his readers. Expressions of this sort on Souvarine's part make all discussions acrimonious.

WALECKI: The *Bulletin Communiste* is under somebody's control. It is a Party organ. You criticize Souvarine. You should also criticize the party leadership.

TREINT: Renoult says that we agree as far as *La Vague* is concerned. Yes, now—before the congress! But I find it inexcusable that four months elapsed between the decision of the comité directeur and the first step toward its implementation. The comité directeur decided to hand over Brizon to the conflicts committee on July 19; this committee tackled the question for the first time only on November 17.

RENOULT: Some of Souvarine's whims are certainly intolerable. We do not want censors. Even without indulging in abuses, one should not accuse comrades of opportunism and excommunicate them in the eyes of Communist opinion.

BRODEL: Shortly thereafter, Souvarine also attacked Verfeuil in the *Bulletin Communiste*.

TREINT: Yes, in the wake of Verfeuil's article in *L'Humanité* where he preached a return to unity.

RENOULT: The editors asked Verfeuil for an article.

TREINT: Did they approve the content of the article?

WALECKI: Be that as it may, according to your text, Souvarine is your only target and the only one criticized. And that is unfair.

RAPPOPORT: If you are attuned to sensibilities in Moscow, we are attuned to French sensibilities.

RENOULT: Rappoport is well aware of them!

RAPPOPORT: Yes, it took me a while, and I suffered a lot because of them. Souvarine did not give you an adequate explanation of the *Journal du Peuple* incident.

Fabre is a nationalist rag seller. But still, this man took some chances during the war, and thanks to his leftist bohemianism, we were able to expose all our ideas in his newspaper.

WALECKI: So you are now repaying it by your conciliatory attitude!

RAPPOPORT: When Fabre went astray, Frossard pointed this out in some brilliant articles. There was a time when, thanks to Fabre, we were able to propagandize our ideas. Even now it gives us access to a whole anarchist-syndicalist circle.

I am not trying to vindicate Fabre. I am just explaining our psychology with respect to the *Journal du Peuple*.

RENOULT: There will be no more of that. We guarantee it.

RAPPOPORT: If only, instead of firing off the big cannon in Moscow, you had communicated by letters.

WALECKI: There were more than ten letters!

TREINT: Yes, but the tone of Souvarine's letters was exploited; it was used to avoid the core of the question.

WALECKI: There is a letter from the Executive Committee written the day after the Moscow congress, wherein the question was examined. Did you not receive Lenin's report?

RAPPOPORT: We feel that Moscow isn't interested in our little troubles.

BORDIGA: But look! Measures to control the press in the entire International were taken. The Executive Committee was willing to make an exception with respect to you. However, it is quite legitimate to wonder how the situation revealed by the Fabre and Brizon cases could exist in a Communist party.

WALECKI: Here is a letter I have just received. It is dated

Moscow, December 19. The gist of the letter is that in the *Journal du Peuple* the resolutions of the International are presented as ukases. Actually, they are not even resolutions but proposals laid before the French party in complete agreement with the French delegation. These proposals were discussed with Humbert-Droz at the time of his trip to Paris. The letter of the Moscow Executive Committee inquires why the French delegation and the party's comité directeur did not stop Fabre's unfair campaign by straightening out the facts!

The *Journal du Peuple,* moreover, has been opposing the strengthening of the party leadership by ridiculing the ideas of a presidium.

Why did the comité directeur not unanimously take a stand against this tendency of the *Journal du Peuple,* which was clearly coming out against the Executive [of the International] and in favor of the "bloc des gauches?"

Rappoport declares, "You are worrying about trifles." And I reply, "Don't you see that the situation has been politically untenable for months?" You say, "It is difficult to establish discipline in France." What have you done to overcome this difficulty?

I am only sorry that the correspondence between Moscow and the French party is not familiar to all Party members.

RENOULT: We promise you that this time there will be deeds rather than words on our part.

WALECKI: In your motion you omit everything which condemns the *Journal du Peuple* on political grounds. And you strike a blow against Souvarine which he may have deserved on formal but not on political grounds. Your conflicts commission serves as the party's political arbitrator. What a cumbersome procedure!

BORDIGA: The presidium is the proper authority for settling these questions which involve the political life of the party.

RAPPOPORT: We do not want to be expelling people all the time.

TREINT: It is serious in my opinion that we have just found out in *L'Humanité* that by a mere censure of the conflicts commission the Fabre affair was settled.

RAPPOPORT: I admit that the commission's declaration did not contain any absolute political condemnation of Fabre.

BRODEL: This congress has been poisoned by a garbage-can-load of controversies dropped on our heads without warning.

WALECKI: This would never have come about if the comité

directeur had done its duty, if it had resolved these questions quickly and definitively. (Walecki reads the passage in the Executive's letter of December 19 on the dilatory treatment of the Brizon case.)

There is no doubt that if the Brizon case had been handled quickly and according to the proper discipline, the *Journal du Peuple* would have been more careful. On the contrary, it was emboldened by the conciliatory attitude shown toward *La Vague*.

RAPPOPORT: We are reluctant to act because of *La Vague's* past reputation.

RAPPOPORT (to Walecki and Bordiga): And as to the controversies, let me give you Souvarine's letters. You will see what name-calling he does with respect to certain party members.

WALECKI: Souvarine is the party's delegate to the Executive. He has never been recalled. Even Bestel confirmed on his recent trip that Souvarine enjoys the confidence of the party.

RAPPOPORT: We do not want to create a scandal.

BORDIGA: Let us return to the organization of the comité directeur. It is paradoxical to say the small bureau shall make decisions on minor matters. The way I see it, minor matters are the ones that could more easily be settled by the comité directeur.

Serious decisions can be made only in a limited circle. They must be left to four, five, or six comrades enjoying the confidence of the party. It is wrong to diminish the role of these comrades by confining them to minor matters.

Of course the small bureau must appear before the comité directeur at regular intervals in order to be given a program and general directives for its work and to account for its policies.

Between the comité directeur meetings, it must have the same powers as the comité directeur—even greater ones, in fact, since it is composed of specialists who devote themselves entirely to the party.

Even in the course of a week, serious and urgent questions may arise demanding immediate decisions. The small bureau must be fully competent to make such decisions, for which it will have to account later on.

If the party is to become an army fighting against the bourgeoisie, it may well be impossible to bring together a large comité directeur. One must reckon with such eventualities. I know what I am talking about: In Italy we had the lesson of fascism.

Remove the word "minor" from your motion.

The question of polemics should not even have arisen. If you had an energetic leadership, all this would already have been settled.

RAPPOPORT: We can add the condemnation of the *Journal du Peuple* in our motion.

BORDIGA: Let me add that to seem to discredit your representative in Moscow in an official document will make a deplorable impression. Could not the thinly veiled allusions contained in your motion be cut out?

I also am astonished that the extreme left wing which seems to have taken over the Seine Federation is concerned about centralism.

SOUTIF: The setting up of a bureau of five members struck us as a form of oligarchic centralism. At any rate, we did not wish to give this bureau political functions. The present text, which gives it minor political functions, is already an important concession on our part.

BORDIGA: And what do you think of the powers of the secretary-general?

SOUTIF: He will be assisted by an administrative secretary.

BORDIGA: If you are going to have a parliamentary system with twenty-four people, you cannot expect to accomplish anything. In Italy we do not have an administrative secretary, but the innermost leadership consists of five interchangeable persons who provide the party with a continuity in its day-to-day work.

We do not distinguish, and it is impossible to distinguish, between what is political and what is administrative.

Even as far as the parliamentary affairs are concerned, one of us may at a moment's notice be compelled to make a declaration in the party's name.

And then, isn't the organization a political problem? The form of the organization varies along with the policies.

The party needs a head to run it. The head must be held accountable. It can be replaced.

BRODEL: I don't know whether my comrades realized what we were going to do here. It seems to me that for the last half hour we have been pushed to reverse our decisions. If we had known, Renoult could have taken the complete text of the proposals at hand.

BORDIGA: We are just deliberating. It will be up to you to decide.

RENOULT: The approval of Frossard's proposal is assured.

TREINT: Frossard's proposal no longer exists. You gave in with respect to the small bureau and you did grant it minor political functions.

BORDIGA: You can guess under what conditions we had to call you together. You are aware that our presence here is clandestine. We have been trying to see you for the last forty-eight hours. We are sorry we could not contact you before.

WALECKI: When you have to act clandestinely, as in our case, one cannot always say: Our hands are tied; the committee's vote has been cast.

Beyond all formal considerations, you must take into account life itself. The life of communism is bound up with the question of organization.

For months your secretariat and Moscow have kept up a continuous correspondence on this subject. Humbert-Droz came on a trip in October. Today I received the letter from Moscow of December 19. Since the opportunity presents itself, we want to inform you of the content of this letter.

The question of the presidium involved the question of the best political leadership of the party. We are sorry that the comité directeur did not itself propose a presidium to the party. We have the stenographic report of the talk with Humbert-Droz. The comrades who were there agreed to constitute a presidium. Why was the *Journal du Peuple* allowed to ridicule the idea of a presidium, whose implementation had been decided upon?

In the Executive Committee's letter of December 19, a whole significant passage is devoted to this question. You owe it to yourselves, in dealing with a question about which your leadership has perhaps not given you sufficient information, not to ignore an opinion of the Executive Committee of the International.

BORDIGA: (reads the passage in the December 19 letter regarding this question).

WALECKI: That is the substance of my talk with Cachin. He told me that an agreement can be reached on this basis.

There is a contradiction between your text and the opinion of the Executive. You state that the comité directeur was ineffective because of minor worries and menial tasks which encumbered its meetings. For that reason, your bureau consisting of five men will be put in charge of minor tasks and worries.

RENOULT: We were under the impression that the Frossard proposal was approved by the party. It certainly cannot just be removed by a stroke of the pen.

WALECKI: This is not an accomplished fact. This is not how the problem must be envisaged. You say, invoking your national autonomy: That is the will of the party. Since when and how has this become an accomplished fact? The stenographic report from October states that the comité directeur agreed with Moscow on the establishment of a presidium. Moscow has not been notified of a change in attitude.

You speak of an accomplished fact. But do your federations know of the about-face of the comité directeur? Did you talk it over with them? The overwhelming majority is completely in the dark about all this.

The political leadership of the party remains problematical. In the Frossard proposal and even in the text of your committee you appoint a certain number of employees to do minor tasks. Well, if you leave it at that, I can predict for sure what will happen. You will not have strengthened your leadership in the least.

There are no routine matters except in a state bureaucracy. Each letter, each conversation even, is a political act.

Be honest about the difference in your attitude toward the party and *L'Humanité*. *L'Humanité* is responsible for three-quarters of the party's political activity. You entrust its editorship to a single man, who must of course account for his actions.

You entrust the control of the party to twenty-four men meeting about once a week. Well, you must pick out a small bureau composed of the five ablest people to handle the party's main business as well as minor matters, and to account for its actions before the comité directeur.

There is something hypocritical in your formulations.

When five men spend eighty hours a week, on a salary, to be sure, working for the party, they will perforce acquire a preponderant influence. These men must enjoy full confidence and a large mandate between two sessions of the comité directeur.

The other side of the coin is that they are accountable. As your organization now stands, when you want someone who is accountable, you never find anyone; all responsibility vanishes.

RENOULT: The overwhelming majority of the congress approved of the comité directeur, except for some details.

WALECKI: You are free to vote any way you wish. But do not

expect to obtain the desired results by putting your texts into practice.

Let me recapitulate my experience here. I am a member of the Polish Communist Party and a delegate to Moscow. I have been chosen to work in the West. I have spent some time in Italy. I have seen the operation of the German party. I have collected some facts and am completely impartial.

The organization of a party's political leadership is a capital question. You have not put this question properly.

If it is not yet too late, leave your comité directeur more leeway. Let it organize your internal activities as it thinks best. Let it select these five delegates, its presidium.

RAPPOPORT: It is true that the motion of the resolutions committee contains some unfortunate expressions.

WALECKI: Twenty-four men can legislate. Twenty-four men are incapable of being in control. We are a fighting army. We are not living in peace. There is no abysmal difference between France and Italy. Well! In Italy, there is not always time to call together a large number of comrades. There have been occasions where a twenty-four-hour delay in making a decision would have turned that decision into a political error.

RAPPOPORT: We will change our method when comparable situations arise.

WALECKI: No, Rappoport, it is not wise to wait with organizing until events point a knife at your throat.

The party is not only an instrument of Communist propaganda; it must also lead the fight of the proletariat, and that is something else entirely. This question is intimately tied to the trade-union question; during strikes the party must step out of its reserve. It must inspire the trade unions through its members. The central organism, which is permanently in session, must be able to step in without delay. That is impossible if you are obliged to assemble twenty-four people.

The German example confirms the truth of my remarks.

With your system, either the letter of your texts is observed—and in that case there is no firm party leadership—or else one or two very strong men will cleverly seize the whole party and turn it into their personal tool. Or else the men delegated to carry out minor tasks will effectively take over the control of the party, and you will have established the presidium according to the conceptions of the International and the theses of the Third Congress.

BRODEL: What if these five or six men are thrown into jail?

WALECKI: I am a member of the comité directeur of an outlawed party. In the trade unions we are 700,000 strong. Our comité directeur consists of nine members. Besides the actual members, there are substitutes. When one member of the comité directeur is arrested, the substitute is entitled to take his place. Even if the substitute does not belong to the comité directeur, he is active in an important federation, which is constantly in touch with the center. He is thus relatively up-to-date in his work.

Last February, of the nine members there were five members at liberty and four imprisoned, so four substitutes were active from the start. And now, after my escape, my place is not empty. While I work here, I have a substitute on the spot.

BRODEL: What happens in case of a wholesale arrest?

WALECKI: Even in Poland, which is in the grip of a serious reaction, this has never happened. There were never more than four members simultaneously in jail.

Of the comité directeur's nine members, four are always traveling, on some mission. Thus there are five left at the center, for the work on the spot.

BORDIGA: The vote of the committee was just referred to as an accomplished fact. There is an earlier accomplished fact: the theses adopted unanimously by the Third Congress, with the concurrence of the French delegation. (Bordiga reads the thesis on the structure of the Communist parties, paragraph 47. This paragraph states: "If the congress considers it expedient it may instruct the central committee to elect from its own membership a smaller committee consisting of the members of the political and organizational bureaus.")

RENOULT: With respect to the more restricted leadership, the text says, "If the congress considers it expedient."

BORDIGA: You are obviously misinterpreting what it says. "If the congress considers it expedient" does not mean that the party can be relieved of organizing a more restricted leadership. What it means is that the congress may, "if it considers it expedient," leave the selection of the smaller group to the comité directeur.

RENOULT: This is a matter of interpretation.

We did receive Humbert-Droz's visit. We used the words "routine matters" and "minor tasks," because that is how we interpreted it. In the light of former habits and the Tours decisions, we feel that the comité directeur provides the leadership.

The immediate creation of a small bureau as you visualize it could have its drawbacks. The relations with the comité directeur as a whole might prove to be delicate. We have strong hopes for Frossard's proposal.

WALECKI: Let me make you a practical proposal.

Let us say in the text that you will vote on something of this sort: the party leadership must be strengthened. The congress leaves it up to the comité directeur to organize its leadership in the light of the proposals presented.

RAPPOPORT: You are asking for a strengthened centralism.

WALECKI: What we want is a strong political leadership.

RAPPOPORT: Since Tours some headway has been made. The theses were imposed on the federations, so to speak.

BORDIGA: It is not a matter of imposing certain theses without discussion. The point is to organize the leadershp of the party and to benefit from international experiences.

WALECKI: Moreover, if the inadequate organization of the party leadership did not prevent the party from doing justice to its tasks, that is only due to the fact that no violent actions came up.

RAPPOPORT: If necessary, the system of strengthened centralism still could be introduced. Under the impact of events, it would be realized with great dispatch, but it can hardly materialize *in abstracto*.

BORDIGA: But still, our experience has an international foundation. What would you say if a federation, invoking its right to organize as it pleases, according to its own experience, were to argue with the party as you do with the International?

WALECKI: And then, Rappoport, remember that you yourself did not happen to invent communism. You received it as a gift.

If you do not prepare now for what the morrow will bring, if you wait for the impact of events, what is the use of working for the future?

You see, Rappoport, it is not so easy to improvise. Your arguments are contradictory. You say that there is a national labor-movement tradition. And then, by claiming to be able to cope with events on the spur of the moment, by asserting that the strengthened centralist organization will spring up naturally when the circumstances call for it, you are blinding yourself to the difficulties in overcoming at the last moment those traditions which you will have done your share in keeping alive.

Let me tell you now what was not accomplished this year for lack of a strong political leadership.

You delayed in broaching the trade union question and are

doing so now only because of the Moscow intervention. The French party has tackled the question only under outside pressure.

The French party has not participated actively in the International. No French debate has touched upon the March action in Germany. You have paid no attention to Italian affairs.

What struck me in the French party is the fact that those who believe they belong to the extreme left are opposing the excesses of centralism. There also is some misunderstanding.

The comité directeur, the party leadership, should not consider it its primary or exclusive function to pass out orders. On the battlefield alone things are done that way. But on a day-to-day basis, a small bureau, a presidium, is essential to play the role of father confessor to the entire party. If one of the party sections is not intensely alive, the party leadership is answerable for it. It is up to the leadership to find out the facts, to nourish, to educate the party. It must say to everyone, "These are the vital problems of the moment. I am giving you the information. Think about it. Study it. And then you will vote, you will take a stand." It is much more desirable that conflicting opinions confront each other inside the party than that each one is left free to do nothing.

The comité directeur, the presidium, is responsible for the whole life of the party.

RAPPOPORT: The more people the better for a task of this sort.

BORDIGA: Then why not two hundred forty instead of twenty four?

WALECKI: You talk of oligarchic centralism. You are battling against a phantom. The truth is that your comité directeur was weak. Where are your pamphlets? After Tours you aroused intellectual curiosities. You failed to satisfy them. All this must be changed. You cannot expect paid employees responsible for handling routine matters to resolve this problem.

BORDIGA: You cannot say: Let the comité directeur handle the important matters and the presidium the minor ones.

You cannot run a party by having sessions two hours a week. At least amend your text to say that the small bureau will be empowered to decide between two sessions of the comité directeur on any urgent matters that might come up.

RENOULT: That goes without saying, if the comité directeur cannot be convened.

BORDIGA: Such emergencies should be planned for in advance. The opposite is likely to happen in periods of crisis. We noticed that in Italy. Our organization is somewhat different from yours. Our comité directeur is a central committee elected for three months. It issues regularly the general directives which are carried out by the narrower executive committee, which is responsible to the central committee but given full authority.

WALECKI: Present the part of your text dealing with the comité directeur and the presidium as a suggestion, as an experiment to try, but nothing with a definitive character. Keep in mind that an important political task is already involved in the preparation of the comité directeur meetings. At worst, your comité directeur could organize its internal activities as it sees fit even without a text. By adhering to the letter of the text, you would be tying down your comité directeur for a year to methods which experience may prove to be unsound. In addition, there seem to be serious disagreements between us.

Think of all these points when you resume your deliberations.

DOCUMENT No. 2:

SUPPLEMENTAL INSTRUCTIONS TO THE DELEGATES OF THE COMMUNIST INTERNATIONAL AT THE SECOND CONGRESS OF THE FRENCH COMMUNIST PARTY IN PARIS, 1922

EDITORS' INTRODUCTION—*The second congress of the French Communist Party took place in Paris, October 15–19, 1922. The congress convened at a time of great intraparty struggles and thus was badly organized. It was so disorderly that Tom Bell, representative of the British Communists, spoke of the "wild scenes" that ensued. The factional struggles helped, however, to establish in France a truly Communist party, a genuine section of the Communist International.*

The Marseille congress eliminated Boris Souvarine from the comité directeur and thus caused the resignation of Loriot, Treint, Vaillant-Couturier, and Dunois; this precipitated publicly a crisis which the delegates of the Comintern believed had been averted by passage of the final resolution worked out with their assistance and indeed under their pressure. At the Tours congress a coalition of the center (Frossard, Cachin) and of the left (Loriot, Souvarine) had given a majority to those who favored joining the Comintern; this coalition now was disrupted.

To understand fully the origins and extent of the intraparty squabbles between the congresses of Marseille and Paris, it is necessary to recall in outline some events that took place from January to October, 1922.

The issue of the united front continued to cloud relations between the Comintern and the French party. On December 18, 1921, the ECCI issued a lengthy directive on the united front; on January 1, 1922, together with the Red International of the Trade Unions, it launched a manifesto calling for "the establishment of a united front of all parties supported by the proletariat, regardless of the differences separating them."[9] The manifesto simultaneously announced the convocation of an enlarged meeting of the ECCI at Moscow on February 19. However, on January 17, 1922, the comité directeur of the French Communist Party, with only Rappoport abstaining, declared that it was impossible to apply united-front tactics in France. Furthermore, at a conference (January 22) convened to consider this question, the majority of regional party secretaries voted against it.

When the enlarged meeting opened in Moscow on February 21, the French delegation (composed of Cachin, Renoult, Sellier and Metayer) was empowered by the French party to oppose the united front. Renoult openly stated that "the French Communist Party registers its opposition to the principle of the united front, and presents a thesis that rejects the premises of the ECCI."[10] Souvarine, Treint and Ker, who were already in Moscow, attacked Renoult's presentation as a distortion of the position of the comité directeur of the French party. Although the French delegation had the support of the representatives of the Italian and Spanish Communist parties, it was clearly in the minority; of the twenty-two delegations who voted on the resolution presented by the ECCI in regard to the principle of the united front, nineteen delegations with forty-six votes were in favor of the proposal, and only three delegations with ten votes voted against it.

After this vote, Cachin read a declaration in the name of the three minority delegations, stating that they "yielded to the majority which had accepted the tactics decided upon by the ECCI." Moreover, Trotsky presented to the conference a written statement from the French delegation, promising in the name of the French party to summon Henri Fabre before the party with the intention of expelling him; to ask the comité directeur to propose to the party's next national council (which had the powers of a congress) the readmission of those leaders who had resigned after the congress of Marseille; to put an end to the harmful polemics; to eliminate factionalism within the party; finally, to achieve the closest possible cooperation in action among all Communists.[11]

After returning to France, the delegates kept their promise; they were, however, unable to convince the party to follow suit. Thus for example, instead of expelling Fabre, the comité directeur declared that his Journal du Peuple *was outside party control and that the commission on disputes was free to examine Fabre's case in whichever manner it pleased. Likewise, the national council of the party, meeting in April 1922, condemned—once again by an overwhelming majority (3,370 against 627)—the tactic of the united front.*

Meanwhile, in Moscow, the ECCI and its special French commission regarded all these actions disapprovingly. Several meetings were held during May to discuss the French question. On May 8, a new delegate of the French party at the Comintern, Lucie Leiciague, member of the comité directeur, submitted a detailed report on the situation. (Lucie Leiciague actually replaced Souvarine, who at the First Plenum of the ECCI had been elected a member of the Presidium.) The ECCI once again made several decisions, one being the expulsion of Fabre from the Comintern, with a request that this decision be carried out by the French comrades. A confidential and explanatory letter was also sent to the comité directeur. "This was an attempt," says Trotsky, "I could say the last attempt, to explain our actions to the comité directeur, thus furthering our mutual understanding and defining the course to be taken and responsibilities to be assumed."[12]

Once again, instead of bringing about a solution, this latest Comintern move served only to alienate further the French leadership, and the commission on disputes suspended its investigation of the Fabre affair. Before Frossard left for Moscow to attend an ECCI meeting in June, the comité directeur instructed him to stress the fact that the party lent no credence to the rumor of Fabre's expulsion by the Comintern. After all, if the latter were true, it would create a precedent threatening the security of all party members. Moreover, Frossard was authorized to declare that the French Communist Party would accept the united front only if it were approved and made mandatory by the supreme authority of the International—that is, the World Congress.

For three days, June 8–11, 1922, the ECCI discussed the case of the French party; at Trotsky's insistence, several peremptory directives to the French party were drawn up. These specified that the next party congress should establish a homogeneous comité directeur, whose membership would form a small bureau (now called politburo). Furthermore, the party press should reflect only the political goals of the party and not the personal opinions of individual journalists; all factional activity should be eschewed and a resolute battle waged against the rightist elements in the party, with the aim of achieving unanimity among the overwhelming majority of the party.

Frossard yielded to Trotsky's influence, promising to work for unity between center and left in order to put an end to intraparty fighting. Once back in France he was ready to carry out his political line, though personally still not convinced of its chances for success. His apprehensions were justified indeed. "My friends did not believe they could follow me. Daniel Renoult, Dondicol, and Meric criticized me sharply for having yielded to Moscow's pressure and inducements. Thus a number of militant party members gathered around them and caused a split in the 'center.' The majority of the center, however, reached an accord with the left on some text rigorously expressing the doctrinal and practical demands of the International."[13]

The "supplemental instructions" of the Comintern to Humbert-Droz and Manuilsky, delegates at the second congress of the French Communist Party, show that in spite of the agreement between the majority of the center and the left, another unexpected source of contention arose to separate the two factions. This time the conflict centered about the distribution of seats claimed by both factions in the party's leading bodies. Early in September, under the guidance of Souvarine who had just returned from Moscow, the left insisted on having two-thirds of all seats on the future comité directeur. Besides, they claimed, Cachin should be expelled from the comité directeur, as well as from the directorship of L'Humanité. By voicing these demands, the left obviously went further than Moscow did; the latter would have been content to weaken the center and expel the right. Prevailed upon to mitigate its claims somewhat, the left finally asked for four seats out of seven in the politburo, and twelve seats out of twenty-four in the comité directeur. Since two delegates of the Communist Youth, possessing the prerogative of membership on the comité directeur, belonged to the left, this meant in effect a leftist majority in both leading organs of the party. Moreover, the leftist Dunois was to replace Cachin as the head of L'Humanité. The center refused to accept these conditions. The Paris congress thus opened without having come to any agreement. This is why it was so "disorderly."

The Comintern delegates once again had a hard time persuading the French party to follow an orthodox course. Since their instructions were not subject to amendment, Frossard, speaking for the center, "objected to the implied choice between obedience and rebellion, and to the total exclusion of the right wing; it was up to the congress to decide the composition of the central bodies."[14] The centrist motion carried the majority: it received 1,698 against 1,516 votes for the motion of the left, with 814 abstentions. Cachin declared in the name of the center that the centrists alone would take the responsibility of leading the party. Following this congress, the leading members of the left wing—Souvarine, Treint, and Dunois—protested, and resigned their posts on the ground that to establish an exclusively centrist leadership in the party implied a break with the International. The centrist comité directeur, sensitive to such accusations, issued an "appeal to the party," asserting that it was up to the Fourth Congress of the Comintern to settle the problems of the French party.

THE INSTRUCTIONS*

In view of the new circumstances, the Executive Committee of the Communist International gives the following supplemental instructions to its delegates:

1) On the occasion of the recent "general strike,"[15] the Communist International could observe that the strike was not in the least organized, that it had been carried out at the instigation of a small group of anarchists, that neither the executive committee of the C.G.T.U. nor the comité directeur of the party had announced any official decisions on the subject of the strike, and that they had done no serious preparatory work. At the moment when such important decisions should have been taken, the requisite numbers of the comité

Ed. note: The French text of these instructions is published by Jules Humbert-Droz in his book, *"L'Oeil de Moscou" à Paris* (Paris: Juillard, 1964), 138–42.

directeur could not be rounded up in Paris; the party was unable to convene a regular gathering; the party's central organ remained without any proper guidance on this question. Consequently, the Executive Committee of the Communist International charges its delegates to state in a suitable manner before the Paris congress and to convey in detail in private conferences with the leading members of the congress that the Communist International considers such an attitude in the face of proletarian mass movements a veritable crime.

The lesson of the last "general strike" must not be lost. The party must be assured that there will be henceforth a real center of control, and that this state of affairs will not recur.

2) The bourgeoisie has set in motion a determined campaign against the *eight-hour day*.[16] The party must at once start a counter-campaign. To postpone it until after the congress would amount to awarding the party a certificate of incompetence. This type of campaign can afford no delay. It calls for immediate action. The Executive Committee of the Communist International insists that the united-front tactics not only be given lip service but applied in practice. *In connection with the bourgeoisie's offensive against the eight-hour day, an official proposal must at once be made to the reformist Labor Confederation and the Socialist party for organizing a common struggle to maintain the eight-hour day.*

3) The Executive commissions its delegates to state at the congress itself in the most categorical and energetic form that, while the Communist International has until now, in view of the circumstances, tolerated the formation of "tendencies" or factions *up to* the time of the party congress, it could under no circumstances accept this state of affairs *thereafter. The Communist International insists categorically on the immediate and absolute dissolution of all factions.* The Communist International emphasizes that in the given situation, maintenance of the factions might literally cost the life of the French party.

4) Having been informed that the left (Souvarine, Treint, and others) is claiming for its tendency two-thirds of the seats in the future comité directeur, the Executive Committee of the Communist International states that it *does not back* this claim and considers it *mistaken.* It is true that the left follows on the whole a very correct course, which expresses exactly the Communist International's decisions; to that extent it has and will have the backing of the Executive. But in our opinion the genuine collaboration of the center and the

left, which the Executive keeps advocating, hinges on having parity and mutual trust between the comrades. The Executive believes that no member of the right nor any comrades who refuse to abide by the Communist International's line on the basic questions (united front, and so forth) should be admitted to the comité directeur. The Executive insists that all members of the new comité directeur be genuine Communists, whose loyalty to the International is unqualified. But that does not mean that two-thirds of the seats should be assured in advance and go automatically to the left wing as it now stands. The Executive insists that each group of comité directeur members (adherents of the left or center) should include a certain number of *workers* having the closest ties with the proletarian masses. The only possible solution to the situation is an agreement between the left and the center on the basis of equality and personal responsibility of each of the comité directeur members before the party and the entire International.

5) The Executive Committee of the Communist International categorically condemns the statement given to the press by Comrade Frossard, according to which he would no longer accept the position of secretary-general and would return to the rank and file. Obviously, Comrade Frossard is formally free to make such a statement. However, under the given circumstances, Comrade Frossard, by raising this sort of personal question, exacerbates to an even greater extent the already grave crisis within the party and does considerable harm to the cause. The Executive strongly urges Comrade Frossard to withdraw his statement. The Executive warns that *it will denounce any declaration of this kind, whatever its source.*

6) To avoid turning the Paris congress into an arena for excessively violent struggles, and to make it actually cement a durable party unity on the basis of the decisions of the Communist International and on the basis of a decisive struggle against the right, the Executive asks the two wings (left and center) *to form at once a small committee with paritary representation, under the chairmanship of two representatives of the Communist International.* This committee is to meet regularly and to prepare, for submission to the decision of the congress (and that of the Executive, if need be) the most important questions.

7) This same committee is also entrusted by the Executive with the task of making a preliminary study of all resolutions drafted for the congress, so that these resolutions can be presented unanimously

to the congress as drafts of the committee. All drafts and amendments must be sent in due course to the Executive in Moscow, so that the latter can, if necessary, express its opinion, by telegram as a last resort.

8) Since Raoul Verfeuil has organized his rightist faction for open combat against the minority[17] of the party and the line of the Communist International, the Executive asks the mentioned committee to prepare a special proposal against the Verfeuil group and send it to Moscow for approval.

9) Since the exacerbation of the intrafaction struggle will doubtless complicate the distribution of the most important functions in the new comité directeur (secretary-general, editorship of *L'Humanité,* composition of the politburo), the Executive Committee offers the future comité directeur its assistance in this matter, and advises it to postpone these decisions until the arrival of the delegation of the French party to the Moscow congress.

We commission the delegation of the Communist International to the Paris congress to communicate the above instruction to the representatives of the two [wings] and to draw it to the attention of the leaders of the main federations, in the course of the congress itself.

(The above instruction was adopted unanimously, with the complete solidarity of Comrade Leiciague, the French party's representative.)

Moscow, September 20, 1922.

(Signed) G. Zinoviev.

[The seal of the Executive Committee of the Communist International]

DOCUMENT No. 3:

A CONFIDENTIAL LETTER FROM THE COMINTERN TO THE LEFT WING OF THE FRENCH COMMUNIST PARTY

EDITORS' INTRODUCTION—*The Fourth Congress of the Comintern (Moscow, November 5–December 5, 1922) made several important decisions with regard to the French Communist Party. It demanded, among other things, that the French party "break off all party ties with Freemasonry as personified by some of its members and its* groups," by January 1, 1923 at the latest. On the eve of the expiration of this ultimatum, Frossard resigned from the Party (although he himself probably was not a Freemason). His resignation, however, did not deprive the party of its leadership. The Comintern congress had resolved that the party's secretariat-general should be shared on the basis of parity, that is, by one person each from the center and the left, with any dispute arising between them to be settled by the politburo. Frossard and Treint had been designated as their party's secretaries, with Louis Sellier as Frossard's alternate. Moreover, the Comintern decided to resolve the acute crisis following the Paris congress by forming the future comité directeur on this basis: the center would have ten full members and three alternates; the left, nine full members and two alternates; the Renoult faction four full members and one alternate; the Renaud Jean faction, one member. The center and the left would likewise each have three members and the Renoult faction one lone member in the future politburo. The congress also selected the persons to represent these various factions in the leading bodies of the party.[18]

The Comintern's Fourth Congress obviously intended either to discipline or to eliminate Frossard, the leader of the center. This, however, did not influence the political position of the center, which maintained its majority within the party, particularly since the Renoult faction stood closer to the center than to the left. During these years of crisis, 1921–23, the left enjoyed greater favor among the Kremlin leaders than the center: Souvarine was the representative at the Comintern and Alfred Rosmer, another left-wing leader, was a close friend of Trotsky. Even though the left was blessed with Moscow's confidence, the center still had a majority in the party. The left's first reaction to Frossard's resignation was to seek to profit from this occasion and get rid of the center. The Comintern, however, reacted otherwise; it needed both the loyalty of the left and the mass support enjoyed by the leaders of the center, and for this reason, as the next document shows, the Comintern asked the left not to break away entirely from the center—especially from its second leader, Marcel Cachin.

The Comintern's directive achieved its purpose: not one of the centrists designated for membership in the comité directeur by the Fourth Comintern Congress followed Frossard's example. Some of them left the Party later (Louis Sellier and Jean Garchery), but others (such as Marcel Cachin and Henri Gourdeaux) spent their

*entire political careers in the Party, following its general line un-
waveringly through almost three decades of Stalinism. Today one of
these early centrists, Georges Marrane, is still among the leaders of
the French Communist Party.*

*The Bukharin letter that follows characterizes the Comintern's
behavior from yet another point of view: factionalism within a Comintern section was forbidden whenever any opposition to the "ukases"
of Moscow was detected. Factions would receive support, however,
when they served the interests of the Comintern. The documents
clearly reveal how the Comintern and the leftist faction of the French
Communist Party communicated with each other over the heads of
the comité directeur: Treint prepared a report for the Comintern in
December 1921 at Marseille; Bukharin, in January 1923, wrote
directly to the left, transmitting formal orders.*

THE LETTER

Prolétaires de tous les pays unissez-vous!

*Comité Exécutif de l'Internationale Communiste
Addresse: Mokhovaja, 16. Addresse Télégramme: Internationale,
Moscou.
Téléphone No. 2-24-12, 56-71, suppl. 62*

No. 68   Moscow, January 15, 1923

To the Left Wing of the French Party

Dear Comrades:

The Presidium of the Executive Committee of the Communist
International confirms once more that it is your duty at present to do
all you can to keep in the party's fold the comrades of the center who
have remained there, and to draw nearer to them. You would expose
the party to a mortal danger if you continue to fight so obstinately
against men like Cachin and if you fail to realize that for the moment
our task is to fight hand in hand with Cachin and the other center
comrades against the dissidents and the deserters. The Presidium of
the ECCI insists strenuously on your applying this fundamental directive inside the party. We ask you to give your attention to the actual

practical work (organization, propaganda, etc.). We ask you to consult with our delegation on all problems.

Best wishes for your success.

THE PRESIDIUM OF THE ECCI
(Signed) N. Bukharine

[The Seal of the Executive Committee
of the Communist International]

DOCUMENT No. 4:

ALBERT TREINT'S LETTER OF RESIGNATION

EDITORS' INTRODUCTION—*Albert Treint, born in 1889, was a schoolteacher who as a member of the Socialist party participated in the Tours congress (December 1920), where he made a significant appearance on the rostrum. At the start of the first session of the congress, he sought modification of the agenda by proposing that the problem of the party's affiliation with the Third International be taken up for consideration forthwith. When a split over this issue ensued, Treint was elected to membership on the new, Communist, comité directeur, in charge of propaganda.*

The preceding documents have shown the prominent role played by Treint in the early history of the French Communist Party. At the Marseille congress, he was chairman of the closed session at which the delegates of the Comintern formulated the views of the ECCI. He later resigned from the comité directeur to demonstrate his solidarity with Souvarine. Early in 1922, at the behest of the Cominterm, he came to Moscow with another delegate to represent the left wing of the French party at the enlarged meeting of the ECCI (February 21–March 4, 1922). Contrary to the views of the official delegation of the comité directeur, he favored the united front.

Back in France, shortly before the Paris congress, Treint was the spokesman of the left at a meeting between the representatives of the center and the left. The meeting, which was held to determine the composition of the party's comité directeur, took place in October under the chairmanship of the Comintern delegates Manuilsky and Humbert-Droz. According to the recollections of Frossard, "in a tone which brooked no contradiction, he [Treint] presented his friends' ultimatum to us." In particular, Treint opposed Marcel Cachin's inclusion in the comité directeur because of the latter's alleged vacillating attitude, and proposed that he be replaced by the leftist Dunois as the director of L'Humanité.[19]

Disappointed by the results of the Paris congress and the center's decision to lead the party alone, Treint resigned from his post as chief of French party propaganda. Two months later, however, at the Fourth Comintern Congress, he and Frossard were jointly named secretaries-general of the French Communist Party by decision of the Comintern. When Frossard resigned from the Party, Treint remained in this post, while Sellier replaced Frossard.

However, Treint did not have the opportunity to settle calmly into his new duties. On orders from the Comintern, the French party was to organize a vast campaign against French imperialism and the occupation of the Ruhr in Germany by French troops, which had entered the Ruhr early in January 1923. From January 6 to 9, together with several other French Communist leaders, Treint participated in a conference at Essen organized jointly with the German Communists. After their return to France, the eight French Communist Party delegates to the Essen conference were arrested and imprisoned for several months. Treint was in jail when he wrote the letter below.

This letter produced no results. Treint's resignation was not accepted because, despite the opposition to him by former centrists in the comité directeur, he still enjoyed Moscow's confidence. He remained secretary-general of the French Communist Party until September 1924, meanwhile adding to this function several others in the Comintern's central apparatus. He was one of the chairmen of the Fifth Comintern Congress in 1924 and was elected a member of the ECCI, as well as of this body's Presidium.

But the fate of Treint's secret and ineffectual letter of resignation is nonetheless indicative of the Comintern's method of procedure. As long as a foreign Communist leader enjoyed Moscow's confidence, he retained his post, even if disavowed by a substantial number of his colleagues and even if he himself wished to resign. But let such a leader oppose Moscow, and he was marked out for purging. This is what happened to Treint.

Close to Zinoviev at the time the conflict between Zinoviev and Stalin arose, Treint was first stripped of some of his functions and then, finally, expelled from the French Communist Party. One step in this squeezing-out process was Treint's expulsion in June 1926 from the politburo of the French party after censure of his leadership at the fifth congress of the party (Lille, June 20–26, 1926) by a new Stalinist, anti-Zinoviev faction—although he remained a member of the ECCI. Zinoviev himself suffered a parallel fate just one month later in the Communist Party of the Soviet Union. In 1927 Albert Treint was removed from both the central committee of the French party and the ECCI. The final blow was his expulsion from the French Communist Party in 1928.

TO THE POLITICAL BUREAU

March 18, 1923

Dear Comrades:

I have succeeded in correcting some tactical errors which occurred during the current united-front phase and threatened to jeopardize the success we expected from it.

There remains to be settled one question to which I attach great importance, not so much because of the facts themselves, but because of their interpretation and because of the precedent they would create were the party to admit their legitimacy.

In January I wrote an article in *L'Humanité* in which I said: "There is no Russian imperialism, only a worker, or Red, imperialism." I showed the legitimacy of the working-class claim on the international stage to rule over the bourgeoisie until its disappearance.

After my imprisonment, *L'Humanité* published an article by Sellier attacking Red militarism, worker imperialism, worker capitalism.

Wishing to avoid a polemical discussion in *L'Humanité,* I wrote an article in *Le Bulletin Communiste* in which I demonstrated

1) that in his definition of militarism, Sellier drew on the dangerous notion of a "collective interest" superior to that of the classes confronting each other;

2) that I had never identified the systematic application of revolutionary violence with militarism;

3) that the notion of Red imperialism is a perfectly proper concept which expresses the will of the proletariat to achieve victory in the class struggle as well as the international solidarity of the proletariats locked in combat;

4) that the notion of worker capitalism is closely tied to the new economic policy considered as one of the phases of Communist construction;

5) that the use of such expressions as "Red imperialism" is as legitimate as the use of expressions like "class struggle" and "dictatorship of the proletariat," and that it is only necessary to clarify its meaning.

This article has not yet been published in *Le Bulletin Communiste*. A few days ago I received the most unconvincing explanations for this. And since that time, no solution [for this impasse] has been found.

This calls for clear words and frankness on my part.

I cannot tolerate that Sellier's article repudiating a preceding article of mine could have been published in *L'Humanité* without the question being discussed among the members of the Bureau, *myself included*.

Since there was no urgency about Sellier's article, I cannot tolerate being left out of such a discussion because of my imprisonment.

I cannot tolerate Sellier's speaking of collective interest in *L'Humanité* without my being given the opportunity in *Le Bulletin Communiste* to attack this notion, which is akin to that of the famous "general interest."

I cannot tolerate that my article was eliminated without any explanation given to me for several weeks.

In the belated explanations, furnished me unofficially, it was stated that certain dangerous expressions such as "Red imperialism" could not be used because they could be exploited by the enemy.

By making explicit the meaning of these expressions, which might be subject to misinterpretation, my article specifically prevents these wrong interpretations.

There is no merit to the argument that citations taken out of context from my article could be used against us.

This argument could be applied to any sort of text that any one of us might write. It is one of the tasks of our press, precisely, to expose the unfair methods our enemies use to fight against us.

Finally, the subject of my article is closely connected with the study of certain aspects of the program of the International to be laid down by the Fifth Comintern Congress.

The discussion in it rests on Communist ground with respect to questions of tactics and doctrine which do not directly involve any action currently in progress. For all these reasons, I cannot tolerate the censorship to which I am being subjected and which is being leveled against me in an insufferably off-hand manner during my present imprisonment.

I have always opposed the right to discuss in the party the fundamental principles of communism and the right to hamper current actions by excessive criticism. By the same token, I shall defend the legitimate right of each one to discuss Communist affairs inside the party.

Since this privilege has been withdrawn from me today under circumstances which are distressing indeed, I can only make myself heard in one way:

I am handing in to you my resignation as secretary of the Communist party.

Only if you decide to reestablish the right of discussing Communist affairs in the party, only if you decide that I should be treated as courteously as if I were at liberty, might I reverse my decision and preserve the title of party secretary until I can actually carry out its functions.

With fraternal greetings,
A. Treint

BIOGRAPHICAL NOTES

As in the case of the documents dealing with the German Communist Party, biographical data are also prepared in connection with the preceding four documents related to the affairs of the French Communist Party. In the present case, however, the editors have tried in vain to make the biographies uniform; some first names, years of birth and death, and other facts could not be determined.

EMILE AUCLAIR. Secretary of the Young Communists of France in Paris district in 1921 and alternate member of the Communist party's comité directeur after the resignation of the left at the Marseille congress in December 1921. He later left the Party and ceased all political activity.

BESTEL. Mechanic, was elected member of the comité directeur of the French Communist Party at the time of its founding at the Tours congress, in December 1920. Toward the end of 1921, he made a trip to Moscow as representative of his party and had occasion to speak with Lenin. At the Marseille congress in 1921, he was made an alternate member of the comité directeur. He quit the Communist Party about 1926–27.

AMADEO BORDIGA. Born in 1889, entered the Italian Socialist Party in 1910. During the First World War he belonged to the extreme left wing of the party; he opposed Italy's entrance into the war, as well as any Socialist participation in parliamentary activities.

In 1919, at its Bologna congress, the Italian Socialist Party, led by Serrati, adopted a favorable stand toward the Third International. At the time, two factions of the extreme left had already affirmed their complete adherence to Russian communism: one group, composed of Gramsci, Tasca, Terracini, Togliatti, and others, edited the review *Ordine Nuovo* in Turin. The animating spark of the other group, in Naples, called the "abstentionists," was Bordiga.[20]

Bordiga took an active part in the work of the Second Comintern Congress held in Moscow July–August, 1920.[21] At the Leghorn congress in January 1921, which ended in the split of the Italian Socialist party and the establishment of the Communist party, Bordiga emerged as leader of the latter organization. He was elected as one of the five members of the executive committee of the new Italian Communist Party—together with Grieco, Terracini, Repossi and Fortichiari—but was in fact "the actual director of all party activity."[22] Moreover, eight out of fifteen members of the central committee of the Italian Communist Party belonged to Bordiga's group, as against two associated with *Ordine Nuovo* (Terracini-Gramsci). Bordiga's prominence at home was paralleled by his career in the hierarchy of the Comintern. He was elected an alternate member of the ECCI at the Fourth Congress and, after the Third Enlarged Plenum of the ECCI in 1923, was promoted to membership of the ECCI Presidium. That same year Bordiga was arrested by the Fascist authorities and imprisoned for ten months. However, when finally summoned before a tribunal with thirty other leading members of the Italian Communist Party, he was ordered released.

Despite his rise in Comintern ranks, Bordiga retained his leftist ideas. From 1922 on, he disagreed with Moscow in regard to the united front, accepting it on the trade-union level only. When Moscow's grip on the foreign Communist parties tightened after the death of Lenin, the Italian party felt the effect of the new Comintern practice of using one faction to destroy the authority of the others. At the Fifth Comintern Congress in 1924, the Italian party was divided into three factions: a right (Tasca); a center, following orders from Moscow (Togliatti); and a left (Bordiga). Thenceforth Bordiga remained part of a minority within the leadership of the Italian Communist Party. His still great prestige, however, helped him win reelection at the close of the congress to membership in the ECCI and its Presidium.

In 1925, Bordiga's position took a turn for the worse. At the Fifth Enlarged Plenum of the Comintern a resolution criticized his alleged association with Trotsky. The process of "isolating" him commenced. Some of his followers, such as Grieco (Garlandi), aligned themselves with the center—that is, with Moscow. Bordiga's influence on Italian Communist youth was undermined systematically; steps also were taken to secure expulsion of several leaders of the leftist opposition, leaving this faction much enfeebled.

At the Lyon congress of the Italian Communist Party (January 1926), the Gramsci–Togliatti group emerged victorious, with Bordiga defeated on every count. Since 1923 he had failed to gain membership on the executive committee of the Italian party; now his last remaining followers were removed from the central committee. A month later he participated in Comintern affairs for the last time, at the Sixth Enlarged Plenum. There, a lone voice in the wilderness, he vigorously attacked the Stalinist leadership, criticized the idea of the united front (drawing a rebuke from Togliatti), assailed the terrorist methods propounded by the new leaders of the Italian Communist Party and accused them of ideological tyranny. It was the last time *Inprecor,* the official organ of the Comintern, was to publish (at least in part) the critical remarks of an opponent; no such forum was available to Trotsky or Vujović in 1927, or to Tasca in 1928.

Bordiga was arrested in Italy at the end of 1926, together with Gramsci and several other leaders. He first was exiled to Sicily, then to the Lipari Islands. Released early in 1930, he drew even closer to the Trotskyites. As a consequence, in March 1930 he was expelled from the Party at a plenary session of the Italian Communist Party's central committee.[23] Bordiga now lives in Naples as an engineer.

PIERRE BRIZON (1878–1923). Socialist deputy from Allier to the National Assembly in 1910. Thanks to his parliamentary immunity, Brizon had been able to render considerable service to the Socialist minority opposing the war. He himself attended the International

Socialist Conference at Kienthal, although he did not later join the Committee for the Reestablishment of International Ties. On February 5, 1918, he published the first issue of a weekly entitled *La Vague,* which continued to appear until his death on August 17, 1923 (during the last month of his life he changed the name of the publication to *Le Bloc des Rouges*). Although he lost his parliamentary seat in the first postwar election in 1919, his former authority combined with the publication of his weekly made him still an influential personality in the ranks of French leftists.

At the Tours congress Brizon followed the new majority, the Communists, although his Socialist federation from Allier had split and his own sympathies lay with Jean Longuet and Paul Faure. This attitude would seem to explain his silence during the congress and the fact that he was not elected to any of the leading organs of the new party. His pent-up opposition to Comintern policies exploded into the open with the "March action" of 1921 in Germany. His description of that action as "a broomstick" insurrection provoked the profound displeasure of the ECCI. But instead of retreating, Brizon actually stepped up his attacks; he denounced "Red militarism," criticized all armies, including the Red Army, and urged the restoration of leftist unity with Longuet and his followers.

Although Brizon was not alone in his criticism of the Comintern, it was he who was singled out for reprisal. On July 19, 1921, at Comintern instigation, the comité directeur of the French Communist Party decided to charge the conflict commission of the party with the examination of Brizon's case. However, the conflict commission proceeded with extraordinary dilatoriness, putting this task off until November. On December 19, 1921, in a letter to the leadership of the French party, the ECCI expressed its annoyance at the fact that the case had not yet been closed. In its view, the swift expulsion of Brizon from the Party would serve as a lesson to other opponents (Fabre, Meric, and others) to be more circumspect in their polemics against the Comintern.

It was not until the Paris congress of the French Communist Party in October 1922 that Pierre Brizon finally was expelled from the Party.

BRODEL. Secretary of the Fédération du Nord of the French Communist Party after the founding of the latter. He was elected a member of the comité directeur at the Marseille congress in December 1921 but left the Party in 1926 or 1927.

MARCEL CACHIN (1869–1958). Professor, member of the French Workers' party led by Jules Guesde. He joined the SFIO when it achieved unity in 1905. Cachin held many positions: in 1905 he was placed in charge of party propaganda, then became municipal councilman and finally, in 1914, a parliamentary deputy. During the course of the war, he advanced with each new majority faction as it emerged within the party: first the "social-patriotic" majority in 1914–15, then the centrist majority in 1917–18. After a visit to Russia with Frossard in 1920, Cachin went over to the Communist majority at the Tours congress (December 1920).

From the first congress of the French Communist Party, Cachin was a member of the comité directeur and thereafter remained as such without interruption. He was likewise a member of the party's politburo and became director of *L'Humanité,* a position he held until his death. He and Frossard led the "centrist" faction, which was in the majority at both the Marseille (1921) and the Paris (1922) congresses. However, Cachin parted with Frossard when the latter decided to break with Moscow. From then on Cachin hewed close to the twistings and turnings of Moscow's policy under Stalin and afterward.

Cachin was reelected deputy in the elections of 1920, 1924, and 1928, and became the first Communist senator in 1935. In 1946, after the Liberation, he regained his parliamentary mandate and held it until his death in February 1956.

He was active as a delegate and speaker at the Second, Fourth and Sixth congresses of the Comintern. A member of the International Control Commission following the Fifth Congress in 1924, he was confirmed in this capacity at the close of the Sixth Congress in 1928. At the last Comintern Congress, in 1935, he was elected to membership in the ECCI and its Presidium.

EUGÈNE DONDICOL. Born in 1874, commercial salesman, for many years a militant Socialist. He belonged to the French Communist Party from its founding and in December 1920, at Tours, joined its first comité directeur. Made party treasurer and then reelected at the Marseille congress of 1921, he later was dropped from the leadership by decision of the Fourth Congress of the Communist International. He resigned from the Party in 1923.

AMÉDÉE DUNOIS (1879–1944). Journalist, anarchist, then militant Socialist. He was named secretary-general of *L'Humanité* in

1918 and became a member of the French Communist Party's comité directeur at the time of the party's founding. Reelected at the Marseille congress in December 1921, he resigned immediately as a sign of solidarity with Boris Souvarine, who had not been reelected. The decisions of the Fourth Comintern Congress, in November 1922, retained him on the central committee of the French party, but he was kept rather at arm's length after the expulsion in 1924 first of Souvarine, then of Monatte and Rosmer. Invited to explain himself (like F. Loriot) at the Clichy congress of the French Communist Party (January 1925), he was severely attacked, after which he quit the French Communist Party and returned to the fold of the SFIO. He was one of the organizers of Socialist resistance during the German occupation, arrested by the Germans, and deported to a concentration camp, where he died.

HENRI FABRE. Born in 1877, he acquired considerable prominence in leftist circles with his publication, between 1908 and 1916, of *Les Hommes du Jour,* a weekly pamphlet which occasionally showed anarchist tendencies. In 1916 its publication was suspended by order of the official censor, but Fabre soon replaced it with a daily, *Journal du Peuple,* which first appeared on January 1, 1917. Its subtitle was "Tribune Libre Pour Tous Les Hommes Libres," a phrase later ridiculed by Zinoviev in his speech at the enlarged First Plenum of the ECCI, in February–March, 1922. Among the collaborators of *Journal du Peuple* were Georges Pioch, Souvarine, Verfeuil, Vaillant-Couturier, Henry Torrès, and others who exercised a decisive influence in orienting a majority in the French Socialist party toward Moscow. To the same circle belonged also some Socialist deputies who favored the pacifist ideas of Kienthal. They supported Briand and defended Caillaux against Clemenceau in 1917, thus creating difficulties for Henri Fabre.

His contact with the Socialists opposed to the war ("Minoritaires de guerre") explains why in 1920 Fabre decided to join the Comintern. At no time, however, was he a true Communist; as may be seen from the preceding documents, his *Journal du Peuple* soon became the forum for all who disagreed with the policy and organizational methods which the ECCI sought to impose upon the French Communist Party. The Comintern's animosity toward Fabre's paper may be seen from the utterance by Trotsky on May 19, 1922 at a session of the ECCI: "Fabre's newspaper is a permanent meeting place for all the elements which paralyze, undermine, and corrupt the

Communist Party. Yes, it is a meeting place for elements hostile to communism, but hiding behind the Communist flag. . . . Fabre is an agent of the bourgeoisie in the Party."[24]

Fabre was expelled from the International, as a result of Trotsky's attack on him, and his expulsion from the French Communist Party followed soon afterward.

PAUL FAURE (1878–1961). Schoolteacher, active in the Socialist movement from 1901. At the end of the First World War, he was one of the leaders of the centrist trend among French Socialists. Prevented from joining the Communist Party at the Tours congress by a decision of the ECCI (Zinoviev's "pistol shot"—a cable forbidding the admission of centrists into the nascent Communist party), he remained a member of the Socialist party and served as its secretary-general from 1921 to 1939. In 1940, he was one of a number of Social deputies who voted to grant full powers to Marshal Pétain. He was ejected from the SFIO after the Liberation.

LOUIS-OSCAR FROSSARD (also called Ludovic-Oscar), 1889–1946. Schoolteacher, from 1905 a member of the Socialist party. He was elected secretary-general of the party in 1918, as spokesman for its new majority, a position held by him until 1920. That year he and Marcel Cachin went to Soviet Russia to exchange views and information. Upon their return, they started a campaign urging adherence of the Socialist party to the Communist International. After the split at the Tours congress, Frossard became secretary of the new Communist party. Soon he got into conflict with Moscow—especially after the ECCI, on December 18, 1921, made known its theses on the united front. Accordingly, in January 1922, under Frossard's guidance, the comité directeur of the French Communist Party unanimously rejected the ECCI's theses; the following month, Frossard managed to avoid going to Moscow for a meeting of the ECCI's enlarged First Plenum. However, he did attend the enlarged Second Plenum in June 1922. Then, in October, Frossard came out once again in open opposition to Moscow. He deliberately stayed away from the Fourth Congress of the Comintern in November 1922, although he had been elected to membership in the ECCI and had been confirmed as one of the French party's two secretaries. Since a resolution dealing with the French question and adopted at this congress stipulated that by January 1, 1923, at the latest, all French leaders had to renounce publicly their ties with Freemasonry, Frossard (although probably not a member of that society) submitted his resignation from the Party on that day.

Immediately thereafter he formed a dissident Communist group, but later rejoined the SFIO. He was a member of parliament until 1940, but in 1936 he left the Socialist parliamentary group and filled ministerial posts in the governments of Chautemps, Blum, and Daladier. He was minister of public works in Marshal Pétain's first government.

JEAN GARCHERY (1872–1957). Socialist from 1890, joined the Communist party at its founding. He was elected to the comité directeur by the Marseille congress in 1921 and was reaffirmed in this status by the Fourth Comintern Congress in November 1922. He was reelected to membership in the central committee at the Lille congress in 1926 but broke with the French Communist Party three years later.

HENRI GOURDEAUX (1881–1961). Postal employee, member of the SFIO from 1908. He belonged to the Communist party from its establishment and was elected at Tours to the comité directeur. Named secretary of the finance commission of the French party, he was reelected to the comité directeur at the next congress (Marseille, December 1921) and confirmed in this capacity by the Fourth Congress of the Comintern. At the Lille congress of 1926 he was once more elected to the central committee. Variously charged with responsibilities for both the CGTU (as secretary of the postal federation) and the Communist party, he was one of the few members of the first comité directeur of the French Communist Party who ultimately was neither expelled from the Party nor left it voluntarily. In 1956, the fourteenth congress of the French party elected him to membership on the central control commission.

MAKSYMILIAN HORWITZ (see Henryk Walecki, pp. 375–76).

JULES HUMBERT-DROZ (see pp. 226, 230–31).

ANTOINE KER (1886–1923). Graduate of commercial studies in Paris and Munich, member of the Committee for the Third International. At the constitutive Tours congress of the French Communist Party, he was elected to membership on the comité directeur and reaffirmed by the congresses of Marseille (1921) and Paris (1922). After the Marseille congress, he was named secretary for international relations and in this capacity participated in the ECCI meeting discussing the question of the united front. Initially a leftist (of the Souvarine-Loriot faction), he joined the center (Cachin-Frossard-Sellier) at the Paris congress and proceeded to denounce the left. In November 1922 he attended the Fourth Comintern Congress; unlike Frossard and many other Freemasons who quit the Comintern rather than yield to the injunction of this congress to give up Freemasonry, Ker yielded but was not reelected to the new central committee of the French Communist Party.

RAOUL LAMOLINAIRIE (see Raoul Verfeuil, pp. 374–75).

ERNEST LAFONT. Born in Lyon in 1879, militant Socialist, elected parliamentary deputy in 1914 and 1919, opted for the Communist party after the split at Tours. In 1921 he had an altercation with Moscow, and a year later he opposed the decisions of the Comintern's Fourth Congress. As a consequence, he established a "resistance committee," but was expelled from the French party in January 1923.

LUCIE LEICIAGUE (married name Le Gléo), (1879–1962). Of Basque origin, militant Socialist before 1914, joined the Communist camp at the Tours congress. Member of the comité directeur until 1926, she represented the French party in the ECCI in 1922–23. She also attended the Fifth Comintern Congress as delegate of the party. The "Bolshevization" decided upon at that congress shook her faith to such a degree that she was removed from the leadership of the French party at its fifth congress in Lille in June 1926.

Her final break with the Party came in 1928, at the time of Stalin's complete victory in the Comintern. She later joined the Socialist party and contributed to the Socialist journals *Le Combat Marxiste* and *Idée et Action*. She specialized in Soviet affairs and was a severe critic of the Soviet Union. After the Second World War, she collaborated for several years with the research association which today publishes in Paris the review *Est & Ouest*.

JEAN LONGUET (1876–1938). Son of Charles Longuet (exiled member of the Paris Commune) and Jenny, second daughter of Karl

Marx. Lawyer, journalist, Socialist deputy in parliament in 1914, he was one of the leaders of the pacifist centrist faction within the SFIO during the war, the faction which at war's end captured the party majority. In April 1916, together with Paul Faure, he established the newspaper *Le Populaire*. Longuet voted in favor of withdrawing the SFIO from the Socialist International, but at the Tours congress Zinoviev's telegram singling him out for attack prevented his being admitted to the French Communist Party. Soon afterward he rejoined the SFIO and remained thereafter in its ranks.

FERNAND LORIOT (1870–1932). Schoolteacher, member of the French Socialist party from 1901, treasurer of the Federation of Teachers' Unions from 1915. He was one of the first opponents of the "defensist" policy of the Socialist and trade-union majority during the early phases of the war. One of the founders of the Committee for the Reestablishment of International Ties, he was appointed its secretary in 1917. That same year he went to Switzerland and, together with ten other European Socialists, signed a declaration affirming their approval of the passage of the Russian revolutionaries, including Lenin, through imperial Germany to Russia.

In 1919, Loriot became one of the three secretaries of the newly established Committee for the Third International. (The others were Pierre Monatte and Boris Souvarine.) While serving as treasurer of the Socialist party, Loriot simultaneously headed its extreme left-wing faction, which had been won over to Bolshevism then triumphant in Russia. In a letter of invitation dated January 24, 1919, urging the convocation of a congress for establishing the Communist International and bearing the signatures of Lenin and Trotsky in the name of the Russian Bolshevik party, reference was made to Loriot as the pivotal figure around whom was clustered a group of Socialists and trade unionists invited to participate.

In May 1920, together with Monatte and Souvarine, Loriot received a ten-month prison sentence, and was thus unable to attend the Tours congress. Nevertheless, he was elected a member of the comité directeur of the new French Communist Party and soon afterward became the party's international secretary. He was chief of the French delegation to the Third Comintern Congress in 1921 and one of the five chairmen of this assembly. After his return from Moscow, Loriot's poor health kept him from participating directly in militant political action. When, after Lenin's death, the first stirrings of the Comintern's "Bolshevization" policy began to be felt, he opposed the new methods and criticized them publicly at the Clichy congress of the French party in 1925.

In 1926, Loriot refrained from renewing his party card and allied himself thereafter with dissident Communist groups who voiced their views in *Bulletin Communiste, Contre le Courant,* and *La Révolution Prolétarienne.* That same year, at the Seventh Plenum of the ECCI, he was denounced violently along with his fellow promoters of the former Committee for the Third International, Monatte, Rosmer, and Souvarine.

PAUL LOUIS. Born in 1872, a publicist of Socialist convictions, author of many works on the history of the workers' movement. An editor of *L'Humanité,* he was elected member of the comité directeur of the French Communist Party at the Tours and Marseille congresses. He was stripped of all official party duties by the Fourth Comintern Congress and finally quit the French party of his own volition in 1923.

GEORGES MARRANE. Born in 1888, watchmaker, member of the French Communist Party from its founding in 1920 to the present day. Administrative secretary of the Communist Federation of the Seine in 1921 and its political secretary in 1927, he was appointed a member of the central committee of the French party by decision of the Fourth Comintern Congress and reelected by the Lille congress of the French Communist Party in 1926. Mayor of Ivry and chairman of the General Council of the Seine in 1936–37, he was one of the leaders of the French Communists during the German occupation. At its 1945 congress, he was elected president of the party's central control commission, and was one of the Communist ministers in the last government of the Fourth Republic headed by Paul Ramadier, January–May 1947, in which the French Communist Party participated. Marrane was elected to the council of the republic (senate) in 1946, 1948, and 1952, and was the Communist choice to oppose General de Gaulle in the presidential election at the end of 1958.

VICTOR MERIC. Born in 1876, writer and journalist, member of the Communist party from its founding, was elected to its comité directeur at the first three congresses of the party (1920, 1921, 1922). After the decisions of the Fourth Comintern Congress, he was one of the three organizers of the resistance committee, which led to his expulsion from the Party in January 1923.

ALPHONSE MERRHEIM (1871–1925). Coppersmith, one of the most important figures of the French trade-union movement. He was the founder of the first trade-union meeting halls (bourses du travail) at Roubaix, 1892. He applied himself zealously to the task of uniting all metalworkers in a single federation, becoming its secretary in 1904. A partisan of revolutionary trade unionism, he was, however, primarily interested in developing the intellectual capacities of workers and their ability to comprehend economic problems. During the years just before the First World War he began evolving a more reformist and more constructive conception of trade-union action.

Opposed during the war to the adherence of trade unionists to the national policy of "union sacrée," and anxious to maintain international ties among the leaders of the working class and to take advantage of any chances for peace that might arise, Merrheim attended the Zimmerwald conference (1915), without, however, sharing Lenin's ideas. He never associated himself with Bolshevism.

After the war, convinced more than ever that reform rather than revolution would lead to the emancipation of the workers, he elaborated a sweeping plan of social reform, which was adopted by the CGT. However, as the result of an invitation to join the International at Moscow—whose acceptance Merrheim vigorously opposed—the CGT split (1921) and, weakened by this schism, was not able to carry through the project it had begun. Severely buffeted by all these tribulations, Merrheim retired in 1923 from active political life.

RENÉ METAYER. Metal worker, member of the French Communist Party from its inception. He was one of the French delegates selected to attend the enlarged plenum of the ECCI in February–March, 1922. He later left the Party.

PIERRE MONATTE (1881–1960). Bookstore employee, proofreader and journalist. He started out as an anarchist, then became a revolutionary trade unionist. In 1909, he founded the revolutionary trade-union journal *La Vie Ouvrière;* in August 1914 he became one of the first to oppose the war. Leader of the pacifist minority within the CGT, he was converted to communism after the Bolshevik revolution and became one of the three secretaries of the Committee for the Third International. Arrested in 1920, he was released by order of the court in March 1921. In 1922 he joined the staff of *L'Humanité* as editor in charge of social questions; the next year he joined the French Communist Party and, at the beginning of 1924, was elected to its central committee. By December of that year he already had been dropped from this post because of his disagreement with the policy of "Bolshevization" instituted after Lenin's death. In 1925 he established the revolutionary trade-union review *La Révolution Prolétarienne,* which is still published in Paris.

GEORGES PIOCH. Born in 1873, poet, journalist, theater and music critic. He joined the SFIO in 1915 and the Communist party upon its establishment. He became secretary of the Seine federation (Paris) of the French Communist Party but came into conflict with the Comintern over the decisions of its Fourth Congress in November 1922. His participation as one of the three organizers of the resistance committee, together with Lafont and Meric, brought about his expulsion from the Party.

CHARLES RAPPOPORT. Born in Russia in 1865, he emigrated to Western Europe in 1887, after having taken part in the Russian revolutionary movement. A militant Socialist revolutionary at first, he joined the Russian Social Democratic party in 1902. He was a contributor to the Russian, Swiss, German and French Socialist press and shared in the work of the Socialist International.

Attracted to communism after October 1917, he joined the French Communist Party at its founding and was elected member of its comité directeur, acting in this capacity until 1923. A writer for *L'Humanité* and editor of the *Revue Communiste,* he became the Paris correspondent of *Izvestia* that same year.

Rappoport was very active in the French party at the time of the Marseille and Paris congresses, particularly in his campaign against Boris Souvarine, the French Communist Party's delegate in Moscow, and in the discussions concerning the united front. Afterward, he maintained aloofness. At the Lille congress of the French party in 1926 he was attacked by the new party leaders, among them Pierre Semard and Jacques Doriot. Still, he broke neither with the Party nor with the Soviets until the time of the great purge trials, the immediate cause of his definite repudiation of communism. He died during the Second World War.

Rappoport was the author of many political pamphlets, as well as of two books: *Jean Jaurès* and *Philosophie de l'Histoire*.

JEAN RENAUD (1887–1961). Farm worker, conscripted in the First World War and wounded in 1915. After his recovery he began a formal program of study and became professor of mechanics in a vocational school. A member of the Socialist party from 1908, he was elected parliamentary deputy in 1920, and reelected Communist deputy in 1924, 1932 and 1936.

A supporter of adherence to the Comintern, he joined the French Communist Party at its inception and was elected to the comité directeur at the Marseille congress. He distinguished himself at this congress by a defense of his views regarding the rural situation in France which brought forth a rebuttal from Lenin. The next year, Renaud was a delegate to the Fourth Congress of the Comintern and spoke in the name of the French party. In 1926, at the Lille congress of the French Communist Party, he was elected a member of its central committee. In 1937, at the party's Arles congress, he was reelected to same post.

Displeased by the Hitler-Stalin pact of 1939, he almost broke with the French Communist Party, but remained in the party to avoid the impression that he was abandoning his comrades in the face of a government campaign of repression. However, the leadership of the French party, led by Thorez, did not forget Renaud's doubts in 1939, and after the Liberation he was never proposed as a party candidate in the elections. He continued in this state of semi-disgrace until his death, discharging the duties of secretary-general of the farmers' association of Lot-et-Garonne.

DANIEL RENOULT (1880–1958). Member of the Socialist party from 1906 and regular representative of its Seine-et-Marne federation at the party congresses. In 1914, he joined the editorial board of *L'Humanité* but was drafted at the beginning of the First World War. His name was not among the minority Socialist faction opposed to the war. From 1920 on, however, he played a prominent role in the Socialist party. As a member of the party's permanent administrative commission, he proposed at the Strasbourg congress of

February 1920 the so-called "resolution on renovation," which recommended the withdrawal of the Socialist party from the Second International and "the renovation of the International through an agreement with the organizations united in the Moscow amalgam," according to his own words at the congress. At the Tours congress he signed the motion in favor of joining the Comintern and delivered a violent tirade against Léon Blum. He had no success, however, in his efforts to persuade the Comintern leaders to sanction the admission of Jean Longuet to the French Communist Party.

At Tours Renoult won a seat on the comité directeur of the French Communist Party, as well as membership on the new administrative staff of *L'Humanité*. The party also charged him with the editorship of a new evening paper, *L'Internationale*, designed to replace *Le Populaire*, which remained in the hands of the Socialists. But this venture proved to be a failure both journalistically and financially.

A supporter of Frossard until the Marseille congress, Renoult defended the position of the French party's majority at the enlarged First Plenum of the ECCI (February–March, 1922). He remained in the Party after Frossard left it. He took part in the Fourth Comintern Congress at the end of 1922, and four members of his faction entered the new comité directeur of the French Communist Party nominated by that Congress. Zinoviev's veto prevented Renoult from becoming a member of the comité directeur. The Comintern's displeasure with Renoult continued for many years: neither at the 1926 congress of the French party nor at later congresses was he elected to the central committee.

An active member of the French Communist resistance during the war, he was arrested by the Nazis but succeeded in escaping from prison in 1944. At the first congress of the French Communist Party after the Liberation, in 1945, he finally joined the central committee of the party and was reconfirmed in that post by the 1947 congress. He was not reelected, however, by the 1950 congress of the party, but remained, until the end of his life a member of the central commission of financial control of the party. From 1944 until his death he was mayor of Montreuil, a suburb of Paris.

LOUIS SELLIER. Born in 1885, postal employee, militant Socialist and trade-unionist from 1909. He joined the French Communist Party at its founding and was elected a member of its first comité directeur. He was not reelected at the Marseille congress, but was sent as one of the French party delegates to the enlarged First Plenum of the ECCI (February–March, 1922). By a decision of the Fourth Comintern Congress in November 1922, he again became a member of the comité directeur of the French party and was promoted to the position of Frossard's deputy in the secretary-generalship of the party, assuming full powers upon Frossard's resignation on January 1, 1923. At the Fifth Comintern Congress in 1924, he became a member of the ECCI and of its Presidium. Although he had discontinued his duties as secretary-general of the party, he gained reelection at the Lille congress (1926) to membership on the central committee and the politburo. He broke with the French Communist Party in 1929.

E. SOUTIF. A militant Socialist, he joined the French Communist Party at its inception and was elected to the comité directeur at the Marseille congress. Associated with L. O. Frossard, for whom he served as assistant in the party secretariat, Soutif was left out of the new comité directeur chosen by the Fourth Comintern Congress. Forced to declare himself by the ultimatum issued at this congress concerning the Freemasons, he quit the Party at the same time as Frossard.

BORIS SOUVARINE (see p. xii).

JOSEPH TOMMASI (1886–1926). Industrial worker, militant Socialist and trade unionist, secretary of the United Trade Unions of the Seine. He joined the French Communist Party at the start, attended the Third Comintern Congress as a delegate, and was elected a member of the comité directeur of the French party by the Marseille congress. The Comintern congress of 1922 reaffirmed his membership in the central committee of the French party. Later implicated in a Soviet-linked espionage case, he had to take refuge in Moscow in 1924, where he died two years later under suspicious circumstances.

HENRY TORRÈS (1891–1966). Attorney, joined the French Communist Party at Tours and was a contributor to *L'Humanité*. He served as defense attorney during the court trial of the three secretaries of the Committee for the Third International—Loriot, Monatte, and Souvarine. When he disagreed with the decisions of the Fourth Comintern Congress concerning the French Communist Party, he joined the resistance committee and was duly expelled from the French party in January 1923. He became a parliamentary deputy in 1932. After the war he became a Gaullist, and twice was elected senator—in 1948 and in 1952—for the *Rassemblement du Peuple Français*.

ALBERT TREINT (see pp. 354–56).

PAUL VAILLANT-COUTURIER. Born in 1892, attorney, joined the Socialist party in 1917 and was elected one of its deputies for Paris in the 1919 elections. He joined the Communists at the Tours congress, at which he was elected a member of the comité directeur of the French Communist Party. He kept this post until his death in 1937. Vaillant-Couturier attended the Third Comintern Congress as a delegate and spokesman for the French party. He served as editor-in-chief of *L'Humanité* from 1926 to 1937 and was elected Communist deputy for Paris in 1936.

RAOUL VERFEUIL (*pseud.* of Raoul Lamolinairie). Born in 1887, politically active among Socialist youth as early as 1905, unsuccessful Socialist party candidate in the elections of 1914. As a writer for the *Midi Socialiste*, he adopted the pseudonym Verfeuil, which he retained permanently. An ardent pacifist during the war and a political associate of Jean Longuet and Paul Faure, he decided after considerable hesitation to throw his lot in with the Communists at the Tours congress. Early in January 1921, he was placed in charge of propaganda by the comité directeur.

Verfeuil's official career in the party lasted only briefly, however. His support of Henri Fabre angered the ECCI, and in July 1922 it forwarded its request to the comité directeur of the French Communist Party that Verfeuil be expelled. This was done by majority vote at a meeting of the comité directeur the following month. Frossard, secretary of the French party and a personal friend of Verfeuil's, was opposed to this decision, which was nevertheless confirmed in October of that year by the Paris congress of the French Communist Party.

Together with other expelled party members (Meric, Pioch, Lafont, Auclair, and Frossard himself after January 1, 1923), Verfeuil established a short-lived group, *L'Union Socialiste Communiste.*

HENRYK WALECKI (*pseud.* of Maksymilian Horwitz). Born in 1877 in Warsaw, to a family of the Polish-Jewish intelligentsia. For his advanced studies he went to the University of Ghent, Belgium, where he received his doctorate in mathematics in 1898. He had joined the Belgian Socialist movement three years earlier, as well as a Socialist group made up of Polish Socialists abroad. Back in Warsaw in 1898, he became active in the Polish Socialist party and soon conflicted with Pilsudski. He was arrested in December 1899 and exiled to Siberia two years later, escaped in the summer of 1902 and managed to reach Switzerland, where he resumed party work. He was a representative of the Polish Socialist party at the 1904 Amsterdam congress of the Second International. For the next few years he led the dangerous life of a revolutionary. He returned to Warsaw in 1905, was arrested several times and again exiled to Siberia in 1906. But he soon repeated his former escape and by the end of 1907 was living intermittently in Cracow and Vienna. He became one of the leaders of the Socialist left wing in opposition to Pilsudski and editor of his faction's organ, *Mysl Socjalistyczna,* which specialized in Socialist theory. It was then that he adopted the pen name Henryk Walecki. He attended all other prewar congresses of the Second International, at which he dissented from the patriotic stand of the Polish Socialist party and leaned toward Rosa Luxemburg's and Julian Marchlewski's Social Democratic Party of Poland and Lithuania (SDKPIL).

After the outbreak of the First World War, Walecki went from Austria to Prussian Upper Silesia, where he was arrested in January 1915 but released by the court. He went to Switzerland, established contact with Lenin, and took part in the Zimmerwald movement. In May 1917, he became editor of the *Volksrecht* in Zurich, one of the organs of the Zimmerwald Left which turned pro-Bolshevik after the October Revolution in Russia. His active participation in the strike of railroad workers in 1918 led to his expulsion from Switzerland. After returning to Warsaw, he was one of the cofounders, in December 1918, of the Communist Labor Party of Poland, which was created by the fusion of the Polish Socialist party's left wing and the Social Democratic party of Poland and Lithuania. He also served on the executive committee of the Warsaw Soviet of Workers' Delegates.

Arrested in the winter of 1919 by the Polish police, he was released from prison on bail in the second part of 1920, and then fled to Russia. There, together with Warski and Wera Kostrzewa, he assumed the leadership of Polish Communists abroad.

In February 1921, Walecki was designated (together with Marchlewski) as Polish representative in the Comintern and Profintern executive committees. He attended and addressed the Third Comintern Congress in July 1921. Although his pamphlet *Tactics and the Attitude Toward Parliamentarianism* (February 1921) had been denounced by the central committee of the Polish party, Walecki continued, as a member of the ECCI, his intense Comintern activity, particularly in Czechoslovakia, France and Italy. (In October 1921 he was a Comintern observer at the Milan congress of Serrati's Socialist party.) He made a report dealing with the united-front tactics at the enlarged First Plenum of the Comintern during February–March, 1922, and was then elected a permanent member of its Presidium. In the middle of 1922, Walecki was sent to the United States to heal the split in the American Communist Party. He took an active part in the debates of the Fourth Comintern Congress, especially in the Polish commission. From February 1923 on, Walecki settled in Berlin, where he contributed to *Rote Fahne* and became coeditor of *Nowy Przeglad* (the central organ of the Polish Communist Party appearing in Silesia). He played an active role in the second congress of the Polish Communist Party (September–October, 1923) and won reelection to the leadership. However, at the Fifth Comintern Congress (June 1924), severe criticism was leveled against the triumvirate policy of Warski, Walecki, and Wera Kostrzewa, with Walecki himself a particular target. He defended himself in an article, "O losach Partii" (The Party's Future) in *Nowy Przeglad* (December 1924), but was censured at the third congress of the Polish party in January 1925, and removed from the party leadership. He thereupon was transferred to duties within the Comintern apparatus and from 1928 to 1935 was deputy head of its Balkan secretariat. He contributed widely to Soviet publications (among them, the Soviet Encyclopedia).

In 1935, Walecki became editor of the *Communist International*, and was elected a member of the Comintern's control commission at the Seventh Comintern Congress.

On June 22, 1937, Walecki was arrested by the NKVD and executed shortly thereafter. He was rehabilitated after 1956.

Notes

Notes

THE COMINTERN'S CLAIM TO MARXIST LEGITIMACY

1. From his preface to the fourth German edition of the *Communist Manifesto*, written in 1890. Karl Marx, Friedrich Engels, *Werke* (Berlin: Dietz Verlag, 1963), XXII, 57. Hereafter cited as *Werke*.
2. *Constitution and Rules of the Communist International*, paragraph 1.
3. From his speech about the Hague congress of the First International, *Werke*, XVIII, 160.
4. The Comintern shared with Bakunin his belief in conspiracy and the absolute need for revolutionary violence. However, it never imitated his childish insurrectional tactics; nor did it follow him in his anarchistic suggestion that a successful uprising should be followed by the immediate abolition of the state.
5. The third condition requested Communists to "create everywhere a parallel illegal apparatus" and also called for "a combination of legal and illegal work." See also the fourth condition, which applied this command to work in military forces.
6. *Werke*, XVII, 655.
7. Some of the conspiratorial methods to which Marx objected most strenuously were listed on July 21, 1873, in the conclusion to "The Alliance of Socialist Democracy and the IWMA." Karl Marx, *Politische Schriften*, ed. by H. S. Lieber (Stuttgart: Cotta, 1960), II, 1012.
8. Karl Marx and Friedrich Engels, *Selected Correspondence* (Moscow: Foreign Languages Publishing House, 1953), 326–29. Hereafter cited as *Selected Correspondence*. Italics in the original.
9. Rudolf Meyer, *Der Emanzipationskampf des Vierten Standes*, 2d ed. (Berlin: Bahr, 1882), II, 545.
10. *Ibid.*, 600.
11. *Werke*, XVII, 422.
12. *Politische Schriften*, II, 968.
13. *Werke*, XVIII, 554.
14. *Ibid.*, 539.
15. *Ibid.*, 529.
16. In a letter of January 24, 1872, to Theodor Cuno, Engels defined the meaning of Bakunin's proposed "abstention from all politics" as follows: "To commit a political act, especially to take part in an election, would be a betrayal of principle. The thing to do is to carry on propaganda, heap abuse upon the state, organize, and when *all* the workers, and hence the majority, are won over, depose all the authorities, abolish the state." *Selected Correspondence*, 335. Italics in the original.
17. In a letter to L. Kugelmann, Marx had stated even earlier, on February 23, 1865, that in England there was good progress on the general suffrage question, "which of course has a *significance here quite different* from what it has in Prussia." *Ibid.*, 206. Italics in the original.
18. The president at the 1872 congress, Gabriel Ranvier, a Blanquist and Communard who had been elected to honor the Commune, "urged the International to establish a permanent committee of barricades." Report by Maltman Barry in *The First Interna-*

tional, Minutes of the Hague Congress of 1872 with Related Documents, ed. by Hans Gerth (Madison: University of Wisconsin Press, 1958), 269. By contrast, Adolf Hepner, a loyal supporter of Marx, opposed "barricadology" on the grounds that "one cannot make revolutions because those arise only in a natural way and are stages of historical development." *Ibid.,* 218.

19. *Werke,* XVIII, 160. In an earlier interview with an American newspaperman on July 3, 1871, Marx stated that the working class had a choice how it would develop its political power. In England, "where through peaceful agitation the objective can be reached more rapidly and safely, an uprising would be a stupidity. In France, a violent solution of the social problem might be necessary, but whether such a solution will be chosen depends on the working class of the particular country." *Ibid.,* XVII, 164.

20. Fr. de J., "Amsterdam Meeting of the First International in 1872," *Bulletin of the International Institute of Social History* (Leiden: E. J. Brill), VI (1951), 1–15.

21. *Selected Correspondence,* 356.

22. Friedrich Engels, "Über das Erfurter Programm," in Karl Marx *Kritik des Gothaer Programms* (Berlin: Neuer Weg, 1946), 75 ff. See also Irving Fetscher, "Marxismus und Bürokratie," *International Review of Social History* (Assen, The Netherlands: Royal Vangorcum), vol. v, no. 3 (1960), 378–99.

23. *Werke,* VII, 511–27. Engels pointed to the successes with parliamentary tactics achieved in Switzerland, Italy, Denmark, Belgium, Rumania, Austria, and, perhaps too hopefully, even Russia (p. 524).

24. *Ibid.,* 526. The reference to the Christians would indicate that Engels had accepted some parts of the Fabian doctrine.

25. *Selected Correspondence,* 568.

26. Benedict Kautsky, ed., *Friedrich Engels' Briefwechsel mit Karl Kautsky* (Vienna: Danubia, 1955), 429.

27. Letter of April 3, 1895. *Selected Correspondence,* 568–69. Italics in the original.

28. Stalin, *Foundations of Leninism* (New York: International Publishers, 1932), chap. iv.

29. The Leninist interpretations of "Marxism" and war date back, it seems, to Eleanor Marx, who, when about ten years of age, commented on the Danish question that "she considers one of the parties to the quarrel as bad as the other, and perhaps worse." Marx to Lion Philips, end of March 1864, in W. Blumenberg, "Ein unbekanntes Kapitel aus Marx's Leben," *International Review of Social History,* I (1956), 97.

30. *Werke,* XVII, 3–7.

31. Letter of September 6, 1870, to Engels. *Briefwechsel* (Berlin: Marx-Engels-Verlag, 1931), IV, 378.

32. *Werke,* XVII, 271–78.

33. *Ibid.,* 277.

34. Meyer, I, 142; II, 613.

35. Neither G. M. Stekloff in *History of the First International* (London: Lawrence, 1928) nor Gustav Jäckh in *Die Internationale* (Leipzig: Leipziger Buchdruckerei, 1904) makes any reference to this phantom plan.

36. James Guillaume, *L'Internationale, documents et souvenirs (1864–1878),* 4 vols. (Paris: Stock, 1905–1910), II, 83.

37. *Ibid.,* 79 ff.

38. Franz Mehring, *Karl Marx, Geschichte seines Lebens,* 4th ed. (Leipzig: Leipziger Buchdruckerei, 1923), 455.

39. In a letter of September 12–17, 1874, to F. A. Sorge, Engels alleged that the Commune was "without any doubt the child of the International intellectually," but added pointedly that "the International did not lift a finger to produce it." *Selected Correspondence,* 350.

40. Hippolyte T. O. Lissagaray, *Histoire de la Commune de 1871* (Buenos Aires: Trident, 1944; originally published in 1876, re-

vised edition 1897), asserted that
the Commune itself allocated only
100,000 francs to organize insurrections in France, because the
Communards wanted to act merely by example (p. 202).

41. Letter of May 13, 1871, to L.
Fränckel and L. E. Varlin.
Selected Correspondence, 321–22.

42. *Ibid.,* 325–26. Italics in the original.

A PARTY OF A NEW TYPE

1. These "rages" are discussed from
time to time in Krupskaya's letters
to Lenin's family as something
familiar to them. They are several
times hinted at in her memoirs,
where she describes them as followed by periods of complete ex-
haustion and a desire only to doze,
or seek solitude in mountain
walks. N. Valentinov describes
Lenin's rages in *Vstrechi s Leninym* (New York, 1953), 182 and
210–12. Lenin himself acknowledged that he was "possessed" by
such a "rage" during the controversies with his fellow Iskrists at
the Second Congress, writing
apologetically concerning his outburst in a letter to Potresov dated
September 13, 1903 (*Sochineniia,*
4th ed., Moscow, 1941–62;
XXXIV (1950), 137–39). He also
spoke of the tempests which "pos-
sess" him in several letters to
Gorky. In one letter he flies into
a fury because Gorky has written
a little coquettishly that he has no
god at this time because he has not
as yet created one. Lenin de-
nounces him in harsh language for
"god creation." "Every god worship is copulation with a corpse."
Since it was Gorky, in whom
Lenin pardoned many things because such a writer was useful to
his cause, Lenin delayed sending
the rude letter until he had cooled
off. But he sent it all the same,
with a lame apology, for Lenin by
no means repudiated in his cool-
er moments what he said in his
rages. Both admission and apology
are omitted from the fourth edition of Lenin's works but may be
found in *Lenin i Gorki* (Moscow,
1958), 105–09.

2. *The Spark (Iskra* in Russian) was
the name he had chosen for the
journal.

3. Lenin, *Sochineniia,* V (1946), 390,
435; VII (1946), 338–39. Here,
as throughout this essay, the italics
are in Lenin's text.

4. *Leninskii Sbornik* (Moscow,
1924–59), VI (1927), 134, 137;
Vtoroi Ocherednoi S"ezd (Geneva, 1903), 241. The *Sbornik*
wrongly attributes the speech to
Rozanov instead of Popov. It is
illustrated with a reproduction of
the handwritten notes which Lenin made while Popov was speaking and used for his own later remarks. When one delegate spoke
of the "rights of party members,"
Lenin wrote in his notes: *"There
are no rights* in party membership.
RESPONSIBILITY. . . . Independent
even of rights, we must not forget
that every member of the party
is responsible for the party and
*the party is responsible for every
member." Vtoroi Ocherednoi
S"ezd,* 254.)

5. *Sochineniia,* VI (1946), 211–15.

6. *Ibid.,* IV (1946), 273.

7. To be sure, there is an ambiva-
lence about leadership and its
functions even in democratic societies: how far shall the leader
follow his followers, how far seek
to lead them? Perhaps in all Marxists, beginning with Marx himself,
because they think they *know*
what path and what doctrine the
working class *must* choose, there
is an unconscious germ of authoritarianism, an intention to indoctrinate, enlighten, instruct and direct, according to a preconceived
formula. But most Marxists, beginning with Marx himself, rejected any intention of dictating to
the working class. They expected
the working class to arrive at its
own "consciousness" out of its
own experiences, form its own
mass parties, select its own leadership, write its own programs.
The Marxists hoped to serve as informed experts and thus reach official positions and the chance to

give leadership because of such selection. It was the opponents of Marx—notably the Pole Makhaiski (Machajski) and the Russian Bakunin — who charged that Marxism aimed at a dictatorship by the intelligentsia, a new official class. Among Marxists, however, Lenin was unique in developing this authoritarian germ to full flower, unique in taking pride in it. It was only gradually in the development of their struggle with Lenin and Leninism that the more democratic Socialists came to reject the authoritarian strain in the Marxist doctrine they themselves had accepted. At the opposite extreme of the spectrum from Lenin was Axelrod, whose organization doctrine of *samodeiatel'nost'* (self-activity of the proletariat) genuinely anticipated the dissolution of the "elite party" in the future mass party of the working class.

8. Plekhanov ran a close second to his disciple, Lenin, in regarding rival views as heresies, to be annihilated at least intellectually. The other *Iskra* editors were, in varying degrees, less doctrinaire and less aggressive in intra-Party controversies.

9. The word "military" has a strange sound in the context of newspaper distribution, but what Lenin wrote would show that he meant the word to be taken literally. His seizure of power in November 1917 was not a mass uprising but a military operation.

10. *Sochineniia*, V, 8–12, 346–50, 355–56, 400–01, 410, 421–22, 431, 440–41, 442–44, 481.

11. *Ibid.*, XXXVI (1957), 80.

12. The verbal difference was trivial, but actually Lenin's definition envisaged a party of "professional revolutionaries" or a revolutionary vanguard elite, while Martov's was intended to be looser and more inclusive, allowing room for anyone who accepted the Party's directives and the Party's program. For an analysis of this point and other aspects of the congress, see the author's *Three Who Made a Revolution* (New York: Dell Pub-

lishing Co., 1964), chaps. xiv and xv.

13. The election of the members of the leading bodies; that is, the issue of the personnel, and thus the personal control of the editorial board of *Iskra*.

14. Lenin's temporary majority had elected Martov also to the editorial board, but he had refused to serve because Axelrod, Zasulich, and Potresov had been excluded.

15. *Leninskii Sbornik,* V, 149.

16. It was to remain the common program of both Bolsheviks and Mensheviks until 1919!

17. See, for instance, G. V. Plekhanov, *Sochineniia* (Peterburg, 1920–27), XII (1925), 138.

18. Karl Marx and Friedrich Engels, *Ausgewählte Werke* (Berlin: Dietz Verlag, 1958); I, 360; II, 8.

19. Maximilien Rubel, "Le Concept de démocratie chez Marx," *Contrat social,* Paris (July–August, 1962), 219.

20. Leon Trotsky, *Lenin* (New York: Minton, Balch, 1925), 43. But when Lenin did not have a majority in the Central Committee, there was no room in his thoughts for the idea of "the subordination of the minority to the majority." Then he would threaten to resign, to mobilize the Party against the Central Committee, or even, as in November 1917, to "go to the sailors," that is, mobilize the non-Party masses against the Party.

21. *Sochineniia*, V, 448.

22. *Ibid.,* VII, 365–66.

23. *Vospominaniya o Lenine* (Moscow, 1956), I, 313.

24. Lenin to the Ninth Party Congress in April 1920; and *II Kongress Kommunisticheskogo Internatsionala,* 576.

25. *Sochineniia*, VI, 221–23 (cf. also VII, 365–66).

26. *Ibid.*

27. Better, a revolutionary with a bureaucratic-*military* mind. Alfred G. Meyer, *Leninism* (Cambridge, Mass.: Harvard University Press, 1957), 98. (The military part of the hyphenated word is my addition to Meyer's formulation.)

28. *Sochineniia*, XXVII (1950), 477.
29. *Ibid.*, IV, 343.
30. See Leopold Haimson, *The Russian Marxists and the Origins of Bolshevism* (Cambridge, Mass.: Harvard University Press, 1955).
31. *Sochineniia*, V, 350 ff.
32. *Ibid.*, 347–48.
33. *Ibid.*, 431.
34. *Ibid.*, 305–06.
35. *Ibid.*, 392.
36. *Ibid.*, 398.
37. *Ibid.*, 410.
38. Of the original *Iskra* six, four were from the hereditary nobility—Plekhanov, Zasulich, Potresov, and Lenin; the other two, Axelrod and Martov, were *raznochintsy,* from those "miscellaneous groups"—neither noble, peasant, nor worker—that did not belong to any of the basic classes or estates of traditional Russian society. All six were students when they became revolutionists.
39. *Sochineniia*, V, 441.
40. *Ibid.*, XXVII, 420.
41. *Ibid.*, V, 421.
42. *Ibid.*, 442–43.
43. *Ibid.*, XXVIII (1950), 54; XXXII (1950), 222; XXVII (1957), 69.

TWO INSTRUMENTS OF CONTROL BY THE COMINTERN

1. A militant Bolshevik since 1904–05, Diogotte lived in Paris in 1908 and there, as a political exile, took part in the political life, along with Lenin and Krupskaya. In August 1919 he was sent from Odessa to Italy and France on a Comintern secret mission which he carried on until his arrest in France in May 1921. He participated in all but the first and last Comintern congresses. After 1928 he was appointed deputy commissar of labor in the government of the Russian Republic. He later became chief prosecutor of the same republic. This, however, did not prevent his arrest in July 1938. He died in deportation in 1944.
2. In August 1915 a Committee for the Reestablishment of International Ties, composed of a group of Socialists and trade unionists opposed to the "defensist" policy of the majority of French Socialist and trade union leaders was established in Paris. The committee was essentially pacifist-minded; after the Bolshevik revolution it endorsed enthusiastically Lenin's goals and activities. Two months after the establishment of the Third International in Moscow, in March 1919, the Committee changed its name to Committee for the Adherence to the Third International, thus becoming the first organized nucleus of the French Communist Party, officially born in December 1920.
3. "L'Internationale Communiste et sa section française" in *Recueil de documents* (Paris: Librairie de *L'Humanité,* 1922), 18.
4. A number of confidential reports which Jules Humbert-Droz sent to Zinoviev were recently published in *L'Oeil de Moscou à Paris* (Paris: Juillard, 1964).
5. Paul Levi, *Unser Weg wider den Putschismus* (Berlin: A. Seehof & Co. Verlag, 1921), 55–56.
6. For an excellent academic analysis of that ill-advised action, see Werner T. Angress, *Stillborn Revolution. The Communist Bid for Power in Germany 1921–1923* (Princeton, N. J.: Princeton University Press, 1963), Part II, "The 'Unauthorized' Bid for Power (1921)."
7. *Ibid.,* Part IV, "The 'Authorized' Bid for Power (1923)."
8. A photocopy of this letter is in the author's possession.
9. Henri Barbé, "Souvenirs de militant et de dirigeant communiste" (unpublished manuscript in possession of the Hoover Institution), 75.
10. Margarete Buber-Neumann, who accompanied Heinz Neumann to Moscow in May 1932 and stayed with him at the Luxe Hotel, made the acquaintance of Williams. She recalls the following: "Our next-door neighbor on the right was the French Communist André Marty, and a few doors away to our left lived 'Williams,' a Russian specialist on India for the Comintern,

whose real name I never learned. 'Williams,' a small, thin man with a complexion of sickly-yellowish tint, walked around mornings and evenings in an oriental-patterned robe that perfectly matched the interior design of his room, the walls of which were adorned with snakeskins, tapestries in bright colors, and foreign-looking ornaments. Besides travel souvenirs, 'Williams' had brought back with him from his mission to the Far East a case of malaria." Margarete Buber-Neumann, *Von Potsdam nach Moskau: Stationen eines Irrweges* (Stuttgart: Deutsche Verlags-Anstalt, 1957), 298.

In the second volume of his history of communism in the United States, Theodore Draper brings supplementary information about "Williams' " role in America or concerning the American Communist Party: in August 1928, during the Sixth Comintern Congress, "Williams" was the secretary of a thirty-two-member commission established by the Comintern's Anglo-American secretariat with the aim of studying the Negro question; he was also the secretary of the Comintern's twelve-member American commission which was instrumental in the removal, in May 1929, of the official leadership of the American party (Benjamin Gitlow, Jay Lovestone, Bertram D. Wolfe); thereafter "Williams" was sent to the United States to act as the Comintern representative (1929–30). *American Communism and Soviet Russia* (New York: The Viking Press, 1960), 345, 406, 423, 170.

By pure chance, André Ferrat happened to run into this same "Williams" one evening in 1945, in Montparnasse. Although he had quit the Communist Party almost ten years before, Ferrat reacted to this encounter as he would have in the old days of conspiracy; he drew close to him and whispered into his ear: "Williams!" The man recognized Ferrat, addressed him by name, but instead of engaging him in conversation, handed him a business card on which was inscribed, "Boris Mihailovich, correspondent for *Izvestia.*"

11. In 1928 Fried was the secretary of the Czechoslovak Communist Party for the industrial region of Liberec; in April 1931, he took part at the Eleventh Enlarged Plenum of the ECCI, as a representative of the Czechoslovak party. He was sent soon afterwards as the Comintern representative to France, where he established himself in the second part of 1931.

12. In disagreement with the Comintern tactical line, and having bad personal relations with Fried, Kagan joined the opposition sparked by André Ferrat and assembled around the review *Que Faire?* He broke with Moscow in 1936 or 1937, and died in December 1943 in New York City where he had lived as a political refugee.

13. From unpublished notes of Albert Vassart, in possession of the Hoover Institution.

14. *Ibid.*

15. *Ibid.*

16. *Bulletin du IVe congrès de l'Internationale communiste,* Moscow, December 11, 1924, no. 28, p. 14.

17. Photocopies of these letters are in the author's possession.

18. In March–April 1924, at the time when Souvarine was in Paris and engaged in a battle about the "Trotsky question," Amédée Dunois was in Moscow as the representative of the French Communist Party with the Comintern. Souvarine returned to Moscow in May 1924 to attend the thirteenth congress of the Russian Communist Party.

19. *Ve congrès de l'Internationale communiste; compte rendu analytique* (Paris: Librairie de l'Humanité, 1924), 464.

20. The original of this letter is in the author's possession. The "Bernard" referred to by Treint was the

pseudonym of another Comintern emissary in France, Alfred Kurella, a German Communist Party worker sent to direct the first central school for leadership cadres of the French party at Bobigny during 1924–25. Kurella is still a member of the Central Committee and an alternate member of the politburo of the Communist Party in East Germany. His brother, Heinrich, was a victim of the Stalinist terror (see p. 157).

21. Stalin, *Sochineniia* (Moscow, 1948), VIII, 102–03.

22. See pp. 165–66.

23. General Leandro A. Sánchez Salazar and Julián Gorkin, *Ainsi fut assassiné Trotsky* (Paris: Editions Self, 1948), 46.

24. In *Les Communistes français pendant la drôle de guerre* (Paris: Les Iles d'Or, 1951), A. Rossi has furnished additional details concerning this affair, including Duclos' part in it, 96–97.

25. Molotov was active in the Little Comission only in 1929 (after Bukharin's fall). He left this post in 1930 and in December of the same year became the head of the Soviet government. Ulbricht was replaced by Wilhelm Pieck, who was considered a nincompoop by everyone at Comintern headquarters.

26. From unpublished notes of Albert Vassart.

27. By "defeatism" is meant an abrupt change in the official attitude of the French Communist Party from full adherence to the national defense, unequivocally proclaimed on August 25, to a complete reversal of position—as a result of Comintern instructions brought back by Raymond Guyot—emphasizing only (after the end of September) a pacifist stand, and assailing not Nazi Germany but the French "200 families" striving to continue the "imperialist" war. For a day-by-day description of this changing attitude, see Rossi, chaps. ii to x.

28. *Ve Congrès de l'Internationale communiste*, 87.

THE EMERGENCE OF A NEW COMINTERN STRATEGY FOR CHINA: 1928

1. (London: Secker and Warburg, 1938), 382.

2. Cambridge, Mass.: Harvard University Press, 1958), 115.

3. *Kuomintang and Chinese Communist Elites* (Stanford, Calif.: Stanford University Press, 1952), 32. Professor North takes a similar position in his book *Moscow and Chinese Communists* (Stanford University Press, 1962), 2d edition, 122.

4. *The United States and China* (New York: Viking Press, 1962), 230.

5. Frank Borkenau, *European Communism* (London: Faber and Faber, 1938), 78 ff., and Robert Daniels, *The Conscience of the Revolution* (Cambridge, Mass.: Harvard University Press, 1960), have described the activities of the "extreme left" factions in the Comintern and in the Russian Communist Party.

6. *Stenografcheskii otchet VI kongress [a] Kominterna* (Moscow: Gos. izdat, 1929–30, 6 vols.) vol. III, 469.

7. *International Press Correspondence*, vol. VIII, no. 1, January 5, 1928, 28. (Hereafter referred to as *Inprecor*.)

8, 9. *Ibid.*, 23.

10. Pavel Mif, *Chung-kuo Ke-ming* (The Chinese Revolution), translated from the Russian (Moscow, 1933), 202; see also *Inprecor*, vol. VIII, no. 76, October 30, 1928, p. 1397.

11. *Inprecor*, vol. VIII, no. 1, January 5, 1928, p. 28. Marx was ambiguous about this, but in at least one place he does say that there are four separate and distinct stages of development: the Asiatic, ancient, feudal and modern bourgeois. See Karl Marx and Friedrich Engels, *Selected Works* (Moscow, 1928), I, 363. For an expression of the view that the Soviets purposely misrepresent Marx on this point and why, see Karl A.

Wittfogel, *Oriental Despotism* (New Haven, Conn.; Yale University Press, 1957), ch. 9, *et. passim.*

12. *Ibid.*

13. *Bolshevik,* no. 3–4, 1928. Besso Lominadze, "Novyi etap Kitaiskoi revoliutsii i zadachi kitaiskikh Kommunistov," 86–107; Pavel Mif, "Spornye Voprosy Kitaiskoi Revoliutsii," 108–22.

14. Pavel Mif, "Agrarnyi Vopros na VI S'ezde Kommunisticheskoi Partii Kitaia," *Kommunisticheskii Internatsional,* no. 43, 1928, 38–47.

15. *Inprecor,* vol. VIII, no. 1, January 5, 1928, pp. 33–34.

16. *Ibid.,* 34.

17. Bukharin, as can be seen from the detailed discussion below, was to propose a policy which would call for continued though limited cooperation with "petty-bourgeois" elements in China. If Lominadze's thesis of a weak and insignificant bourgeoisie were declared valid, there would be little point in pursuing a policy of cooperation with the bourgeoisie.

18. *Kommunisticheskii Internatsional v Dokumentakh,* Bela Kun, ed. (Moscow, 1933), vol. II, 763. Hereafter cited as *KIVD.*

19. "Resolution on the Chinese Question," *Inprecor,* vol. VIII, no. 16, March 15, 1928, p. 321. Apparently, Ch'ü Ch'iu-pai attempted to insert the concept of the Asiatic mode of production into the first draft of the resolution on the agrarian question at the CCP Sixth Congress, but it was eliminated from the final draft. See Wittfogel, *op. cit.,* 405.

20. Other sources suggest that Ch'ü was a "terrorist" (North, *Moscow and Chinese Communists,* 128), that he was the leader of a separate extremist faction in the left wing of the CCP, and that he was "influenced" by Lominadze (*Pu er sa wei k'o,* (Bolshevik), vol. IV, no. 3, May 10, 1931. See pp. 13–14 "Li-san's report;" pp. 35–37 "remarks of Ts'ai Ho'shen;" pp. 61–66 "Li-san's conclusions.")

Conflict between the extreme left and the left proper is suggested by the fact that Li-san was one of the coauthors with Stalin of the Ninth Plenum resolution which Ch'ü opposed: "Resolution on the Chinese Question" (*Inprecor,* vol. VIII, no. 16, March 15, 1928, p. 321).

21. Pavel Mif, "VI S'ezd Kommunisticheskoi Partii Kitaia," *Kommunisticheskii Internatsional,* no. 39–40, 1928, 23.

22, 23, 24. *Ibid.,* 22.

25. Pavel Mif, *Bolshevik,* no. 3–4, 1928, 119.

26. *Chung-kuo Ke-ming ho Chung-Kung te Jen-wu* (The Chinese Revolution and the Tasks of the CCP), a political report delivered to the sixth CCP congress by an unidentified Comintern representative. (Moscow, 1929), 36–37. Because of its importance, I quote from the speech at length. Theoretically, during the bourgeois-democratic stage of the revolution the "working class" could not take power alone. However, it would be perfectly all right for the working class to take power in conjunction with some portion of the bourgeoisie. Recall, for instance, Lenin's formula of a dictatorship of the proletariat and peasantry in 1905 when the revolution was still considered to be in its bourgeois-democratic stage.

27. *Ibid.,* 70.

28. *Ibid.,* 71.

29. *Ibid.,* 73.

30. *Ibid.,* 74.

31, 32. *Ibid.,* 75.

33. *Ibid.,* 76.

34. *Ibid.,* 106–07 (italics supplied).

35. *Ibid.,* 104 (italics supplied).

36. The remarks of Lominadze at the fourteenth session, *Stenograficheskii otchet VI kongress* [a] *Kominterna,* III, 469; see also *Inprecor,* vol. VIII, no. 53, August 23, 1928, p. 933 (italics supplied).

37. Daniels, 378–79. According to Margarete Buber-Neumann (*Von Potsdam nach Moskau,* Stuttgart: Deutsche Verlag-Anstalt, 1957) Lominadze had committed suicide

shortly after Kirov's assassination in December 1934, 400–01; 406.

38. The remarks of Neumann at the thirty-seventh session, *Stenograficheskii otchet VI kongress [a] Kominterna*, IV, 380; for an English translation, see *Inprecor*, vol. VIII, no. 76, October 30, 1928, pp. 1417–18.

39, 40. *Ibid.*, 383, 1418.

41. *Ibid.*, 384, 1418.

42. The Ninth Plenum "resolution on the Chinese Question," *KIVD*, 763.

43. Theses on the Revolutionary Movement in the Colonies and Semi-Colonies, *KIVD*, 778 (italics supplied).

44. Neumann's remarks at the thirty-seventh session, *Stenograficheskii otchet VI kongress [a] Kominterna*, IV, 384.

45. Ch'ü Ch'iu-pai, *To Yü te Hua* (Superfluous Words), 144, an appendix in Sz Ma-lo, *Ch'ü Ch'iu-pai Ch'uan* (The Story of Ch'ü Ch'iu-pai, Hong Kong: Tzu Lien Press, 1962).

46. The Concluding Remarks of Strakhov (Ch'ü Ch'iu-pai) at the thirty-ninth session, *Stenograficheskii otchet VI kongress [a] Kominterna*, IV, 494. An English translation which omits parts of Ch'ü's speech can be found in *Inprecor*, vol. VIII, no. 78, 1474–76.

47. *Ibid.*, 497.

48. *Ibid.*, 496–97.

49. *Ibid.*, 499.

50, 51. *Ibid.*

52. *Ibid.*, 493.

53, 54, 55, 56. *Ibid.*

57. *Ibid.*, 500.

58. "Remarks of Comrade Lozovsky," *Inprecor*, vol. VIII, no. 76, October 30, 1928, p. 1413.

59. "Theses and Resolutions: Theses on the Revolutionary Movement in the Colonies and Semi-Colonies," *Inprecor*, vol. VIII, no. 88, December 12, 1928, pp. 1662–64.

60. *Inprecor*, vol. VII, no. 73, 1927. 1678.

61. *Ibid.*, 1678–79.

62. *Ibid.*, 1679.

63, 64. *Inprecor*, vol. VIII, no. 1, January 5, 1928, p. 28.

65. *Ibid.*, 29.

66. *Ibid.*, 33–34.

67, 68. *Ibid.*, 34.

69. "Resolution on the Chinese Question, *KIVD*, 763.

70. *Programmnye Dokumenty Kommunisticheskikh Partii Vostoka* (Moscow, 1934), 31. A Chinese translation can be found in *Chung-kuo kung ch'an tang ti liu tz'u ch'üan-kuo ta-hui i-chüeh-an* (Resolutions of the Sixth Congress of the CCP), n.p., n.d., 56–57. For an English translation, see Conrad Brandt, Benjamin Schwartz and John Fairbank, *A Documentary History of Chinese Communism* (Cambridge, Mass.: Harvard University Press, 1952), 152. (Hereafter the respective references will be *Programmnye Dokumenty, CCP Sixth Chinese Text,* and *Documentary History*.)

71. *CCP Sixth Chinese Text,* 178; *Documentary History,* 157.

72. *Chung-yang t'ung-hsin ti erh hao* (Central Circular No. 2), "The Spirit and Conclusions of the CCP Sixth Congress," September 17, 1928, p. 4.

73. *Ibid.*, 7.

74, 75. *Inprecor*, vol. VIII, no. 70, 1928, 1274.

76. *Ibid.*, 1276.

77. Bukharin to Humbert-Droz, September, 1928; Humbert-Droz Archive, quoted in Daniels, 335–36.

78. *Strategiia i taktika Kominterna v natsional'no-kolonial'noi revoliutsii, na primere Kitaia;* edited by Pavel Mif (Moscow, 1934), 236–45.

79. The Ninth Plenum resolution on the Chinese Question, *KIVD*, 765.

80. For instance, see Martin S. Wilbur's "Ashes of Defeat" in *China Quarterly,* no. 18, April–June 1964, pp. 3–54, for Chinese Communist leaders' own interpretations of the Nanchang uprising and its aftermath.

81. *KIVD.*, 763–67.

82. *Ibid.*, 763.

83. *Ibid.* The Comintern apparently made its first call for the establishment of soviets the previous September.

84, 85, 86, 87. *Ibid.*, 764.

88. *Ibid.* (italics supplied).
89. *Ibid.*
90, 91, 92, 93. *Ibid.*, 765.
94. See pp. 101–104 for discussion.
95. *KIVD*, 765.
96. Jan Valtin (Richard Krebs) in his book *Out of the Night* (New York: Alliance Book Co., 1941), 106 ff., presents a discussion of the methods of "workers fraternities" in Europe.
97, 98, 99, 100. *KIVD*, 765.
101, 102. *Ibid.*, 766.
103. *Ibid.*, 767.
104. Correspondence with author, April 26, 1963.
105. *Ocherki istorii Kitaia v noveishie vremia*, N. Perevertailo, gen. ed. (Moscow, 1959), 214.
106. Li Ang, *Hung Se Wu T'ai* (Red Stage), (Chungking, 1942), 64. According to Li, a former Communist who later came over to the Kuomintang and is a hostile source, there was no Chinese faction opposing the Comintern at this time. Nevertheless, Li himself was not permitted to proceed to Moscow to attend the sixth congress. He and several others were detained en route at Irkutsk for a few days, then sent back to China.
107. Perevertailo, *loc. cit.;* Wang Shih, et al., *Chung-Kuo Kung Ch'an Tang Li-Shih Chien-Pien* (An Abridged History of the Chinese Communist Party), (Shanghai, 1958), 105; North, *KMT and CCP Elites*, 110. Party membership is conservatively listed by North as 15,000 in 1928.
108. Russian-language translations of the political resolution, the resolution on the agrarian question and the resolution on the organization of soviets can be found in *Programmnye Dokumenty*, 14–68. Chinese translations of these and other resolutions of the CCP sixth congress can be found in *CCP Sixth Chinese Text*. Both of these are on file at the Hoover Institution, Stanford University. English translations of the resolution on the peasant movement and the political resolution are given, not without errors, in Conrad Brandt, Benjamin Schwartz and John Fairbank, *Documentary History*, 149–64.
109. North, *Moscow and Chinese Communists*, 146; Schwartz, *op. cit.*, more cautiously calls Comintern directives "slippery" (p. 128).
110. The Russian-language original of the political resolution is used here. The Chinese version contains ambiguities not found in the Russian. The English translation found in the *Documentary History* contains errors.
111. The "correct tactical view" of armed uprisings was discussed in a lengthy political report by a Comintern representative (probably Pavel Mif) to the sixth congress of the Chinese party. In it he said that an insurrectionary line should be continued, but that "the present meaning of the insurrectionary line is completely different from certain previous periods, like the Kwangtung uprising or the period directly preceding the Kwangtung uprising" (presumably the Nanchang and Autumn Harvest uprisings). For reference, see Note 26 above, 100.
112. *Programmnye Dokumenty*, 28–29; *CCP Sixth Chinese Text*, 49–50. Compare *Documentary History's* translation, 149.
113. *Ibid.*, 29, 51–52, and 149–50, respectively.
114. *Ibid.*, 29–30, 53–54, and 150–51, respectively.
115. A separate resolution was devoted to this problem (see footnote 133).
116. See pp. 107–109 of this paper.
117. See footnote 133.
118. *Programmnye Dokumenty*, 30, 54–55, and 151–52, respectively.
119. *Ibid.*, 31, 54–57, and 152, respectively.
120. Schwartz, *Rise of Mao*, 127.
121. See James Cross, *Conflict in the Shadows, the Nature and Politics of Guerrilla War* (New York: Doubleday, 1963), 53.
122. *CCP Sixth Chinese Text*, 177–78.
123. *Ibid.*, 179–80.

124, 125. *Ibid.*, 180.
126. *Ibid.*, 180–81.
127. *Ibid.*, 185.
128. *Ibid.*, 185–87.
129. *Ibid.*, 187.
130. *Ibid.*, 187–88 (italics supplied). Cf. Schwartz' discussion of the resolution on the peasant movement in *Rise of Mao*, 123–24. The specific preparations are discussed in the resolution on the organization of soviet power below.
131. See Schwartz, *Rise of Mao*, 124, for an interesting discussion of this question.
132. *Mao Tse-Tung Hsüan-chi* (The Selected Works of Mao Tse-Tung), (Peking, 1961), I, 182 (italics supplied).
133. "Resolution on the Question of Organizing Soviet Power," *Programmnye Dokumenty*, 51–68. Above quote is on p. 51. I quote this resolution extensively because it is vital to the general argument and, to my knowledge, has not been referred to previously. See *CCP Sixth Chinese Text*, 191–222.
134. *Programmnye Dokumenty*, 52. *CCP Sixth Chinese Text*, 193.
135, 136. *Ibid.*, 54 and 196, respectively.
137. *Ibid.*, 66 and 220.
138. *Ibid.*, 54–55 and 197.
139, 140. *Ibid.*, 55 and 197–98.
141. *Ibid.*, 55–56 and 199.
142. *Ibid.*, 58, 202.
143. *Ibid.*, 59, 202–03.
144. *Ibid.*, 57, 201–02.
145, 146. *Ibid.*, 56, 201.
147. *Ibid.*, 61, 209.
148. *Ibid.*, 63, 213.
149. *Ibid.*, 62–63, 212–13.
150. *Ibid.*, 63, 213.
151. *Ibid.*, 64, 215.
152. *Ibid.*, 65, 217.
153. *Ibid.*, 67–68, 221.
154. *Ibid.*, "Resolution on the Agrarian Question," 34–50.
155. *Ibid.*, 50.

THE GERMAN COMMUNISTS' UNITED-FRONT AND POPULAR-FRONT VENTURES

1. The terms "united front" and "popular front" should be distinguished. The "united front" tactics, inaugurated by the Comintern at its Third Congress in 1921, aimed essentially at widening the scope of Communist influence among the Socialist rank and file. The "popular front" tactics, in use since 1934, went a step further and appealed to Socialists in general as well as to non-Socialist democrats—that is, to all those willing to join the Communists in the antifascist struggle. A further political and semantic extension of the "popular front" scheme was the slogan of "national fronts," launched after the Nazi attack on the Soviet Union in June 1941. It was the broadest extension of the Communist "front" appeals for cooperation with the non-Communists.

2. For Otto Bauer's speech at the Linz congress, see *Parteitagsprotokoll der Sozialistischen Partei Oesterreichs* (Vienna, 1926), 267–68. For Bukharin's criticism, "Das neue Programm der Oesterreichischen Sozialdemokratie," *Die Kommunistische Internationale*, VII (1926), September 17, 1926, 8–17.

3. *Thesen und Resolutionen des V. Weltkongresses der Kommunistischen Internationale* (Hamburg: Carl Hoym, 1924), 7.

4. *International Press Correspondence*, March 4 and March 10, 1926, pp. 254, 257 ff.

5. Stalin, *Sochineniia* (Moscow, 1947), VI, 282.

6. *Protokoll des 10. Plenums des Exekutivkomitees der Kommunistischen Internationale. Juli 1929* (Hamburg-Berlin: Carl Hoym, 1929), 575.

7. Ernst Thälmann, "Die KPD im Vormarsch," *Die Kommunistische Internationale*, Berlin, February 15, 1931, p. 194. Italics in the original.

8. Quoted in Margarete Buber-Neumann, *Von Potsdam nach Moskau: Stationen eines Irrweges* (Stuttgart: Deutsche Verlags-Anstalt, 1957), 285.

9. Frick had been picked as Minister of the Interior in Thuringia by a

conservative majority. During his term of office, he tried to block legislative activity on the part of the diet through special enabling legislation. In all his official capacities he acted according to his National Socialist convictions. After his fall it became known that he had tried to secure German citizenship for Hitler by appointing him police commissioner in Hildburghausen. Hitler declined the appointment; shortly thereafter he secured German citizenship by his appointment at Regierungsrat in Braunschweig.

10. The Young Plan, named after the American economist Owen Young, was drawn up at the Hague conference in 1929. It was based on the Young Committee report of June 7, 1929, which required the Germans to pay reparations for fifty-nine more years. The plan called for a new scheme to ease the pressure on the German economy. Specifically, it provided for a substantial reduction of payments and for the elimination of other unpopular features of the earlier Dawes Plan, such as the cost-of-living index, the so-called "index of prosperity", and international controls over Germany's economy.

11. *Rote Fahne,* Berlin, August 24, 1930.

12. To Toni Waibel, Communist functionary since 1919 and personal friend of Pieck.

13. To Willi Münzenberg in Moscow, January 1933.

14. Margarete Buber-Neumann, 284.

15. *L'Humanité,* April 1, 1933.

16. *Rundschau,* Basel, January 2, 1934.

17. According to Herbert Wehner, who took part at the conference and later gave a vivid description of it, the official name of "Brussels conference" was adopted in order to confuse the Gestapo. Cf. Wehner's *Erinnerungen* (Bonn, 1957; mimeographed), 101 ff.

18. This was a group composed of younger Communists in opposition to the official Communist party, and of left-wing Socialists.

19. Heinz Neumann was sent to the German Communist Party in Berlin by Stalin in 1928. Before that he had been delegate of the Communist International in Canton, where in justification of Stalin's Chinese policy he instigated an uprising which was suppressed by Chiang Kai-shek.

Neumann had the reputation of being aggressive and a leftist, a man willing to enforce the Stalinist line against Social Democratic deviations. When the National Socialists grew powerful in 1930, he advocated an uncompromising struggle against the Nazis. "Down with the fascists, wherever you run into them!" was his motto. Stalin tried repeatedly to moderate Neumann's attitude toward the National Socialists. When these attempts failed and Neumann displayed a lack of discipline within the German leadership, causing constant friction, he was removed from his post in the politburo in February 1932, for "party-damaging group activity" and recalled to Moscow.

Stalin's decision to drop Neumann as a political instrument undoubtedly was influenced by the fact that Neumann had been in close contact since 1924 with a Soviet group composed of Lominadze, Shatskin, and their friends.

In 1930 Stalin assigned these young officials to key political positions in Transcaucasia, Georgia and Armenia to act as whips for forced collectivization. The resolute resistance of the peasants in these areas gave rise to bloody conflicts, in the course of which Lominadze and others demanded that the coercive measures and brutal methods be discarded, subjecting Stalin's economic policies to violent internal criticism. A group of like-minded men was formed and was quickly betrayed by the GPU. In November-December 1930, the members of this group—Syrtsov, Lominadze, Shatskin, Reznik, Chaplin, Akhunov, Goguberidze and Rakhmanov—were publicly branded as "rightists and followers of Rykov and Tomsky" and excluded from the Central Committee of the Soviet Communist Party.

20. Wilhelm Pieck, *Der Neue Weg zum gemeinsamen Kampf für den Sturz der Hitlerdiktatur* (Strasbourg: Editions Prométhée, n.d.), 14.

21. Cf. *Dokumente zur Geschichte der KPD aus den Jahren 1935 bis 1939* ([East] Berlin: Herausgegeben von der SED, n.d.), 22–35.

22. When the Social Democrats raised the question about what the situation would be in Germany once bourgeois-democratic liberties had been won back with the help of the united front, Ulbricht stated in reply: "Let the German people freely choose what kind of government it wishes. If it rejects a soviet regime, the choice should be left up to a national assembly." Dahlem added, "If a popular majority does not want soviets, we shall abide by the will of the people." (From unpublished correspondence in the Archives of the German Social Democratic party, Bonn, Germany.)

23. *Neuer Vorwärts,* Prague, December 1935.

24. Internationaler Sozialistischer Kampfbund, a Socialist group of anti-Marxist inclination, following the ideas of the German philosopher Rudolf Nelson; after 1945 it reintegrated the German Socialist party.

25. *Pariser Tageblatt,* February 13, 1936.

26. *Neue Rundschau,* Baden-Baden, May, 1957.

27. *Mitteilungen der Deutschen Freiheitsbibliothek,* Paris, no. 12, May 1, 1936, p. 5.

28. This group called the Kommunistische Partei Deutschlands (Opposition) — KPD (O) — was a right wing opposition group expelled from the German Communist Party in 1929–30; its head was Heinrich Brandler, former leader of the German Communist Party.

29. *Neue Front,* Paris, no. 6, March 15, 1936.

30. *Ibid.*

31. These drafts for a constitution by Schwarzschild-Bernhard were published in an underground leaflet in Paris, in 1937, by the "Auslandskomitee" of the KPD (O) as mimeographed material for its followers.

32. *Das Neue Tagebuch,* Paris, January 1937.

33. From the first *Freiheitsbriefe* written by Otto Klepper. Concerning these "Freedom Letters" see below in the text.

34. *Deutsche Berichte der SOPADE* [*Sozialdemokratische Partei Deutschlands*], Prague, September 1936.

35. Curt Geyer, a prominent Socialist leader and writer, joined the German Communist Party at the Halle congress of German Independent Socialists (October 1920), but broke away from the Comintern in 1921, together with Paul Levi. During the post-1933 emigration, he was a member of the "Parteivorstand," the supreme body of the German Social Democrats in exile.

36. Friedrich Stampfer, also a member of the "Parteivorstand" and for years chief editor of *Vorwärts,* the official organ of the German Social Democratic party.

37. *Neuer Vorwärts,* Prague, December 1937.

38. Hermann Brill, *Gegen den Strom* (Offenbach/Main: Bollwerk-Verlag Karl Drott, 1946), 15.

39. According to a private communication by A. Blumel, one of Blum's collaborators in the first French popular front cabinet.

40. Brill was thoroughly anti-Communist during the illegal popular front activities. Later, in the concentration camp, he believed there could be a possibility of collaboration with the Communists. But as early as 1945, after his release, he became sharply anti-Communist and fought against them until his death.

41. Georgi Dimitrov, *Communism and the War* (London: Modern Books, 1939), 15. Italics in the original.

STALIN'S MASSACRE OF THE FOREIGN COMMUNIST LEADERS

1. Arvo Tuominen, *Kremls Klockor* (Helsingfors: Söderström, 1958), 216.
2. Božidar Maslarić, *Moskva-Madrid-Moskva* (Zagreb: Prosvjeta, 1952), 103.
3. Cf. Alfred Burmeister, *Dissolution and Aftermath of the Comintern; Experiences and Observations 1937–1947* (New York: Research Program on the U.S.S.R., 1955), 4–8.
4. Milovan Djilas, *Conversations with Stalin* (New York: Harcourt, Brace & World, 1962), 34.
5. Tuominen, 9.
6. Nadezhda Kroupskaia [Krupskaya], *Ma vie avec Lénine* (Paris: Payot, 1933), 265.
7. To preserve uniformity for the various names in this essay, the original family names will be given first, followed by a pseudonym or pseudonyms in parentheses. Later in the text, those names will be used under which a person was best known in Comintern circles.
8. *Malaia Sovetskaia Entsiklopediia,* 3d ed. (Moscow, 1958), II, 151.
9. *Vospominaniia o Vladimire Il'iche Lenine* (Moscow, 1957), II, 713.
10. *Malaia Sovetskaia Entsiklopediia,* 1st ed. (Moscow, 1930), VI, 584.
11. *Neue Zürcher Zeitung,* October 10, 1956. This information was confirmed by the Soviet press in connection with the posthumous rehabilitation of Platten, made public in July 1963, on his eightieth birthday.
12. Willi Münzenberg, *S Libknekhtom i Leninym* (Moscow-Leningrad, 1930), 139.
13. *Kommunisticheskii Internatsional,* No. 4, April 1939, pp. 126–28.
14. *Malaia Sovetskaia Entsiklopediia,* 3d ed. (Moscow, 1958), I, 954.
15. *Ibid.,* 3d ed. (Moscow, 1960), IX, 770.
16. *World News and Views* [formerly *Inprecor*], April 6, 1939, p. 382.
17. *La Correspondance Internationale,* November 11, 1924, p. 839.

18. *La Question Polonaise au Vᵉ Congrès de l'Internationale Communiste* (Moscow, 1924), 91.
19. Cf. Alfred Burmeister, "Rehabilitierte NKWD-Opfer," *Ost-Probleme,* Frankfurt am Main, August 12, 1955. (According to other information he committed suicide in 1937, anticipating his immediate arrest.)
20. Herbert Wehner, *Erinnerungen* (Bonn, 1957), 141–42.
21. *La Correspondance Internationale,* March 28, 1923, pp. 183–84.
22. Vladimir Dedijer, *Tito Speaks* (London: Weidenfeld and Nicolson, 1953), 391.
23. *Sindikalni pokret u Srbiji (1903–1919).* (Belgrade: Rad, 1958), 600.
24. *Borba,* Belgrade, June 10, 1962.
25. *International Press Correspondence,* April 13, 1934, p. 599.
26. Wehner, 160.
27. Margarete Buber-Neumann, *Von Potsdam nach Moskau: Stationen eines Irrweges* (Stuttgart: Deutsche Verlags-Anstalt, 1957), 203.
28. Wehner, 150.
29. Buber-Neumann, 70.
30. *Ibid.,* 71.
31. W. G. Krivitsky, *In Stalin's Secret Service* (New York: Harper, 1939), 35.
32. Tuominen, 208.
33. *Ibid.,* 209.
34. *Ocherki Istorii Komunisticheskoi Partii Estonii* (Tallinn, 1961), I, 82.
35. Maslarić, 43.
36. Tuominen, 210.
37. *International Press Correspondence,* No. 67, August 11, 1922, p. 501.
38. Ivan Karaivanov, *Ljudi i pigmeji* (Belgrade, 1953), 112.
39. A copy of this letter is in my possession.
40. Pierre Naville, *Trotsky vivant* (Paris: Juillard, 1962), 24.
41. Henri Barbé, "Souvenirs de militant et de dirigeant communiste" (unpublished manuscript at the Hoover Institution), 111–12.
42. According to William Henry Chamberlin, "He [Andreichin] had been released from the con-

centration camp, employed in translation during the war, and finally permitted to return to his native Bulgaria, but by 1947 he was purged while serving as the 'head of the Anglo-American Department of the Foreign Ministry.' " *Russian Review,* October 1962, p. 338.

43. Barbé, 300.
44. Tuominen, 215.
45. J. T. Murphy, *New Horizons* (London: John Lane, 1941), 242.
46. Walter Z. Laquer, *The Soviet Union and the Middle East* (New York: Praeger, 1959), 30.
47. Two books published in Italy in 1964 provide information about the fate of Italian Communists who were refugees in the Soviet Union at the time of the big purge: Renato Mieli, *Togliatti 1937* (Milano: Ed. Rizzoli), and Guelfa Zaccaria, *200 Comunisti italiani tra le vittime dello stalinismo* (Milan: Ed. Azione Comune).
48. Djilas, 34.
49. *Ibid.*
50. Wehner, 161.
51. Popov, husband of Otto Kuusinen's daughter, had been named an alternate member of the ECCI at the 1935 congress.
52. *Rabotnitchesko Delo,* Sofia, September 5, 1962.
53. *Ibid.,* November 10, 1963.
54. Wehner, 151, 157.
55. M. K. Dziewanowski, *The Communist Party of Poland: An Outline of History.* (Cambridge, Mass.: Harvard University Press, 1959), 154.
56. *Survey,* October 1962, p. 162.
57. Boris Souvarine, *Stalin. A Critical Survey of Bolshevism* (London: Secker and Warburg, n.d.), 586. Italics in the text.
58. Wehner, 165.

THE COMINTERN AND THE INSURRECTIONAL ACTIVITY OF THE COMMUNIST PARTY OF YUGOSLAVIA IN 1941–42

1. The condensation is from the complete report by Dimitrov in his *The United Front: The Struggle Against Fascism and War* (New York: International Publishers, 1938), 9–93.
2. "Resolution on the Report of Comrade Dimitrov," *Report of the Seventh World Congress of the Communist International* (London: Modern Books, 1936), 19. Italics in the text.
3. From Tito's report "On the Work and Tasks of the Party," delivered to the fifth conference of the Communist Party of Yugoslavia in Zagreb, November 1940. *Komunist,* organ of the central committee of the party, October 1946, 64.
4. Quoted in *Istorijski arhiv komunističke partije Jugoslavije* (Belgrade, 1950), II, 421.
5. *Ibid.,* 369.
6. Arsa Lazarević, *Istaknuti graditelji socijalističke Jugoslavije* (Belgrade: Omladina, 1957), 40.
7. "Yugoslav volunteers fought in Spain in the units of all international brigades, but mostly in the 129th International Brigade in the battalions Djuro Djaković, Dimitrov, Masaryk, and in the independent battalion Divizionario.... For their merits in Spain about 280 Yugoslavs were promoted to various commissioned ranks or were made commanding officers in various units of the Spanish Republican Army. Two Yugoslavs were promoted to the rank of lieutenant-colonel, eight to the rank of major, 35 of captain, 105 of lieutenant, etc. Thirty-nine Yugoslavs were political commissars." "Association of Yugoslav Volunteers in the Spanish Republican Army," *Yugoslav Survey,* October–December 1961, 958.
8. *Ibid.,* 959.
9. Another prominent Yugoslav Communist, Filip Filipović (writing and acting under the pseudonym of "Bošković"), took part in the seventh Congress as a member of the Comintern Presidium.
10. From scattered and incomplete information it is possible to say the following about the fate of the majority of Yugoslav Communists

who had attended the Seventh Congress: Gorkić and Filipović lost their lives during Stalin's purges; Parović perished in Spain; two other delegates who returned to Yugoslavia after the congress, Milenković from Zagreb and Ivo Marić-"Željezar" from Split, were arrested by police and because of their allegedly spineless behavior in jail were expelled from the Communist Party of Yugoslavia; Miladin Radovanović—"Simonović —remained in the Soviet Union, and his name never appeared later in connection with Party activities; Lovro Kuhar–"Valić" died in 1950 in Yugoslavia. See *Komunist* of January 8, and September 3, 1959. The official *Pregled istorije saveza komunista Jugoslavije* (Belgrade: Institut za izučavanje radničkog pokreta, 1963) makes no mention of the names and fate of the Yugoslav delegates at the Comintern's Seventh Congress.

11. Milovan Djilas, *Conversations with Stalin* (New York: Harcourt, Brace & World, 1962), 34.

12. On the same problem, see the section of Branko Lazitch's essay in this book discussing the Yugoslav Communists massacred by Stalin's police.

13. From Tito's report to the fifth conference of the Communist Party of Yugoslavia, 69.

14. "Za čistoću i boljševizaciju partije" in *Materijal za ideološko-političko vaspitanje* (Belgrade, 1946), VIII, 34.

15. Djilas, 11–12.

16. Hannah Arendt, *On Revolution* (New York: Viking Press, 1963), 263.

17. The Communist Party of Yugoslavia had 1,500 members at the end of 1937; 6,000 in November 1940; 8,000 in May 1941; 12,000 in July 1941. Jovan Marjanović, *Potsetnik iz istorije komunističke partije Jugoslavije (1919–1941)*, (Belgrade: Rad, 1953), 56, 64. Moma Marković and Ivan Laća, *Organizacioni razvitak komunističke partije Jugoslavije* (Belgrade: Kultura, 1960), 69, 80, 83. To

these figures one should add the membership of the Alliance of the Communist Youth of Yugoslavia, which in September 1940, had 18,000 members and in July 1941, 30,000. See Aleksandar Ranković, *Report of the Central Committee of the Communist Party of Yugoslavia on the Organizational Work of the CPY*, delivered to the fifth congress of the Communist Party of Yugoslavia (Belgrade, 1948), 26, 32.

18. A detailed analysis of the Communist Party of Yugoslavia between the two world wars will be found in my forthcoming book, *The Comintern and the Communist Party of Yugoslavia, 1919–1941*, to be published by the Hoover Institution, Stanford, California.

19. The text of this telegram is quoted in an article by a noted historian of the Yugoslav party, Jovan Marjanović, "Forme borbe i rada KPJ u narodnoj revoluciji," *Komunist*, January 1951, 116.

20. *Komunistička partija Jugoslavije, 1919–1941: Izabrani dokumenti* (Zagreb: Školska knjiga, 1959), 255–56.

21. For the full text of this telegram, see Marjanović, 117.

22. Jovan Marjanović and Pero Morača, *Naš oslobodilački rat i narodna revolucija* (Belgrade: Prosveta, 1959), 45. "A manifesto of the central committee of the Communist Party of Yugoslavia calling the peoples of Yugoslavia to an armed struggle was announced on July 12, 1941. The central committee urged the peoples of Yugoslavia to turn their land into a besieged fortress for the fascist invaders; it appealed to the Communists to organize without hesitation partisan detachments and put themselves at the front of the people's liberation struggle." *Pregled istorije saveza komunista Jugoslavije*, 330.

23. Cf. Tomo Čubelić and Milovan Milostić, *Pregled historije narodnooslobodilačkog rata i revolucije naroda Jugoslavije* (Zagreb: Matica Hrvatska, 1961), 83–84.

24. For a brief description of Jovano-vić's political career (he perished as a prominent political and military figure among the partisans in Serbia in March 1942), see *Narodni heroji Srbije* (Belgrade, 1951), 38.

25. For the text of the Comintern's decision, see *Istorijski arhiv komunističke partije Jugoslavije*, VII, 50. The same volume contains abundant material concerning the dispute between the two parties over Macedonia; the Comintern's decision in favor of the Yugoslavs is particularly significant if viewed against the background of the interwar experience when the Bulgarian Communists, unlike those of Yugoslavia, enjoyed great prestige and hierarchical importance in the Comintern apparatus. See on the same subject Lazar Mojsov, *Bugarska radnička partija (Komunista) i makedonsko nacionalno pitanje* (Belgrade: Borba, 1948), 110.

26. Cf. Vladimir Dedijer, *Jugoslovensko-albanski odnosi (1939–1948)*, (Belgrade: Borba, 1949), 25–26.

27. All public pronouncements of the Communist Party of Yugoslavia in the period between the dismemberment of Yugoslavia and June 22 had a typical "class" character, reminiscent of the "class against class" phraseology following the Sixth Comintern Congress. The attack of Germany against the USSR—like Hitler's coming to power eight years earlier—served as the impetus for a change in the political line. And since 1941 was deadlier than 1933, the "popular front" phraseology of 1935 had to be strengthened by the introduction of "national front" slogans.

28. *Yugoslavia's Way: The Program of the League of the Communists of Yugoslavia* (New York: All Nations Press, 1958). The quoted words are taken from the 1958 program of the League of the Communists of Yugoslavia (as the Communist Party of Yugoslavia was officially called after its sixth congress in November 1952), 98; the statement about transforming the partisan war into an instrument for seizing power is in keeping with the essence of an entire section of that program, 94–103.

29. As Milovan Djilas, head of the official mission of the Yugoslav partisans to the Soviet Union, tried to explain to his Soviet hosts in March of 1944, the central problem of the uprising in Yugoslavia was reduced to achieving a tie "between a peasant rebellion and the Communist avant-guard." Djilas, 30.

30. Vladimir Dedijer, *Dnevnik* (Belgrade, 1945), I, 88. Dedijer reports here on the conclusions of a party meeting in the small town of Foča, in eastern Bosnia, on February 13, 1942, attended by Tito. It was decided to intensify political work among the peasantry, to recruit the youth, and to build systematically the party cadres. ("We must open wide the gates of the party.")

31. *Yugoslavia's Way*, 98.

32. *Zbornik dokumenata i podataka o narodnooslobodilačkom ratu jugoslovenskih naroda* (Belgrade: Vojno-Istoriski Institut Jugoslovenske Armije, 1949), vol. II, book 1, p. 11.

33. *Political Report of the Central Committee of the Communist Party of Yugoslavia*, delivered at the fifth congress of the party (Belgrade, 1948), 53.

34. Josip Broz Tito, *Stvaranje i razvoj jugoslovenske armije* (Belgrade: Glavna Politička Uprava Jugoslovenske Armije, 1949), 64.

35. *Political Report . . .*, 65.

36. *Istorijski arhiv komunističke partije Jugoslavije*, vol. I, book 1, pp. 18–20.

37. *Ibid*. Italics in the text.

38. From Pijade's speech about the project of the general bill on people's committees, made before both houses of the Yugoslav Assembly, on May 18, 1946. This speech contains an interesting survey of the "historical development of the people's committees." *Izabrani govori i članci* (Belgrade: Kultura, 1948), 131.

39. *Ibid.*, 145–46. Italics in the text.

40. Marjanović, "Forme borbe i rada KPJ u narodnoj revoluciji," (see Note 19 above), 133.

41. Moša Pijade, "Trideset godina KPJ," *Komunist,* March 1949, 20.

42. Analyzing the mistakes committed by the Communist Party during the war in Montenegro, in 1941, Tito stated in his report to the fifth congress: "Force was used rather than persuasion, which embittered one section of the people even more and they then fell under the influence of Mihailović's četniks." *Political Report . . . ,* 107. Speaking at the same congress, Aleksandar Ranković said that in Bosnia and Herzegovina the party organizations had also been guilty of several mistakes and shortcomings: "The mistakes in Herzegovina were reflected in sectarian deviation from the correct political line, in the sectarian slogan, Let Us Sovietize Herzegovina," *Report of the CC of the CPY on the Organizational Work of the CPY,* 37. Similarly, in an article published in July 1942, Edvard Kardelj criticized "the sectarianism which lately has taken over so strongly in a full range of party organizations that it endangers many of the achievements of our party in recent years." *Put nove Jugoslavije, 1941–1945* (Belgrade: Kultura, 1949), 286.

43. This description appears in Tito's order of February 18, 1942. *Zbornik,* vol. II, book 2, p. 379.

44. *Ibid.,* 134. In another letter to Djilas, dated February 5, 1942, Tito stressed that the task of the proletarian brigade was primarily to fight the "fifth column" and only secondarily the occupiers; *ibid.,* 320, see also 156, 187–88, 233, 284, 317, 406.

45. The text of the statute was published in the February–March 1942 issue of the *Bulletin* of the supreme headquarters. *Zbornik,* vol. II, book 1, pp. 134–37.

46. From an interview with the director of Radio Belgrade, as published in Belgrade's *Borba,* July 7, 1953.

47. In a letter to Tito from Croatia, written on August 2, 1941, Edvard Kardelj complained about the "N. N. affair." According to Kardelj, N. N. was unable to understand the existing situation in Croatia. Moreover, wrote Kardelj, "I am thoroughly convinced that he is, perhaps subconsciously, set against you and our entire leadership. I say subconsciously, but this does not mean that there were not some clear intentions. He lied to 'Grandfather' at the most difficult time; he was wrecking the 'firm' [party]. The fact is he played a provocative role." *Zbornik,* vol. II, book 2, p. 28. (I was unable to solve the mystery of who N. N. was and what became of him later. *Zbornik* abounds in explanatory notes about practically everybody mentioned in the text, but the identity of N. N. is not revealed.) About Tito's doubts (in a letter from September 12, 1941) as to whether N. N. was even sending his messages to the Comintern, see *ibid.,* 63.

48. *Ibid.,* 429–30.

49. Quoted in Moša Pijade, *About the Legend That the Yugoslav Uprising Owed Its Existence to Soviet Assistance* (London, 1950), 9.

50. *Ibid.,* 11.

51. *Ibid.*

52. Pijade's interesting and important pamphlet contains only a small number of texts exchanged between the Comintern and the Yugoslav party during 1942 and 1943. (He mentions at one point the Comintern's telegram No. 78.) The bulk of these exchanges was not published, and it is indeed regrettable that scholars in the West cannot get hold of them in their entirety.

53. Dušan Plenča, *Medjunarodni odnosi Jugoslavije u toku Drugog svjetskog rata* (Belgrade: Institut društvenih nauka, 1962), 153 n.

54. An example of this attitude was given by Stalin during Tito's visit to Moscow in September 1944. To Tito's remonstrances over any reinstatement of King Peter, Stalin stated, "You need not restore him

forever. Take him back temporarily, and then you can slip a knife in his back at a suitable moment." Vladimir Dedijer, *Tito Speaks* (London: Weidenfeld & Nicolson, 1953), 234.

55. Pijade, 12. Soviet inability or unwillingness to supply Tito with war materials during the earlier phases of the partisan struggle had certainly caused deep disappointment among the leaders of the Yugoslav party. Likewise, according to Dedijer (*Tito Speaks,* 233), some of Tito's reproaches on the same subject provoked Stalin's anger. On the other hand, as frequently noted by Dedijer in his *Dnevnik,* "Radio Free Yugoslavia" transmitting from Tiflis, and Radio Moscow's broadcasts in Serbo-Croatian played a primary role in partisan propaganda at home. Moreover, the exaltation of Soviet Russia, and of Stalin in particular, was an important element in the emotional and political conditioning of partisan fighters.

56. Djilas, 24.

57. In the undated telegram, No. 78, sent sometime in March 1942, by the Comintern to Tito, it was termed inopportune "to emphasize that the [partisan] struggle was mainly against the četniks." Pijade, 12.

58. *Ibid.,* 20.

59. *Ibid.* Italics added. In his book *The Heretic* (New York: Harper, 1957), 158, Fitzroy Maclean calls this Comintern reply "fussy and discouraging." He quotes parts of the same telegram, but he omits in his quotation the sentence placed here in italics. In fact, when this sentence remains where it belongs, it shows the Comintern's answer was not "discouraging" at all, but conformed to the pattern of Comintern-Tito relations just outlined.

60. Ivan Ribar, *Uspomene iz narodnooslobodilačke borbe* (Belgrade: Vojno delo, 1961), 57.

61. Ferdo Čulinović, *Stvaranje nove jugoslavenske države* (Zagreb: Školska knijga, 1959), 191.

62. Ribar, 59.

63. Dedijer, *Dnevnik,* I, 360.

64. For the text of Masleša's report, see his *Dela* (Sarajevo: Svjetlost, 1954), II, 117–23.

65. It is revealing for a study of Communist methods in general, and for synchronization of the Comintern's directives and Tito's compliance in particular, that one cannot find anywhere in postwar Yugoslav books and published documents the *entire* text of the Bihać manifesto. Or, to put it more precisely, the Yugoslav authors never quote the six specific points of this manifesto as published in Stephen Clissold's *Whirlwind: An Account of Marshal Tito's Rise to Power* (London: Cresset Press, 1949), 113–14. The first two points formulate in the following ways the aims of the Yugoslav National Liberation Movement: "(1) The liberation of the country from the invaders and the achievement of independence and true democratic rights for all the peoples of Yugoslavia. (2) The inviolability of private property and the providing of every possibility for individual initiative in industry, trade and agriculture." These and later similar points correspond exactly to "Grandfather's" advice to Tito to proclaim at that time only the broadest national and democratic aims. Is it astonishing, then, that when it became obvious after the war that the Bihać manifesto was a Stalinist stratagem designed for foreign consumption, the Yugoslav writers and historians preferred to leave unmentioned the broken promises?

66. Djilas, 29–30.

67. Pijade, 20–21.

68. *The Russian Revolution: The Overthrow of Tsarism and the Triumph of the Soviets,* selected and edited by F. W. Dupee from the *History of the Russian Revolution* by Leon Trotsky (New York: Doubleday Anchor Book, 1959), 307.

THE FOUNDING OF THE COMINFORM

1. Eugenio Reale, *Nascita del Cominform* (Milano: Mondadori, 1958). French edition, *Avec Jacques Duclos au Banc des Accusés à la Réunion Constitutive du Kominform à Szklarska Poreba (22–27 Septembre 1947),* (Paris: Librairie Plon, 1958).
2. Zoltan Pfeiffer was the leader of the Hungarian Independence Party which at the August 31, 1947 elections rallied the anti-Communist votes. Three months later his party was dissolved, as advocated by Révai in Szklarska Poreba, and Pfeiffer fled to the West.
3. *Conversations with Stalin* (New York: Harcourt, Brace & World, 1962), 129.
4. *Ibid.,* 129–30.
5. Cf. Imre Nagy, *On Communism. In Defense of the New Course* (New York: Praeger, 1957).
6. Vladimir Dedijer, *Tito Speaks* (London: Weidenfeld and Nicolson, 1953), 331.

PAUL LEVI AND MOSCOW

1. Filippo Turati (1857–1932) was one of the founders and leaders of the Italian Socialist Party before the First World War. After the war he took a consistently moderate position, and at the Leghorn congress he was heading the reformist wing (the smallest numerically) of the Italian Socialist Party. Target of Communist and "Maximalist" attacks at that time, and persecuted by the Fascist regime, he escaped Italy in 1927 and died in exile in France.
2. Victor Kopp, the former Menshevik, was sent in November 1919 to Berlin as a Soviet plenipotentiary for prisoner-of-war affairs. In addition to his official function, he established there, on Trotsky's behalf, secret contacts with big German industrial concerns, probing the possibility of German technological and military assistance to Soviet Russia.
3. Rudolf Hilferding, one of the leaders of the Independent Social Democratic party of Germany, was included together with Karl Kautsky among the "notorious opportunists" in the language of the "twenty-one conditions for the admission in the Communist International," adopted at the Second Comintern Congress. Later, at the Halle congress of his party, Hilferding was the main antagonist of Zinoviev in the battle for the future orientation of German Independent Socialists.
4. Radek's reference here concerns an open letter, drafted by Levi with Radek's blessing and published on January 8, 1921 in *Die Rote Fahne.* The letter was addressed to a number of German labor organizations. It made an appeal for working-class solidarity and as such foreshadowed the united-front tactics of the future. Cf. Werner T. Angress, *Stillborn Revolution: The Communist Bid for Power in Germany, 1921–1923* (Princeton, N. J.: Princeton University Press, 1963), 91–92.
5. The KAPD (Kommunistiche Arbeiterpartei Deutschlands) was founded as the rival to the German Communist Party in April 1920. A typical "left-wing" Communist group with strong anarcho-syndicalist features, it never became a significant political force but gave considerable trouble to the official Communist party. It had sent its delegates to the Second and Third Comintern congresses, but was never accepted as a full-fledged Comintern section. It was criticized by Lenin at the Third Congress. In 1923 it was virtually extinct.
6. Fritz Wolffheim, leader, with Heinrich Laufenberg, of the earliest left-wing faction within the German Communist Party, resigned from the Party at the Heidelberg congress (October 1919). His "national Bolshevism" was assailed by Lenin in *"Left-Wing Communism," an Infantile Disorder* as a "Communist heresy."
7. See the biographical notes following the documents dealing with the Comintern's interference in

Index

401

tioned, 129, 300, 302, 310, 311, 315, 391, 398, 399
LEVIN (LEVIEN), MAX, 158–59
LEWINSON, PAWEL (*pseud.* Stanislaw Łapiński), 144, 179
LI ANG, 388
LI LI-SAN, 67, 68
LI-SAN, 386
LIEBKNECHT, KARL, 304, 308–09
LIEBKNECHT, WILHELM, 11, 12
LINDAU, RUDOLF, 155
Lithuania: Communist Party of, 160, 161; mentioned, 161
LITVINOV, MAXIM, 121, 239
LIUBARSKY, ("Comrade Carlo"), Russian Communist, 274, 281
LOMINADZE, BESSO: his "extreme left" position, 68, 72; report to Fifteenth congress of Russian Communist Party, 68–70; views expressed in Party journals, 71; views on China linked to Trotsky's, 71; recantation, 76–77; later career and suicide, 77; mentioned, 75, 80, 81, 82, 84, 162, 172, 386, 390
LONGO, LUIGI, 253, 259, 266
LONGUET, CHARLES, 15
LONGUET, JEAN: and "Zinoviev's pistol shot," 311; highlights of political career, 366–67; mentioned, 361, 374
LORIOT, FERNAND: highlights of political career, 367–68; mentioned, 54, 318, 329, 344, 363, 366, 373
LOUIS, PAUL, 333, 368
LOVESTONE, JAY, 147, 384
LOZOVSKY, SOLOMON A.: criticizes "hinterland" ("world rural districts") theory, 82; mentioned, 220, 228
LUDWIG, EMIL, 125
LUNACHARSKY, ANATOL VASILYEVICH, 32, 54
LUXEMBURG, ROSA, 176, 294, 304, 375

LVOV, PRINCE GEORGI EVGENIEVICH, 16

Macedonia, *see* Yugoslavia
MAČEK, VLADKO, 211
MACLEAN, FITZROY: quotation disputed, 397
MAGYAR, ALICE, 162–63
MAGYAR, L., 162
MAKHAISKI (MACHAJSKI), W., 382
MALENKOV, GEORGI, 253, 257, 258, 261, 262, 264, 266
MALIŠIĆ-MARTINOVIĆ, JOVAN, 153–54
MANN, HEINRICH, 125, 128, 133, 137
MANN, KLAUS, 125
MANNER, KULLERVO, 159
MANUILSKY, DMITRII: 1919 arrival in France, 47; visits France (1922, 1924), 48; 1925 mission to France, 52; assails united-front tactics (1929), 115; attacks Social Democrats (1931), 116, underestimates Hitler, 237; calls Polish Communists fascist spies, 147; attacks Tasca, 230; criticizes Thorez, 241; favors tactical change in France, 243–44, 246; assails French Communists, 246, 248–49; absent from Cominform, 257; as Comintern delegate at Second congress of French Communist Party, 347–48; mentioned 49, 50, 51, 53, 56, 59, 60, 61, 62, 173, 189, 218, 231, 233, 304, 354
MAO TSE-TUNG: approves theoretical line of Sixth congress of Chinese Communists, 104; develops and refines Comintern's policy for China, 109; mentioned, 43
MARCHLEWSKI, JULIAN, 375
MARCU, VALERIU, 129
MARCUSE, LUDWIG, 125
MARIĆ-"ŽELJEZAR", IVO, 394
MARINA, *see* PAUKER, ANNA
MARION, PAUL, 224

THOMAS, *see* REICH, J.

THOREZ, AURORE, 53

THOREZ, MAURICE: adheres to "class against class" tactic, 236, 242; relations with Doriot, 236, 241, 242, 244–45; criticized at Thirteenth Comintern Plenum, 240; trails behind Comintern, 240–41; echoes Stalin in *Fils du Peuple*, 242; compares Doriot with Trotsky, 245; brings about shift in party line, 251; mentioned, 52, 58, 60, 233, 234, 235, 257, 266, 371.

TITO, *see* BROZ, JOSIP

TKACHEV, P. N., 8, 43

TOGLIATTI, PALMIRO (*pseud.* Ercoli): assailed by Silone, 226; attacks Tasca at Tenth Plenum of ECCI, 230; accuser of Yugoslav Communists, 262; mentioned, 59, 61, 146, 157, 158, 168, 173, 189, 220, 225, 229, 246, 256, 258, 265, 267, 268, 304, 359, 360

TOLLER, ERNST, 125

TOMMASI, JOSEPH, 165, 373

TOMSKY, M. P., 219, 231, 391

TORRÈS, HENRY: highlights of political career, 373–74; mentioned, 363

Transylvania, 164, 302

TREINT, ALBERT: and his January 1922 letter to Comintern, 319–20; text of his report to Comintern, 320ff; highlights of political career, 354–56; letter of resignation, 356–58; mentioned, 45, 48, 50, 52, 56–57, 58, 312, 313, 318, 319, 323, 328–29, 331, 332, 333, 334, 335, 338, 344, 345, 348, 349, 352, 353, 374, 384

Tribuna Ludu (organ of the Polish Communist Party), 150

TRILISSER, M. A. (*pseud.* M. A. Moskvin), 140

TROTSKY, LEON: Zinoviev and Stalin campaign against, 49; praising

Louis Sellier, 55; on GPU role in Comintern, 58; views on China criticized by Comintern, 71; defeated by Stalin, 84; defends Souvarine, 317–18; defended by Polish Communists, 147; intervenes in affairs of French Communist Party, 345–46, 347, 364; mentioned, xii, 48, 50, 56, 94, 148, 153, 157, 158, 159, 165, 166, 167, 170, 176, 177, 178, 180, 181, 182, 213, 219, 229, 232, 245, 303, 304, 306, 314, 322, 352, 360, 363, 367, 384, 398

—, Trotskyites: in Spain, 131; mentioned, 130, 144, 147, 170, 171, 360, 399

TUKHACHEVSKY, M. N., 178, 236, 307

TUOMINEN, ARVO, 140, 141, 160, 173

TURATI, FILIPPO, 273, 275–76, 277, 278, 290, 398

Ukraine: Communist Party of, 163; mentioned, 146

ULBRICHT, WALTER, 59, 119, 122, 123, 133, 137, 230, 385, 391

L'Union Socialiste Communiste, 375

L'Unità (Italian Communist paper), 267

United front: emergence of, 111, 314; limits to, 112; and the popular front, 112–13; and Dimitrov, 119–21; mentioned, 321, 325, 326, 360, 389

—, in Germany: beginnings, 113, 274, 314–15; 1923 experience in Saxony, 113–14; successful 1926 action, 114; abandoned in 1929, 115; "Against Social Democracy, for a United Front from Below," 118; in the Saar, 119; grows to popular front, 119–20; mentioned, 124, 321, 324, 391, 398

DATE

GAYLORD